ARCHAEOLOGY, LANGUAGE, AND HISTORY

ARCHAEOLOGY, LANGUAGE, AND HISTORY

Essays on Culture and Ethnicity

Edited by
John Edward Terrell

Scientific Archaeology for the Third Millennium

BERGIN & GARVEY
Westport, Connecticut • London

Library of Congress Cataloging-in-Publication Data

Archaeology, language, and history : essays on culture and ethnicity / edited by John
Edward Terrell.
     p. cm. — (Scientific archaeology for the Third Millennium, ISSN 1529–4439)
    Includes bibliographical references and index.
    ISBN 0–89789–724–2 (alk. paper)
    1. Ethnoarchaeology. 2. Social archaeology. 3. Archaeology and history. 4. Language
and culture—History. 5. Ethnicity—History. 6. Anthropological linguistics. I. Terrell,
John. II. Series.
CC79.E85A75 2001
930.1—dc21   00–037835

British Library Cataloguing in Publication Data is available.

Library of Congress Catalog Card Number: 00–037835
ISBN: 0–89789–724–2
ISSN: 1529–4439

First published in 2001

Bergin & Garvey, 88 Post Road West, Westport, CT 06881
An imprint of Greenwood Publishing Group, Inc.
www.greenwood.com

Printed in the United States of America

The paper used in this book complies with the
Permanent Paper Standard issued by the National
Information Standards Organization (Z39.48–1984).

10 9 8 7 6 5 4 3 2 1

FOR GABRIEL

Contents

Series Foreword

Few would deny that archaeology has undergone a number of theoretical and methodological changes in recent years. These developments have brought archaeology into new relationships with several sciences—biology, geology, physics, chemistry, and computer science—and have modified archaeology's earlier relationships with other disciplines such as history, ethnography, and anthropology. No matter when we got our degrees, none of us can deny that archaeology today is different from the archaeology we studied as graduate students.

To confront, to incorporate, and to advance beyond the recent theoretical upheavals are challenges that archaeology will face early in the new millennium. Maintaining scientific rigor in the midst of vaporous theoretical debates may be the biggest challenge of all. This is the reason we are launching the series "Scientific Archaeology for the Third Millennium," which we hope will be a medium of academic and scientific discussion in contemporary archaeology. The general goal of the series is to promote new scientific perspectives in archaeology by drawing on new theories, methods, and techniques that archaeologists are developing in different parts of the world.

Archaeology's current challenges involve all professional archaeologists regardless of nationality and/or theoretical orientation. As practitioners of a young science, we have gone through a process of searching and experimenting that has given us the theoretical-methodological diversity that we see today. Now we must begin to evaluate the contributions of the various perspectives by putting them to work in building scientific understanding of the past.

We thank Greenwood Publishing Group and especially our editor, Jane Garry, for the opportunity to disseminate studies that promote archaeological science. We also thank the members of our Advisory Board for their helpful and frank advice about which manuscripts might be appropriate as initial issues in our series.

We invite colleagues who view archaeology as a science to join us in meeting the challenges that face us during the first decades of the third millennium.

Jose Luis Lanata
Department of Anthropology
University of Buenos Aires

Mark Aldenderfer
Department of Anthropology
University of California, Santa Barbara

Hector Neff
Missouri University Research Reactor
University of Missouri

1

Introduction
John Edward Terrell

Language is often taken as a sign of ethnic identity and origins; language differences are commonly seen as barriers isolating people from one another. On this basis, as Franz Boas observed years ago and some still insist, language history ought to parallel culture history and the history of human populations. Archaeologists, linguists, and others have often argued the case against this commonsense proposition in ambiguous, even ambivalent ways. The authors of these chapters start with a much stronger position in mind: language, culture, and biology always vary independently except under special conditions. What are those conditions? When do they apply?—Editor

My mother used to say that you must not call something an antique before it is at least 75 years old; anything younger is merely an antique-in-the-making. There must be a similar age requirement before we can call a group of people an ethnic group. Where I live in Wisconsin, an annual event for many Norwegians is the family gathering at our local park and American Legion hall. The living descendants of the same foreign-born immigrant couple several generations back assemble for a potluck meal and a chance to catch up on what has happened "in the family" over the past year. It would occur to nobody at these gatherings of closely related kin—who may be named, say, Erickson, Larson, or Rygh—to identify themselves as an ethnic group. They are "just family." Probably most of those attending would classify themselves instead, if asked, as Norwegian or Norwegian American, although many might admit (since marriage across ethnic lines is not uncommon in southwestern Wisconsin) that they also have at least an ancestor or two who came from Switzerland, Germany, or maybe even England, Ireland, Mexico, or farther afield. Evidently the simple fact of being able to trace one's ancestry back to a common ancestor is not enough to qualify the people meeting at these family gatherings as an ethnic group. "They may be family," my mother might say if she were alive, "but they are not old-enough family." In this part of the world where people often live into their 80s, 90s, and sometimes over 100, being "old enough" is obviously not just 75 years.

But what is the minimal age that a group of related people must attain to qualify as a genuine ethnic group? What minimal proof is needed to certify that people claiming to have a common background truly do? For that matter, with so much marrying in and out, what does it mean to claim "common ancestry"? It is well known that many application forms ask the applicant to state his or her "race or ethnic group." This would seem to be proof enough that while the minimal age needed to qualify as a real ethnic group may be more than 75 years, it is less than 500 years. People who check "Hispanic" on such forms, after all, did not exist in the New World before 1492. But many would retort that Hispanics in the Americas are a "mixed race," a recent ethnic blend of African, European, and Native American genes and cultures. They are not really old enough as an ethnic group to be a real group in their own right—what plain folks would call "a race." They are "mixed," or, as some biologists like to phrase it, they are an "admixed population." Does this mean, therefore, that genuine ethnic groups—true races—must be more than 500 years old? If so, how much older do they need to be to qualify? Is it necessary, say, for people to be able to trace their roots back to prehistoric times? What proof is needed to establish the authenticity, the credibility, of such claims of great antiquity?

These are vexing questions in part because the geography of human variation has stubbornly resisted attempts by social scientists to see the world as a great jigsaw puzzle of distinct, bounded, nonoverlapping pieces that can be labeled as different races, culture areas, or ethnic groups (Lewis 1991). One clue that many are looking for better ways to map our diversity is that the generic word *tribe* for ancient or primitive social aggregates bigger and longer-lived than family groups and small face-to-face communities is unpopular (Banks 1996: 11, 25). Some nowadays favor instead the phrase *ethnic group*; others use the expression *ethnolinguistic group* (Breton 1991; Lewis 1991; Welsch 1996). Usage varies more or less with context (Alonso 1994; Jones 1997; Linnekin and Poyer 1990; Williams 1989). "Ethnic group" is frequently used when people are talking about the diversity of modern nation states; "ethnolinguistic group" is basically a synonym for what used to be called a tribe (Cohen 1978; Nettle 1998:359–360). Put simply, therefore, these differing ways of talking about our diversity as a species may signal that many are unhappy with established ways of parsing that diversity, but these new conventions may obscure the underlying reality that no one is certain how our diversity should be categorized and mapped geographically.[1]

Similarly, decades of debate in the social sciences have underscored that there

Figure 1.1
Images of History

Note: (a) "The tree of life" (left); (b) "The tree of the knowledge of good and evil—that is, of human culture" (center); (c) "The trellis model of recent human evolution" (right).

Source: Figures 1.1a and 1.1b from *Anthropology*, by Alfred L. Kroeber, new revised edition (260, fig. 18), copyright 1948 by Harcourt, Inc., and renewed 1972 by T. Kroeber Quinn. Reproduced by permission of the publisher. Figure 1.1c reproduced by permission of the American Anthropological Association from *American Anthropologist* 100(3), September 1998. Not for further reproduction.

is little agreement on how our diversity should be ordered and charted historically (Banks 1996; Barth 1969). Some continue to depict our human accomplishments as if our history were a temporal jigsaw puzzle, or time mosaic, of separate cultural traditions or cultural lineages—many of which are extinct, but some of which lead down through time directly to what we see around us today (Bellwood 1996; Mace and Pagel 1994; Nettle 1998). Others emphasize instead the universality of human contact and influence (Lesser 1961) and see no more value in saying that history can be divided into separate cultural lineages or ethnic traditions than in still trying to carve up the world into separate ethnic societies or races. Advocacy for one or the other of these two contrasting ways of characterizing the temporal geography (Terrell and Welsch 1997) of our species is at times rancorous (Moore and Romney 1994, 1995, 1996), which hints that how to chart our long history on earth is no more certain than how to map our global diversity.

It is now common to describe these alternative ways of talking about temporal geography using two contrasting images (Dewar 1995). Those who say that the past is more or less the sum of many separate ethnic lineages often liken human history to a *family tree, dendrogram,* or *cladogram* (Figure 1.1a), showing separate cultural traditions as "limbs" branching off from a common "root" or "trunk" (Alter 1999; Bouquet 1996; Hoenigswald 1987). Alternatively, those who emphasize that "separate ethnic lineages" are simply convenient analytical fictions, not real phenomena, describe history instead as like a *trellis, lattice,* or *reticulated graph* (Figure 1.1c), showing many local traditions linked together by crosscutting ties of contact, diffusion, borrowing, and human movement—a characterization that a previous generation of scholars likened to a woven textile.

In 1928, for example, the Harvard anthropologist Roland B. Dixon wrote that the "warp" or foundation of any group's "cultural fabric" is its heritage plus all the innovations and local adaptations that the group has made over time; exotic traits derived by diffusion from other groups supply the weft (Dixon 1928:269–272, 284–285). All cultures, therefore, can be seen as "blends" both of what is local and culture-historical and of what is acquired via currents of diffusion that bring in culture traits that have arisen under alien skies:

> To any people, thus, there comes a greater or lesser wealth of such varied, exotic traits, which may be adopted or fail of adoption, or may serve merely as stimuli to special local development according as circumstances may decree. And of these two sets of elements—exotic traits brought by diffusion and local traits arising either out of their cultural heritage by adaptation or discovered and invented by their own genius and correlated in some degree often with their environment—of these two elements the fabric of a people's culture is woven. (Dixon 1928:271)

It is now widely recognized that family trees and reticulated trellises, however portrayed, are polarized ways of thinking about our diversity and history. Intermediate imagery would be more realistic, although such representations may be harder to draw or describe. Alfred Kroeber observed over 50 years ago, for instance, that while biological evolution can be reasonably depicted as a family tree, "the course of development of human culture in history cannot be so described, even metaphorically. There is a constant branching-out, but the branches also grow together again, wholly or partially, all the time" (Kroeber 1948:260). Hence the "tree of culture" is drastically different; it is a ramification of "coalescences, assimilations, or acculturations" (1948:261). Kroeber labeled his way of drawing human history "The Tree of Knowledge of Good and Evil" (Figure 1.1b). His contemporary Ralph Linton was even specific as to the kind of tree. He likened our history to "the banyan tree of the tropics" (Linton 1955:v). Recently, John Moore (1994b) offered yet a third image of the past, the "braided river channel," to make the same point that a strict biological (i.e., genetic) tree showing human history as a monophyletic branching off from a common trunk does not work well as a way of representing our history and diversity.

How one phrases a question may determine how one answers it. Similarly, how one sketches an issue may affect how one studies it (Miller 1986). We should not forget, therefore, that other ways of depicting human history have also been popular at one time or another during the twentieth century and before. Perhaps among the best known is the portrayal of cultural diffusion as a question of "centers and margins" or "cores and peripheries" that can be drawn as an "age-area" stepped pyramid or as an imaginary volcano formed by "successive lava flows, of which the latest covers the smallest area" (Dixon 1928:68).

Even when such three-dimensional portrayals have been popular, it has been noted (Wissler 1923:156) that our diversity and its history should not be "conceived of as so many separate blocks" but rather as a gigantic, complex structure in which only partial segregations occur:

What we see, then, as we look about over the earth, are a number of culture nuclei, more or less in touch with each other. We all know the history of the world's great centers and how they were mutually influenced, but even among the primitives something filtered through. . . . What we see is strikingly analogous to volcanic activity, these different centers appearing as so many crater cones of varying diameter, all belching forth the molten lava of culture, their respective lava fields meeting and overlapping, but, as in true volcanoes, the lavas differ one from the other and from time to time, and each crater contributes something new to the growing terrain. Again craters become extinct and new ones break forth in between. But the important point is that in all of them once burned the fire of originality. (1923:156–157)

Regardless of how we portray history and chart our diversity as a species, there must be some agreement on what it is about the past that is worth researching. It may be easy enough to use measures of time and space as our yardsticks for calibrating happenings and historical relationships, but what sort of happenings and relationships are important? Said differently, what is it about our diversity and history that we need to pay attention to?

Some say that people can be classified into different tribes, cultures, ethnic populations, or ethnolinguistic groups by the language they speak. Note the presumption that people are normally monolingual, or at least that one's "true language" is one's mother tongue. In like manner, some say that historical linguistics can be used to chart the "cultural phylogeny" of human groups—note the further assumption that culture history looks like a family tree—showing how people and their cultures are related historically to one another. Ruth Mace and Mark Pagel (1994:557) have written, for instance, that "if there are no other clues to phylogeny, language at least is always known."

These claims are grounded on several key assumptions: (1) human populations, ethnic groups, cultures, and languages are real things—actual empirical phenomena—and not just convenient analytical fictions; (2) despite births and deaths—and people coming and going—these corporate entities are also historically enduring phenomena (Wiley, Comuzzie, and Bamshad 1990:314); (3) like individuals, such corporate things have ancestors, descendants, relatives, and "patterns of hierarchical descent" (Mace and Pagel 1994:551); and (4) linguistic relationships between these alleged corporate entities, like kinship relationships within families, may be used to chart the genealogy, so to speak, of human history.

These assumptions are problematic (John Moore 1994a, 1994b; Terrell and Stewart 1996; Terrell, Hunt, and Gosden 1997). Even those who say "that cultures are real, that they persist through time, and that they occasionally give rise to daughter cultures" (Mace and Pagel 1994:563) acknowledge that the coincidence or coevolution of biology, language, and culture within historically en-during groups or similar corporate entities may be imperfect due to population interbreeding and the horizontal transmission (e.g., between neighbors) of cultural elements. "We shall have to accept, then, that a cultural phylogeny represents only broadly the cultural path that most of the ancestors of the majority of members of that culture followed" (1994:552). Yet even this statement is questionable. It has long been thought self-evident in anthropology and other social sciences that race, language, and culture are separate dimensions of what it means to be human. Consequently, "it is permissible to treat mankind as a whole" (Boas 1938:31), and to study language and culture apart from human biology.

It is true, nonetheless, that language is often still taken as a marker of ethnic identity and origins; language differences are ordinarily seen as barriers isolating us from other people. On this basis, as Franz Boas noted years ago and some still insist, language history ought to parallel culture history and the history of human populations. "Attempts to classify mankind from any one of the three points of view would necessarily lead to the same results; in other words, each point of view could be used independently or in combination with the other ones, to study the relations between the different groups of mankind" (Boas 1911:125).

Today, as yesterday, in short, not everyone accepts that how we look, how we speak, and how we behave are characteristics that march to different drummers. There are still those who insist that at least under favorable circumstances, examining humankind from any one of these three points of view will lead to the same analytical conclusions about history and ethnicity (Mace and Pagel 1994; Renfrew 1992). Just as Boas (1911:125) wrote 90 years ago, "the opinion is still held by some investigators that linguistic relationships and racial relationships are in a way interchangeable terms"; and language continues to be used by many people—including scholars, bureaucrats, and journalists—as a convenient, if perhaps imperfect, index of biological and cultural relationships among human groups. Not long ago, to offer one example (and others will be found in the chapters to follow), the geneticist L. L. Cavalli-Sforza and his colleagues (1994:23) wrote: "Except for the very few widely spoken languages, there tends to be a one-to-one correspondence of tribal names to language names. Thus, except in the case of large modern nations in which the identity of original tribes is usually—though not entirely—lost, languages offer a powerful ethnic guidebook, which is essentially complete, unlike strictly ethnographic information." (These scholars were evidently unaware that the correspondence between tribal names and language names is mostly one of Western colonialism's more obvious legacies; see Cohen 1978; Wolf 1982; MacEachern, this volume.)

The authors of the chapters in this book want to bridge the gap thus evidenced between common sense and one of anthropology's most important doctrines. As editor of this collection of invited essays, I asked them to take a hard look at the old issue of "race, language, and culture." As my opening chapter recounts, the founding fathers of American anthropology generally accepted what might be called the "Boas hypothesis" about our diversity as a species. This is the relatively indifferent observation that language, culture, and biology do not have to go with one another—that is, they do not have to change in step with each other. In Boas's day, Jews were commonly seen as perhaps the most obvious example showing how race, language, and culture may vary independently.

I asked these authors to tackle this old issue of how firmly these dimensions of our humanity are tied to one another from the opposite direction, so to speak. I asked them to begin with a much stronger proposition about our diversity, one I like to call the "strong Boas hypothesis." This is the axiom that language, culture, and biology always vary independently of one another except under specific circumstances. What are those circumstances? How can we tell if they are (or in the past, were) present?

As I explain in my opening chapter, one reason it is still necessary to ask if it is the exception or the rule for race, language, and culture to be closely tied is that anthropologists, linguists, and others have often stated the case for saying that these dimensions of our variability are independent in ambiguous, even ambivalent, ways (Boas 1940:159, 171). I suspect that many scholars would even now subscribe themselves to the idea that these ways in which we vary as human beings normally go together provided they may attach the learned reservation "but they do not have to." But this qualifying rider, this amendment to common sense, explains nothing. Why would they usually go together? When do they not?

The authors of these chapters—linguists, archaeologists, and ethnographers—do more than explore the commonsense idea that "different peoples speak different languages" and, therefore, language is a reliable guide to our biological heritage and ethnic identity. They also assess a more sophisticated notion. This is the claim popular today that the methods of historical linguistics can be used to reconstruct the genealogy (or phylogeny) of culture history. According to some writers, there may even be an advantage to letting language be our guide to the past. "Language differences typically evolve much more rapidly than genetic differences and therefore can be used to separate groups that may be difficult to distinguish on common genetic indices" (Mace and Pagel 1994:552). The authors of the chapters in this volume look closely at the notion that historical linguistics can be used to chart the hereditary relationships between different societies just as kinship is used to chart human relationships within societies. As we shall see, this presumption makes little sense if race, language, and culture are not intimately bound to one another.

These essays, therefore, are important for two reasons. They show why the commonsense assumption that studies of language, biology, and culture lead to similar results may lead instead to misguided science. More important, uncritically accepting this opinion easily lends the weight of science to the more dubious claims that human races exist, that people who speak different languages belong to fundamentally different biological lineages, and that the human achievements we should be celebrating are telling us instead how far apart we are from one another. That these ideas continue to look like good common sense to many people shows why we need essays such as these to show us that it is the exception, not the rule, for race, language, and culture to "go together."

NOTES

I thank Joseph Marlin for his assistance with historical research, and both Esther Schechter and Jennifer Ringberg for their production assistance.

1. One sign of this uncertainty is that there is no current agreement on what words like "ethnic," "ethnicity," and "ethnic group" should mean (Banks 1996:4–6; Jones 1997: 56–87). Older dictionaries define *ethnic* as "neither Christian nor Jewish, heathen" and also "of or relating to races or large groups of people classed according to common traits or customs" (*Webster's Seventh New Collegiate Dictionary*, 1965). A more recent dictionary adds: "of or relating to sizable groups of people sharing a common and distinctive racial, national, religious, linguistic, or cultural heritage" (*American Heritage Dictionary of the English Language*, 3rd ed., 1992). In general parlance, therefore, "ethnic" presupposes that ethnic groups actually exist. This presumption has led many to ask not "What does 'ethnic' mean?" but instead, "What defines or determines the boundaries of ethnic groups?" It may be more helpful, however, to see ethnicity as a nested set of analytical (and vernacular) ideas. The most basic concept would seem to be that the word "ethnic" and its variants refer to the sense that many of us may have that we "belong to" or "are part of" a group of people who all share with us some distinguishing trait (or traits), and that this trait (or traits) is not something of our own choosing. Like gender, stature, or sexual orientation, our "ethnicity" may be commonly thought of as predestined by where we were born, who our parents happened to be, what language we learned at our mother's knee, and so on. Many, if not most, might add that ethnic traits, like the color of our skin, cannot be changed; they define "who we really are" in spite of all we might do to "pass as something else." In this sense, some say that ethnicity is "primordial"—our ethnic heritage is so much a primal part of our "identity" as a person even at birth that it predetermines not only what we are like but also what everyone else "in my ethnic group" will be like, as well. As Linnekin and Poyer (1990:2) observe, "In this view, people are as they are because they were born to be so."

REFERENCES

Alonso, Ana María
1994 The Politics of Space, Time, and Substance: State Formation, Nationalism, and Ethnicity. *Annual Review of Anthropology* 23:379–405.
Alter, Stephen G.
1999 *Darwinism and the Linguistic Image: Language, Race, and Natural Theology in the Nineteenth Century*. Baltimore: Johns Hopkins University Press.
Banks, Marcus
1996 *Ethnicity: Anthropological Constructions*. London: Routledge.
Barth, Fredrik
1969 Introduction. In *Ethnic Groups and Boundaries: The Social Organization of Culture Difference*. Fredrik Barth, ed. Pp. 9–38. Boston: Little, Brown.

Bellwood, Peter
1996 Phylogeny vs Reticulation in Prehistory. *Antiquity* 70:881–890.
Boas, Franz
1911 *The Mind of Primitive Man*. New York: Macmillan.
1938 *The Mind of Primitive Man*. Rev. ed. Paperback ed., 1965. New York: Free Press.
1940 *Race, Language, and Culture*. Paperback ed., 1966. New York: Free Press.
Bouquet, Mary
1996 Family Trees and Their Affinities: The Visual Imperative of the Genealogical Diagram. *Journal of the Royal Anthropological Institute*, n.s., 2:43–66.
Breton, Roland J.-L.
1991 *Geolinguistics: Language Dynamics and Ethnolinguistic Geography*. Translated and expanded by Harold F. Schiffman. Ottawa: University of Ottawa Press.
Cavalli-Sforza, Luigi Luca, Paolo Menozzi, and Alberto Piazza
1994 *The History and Geography of Human Genes*. Princeton: Princeton University Press.
Cohen, Ronald
1978 Ethnicity: Problem and Focus in Anthropology. *Annual Review of Anthropology* 7:379–403.
Dewar, Robert E.
1995 Of Nets and Trees: Untangling the Reticulate and Dendritic in Madagascar's Prehistory. *World Archaeology* 26:301–318.
Dixon, Roland B.
1928 *The Building of Cultures*. New York: Charles Scribner's Sons.
Hoenigswald, Henry M.
1987 Language Family Trees, Topological and Metrical. In *Biological Metaphor and Cladistic Classification: An Interdisciplinary Perspective*. Henry M. Hoenigswald and Linda F. Wiener, eds. Pp. 257–267. Philadelphia: University of Pennsylvania Press.
Jones, Siân
1997 *The Archaeology of Ethnicity: Constructing Identities in the Past and Present*. London: Routledge.
Kroeber, Alfred L.
1948 *Anthropology: Race, Language, Culture, Psychology, Prehistory*. New York: Harcourt, Brace.
Lesser, Alexander
1961 Social Fields and the Evolution of Society. *Southwestern Journal of Anthropology* 17:40–48.
Lewis, Martin W.
1991 Elusive Societies: A Regional-Cartographical Approach to the Study of Human Relatedness. *Annals of the Association of American Geographers* 81:605–626.
Linnekin, Jocelyn, and Lin Poyer, eds.
1990 *Cultural Identity and Ethnicity in the Pacific*. Honolulu: University of Hawaii Press.
Linton, Ralph
1955 *The Tree of Culture*. New York: Alfred A. Knopf.
Mace, Ruth, and Mark Pagel
1994 The Comparative Method in Anthropology. *Current Anthropology* 35:549–564.

Miller, Arthur I.

1986. *Imagery in Scientific Thought: Creating 20th-Century Physics*. Cambridge, MA: MIT Press.

Moore, Carmella C., and A. Kimball Romney

1994 Material Culture, Geographic Propinquity, and Linguistic Affiliation on the North Coast of New Guinea: A Reanalysis of Welsch, Terrell, and Nadolski (1992). *American Anthropologist* 96:370–392.

1995 Commentary on Welsch and Terrell's (1994) Reply to Moore and Romney (1994). *Journal of Quantitative Anthropology* 5:75–84.

1996 Will the "Real" Data Please Stand Up? Reply to Welsch (1996). *Journal of Quantitative Anthropology* 6:235–261.

Moore, John

1994a Ethnogenetic Theory of Human Evolution. *National Geographic Research and Exploration* 10(1):10–23.

1994b Putting Anthropology Back Together Again: The Ethnogenetic Critique of Cladistic Theory. *American Anthropologist* 96:925–48.

Nettle, Daniel

1998 Explaining Global Patterns of Language Diversity. *Journal of Anthropological Archaeology* 17:354–374.

Renfrew, Colin

1992 Archaeology, Genetics, and Linguistic Diversity. *Man*, n.s., 27:445–478.

Terrell, John Edward, Terry L. Hunt, and Chris Gosden

1997 The Dimensions of Social Life in the Pacific: Human Diversity and the Myth of the Primitive Isolate. *Current Anthropology* 38:155–195.

Terrell, John Edward, and Pamela J. Stewart

1996 The Paradox of Human Population Genetics at the End of the Twentieth Century. *Reviews in Anthropology* 26:13–33.

Terrell, John Edward, and Robert L. Welsch

1997 Lapita and the Temporal Geography of Prehistory. *Antiquity* 71:548–572.

Welsch, Robert L.

1996 Collaborative Regional Anthropology in New Guinea: From the New Guinea Micro-Evolution Project to the A. B. Lewis Project and Beyond. *Pacific Studies* 19(3):143–186.

Wiley, E. O., Anthony Comuzzie, and Michael Bamshad

1990 Comments on "Speaking of Forked Tongues" by Richard Bateman, Ives Goddard, Richard O'Grady, V. A. Funk, Rich Mooi, W. John Kress, and Peter Cannell. *Current Anthropology* 31:314–315.

Williams, Brackette F.

1989 A Class Act: Anthropology and the Race to Nation across Ethnic Terrain. *Annual Review of Anthropology* 18:401–444.

Wissler, Clark

1923 *Man and Culture*. New York: Thomas Y. Crowell Company.

Wolf, Eric R.

1982 *Europe and the People without History*. Berkeley: University of California Press.

2

The Uncommon Sense of Race, Language, and Culture

John Edward Terrell

Forty years ago the influential British historian E. H. Carr wrote a book simply entitled *What Is History?* Historians recognize today that an equally important question is "Whose history?" What three of the founding fathers of twentieth-century American anthropology wrote about our variation and diversity as a species shows unmistakably that it is not as easy as some may think to describe and classify groups of people by their collective traits of biology, language, and culture so that we can write history. Nor is it obvious whose history this kind of history would be.—Editor

In this opening chapter I examine the issues that the authors of the chapters in this book explore in their essays by looking at what three of the founding fathers of twentieth-century American anthropology wrote about race, language, and culture—Franz Boas, Edward Sapir, and Alfred Kroeber. As George Santayana observed, those who do not remember the past are condemned to repeat it. Modern debates about ethnicity and human diversity are more repetitious than some may realize. What each of these distinguished scholars said about ourselves illustrates the basic ambiguity of what has often been written by twentieth-century scholars about our variation as a species.

Common sense tells us that different kinds of people inhabit the earth. If so, we should be able to classify them and write their history. Boas, Sapir, and Kroeber basically accepted this commonsense way of thinking about our diversity as a species. They agreed that races as conventional as "Europeans," "Negroes," and "Mongols" exist. No wonder, therefore, that Sapir wrote in 1921: "Language, race, and culture are not necessarily correlated. This does not mean that they never are. There is some tendency, as a matter of fact, for racial and cultural lines of cleavage to correspond to linguistic ones, though in any given case the latter may not be of the same degree of importance as the others" (Sapir 1921:230). But what such a statement means is not easy to decide. And is common sense truly able to make sense of our diversity?

COMMON SENSE

Common sense—our "native good judgment"—makes good sense in many situations. A fine example of common sense gone wrong, however, is the ancient view made authoritative and scientific by Ptolemy and his followers that the earth sits motionless at the center of the universe while the sun, moon, and planets move around it. Judged by common sense, the opposite idea that the earth moves is absurd. "Our senses tell us all we know of motion, and they indicate no motion for the earth" (Kuhn 1957:43). It takes no great wisdom to see that if the earth were in motion, all things not firmly attached to it would be "hurled from a rotating earth as a stone flies from a rotating sling" (1957:44).

Unhappily, astronomical arguments born from our everyday wisdom cannot effectively account for the erratic movement of the planets. Copernicus wrote his highly technical treatise *De revolutionibus orbium caelestium*, published just before his death in 1543, to solve the riddle of these "wandering stars" (Kuhn 1957:136). He broke with common sense and Ptolemaic tradition to argue that the earth spins on its axis once each day and travels around the sun once each year for what looks like an obscure reason. He wanted to improve the simplicity and accuracy of predicting the astronomical positions of these shifting celestial bodies.

Until its revision by Kepler more than sixty years after his death, however, Copernicus's heliocentric approach was no more accurate at this task than Ptolemaic astronomy. Worse than that, the Copernican world view was incompatible with a host of other valuable scientific ideas and useful procedures then popular "which explained, among other things, how stones fall, how water pumps function, and why the clouds move slowly across the skies" (Kuhn 1977:323). It is sobering to know that both common sense and good practical (and scholarly) reasoning in the sixteenth century spoke unequivocally against Copernicus and in favor of the established geocentric tradition.

We know that Copernicus, with help from his followers after his death, finally won out over Ptolemaic tradition. Yet we also know that common sense continues to rule in other domains of our daily life, and quite rightly so. Based as it is on everyday earthly experiences, common sense is the way that most of us navigate successfully through life and meet its challenges and demands. The story of Copernicus and the beginnings of modern science, nonetheless, suggests a helpful rule of thumb: *Judgments born from our worldly experiences lose their force the further we go beyond the here and now of our daily lives.* Common sense may work for handling everyday problems, but it breaks down when we deal with issues and events that are more complicated or more remote in time and space.

Questions about race, language, and culture meet both of these criteria. Our variation is complicated. After years of careful investigation, anthropologists, linguists, and human biologists are still struggling to make sense of human diversity. Our beginnings are remote in time and space. Our history goes back millions of years; there is little solid evidence to work with for most of our story; and what we have is often open to conflicting interpretation. There are grounds for thinking that common sense may not be able to handle our history and diversity as a species. However, the long and successful record of Ptolemaic astronomy shows that *common sense makes sense even when it is wrong*. Therefore, what do we need to have in hand to see that what common sense tells us may not work as well as some might think?

Everyday logic suggests that researching race, language, and culture ought to lead to the same conclusions about ethnicity and human diversity if speaking different languages creates social, economic, political, and perhaps psychological barriers that are likely to divide and isolate people from one another (as possibly French and English may do in Canada), especially if language barriers, once erected, are difficult to overcome. As Alfred Kroeber wrote many years ago: "While populations can learn and unlearn languages, they tend to do so with reluctance and infinite slowness, especially while they remain in their inherited territories. Speech tends to be one of the most persistent population characters; and 'ethnic' boundaries are most often speech boundaries" (Kroeber 1948:221). If so, then it should be possible to tell where someone is from and maybe what he or she is like, all other things being equal, by identifying the language he or she speaks. But what if all other things are not equal? Can we really trust language, for instance, as a reliable guide or guidebook to human diversity?

LANGUAGE AS A GUIDEBOOK

The linguist George Lakoff and his colleague Mark Johnson have argued that "our experiences with physical objects (especially our own bodies) provide the basis for an extraordinarily wide variety of ontological metaphors, that is, ways of viewing events, activities, emotions, ideas, etc., as entities and substances" (1980:25). Kroeber's conviction that language is one of the most persistent populational characters and that ethnic boundaries are often speech boundaries is in keeping with the conventional wisdom that treats languages as if they were tangible objects. Consider these examples that come to mind:

Language as an Object

My German is *rusty*.

Russian *frightens* me.

I find Spanish easy to *grasp.*

These languages have been *in contact* for a long time.

Languages *offer* us a *powerful ethnic guidebook.*

Language as a Substance

Her French is *fluent.*

German is *hard.*

I find his accent *impenetrable.*

What he had to say was very *dense.*

Language as a Container

Can you put that *into* words?

Can you please put that *into* plain English?

Did you get anything *out of* what she said?

Can that be translated *from* English *into* Dutch?

Language as a Place

How do you say that *in* French?

I get *lost* in Russian.

She can't *get very far* in Polish.

Oh, I can *find my way* around Norwegian easily enough.

In the middle of the conversation, he *slipped into* Yiddish.

All of these examples illustrate how common it is to talk about languages as if they were bounded entities, substances, or objects.

Lakoff and Johnson also say that ontological metaphors are generally seen as self-evident, direct descriptions of the way things are, for such expressions seem natural and are pervasive in our everyday speech. That languages are not objects but are instead learned repertoires of vocal and mental activities may seem unimportant. It may look pedantic to point out that talking this way about language does not prove that languages have boundaries, that language boundaries isolate people, or that languages "contain" people inside them who are similarly discrete and identifiable—notably in their appearance (their race) and in their ways of living (their culture).

A commonsense view of language and who we are is not completely wrong. If we parse the world carefully, it is always possible to find—or, at any rate, to define—instances where race, language, and culture all appear to be, metaphorically speaking, "packaged" together, that is, where people do seem to live in their own world, where they speak in their own distinctive ways and have their own exclusive cultural traits and practices. The challenge, therefore, does not lie in finding places where these three dimensions of our diversity seem to go together as a package at any single moment or "snapshot" of time. The challenge is finding places where they stay together over the course of time.

Consider the metaphor that language is an ethnic guidebook. Every traveler knows how worse than worthless an outdated guidebook can be: some of the information is probably still true; some is hopelessly out-of-date. In all likelihood, there may be no way to tell what is still true and what has changed. Seen in this light, how likely is it that language is a reliable guide to anything as complicated as ethnicity and human history?

To answer this question, we need to acknowledge that common sense draws on more than metaphorical language and our sense impressions of the world around us. Inherited notions and presumptions are also involved. From this perspective, our sense of common sense struggles with a conundrum that is biblically inspired. On the one hand, Judeo-Christian tradition supports our sense impressions that the diversity of life we see all around us is timeless by saying that it is God created. It took Darwin, not Copernicus, to convince thoughtful people that life evolves and that change in kind as well as variation in form is the nature of all biological things. On the other hand, the Bible also asks us to look on our own variation in quite a different light. The Bible insists that our kind, unlike all of God's other creatures, has been cursed by evolution: our wanderings away from Eden, generation after generation, have transformed the children of Adam. We are all "descendants of a single family," the Bible and its interpreters tell us, that was "divided by language at the tower of Babel, and had thence degenerated both physically and culturally during the ensuing four millennia as they moved—or were driven—through inhospitable environments toward the farther corners of the earth" (Stocking 1988:4).

From a biblical perspective, therefore, human beings have changed in fundamental ways since our time in the Garden of Eden. We are the conspicuous exception to common sense. Until Darwin taught us otherwise, it was reasonable to think that all of the world's diversity that God created is timeless except our own, and that our colorful variation is the price we pay for our sin of becoming sapient. No wonder (according to historian George Stocking) that there is "a continuing dialectical tension between human unity and diversity" (Stocking 1988:3) in Western thought.

While granting the power of inherited wisdom, I would argue that common sense based on our everyday impressions more often than not directs our thoughts. If so, it is hardly surprising that language might be seen as a powerful and trustworthy ethnic guidebook. True, from a biblical perspective, we started off as one in the Garden of Eden, and our diversity as a species has been created since that time. Yet even when many people once accepted that our differences evolved after Eden and Babel, there was little compelling evidence to doubt that the different races into which we have degenerated are basically fixed and pure (if not perfect), except perhaps in those instances where racial "mixing" or "admixture" between the different basic races of our kind has led to new, mixed varieties or hybrids. It was (and is) not obvious why anyone should think instead that our kind is so open to variation and change over time that a guidebook to our traits of race, language, and culture would not be trustworthy enough to use year after year. The Bible and Charles Darwin may tell us that we have evolved, but surely not everything about who we are is so up for grabs that we ought to think of language, say, only as an encyclopedia that is in constant need of updating rather than as a guidebook we can trust for all time. In fact, is not writing the ultimate guidebook to human beings one of the basic goals of anthropology, linguistics, and other social sciences?

FRANZ BOAS

Perhaps no scholar is more closely identified with the study of race, language, and culture than Franz Boas (1858–1942). It was he who declared in his popular classic *The Mind of Primitive Man* that "we are led to the conclusion that [racial] type, language, and type of culture, may not be closely and permanently connected" (Boas 1911:127). It is evident, he said, "that in many cases a people, without undergoing a considerable change in type by mixture, has changed completely its language and culture, still other cases may be adduced in which it can be shown that a people has retained its language while undergoing material changes in blood and culture, or in both" (1911:129–30).

Note, however, that these are not exceptionally strong claims. In the second edition (1938) of *The Mind of Primitive Man*, Boas did change the words "may not be closely and permanently connected" to read "are not closely and permanently connected" (1938:138). But how he phrased these pivotal observations paradoxically shows that ambiguity about ethnicity and human variation—the tension in Western thought about our unity and diversity as a species—may be nowhere more apparent than in what Boas himself wrote about the sensitive issue of race.

Consider how he began the 1938 edition of *The Mind of Primitive Man*, published at a time when the world was under the threat of Nazi Germany:

A survey of our globe shows the continents inhabited by a great diversity of peoples different in appearance, different in language and in cultural life.... Each human type seems to have its own inventions, its own customs and beliefs, and it is very generally assumed that race and culture must be intimately associated, that racial descent determines cultural life. (1938:19)

Here he uses the words *type, race,* and *culture* without questioning the appropriateness of this terminology. As his book unfolds, Boas is careful not to leave these terms unexamined. Yet he never directly tells us that we should wonder whether types, races, or cultures exist not only as convenient and useful concepts but also as entities or objects. Indeed, he repeatedly refers to "the White race," "the White type," "the European," "the Negro," "the Mongol," and so on as if this nomenclature were unproblematic (see also Boas 1940[1899a]:157; Boas 1940[1936b]:173).

Boas did give a definition of *race* that would please most modern evolutionary biologists:

A race must not be identified with a subjectively established type but must be conceived as a biological unit, as a population derived from a common ancestry and by virtue of its descent endowed with definite biological characteristics. To a certain extent these may be unstable because subject to a multitude of outer influences, for the biological character of the genealogical group finds expression in the way in which the body is shaped under varying conditions of life. (1938:46–47)

Yet again this definition shows unmistakably that he was willing to grant that distinct "biological units" can be established for our species, cautioning only that they must not be determined subjectively.

Said differently, Boas talks about race in *The Mind of Primitive Man* as a methodological, not an ontological, issue. While modern writers would deny that extreme local forms exist within *Homo sapiens* (Templeton 1998), Boas immediately goes on to note that Europeans, Melanesians, African Negroes, Northern Mongolids, Malay groups, Australians, perhaps some American Indian groups, and others would be such racial types (1938:58).

BOAS'S DILEMMA

Given what Boas wrote about race, it is hardly surprising that people might find his (and perhaps anthropology's) stand on human variation and diversity ambiguous. To offer examples taken from some of his other writings, Boas made a point of saying on the one hand that (1) the history of any selected group or of humankind as a whole is so complex that all explanatory systems and classifications will be subjective, unrevealing, and misleading (1940[1936a]:310); (2) anthropologists "have not been able to find any criterion by which an individual skeleton of any one race can be distinguished with certainty from a skeleton belonging to another race, except in a very general way" (1940[1899b]: 166); (3) anthropological classifications are only statistical studies of "the distribution of forms" occurring in "local or social varieties" (1940[1899b]:166); (4) "the fact that individuals cannot be classified as belonging to a certain type shows that physical anthropology cannot possibly lead to a classification of mankind as detailed as does the classification based on language" (1940[1899b]: 171); and (5) "the analysis of distributions of measurements [must] be carried much further than it has proceeded up to the present time" (1940[1889b]:170). But he then immediately added: "This done, I believe we shall obtain a means of determining with considerable accuracy the blood-relationships of the geographical varieties of man" (1940[1899b]:170–171).

Judging by these words, Boas plainly accepted that human beings can be classified into diverse geographical varieties or biological units as conventional as "Europeans," "Negroes," and "Mongols."

It is easy to describe what distinguishes a lion from a mouse. It is almost as easy to give a satisfactory description that enables us to distinguish the type of the Swede from the

type of the Central African Negro. It is, however, difficult to give a satisfactory description that will set off a Swede against a North German, or a lion of North Africa against
a lion from Rhodesia. The reason is clear. Not all Swedes are alike, and some cannot be
distinguished from North Germans, and the same is true of lions of different localities.
The variability of each group is considerable, and if we want to know what a Swede is
we must know all the different forms that may be found among the descendants of a
group of "pure" Swedes. (1938:47)

Why did Boas interject here the idea of pure races (to the possible dismay of
those who know that Boas was an ardent foe of Nazi racism)? The answer may
lie in how he explained racial variation.

In both the 1911 and 1938 editions of *The Mind of Primitive Man*, Boas has
only a few words to say about human genetics, concluding in both editions that
how far human traits follow the laws of genetic inheritance is "a question that
cannot be answered definitely at the present time" (1911:84; 1938:61–62). Nonetheless, the reason for human biological variation is easily understood. It is a
characteristic of all living creatures that individuals descended from the same
ancestors are not identical because there are so many uncontrollable conditions
that affect the growth of an organism. Even with identical ancestry, the outcome
cannot always be the same, although if we could somehow control all the relevant conditions from conception to adulthood, "then we should, of course,
expect the same result in every case" (1938:48). In other words, pure human
types would exist were it not for the vagaries of biological development. Hence
to decide whether two "distinct individual human forms" are two different races
or are merely extreme varieties of a single human type, "we ought to prove that
the ancestral forms do not vary in such a way that both forms might have
developed from the same single uniform ancestry." To do so, Boas instructs us,
"we must describe the frequency of the various forms that occur in each local
or social unit." Only then can we decide "whether the variations are due to
varying internal organic conditions or whether we are dealing with a mixed
population in which genetically distinct types occur. In some cases a careful
[statistical] analysis of the interrelations of measurements makes it possible to
answer this question" (1938:50).

Observe, however, that Boas reached this admittedly cautious conclusion
without commenting on what might be seen as an obvious dilemma: *How do
we decide who are the proper individuals to measure and enumerate? How do
we know what are the right "local or social units" to compare?*

WHY DO RACES EXIST?

This is the catch and the ambiguity at the heart of what Boas wrote about
race, language, and culture. He gave an admirable and quite modern definition
of what the word *race* should mean (a population of individuals having common
ancestry). Yet since he was evidently willing to grant that racial types (of

a statistical sort) exist, his solution to "the problem of the biological relation of races" puts the cart before the horse. His recipe for writing a guidebook to human variation and diversity asks us to identify racial groups before we compare individuals to see what racial groups they belong to. Somehow we have got to know what we want to know before we have a way of knowing it. Since this is not possible, we need to backtrack and ask again, Why was Boas convinced that races exist?

The Bible says that our diversity began when God, to keep us weak, used language to divide us (Genesis 11:1–9). Boas did not cite the same reason, but he accepted the same result: local types (i.e., races) develop only when small groups are isolated and the people in them "show peculiarities" (1938:74). This answer begs the question. For both Boas and the Bible, isolation is the major reason for humankind's evolution (or degeneration) into recognizably distinct types of people speaking different languages and having different cultural practices and traits. But what isolates small groups of people? Would it not make sense to think that they are the last people on earth who can afford to be isolated? Would they not need ties with people in other places so that they could call upon friends in times of need and find suitable mates to woo as wives or husbands?

It might be thought that these hesitations, being so elementary, would be enough to undermine the wisdom that primitive people have lived isolated lives in small hordes, bands, or "social units," but apparently not. Boas's account of early times in another famous book, *Anthropology and Modern Life*, is colorful but not unusual. Remarking that "in primitive human society every tribe forms a closed society," he explains:

In the early days of mankind our earth was thinly settled. Small groups of human beings were scattered here and there; the members of each horde were one in speech, one in customs, one in superstitious beliefs. . . . They were held together by strong bands of habit. The gain of one member of the horde was the gain of the whole group. . . . Beyond the limits of the hunting grounds lived other groups, different in speech, different in customs, perhaps even different in appearance, whose very existence was a source of danger. . . . They acted in a different manner; their reasoning and feeling were unintelligible; they had no part in the interests of the horde. Thus they stood opposed to it as being of another kind, with whom there could be no community of interest. . . . Thus the most primitive form of society presents to us the picture of continuous strife. . . . Always on the alert to protect himself and his kindred, man considered it an act of high merit to kill the stranger. (1928:67–68)

This picture of humankind's early days is, of course, wholly speculative (and in some of its elements, almost biblical). As Boas acknowledged in *The Mind of Primitive Man*:

It must be granted that in a theoretical consideration of the history of the types of mankind, of languages, and of cultures, we are led back to the assumption of early conditions, during which each type was much more isolated from the rest of mankind than it is at the present time. For this reason the culture and the language belonging to a single type must have been much more sharply separated from those of other types than we find them to be at the present period. It is true that such a condition has nowhere been observed; but the knowledge of historical developments almost compels us to assume its existence at a very early period in the development of mankind. (1911:134; 1938:142–143)

This portrayal is an unequivocal example of what the anthropologist Alexander Lesser (1961) once labeled "the myth of the primitive isolate": the view of early or primitive human life as a world of closed social aggregates, each out of contact with other humans. This myth is enticing, for it explains our variation and diversity as a species in a way that is simple, easy to understand, and logically sensible and does not require the hand of God or the tower of Babel.

MYTH OF THE PRIMITIVE ISOLATE

If Boas were alive, it is conceivable that his "unrelenting empiricism" (Steward 1961:1049) and his strong inductivist leaning in science (Boas 1940[1932]: 243–259), together with all the advances in human genetics since his death in 1942, would have led him long ago to revise his views on race. He would have seen by now that genes can travel the earth (via sexual intercourse) unaccompanied by the "biological units" or "local or social units" that individuals are part of at any given moment. He would have accepted that genes can "flow" via the mobility and mating of individuals just as traits of culture and language may be "borrowed" and "diffused" between places as individual elements of variation and diversity. Consequently, attempts to classify people by genes, like attempts to do so by cultural and linguistic traits, "must lead to contradictions" (Boas 1938:145).

It is harder to say whether Boas would have rejected the myth of the primitive isolate. When Alexander Lesser proffered this phrase in November 1960 at the meetings of the American Anthropological Association, he observed that "the myth of the primitive isolate is still with us, still embedded in current concept and theory" (1961:42). Its adherents recognize that it may be impossible to find, even difficult to conceive of, a society that is physically or socially isolated in an absolute sense:

Yet they imply that isolation, as the extreme opposite of the contact so obvious in complex social situations, [should] be imagined to have been the condition at the beginning; and draw from this hypothetical notion the idea of the primitive isolate as a conceptual tool. One is reminded of how some 19th century evolutionists postulated promiscuity—the absence of patterned interpersonal sexual relations—as the primitive social condition from which marriage and the family had evolved. (1961:42)

Lesser asked us instead to adopt "the universality of human contact and influence" as our working hypothesis—as one of our fundamental assumptions about human history. We need to regard, he said, different social aggregates ("groups, tribes, communities, settlements") not as isolated, not as separated from others by some kind of wall, but "as inextricably involved with other aggregates, near and far, in weblike, netlike connections." Then we would be able to see that "there is a communications process between any social aggregate, primitive or more advanced, and others. The communications process has evolved, but it has not evolved out of conditions in which it was absent, but from the primitive communications process which links social aggregates even in the earliest time of which we have evidence" (1961:47).

Lesser was one of Boas's most unwavering students (Belmonte 1985). He helped Boas select the essays to be reprinted in *Race, Language, and Culture* (Boas 1940). It may not be farfetched, therefore, to think that Boas would have come around eventually to Lesser's way of thinking about the myth of the primitive isolate. It is anyone's guess how many others by now would have come around, too. The thought that once upon a time we were all the same, but then something happened that made us different (if not the hand of God, then perhaps our primitive impulse to kill all strangers who show up at the borders of our hunting grounds), would seem to be such good common sense that if we do not accept the Bible's explanation for our degeneration into different kinds, we need something like the myth of the primitive isolate to explain why we have left our original state of unity and perfection behind us.

Although Boas may have accepted "the primitive isolate" as a way of explaining why human beings came to be divided into different races, we do know that he did not find a common inference based on this argument equally convincing. Reconstructing the character of our early social life as a time of isolation and hostility between human hordes can be seen (and has been seen) as grounds for saying that early in our history as a species, each of the different races, or primal bloodlines, that human beings were soon subdivided into must have had its own particular characteristics of language and culture. It is often said that only more recently—except in the case of people who are still living "Stone Age" lives—have the development of agriculture, the growth of urbanism, and the progress of technology led to larger, more fluid human populations and to the decline in the uniqueness and authenticity of our prehistoric bloodlines (and, unfortunately, also to a decline in the odds of writing a complete and easy-to-understand book about the major types of human beings). Boas himself wrote, however:

The historical development of mankind would afford a simpler and clearer picture if we were justified in assuming that in primitive communities the three phenomena had been intimately associated. No proof, however, of such an assumption, can be given. On the contrary, the present distribution of languages, as compared with the distribution of [racial] types, makes it plausible that even at the earliest times the biological units may have been wider than the linguistic units, and presumably also wider than the cultural units. I believe it may be safely said that all over the world the biological unit—disregarding minute local differences—is much larger than the linguistic unit; in other words, that groups of men who are so closely related in bodily appearance that we must consider them as representatives of the same variety of mankind, embrace a much larger number of individuals than the number of men speaking languages which we know to be genetically related. (1911:135; 1938:143; see also 1940[1920]:212)

Consequently, attempts to classify people from more than one of these points of view will lead to contradictions (1938:145; variant phrasing, 1911:139).

Boas had other reasons, too, for rejecting the primordial union of race, language, and culture. One is the mobility of human populations. "From earliest times on we have a picture of continued movements, and with it of mixtures of diverse people. It may well be that the lack of clean-cut geographical and biological lines between the races of man is entirely due to these circumstances" (Boas 1928:29). Another is the rapidity of language change. "Languages that have sprung from the same source may become so distinct that, without documents illustrating their historical development, relationships are difficult to discover; so much so, that in some cases this task might even be impossible" (1940[1917]:202). As a result, contradictions between classifications based on race, language, and culture are inevitable, even if we accept that these dimensions of our diversity were once closely unified by the (purported) isolation of early and primitive societies.

Did Boas's contemporaries, however, agree? It is instructive to look at what two other prominent anthropologists who were among Boas's most successful students say about human ethnicity and history: the anthropologist and linguist Edward Sapir (1884–1939) and the anthropologist Alfred Kroeber (1876–1960).

EDWARD SAPIR

Franz Boas is often said to have been the single most influential American anthropologist in the first half of the twentieth century. He was not, however, the only leading scholar of his day to write definitively about race, language, and culture. In 1936, for example, Ralph Linton observed in *The Study of Man*:

The social horizon of uncivilized groups is always very limited. They know only the members of their own band and possibly those of the bands whose territory immediately adjoins theirs. They are often on hostile terms even with these close neighbors. The result of this is fairly close and continuing inbreeding. (1936:25)

While Linton observed that biological differences between even the most diverse human varieties are not very great (1936:24–25), he concluded that the consequences of our early isolation and inbreeding are apparent:

Throughout the history of our species two forces have constantly been at work. On the one hand the combined factors of variation, selection, and fixation of traits by inbreeding have worked steadily toward the production of a greater and greater number of human varieties. On the other hand, the ease with which human strains can and do cross has worked to blur the outlines of these varieties and to produce multitudes of individuals of mixed heredity and variable physical type. The first of these forces [the factors favoring diversity] was dominant during the early period of man's existence. The second [that favoring unity] became increasingly important as time passed and has risen to a crescendo with the elimination of space and the breakdown of old local groupings which are characteristic of modern civilization. (1936:32)

Given this depiction, it is hardly surprising that "every band has a culture of its own" (1936:221) and that "aggregations of bands into a tribe" are (or were) marked by "community of language, culture, and origin" (1936:233). In fairness, however, we should add that Linton insists in *The Study of Man* that diffusion from other places has played a role in establishing the content of all cultures, and that "we know from direct observation that language distributions are only superficially related to those of any other elements of culture, and [therefore] classifications based upon them are useful only for linguistic studies" (1936: 390).

Judging by what Edward Sapir wrote in *Time Perspective in Aboriginal American Culture: A Study in Method*, which was published in 1916, he did not agree with Linton:

It is customary to insist on the mutual independence of racial, cultural, and linguistic factors. This caution of method must, however, not be understood to mean that conclusions of direct value for the history of culture can not be derived from the data of physical anthropology and linguistics. In actual practice the units of distribution of these three sciences, while never coinciding throughout, do nevertheless show significant lines of accord. . . . That differences in culture ever neatly correspond to differences of race and language can not be maintained, but I wish to point out that the numerous homologies are of at least as great historical importance as the discordances. (Sapir 1916:10–11; see also Sapir 1921:230)

Sapir also insisted that anthropology is "a strictly historical science" and that its data cannot be understood, either in themselves or in their relation to one another, "except as the end-points of specific sequences of events reaching back into the remote past" (1916:1). Primitive culture, he wrote,

consists throughout of phenomena that, so far as the ethnologist is concerned, must be worked out historically, that is, in terms of actual happenings, however inferred, that are conceived to have a specific sequence, a specific localization, and specific relations among themselves. Few would be so bold as to maintain that the vast and ever growing mass of ethnological material will ever completely yield to such an historical interpretation, but it is highly important than an historical understanding of the facts be held up as the properly ethnological goal of the student. (1916:2)

He repeats this theme throughout this short but extremely influential 1916 monograph as a subtle (or not-so-subtle) rejoinder to those who would use intellectual shortcuts to arrive at sweeping statements about the psychology and evolution of primitive peoples or about the diffusion of "cultural elements" torn loose from their "psychological and geographical (*i.e.*, distributional) setting" (1916:87).

These sentiments are fitting, and yet *Time Perspective in Aboriginal American Culture* is a puzzling book. Sapir championed anthropology as a historical science, but it is not clear what history for Sapir is all about. "It is evident at the outset," he observes, speaking as a student of aboriginal American culture, "that the nature of our material imposes limitations not felt, or not felt so keenly, by the historian" (1916:3). One limitation, he says, is that anthropologists are rarely able to assign absolute dates to the events they study. A second limitation hints more directly at what Sapir means by the "history of culture":

One of the characteristic traits of history is its emphasis on the individual and personal. While the importance of individual events and personalities for the progress of human affairs is not to be underestimated, the historical reconstructions of the cultural anthropologist can only deal, with comparatively few exceptions, with generalized events and individualities. (1916:3)

He says, however, that we should not be overly worried about this second limitation: "the nature of the social units, whether individual or collective," introduces "a purely quantitative, not qualitative, correction" (1916:3). True, we may be unable to discover "the specific influence exerted by a particular shaman of a tribe at an inaccessible period in the past," but we can "lump together a number of such phenomena" and thereby "generalize as to the influence exerted by the class of shamans at a more or less well defined time and place." Similarly,

if it is a question of the social relations between two tribes, say the Haida and Tsimshian, [we] may in a number of cases have to content [ourselves] with a broad definition of such relations, taking, for instance, the Haida and Tsimshian as such as the units directly involved, though perfectly aware that the actual mechanism of the relation is in every case borne by individuals, house-groups, or clans, that is, by subdivisions of the historical units ostensibly concerned. A great deal of such substitution of the whole for the part is unavoidable in ethnology. (1916:3)

However, Sapir is not confronting a key issue that is none other than Boas's dilemma in new clothing. Recall that Boas's methodological approach to race asks us to identify racial groups ("biological units," "local or social units," and so on) before we compare individuals to see what racial groups they belong to. In like fashion, Sapir directs us to be historians of aboriginal culture, but he does not tell us how to recognize the proper "wholes" (as in the quotation just given) to study so that we can substitute "the whole for the part," that is, he does not explain how we are to identify the right "historical units."

In his famous book *Language*, published several years after *Time Perspective in Aboriginal American Culture*, Sapir returned to the issue of how closely race, language, and culture may be tied to each other. The position he takes in this later book is once again confusing. He writes that "historians and anthropologists find that races, languages, and cultures are not distributed in parallel fashion, that their areas of distribution intercross in the most bewildering fashion, and that the history of each is apt to follow a distinctive course" (1921:222). He notes that many striking examples of the lack of correspondence between race and language can be given (1921:227). In a chapter on how languages influence each other, he even seems to be arguing against the myth of the primitive isolate: "It would be difficult to point to a completely isolated language or dialect, least of all among the primitive peoples. The tribe is often so small that intermarriages with alien tribes that speak other dialects or even totally unrelated languages are not uncommon. It may even be doubted whether intermarriage, intertribal trade, and general cultural interchanges are not of greater relative significance on primitive levels than on our own" (1921:205). Nonetheless, he claims elsewhere in this same book that "under primitive conditions the political groups are small, the tendency to localism exceedingly strong. It is natural, therefore, that the languages of primitive folk or of non-urban populations in general are differentiated into a great number of dialects. . . . The life of the geographically limited community is narrow and intense; its speech is correspondingly peculiar to itself" (1921:161).

To archaeologists, at least, Sapir's insistence that anthropology is a strictly historical science sounds right, and it is impossible not to admire his extraordinary scholarship and insights. Yet, to put it mildly, the uncertain character of his position on human variation and diversity is disappointing. He says in 1916, for example, that if we succeed "in putting the changing face of culture into relation with the changing face of language, we shall have obtained a measure, vague or precise according to specific circumstances, of the relative ages of . . . culture elements" (1916:52). He also says that "the simple fact that the bearers of a distinctive culture are often marked off from the bearers of other cultures by a distinctive physical type enables us not infrequently to employ the racial evidence for cultural purposes" (1916:11). However, he promised more than this. He says that we shall be able to get "conclusions of direct value for the history of culture" from the data of physical anthropology and linguistics if we follow the methodological guidelines he sketches for us in *Time Perspective in Aboriginal American Culture*. But it is simply not obvious *whose* history or *what kind* of history we will be writing if we labor in the fields of biology, linguistics, and cultural anthropology in the ways he says that we should.

Alfred Kroeber, Sapir's equally famous contemporary, also insisted on the importance of history to anthropology. Perhaps his writings can explain in a more compelling way why it is worthwhile to look for connections between race, language, and culture.

ALFRED KROEBER

When Alfred Louis Kroeber died in 1960, he was widely considered the dean of American anthropology. After his death, Julian H. Steward called Kroeber's textbook *Anthropology* (1923, 1948) perhaps the single most important work ever written in the field: "It constitutes a basic survey of modern anthropology which well serves Ph.D. candidates and all others wishing a sophisticated view" (Steward 1961:1058). It may be noteworthy, therefore, that the position Kroeber takes on race, language, and culture in this classic textbook is even more equivocal than that taken by Boas and Sapir:

As to the relative permanence of race and speech, everything depends on the side from which the question is approached. . . . It is a fallacy to think, because one can learn French or become a Christian and yet is powerless to change his eye color or head shape, that language and culture are altogether less stable than race. Speech and culture have an existence of their own, whose integrity does not depend on hereditary integrity. The two [race and language] may move together or separately. (Kroeber 1923:105–106; variant phrasing, Kroeber 1948:221–222)

However indecisive this statement may be, it does not obscure that Kroeber saw race as a valid biological concept. Elsewhere in *Anthropology*, he defines race, as if paraphrasing Boas, as "a group united by heredity: a breed or genetic strain or subspecies" (1948:124; also 1923:56). Like Boas, he claims that the difficulty with race is not whether "the desirability of a trustworthy classification of the human races" is questionable. The value of racial classifications can be "generally accepted without further argument," and "some general truths can be discovered from a careful race classification and certain constant principles of importance emerge from all the diversity" (1923:36; 1948:126). But there is a problem with race, nonetheless. Making trustworthy racial classifications is more difficult work than might be imagined:

It is true that a Negro and a northern European cannot possibly be confused: they happen to represent extreme types. Yet as soon as we operate with less divergent races we find that variations between individuals of the same race are often greater than differences between the races. . . . This is called *overlapping*; and it occurs to such an extent as to make it frequently difficult for the physical anthropologist to establish clear-cut types. (1923:36, 1948:126)

It is worth noting that Kroeber here uses the word *overlapping*, a word we have seen Boas and Sapir also using. As my dictionary would put it, "overlapping" means that a part or portion of one thing extends over and covers part of something else. Like Boas, Kroeber did not see "overlapping" as an insurmountable hurdle to race classification. He did not opt for the solution to the problem of race that says that all geographic variation within *Homo sapiens* is "overlapping," and therefore we need a more appropriate word to use, perhaps a verb like "grades" or "shades," to signal that our variation expresses itself in complicated ways throughout the geographic range of our species.

Kroeber did complain, nonetheless, that making good racial classifications is hampered by the popular use of the word "race" to refer to people "having any traits in common, be they hereditary or non-hereditary, biological or social" (1923:56; variant phrasing, 1948:175). Thus it is not uncommon "but mainly inaccurate" to hear people talking about "the French race, the Anglo-Saxon race, the Gypsy race, the Jewish race." In the latter case, for example, Jews evince little hereditary type (1923:57; 1948:144), and "at any rate, attitudes toward Jews obviously depend immeasurably more on emotional reaction to the social functioning of Jews than on their biology" (1948:175).

Kroeber concludes, censoriously, that it may not seem important whether the word *race* is limited to its "strict biological sense or used more loosely." However, "untold loose reasoning has resulted from the loose terminology." When people have spoken a dozen times about "the French race," it is only natural that they begin to think of the inhabitants of France as a biological unit, which (he insists) they are not: "That civilizations, languages, and nationalities go on for generations is obviously a different thing from their being caused by [biological] generation. Slovenly thought, tending to deal with results rather than causes or processes, does not trouble to make this discrimination, and everyday speech, dating from a pre-scientific period, is ambiguous about it" (1923: 57; 1948:176).

THE LION AND THE MOUSE

On Boas's death, Ruth Benedict wrote that he had "found anthropology a collection of wild guesses and a happy hunting ground for the romantic lover of primitive things; he left it a discipline in which theories could be tested and in which he had delimited possibilities from impossibilities" (quoted in Stocking 1996:3–4). I have stressed, however, the ambiguity of his position on the character and causes of human variation and diversity. I have argued that by not challenging the impression that human beings belong to racial groups and the conventional "myth of the primitive isolate," Boas weakened the clarity and force of what he wanted us to think about the freedom that race, language, and culture have to change in separate ways—a shortcoming that undermines his profession that race is not a factor in human affairs and that the concept of race should not be turned to political ends.

We have also seen that Edward Sapir and Alfred Kroeber took positions on ethnicity and human history that differed somewhat from what their mentor wrote about these matters, yet they took it more or less for granted, as well, that races are real. Each of these noted scholars—they were neither the first nor the last to do so—made pronouncements about how and why we should study ourselves from the "three points of view" of race, language, and culture without answering the most important question of all. Both metaphorically and quite literally, What is the object of such investigations?

Nobody doubts, I suspect, that we can describe and classify human beings according to their traits of race, language, and culture, although it may not be easy to select and define the specific traits to be used, and it may be hard to decide whether classifying people in these ways is worthwhile. (Classifying me as a native speaker of American English whose ancestors came from England, Ireland, and Germany and who still uses Aladdin kerosene lamps to light my home in Wisconsin tells something but not very much about who I am, my personal history, and how I relate to other people.) But what if we move up a step? What if we attempt to describe and classify groups of people by their collective traits of race, language, and culture? What human groups should we look at? Would classifying them according to these "three points of view" actually tell us something about their collective history, relations, and character?

We cannot turn to what Boas, Sapir, and Kroeber wrote for help in picking our human groups to study. Look at the many words and phrases Boas, Linton, Sapir, and Kroeber use to refer to human social aggregates (to borrow Lesser's expression): "group," "group of mankind," "racial group," "tribe," "class," "people," "population," "local or social unit," "historical unit," "race," "biological unit," "genealogical group," "extreme local form," "local or social variety," "geographical variety of man," "local form," "pure type," "more or less specialized local type," "small group," "horde," "band," "primitive community," "variety of mankind," "the whole," and "breed." They do not tell us what these words and phrases mean. There is no dictionary or guidebook that can tell us in a fashion that would equip us to go out into the real world and find them, although nowadays the word *tribe* has a legal meaning in the United States. But what is legally a tribe may not actually be a meaningful social aggregate.

In short, while there is general agreement that humans are a social animal and that people usually participate in collective activities and tasks, these two commonsense facts do not mean that the seemingly diverse kinds of social aggregates named by Boas, Sapir, and Kroeber exist in the world as real objects suitable for study in the way that you and I exist and can be studied. But then how are we to describe and classify groups, tribes, hordes, local forms, and the like according to their biological, linguistic, and cultural traits? How can we discover their relationships to one another? If races, ethnic groups, tribes, varieties, and so on are not real the way you and I are real, how are we to avoid what might be called "Ptolemy's fallacy," namely, getting results but for the wrong reasons? This may be fine if all we want to know is where the planets will be on such and such a date so that we can make astrological predictions, but it will not do if we want to really understand our history and variation as a species.

REFERENCES

Belmonte, Thomas
1985 Alexander Lesser (1902–1982). *American Anthropologist* 87:637–644.
Boas, Franz
1911 *The Mind of Primitive Man.* New York: Macmillan.
1928 *Anthropology and Modern Life.* New York: W. W. Norton.
1938 *The Mind of Primitive Man.* Rev. ed. Paperback ed., 1965. New York: Free Press
    (Macmillan).
1940 *Race, Language, and Culture.* Paperback ed., 1966. New York: Free Press.
1940 [1899a] Review of William Z. Ripley, "The Races of Europe." Pages 155–159 in
    Boas 1940.
1940 [1899b] Some Recent Criticisms of Physical Anthropology. Pages 165–171 in Boas
    1940.
1940[1917] Introduction, International Journal of American Linguistics. Pages 199–210
    in Boas 1940.
1940[1920] The Classification of American Languages. Pages 211–218 in Boas 1940.
1940[1932] The Aims of Anthropological Research. Pages 243–259 in Boas 1940.
1940[1936a] History and Science in Anthropology: A Reply. Pages 305–311 in Boas
    1940.
1940[1936b] The Relations between Physical and Social Anthropology. Pages 172–175
    in Boas 1940.
Kroeber, Alfred L.
1923 *Anthropology.* New York: Harcourt, Brace, and Company.
1948 *Anthropology.* New York: Harcourt, Brace.
Kuhn, Thomas S.
1957 *The Copernican Revolution: Planetary Astronomy in the Development of Western
    Thought.* Chicago: University of Chicago Press.
1977 *The Essential Tension: Selected Studies in Scientific Tradition and Change.* Chi-
    cago: University of Chicago Press.
Lakoff, George, and Mark Johnson
1980 *Metaphors We Live By.* Chicago: University of Chicago Press.
Lesser, Alexander
1961 Social Fields and the Evolution of Society. *Southwestern Journal of Anthropology.*
    17:40–48.
Linton, Ralph
1936 *The Study of Man: An Introduction.* New York: D. Appleton-Century.
Sapir, Edward
1916 *Time Perspective in Aboriginal American Culture: A Study in Method.* Canada,
    Geological Survey, Department of Mines, Memoir 90; Anthropological Series,
    No. 13. Ottawa: Government Printing Bureau.
1921 *Language: An Introduction to the Study of Speech.* New York: Harcourt, Brace,
    and Company.
Steward, Julian H.
1961 Alfred Louis Kroeber, 1876–1960. *American Anthropologist* 63:1038–1060.
Stocking, George W., Jr.
1988 Bones, Bodies, Behavior. In *Bones, Bodies, Behavior: Essays on Biological An-*

thropology. George W. Stocking, Jr., ed. Pp. 3–17. Madison: University of Wisconsin Press.

1996 Boasian Ethnography and the German Anthropological Tradition. In *Volksgeist as Method and Ethic: Essays on Boasian Ethnography and the German Anthropological Tradition*. George W. Stocking, Jr., ed. Pp. 3–8. Madison: University of Wisconsin Press.

Templeton, Alan

1998 Human Races: A Genetic and Evolutionary Perspective. *American Anthropologist* 100:632–650.

3

Ethnogenetic Patterns in Native North America

John H. Moore

Proponents of ethnogenetic models of human history and evolution argue that human societies periodically reorganize themselves and that the resulting new social formations are likely to have their "roots" or "origins" in several antecedent societies (which may be greatly dissimilar), not just in one. The resulting patterns of diversity in biology, language, and culture can be said to be more like a "tapestry" than a "family tree."—Editor

In current anthropological discourse, contrasts are being drawn between two models of human evolution, one that is friendly to the analytic importance of "racial" differences among human groups, and another that calls attention to a basic and underlying homogeneity of the human species (Bellwood 1996; Hill 1996; Moore 1994). The former model is cladistic in nature and emphasizes the extent to which human populations separate, evolve independently, and become progressively more dissimilar as time passes, thereby producing a "mosaic" pattern of human diversity, expressed geographically as clearly bounded separate populations. The other model is reticulate in form, embodies ethnogenetic processes, and emphasizes that human societies periodically reorganize themselves so that each new society is rooted in several antecedent societies that may be very different from one another. The pattern resulting from the operation of ethnogenetic forces can be called a "tapestry" of variation, expressed geographically by gradual and continual variation within and among local human populations.

In addition to having biological significance, these two models are alleged to have linguistic and cultural significance as well. In cladistic theory, genes, lan-

guage, and culture are said to evolve as a "package," so that all three aspects
of human life tend to experience congruent or parallel changes.[1] A biological
taxonomy of human populations showing their overall genetic relatedness should
be compatible with a taxonomy of their languages, technology, or other aspects
of culture. By knowing a group's genetic structure, we should be able to predict
such traits as their linguistic affiliations, their social structure, and their religion.
By contrast, the ethnogenetic view emphasizes the novel and hybrid nature of
each human population, its language and culture. Alfred Kroeber's famous tree
of culture (Figure 1.1b) represents a basically reticulate and ethnogenetic view
of human evolution.

While no one would deny that ethnogenesis (the development of new hybrid
ethnic groups) happens, there are important differences of opinion between cladistic and ethnogenetic theorists regarding the overall importance of ethnogenetic
events—their speed, frequency, and global distribution—and the historical conditions that bring them about. One condition that at least encourages ethnogenesis, if it is not in fact essential, is the presence in one society of people of
diverse linguistic and cultural backgrounds who can provide the raw material
for a new cultural synthesis, as well as creating a greater genetic diversity in
the group. In this chapter, I will argue that among human societies of small
scale, which characterizes all but the last several millennia of human existence,
this kind of diversity is achieved predominantly by intermarriage across linguistic, ethnic, and "racial" boundaries, that is, marriage with "foreigners." Using ethnohistorical evidence from aboriginal North America, I will argue that
foreign intermarriage and resulting ethnogenetic episodes were very common in
the sixteenth through the nineteenth centuries. After establishing empirically in
the first part of this chapter that intermarriage and ethnogenesis did occur, I will
then use demographic models to show why and how these small-scale "tribal"
societies were driven to seek far-flung marriages, not only by their desire for
trade and political alliance, but by the operation of their own marriage rules.
Last, I will outline a typology of ethnogenetic processes observed in North
America, hoping that they might prove to have a broader application to ethnogenetic processes as seen in other places and other times.

ETHNOHISTORICAL EXAMPLES

To observe and understand diversity in a tribal society, one first has to cure
oneself of the normative expectations created by three prominent schools of
thought in anthropology—structuralism, structural functionalism, and the "historical particularism" of the students of Franz Boas (see Harris 1968). The theoretical assumptions of these schools have necessarily led to normative
approaches in ethnography so that the scholarly observer comes to expect that
every person within a society, and every band or village within a tribal polity,
will be culturally the same. In the period 1900–1950, for example, few ethnographers of Native North American societies recorded data on diversity and

change or concerning bilingualism, foreign origins of citizens, or recent and novel institutions within a native society.[2] Instead, the ethnographic emphasis was on the homogeneity and antiquity of a "tribe" and its people. Lines were drawn on maps of North America to show the territory within which a tribe and its culture were dominant, as if these societies were fully analogous with the great nation-states of Europe or Asia.

My first professional experience as a field ethnographer was with the Cheyennes of the Great Plains during the 1970s, and early in that fieldwork it became apparent to me that a normative perspective would not work if one wanted to understand process, change, and the origins of institutions among these equestrian buffalo hunters. In talking to Cheyenne elders, it became clear that the classic ethnographers of the Cheyennes, in their desire to present a normative picture, had inadvertently covered up exactly the kinds of issues that are crucial for understanding diversity and change—factionalism, familism, adoptions, intermarriage, even treason and civil warfare. Theoretically, the normative perspective, which explains how a society is ideally supposed to function rather than how it does function, supports a cladistic view of history in which homogeneous human societies evolve slowly from one steady state to the next without the traumas of such matters as secession and marriage with enemies. But I would argue instead that such events should not be regarded as traumatic or unusual, but as normal and necessary occurrences in human evolution.[3] It is exactly these events that have produced the diversity and change that are crucial for the continuation of human evolution.

As I have explained in a series of books and articles, the Cheyennes have had many disputes and traumas in their time, some of them very serious (Moore 1987). One residue of these disputes, ethnonymically, is the continuing controversies among Cheyennes over which names should be used to designate the tribe and its component bands. For example, the modern descendants of the Dog Soldiers use the term "Cheyenne" only to designate the "peace faction," whom they still regard as collaborators. For another example, the Southern Cheyennes of Oklahoma refer to the Northern Cheyennes of Montana as Sutaio, implying that they are only one band rather than half the tribe. The Northerners employ the same practice in designating the Southerners as Hevhaitanio, as if they were only one band. Also, the use of the term "Cheyenne" or "Tsistsistas" as a national designation is contested among different bands and factions, for parochial reasons. Many terms such as *cheyenne, hevhaitanio, sutaio,* and *tsistsistas* are nested ethnonymically, and this nesting is used politically so that particular groups are alleged to be more or less important depending on the speaker's sociological and political viewpoint. The point is that ethnonymy and the mutual perspectives represented in ethnonymy are a sensitive indicator of social and political issues, past and present.

The aspect of ethnonymy that I wish to emphasize here, however, is that the names used for several of the twenty or so traditional bands of the nation explicitly state that the band originated from intermarriage with foreign tribes or

Table 3.1
Cheyenne Bands of Foreign Derivation

Band	Affiliation
Hevhaitanio	Arapaho
Hotamhetaneo (Dog Soldiers)	Lakota
Masikota	Lakota
Moiseyu	Lakota
Oivimana	Arapaho
Plains Apache	Adoptees
Ree Band	Arikara
Sutaio	Adoptees
Two Strike	Lakota
Wotapio	Kiowa

nations, as indicated in Table 3.1. Elsewhere I have explained how these foreign elements were collected together to form the Cheyenne Nation around 1700, under the leadership of the prophet Sweet Medicine. Under his guidance, the Cheyennes transformed themselves from a sedentary horticultural society into a militaristic, buffalo-hunting society—an example of ethnogenesis. In this case, the cultural components for the transformation were provided by their inter-marriages with Arikaras, Apaches, and Arapahoes, tribes who were already on the Plains when the Cheyennes got there. Their new political system, the Council of Forty-four Chiefs, was inspired by the Assiniboins through the agency of a Cheyenne woman who had been captured by the Assiniboins but had returned to her native tribe (Grinnell 1962, vol. 1:345–348). Horses and horsemanship they received through intermarriages with the Apaches and Arapahoes. Their Sun Dance came either from the Mandans or the Arapahoes, depending on which historical accounts one prefers. All of these episodes have been explicitly re-corded from Cheyenne oral tradition (Moore 1996:176–198).

The intermarriage of Cheyennes with other tribes is also attested in their system of personal names, as these names were recorded on official government censuses in the late nineteenth century. Foreign women who married into a Cheyenne family were at first known merely by the name of their tribe: "Arapaho Woman," "Pawnee Woman," and so on. But these names only lasted one generation at most, since personal names were traditionally taken from the pa-trilateral side of the family, not the mother's side, and were bestowed by the father's eldest sister. Since a foreign woman would most likely not have a brother among the Cheyennes, her name would not be passed on to his children. Consequently, the number of "foreign-woman names" gives us a rough, mini-

Table 3.2
Number of Foreign-Born Cheyenne Women by Tribe in 1892

Tribe	Number
Apache	2
Arapaho	17
Arikara	1
Blackfeet	1
Caddo	2
Creek	1
Crow	2
Kiowa	3
Oto	1
Pawnee	2
Ponca	3
Sioux (Lakota)	15
Ute	2
Total	**52**

Source: Moore (1994).

mum measure of the amount of intermarriage for each generation, distributed by tribe, as shown in Table 3.2. Significantly, these foreign women were not distributed randomly among Cheyenne bands, but certain bands tended to marry into certain foreign tribes, confirming the patterns of intermarriage reflected in the band names. Not surprisingly, the bands on the edge of Cheyenne territory tended to marry with the foreign bands most proximate to them.

The Cheyennes were not unique among Plains Indian societies in marrying their foreign neighbors and thereby creating bands that were multilingual and multiethnic in composition. A survey of standard sources on other tribes shows that nearly every pair of contiguous Plains tribes in the nineteenth century generated at least one and sometimes several bands that were biologically and culturally hybrid, and often bilingual.[4] A schematic diagram of these tribes, showing the existence of a hybrid band or bands as a diamond, is presented here as Figure 3.1, redrawn from several published sources. For those pairs of tribal nations that are not connected with a double line, I have been unable to find a documentary source specifying that they generated a hybrid band in the ethnohistorical period.[5] But in most cases, there were hybrid bands between contiguous groups regardless of cultural and linguistic differences, and in fact

Figure 3.1
Hybrid Bands among Plains Indian Tribes about 1870

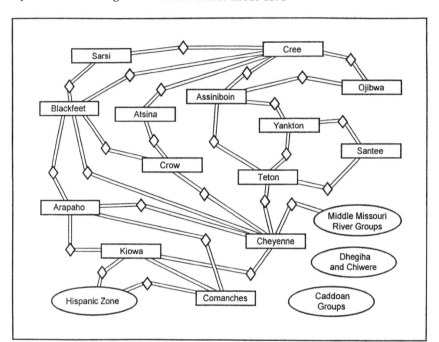

the tribes of the Plains are very different among themselves, comprising languages of about six different language families.

Scholars attempting to write general descriptions of Plains Indians have often had difficulty characterizing the tribes as unique or different from other tribes. Particular soldier societies, for example, or the rituals of the Sun Dance are not peculiar to one tribe, but tend to occur in clusters that do not correspond to language groupings (Jorgensen 1972; Lowie 1963). I wish to suggest here that the reason for this, and the reason why the tribes of the Plains "culture area" are so homogeneous culturally, is the continued intermarriage among contiguous bands, constantly disseminating a cultural inventory each generation over hundreds of miles.

I believe that a closer inspection of ethnohistorical narratives, especially unpublished ones, would show for all the Plains tribes the same pattern I have detected for the Cheyennes. The examples of intertribal marriage listed in major published sources and illustrated in Figure 3.1 represent only the best-known examples. But in the Cheyenne case, archival sources and interviews with Cheyenne elders revealed a pattern of intermarriage that was more intensive and more complex than that indicated by a superficial examination.

As I began to realize, about 1981, the pervasive extent of intermarriage among contiguous tribal groups on the Plains in the aboriginal period, two ethnographic episodes conspired to help me understand the reasons for this phenomenon. First, in that year I interviewed Mrs. Vinnie Hoffman, an elderly woman monolingual in Cheyenne who narrated to me the story of how a local Cheyenne community, around 1900, actually held a meeting at which they invented a clan system, and their reasons for doing so.

The Cheyennes were traditionally a bilateral society with marriage forbidden among known relatives, but in reservation years, beginning about 1880, their marriage system was increasingly impeded by a government system of administration that did not allow the kind of long-term visiting and courtship among bands and with neighboring tribes that had been typical of the aboriginal period. Also, a system of government record keeping was created on the reservation that preserved a knowledge of genealogical connections among young people long past the normal operation of what demographers call "genealogical amnesia." Consequently, young Cheyennes were increasingly faced with a situation in which they could find no marriageable nonrelatives in their community, or even in their county or district. To solve this problem, and to allow children to maintain residence in their home community, Chief White Shield (Photo 3.1) convened a meeting at which it was decided that henceforth all members of the community would be divided into one of two groups, the descendants of Red Moon or the descendants of White Shield, both figured patrilineally. When a patrilineal descendant of Red Moon married a patrilineal descendant of White Shield, it would thereafter not be regarded as an incestuous union.

At about the same time as I talked with Mrs. Hoffman, I happened to be reviewing some deep genealogies of Mvskoke Creek Indians living in eastern Oklahoma that had been collected by myself and others to help prepare for health research concerning the incidence of type II, or adult-onset, diabetes. The participants supplying information for the genealogies were rural Indian people associated with the villages, called "tribal towns," of Okfuskee, Nuyaka, Greenleaf, and Fish Pond.[6] Traditionally, from their earliest times in what are now the states of Alabama and Georgia, the Mvskoke people have maintained a social system in which clans and phratries have been matrilineal, and tribal towns have been both matrilineal and matrilocal. In collecting genealogies, we asked about clan and tribal-town membership as a way of finding or verifying genealogical relationships where we had partial information from personal names and mailing addresses.

When the field genealogies were collated and entered on a computer, and when these genealogies were linked to each other and to official censuses and rosters of the nineteenth century, it was surprising to discover that at the level of the third or fourth ascending generation, large segments of the populations of different clans and tribal towns were shown to be related. At the fifth or sixth generational level, we discovered that nearly every living person in the genealogies, which comprised about 1,800 persons altogether, were related to one another in some manner, often by multiple routes. That is, at a level that rep-

Photo 3.1
White Shield, Chief of the Hammon Band, during the Early Reservation Period

Source: Photographer and date not recorded; prior to 1877. Reprinted courtesy of the Smithsonian Institution National Anthropological Archives, Bureau of American Ethnology Collection.

resented only about 100 to 150 years, many of the ancestors became ubiquitous, serving as antecedents to nearly everyone in these tribal towns.[7]

Coming on the heels of my interview with Mrs. Hoffman concerning White Shield's attempt to invent Cheyenne clans, the empirical conclusion seemed compelling: Unilineal clans, far from constraining marriage choices as one might think, actually enable young people to marry close kin, cousins who otherwise would have to be excluded from the marriage pool because of incest rules. In addition, it seems apparent that the existence of exogamous clans also encourages genealogical amnesia. In courting a potential spouse, a person in a clan system does not have to know the person's genealogy, only his or her clan. White Shield's prescription and expectation for Cheyenne society, then, was confirmed by the Mvskoke genealogies. Thus, having good genealogical data on societies with contrasting kinship systems, I had the opportunity to compare Cheyenne and Mvskoke marriage patterns, with special attention to the extent to which each system forces a young person to marry outside the local community.

Such studies of marriage patterns, and specifically the consideration of how far people will or must travel to find spouses, relates of course to issues of gene flow and population diversity in human biological evolution (Mielke and Swedlund 1993). If intermarriage among tribal groups is far-flung and extensive, then any gene in a population has the opportunity of being quickly distributed across a region or even a continent, increasing its frequency in a population if it has some adaptive advantage. If marriage is intensive, however, closely circumscribed by a system of endogamy within a tribal society, then marriages will tend to stay within the society, and genes will not travel as far or as quickly. In this case, societies will differentiate from their neighbors over time, and evolution will be cladistic rather than reticulate. In the former case, with extensive, far-flung marriages, evolution will be reticulate.

At first glance, the Mvskoke Creeks would seem to have the sociological equipment for intensive endogamy and cladistic evolution, exhibiting a clan structure that makes it possible for people to marry close relatives within a restricted geographical area. But historically they did not. In fact, the Mvskokes are notorious among ethnohistorians for exhibiting the opposite kind of behavior—for marrying, adopting, and incorporating immigrants and refugees from a large number of other diverse Native North American nations (Bartram 1980: 463). They essentially practiced an "open-door" policy toward individuals, families, towns, and even whole tribes of foreigners who wanted to be incorporated into the Mvskoke Confederacy. These episodes of incorporation are described in several scores of narratives and historical maps of the Southeast, beginning with a 1544 map emerging from the de Soto expedition of 1540 and continuing to the modern and recent maps produced by anthropologists and by my own Mvskoke consultants in Oklahoma and Florida.[8]

Map 3.1 shows the results of ethnohistorical research currently under way, indicating the locations of Creek tribal towns in Alabama and Georgia according

Map 3.1
Ethnicity of Mvskoke Tribal Towns about 1800

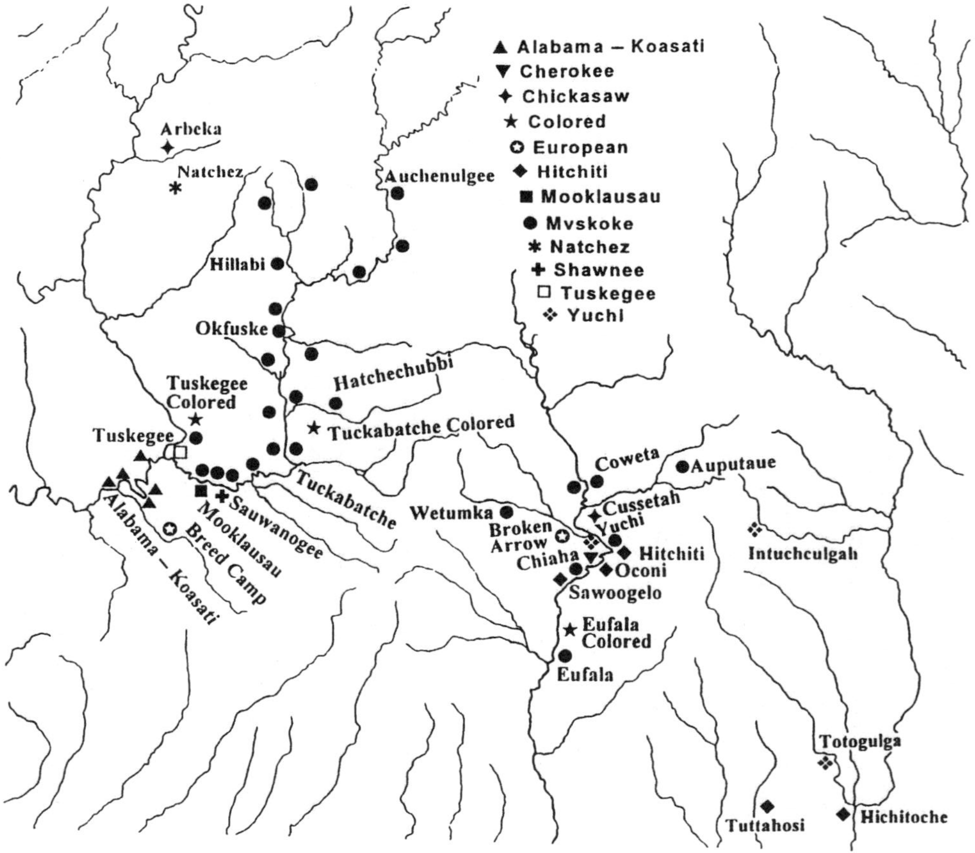

to Benjamin Hawkins in 1799, onto which I have added symbolic codes showing the ethnic/linguistic origins of the groups (Hawkins 1982). In some cases, the codes indicate entire towns who were invited in; in other cases, the codes indicate massive intermarriage. In a few cases, the codes indicate only the presence of substantial bilingualism or the recognition by the citizens (and the Europeans who provided the narratives) that there had been an immigration worth mentioning, or that their origins and ethnicity were originally something different from Mvskoke. To avoid cluttering the map, I have not added names to all the solid circles, which represent towns that were exclusively Mvskoke in their language and ethnicity, according to the historical accounts examined so far.

The historical depth of the Mvskoke maps and documents over the span of 450 years allows the opportunity to examine processes of ethnogenesis in some detail. But before I attempt to generalize about these processes, I will describe another compelling body of data, recently come to light, that shows the extent of tribal intermarriage among many tribes in aboriginal North America in the nineteenth century.

Between 1888 and 1903, Franz Boas and his associates collected biophysical and cultural data from about 15,000 Native Americans representing more than 100 U.S. tribes from coast to coast. After some sketchy analysis, the survey schedules disappeared from view. In a special issue of *Human Biology*, Richard Jantz has related the circumstances by which, 90 years later, he discovered this enormous data set in the basement of the American Museum of Natural History in New York City, and how he sought and received a grant for entering and analyzing the data.[9] My colleague Janis Campbell and I were privileged to analyze intermarriage in the data set for an article that was published in the special issue (Moore and Campbell 1995).

Table 3.3 is modified from a table in our original article to show the extent of Indian-Indian tribal intermarriage in the Boas material. Column A shows the tribes represented in the sample for which we had a sufficient number of schedules to include them in the analysis. Column B shows the total number of persons in each tribe, according to the 1900 U.S. Census, which was not conducted by Boas. Column C is the number of persons interviewed in each tribe, and column D shows the percentage of the whole represented by the people interviewed, C/B. Column E is the number of persons in each tribe who reported European ancestry, and column G is the number of persons who reported ancestry in foreign Indian tribes. Columns F and H, respectively, translate these numbers into a percentage of the number of persons in the tribal sample. For column H, I have subtracted the number of people with European ancestry from the denominator to approximate the extent of foreign intermarriage, excluding Europeans.

These numbers, of course, constitute an imperfect estimate of the rate of intertribal marriage in the ethnohistorical period because of the interference caused by the marriages with Europeans. One might argue that the rates of intermarriage with foreign tribes would have been higher if Europeans had not

Table 3.3

Statistics for Individuals from 52 Tribes Selected from the Boas Schedules, Incorporating Data from the 1900 U.S. Census

A Tribe or Nation	B Total 1900 Population	C Sample Size	D C/B (%)	E European Ancestry	F E/C (%)	G Foreign Indian Ancestry	H G/(C-E) (%)
Apache	6,268	367	6	9	2	19	5
Arapaho	1,782	95	5	1	1	12	13
Caddo	497	62	12	7	11	7	13
Catawba	60	55	92	53	96	2	100
Cherokee	36,376	700	2	179	26	3	—
Cheyenne	3,416	55	2	7	13	5	10
Chickasaw	10,500	218	2	51	23	24	14
Chippewa	22,429	876	4	435	50	35	8
Choctaw	20,250	522	3	35	7	5	1
Coeur D'Alene	450	49	11	2	4	1	2
Comanche	1,499	194	13	23	12	4	2
Concow	164	64	39	14	22	6	12
Creek	16,000	104	1	10	10	2	2
Crow	1,941	607	31	55	9	15	3
Hoopa	421	88	21	12	14	0	0
Kiowa	1,136	203	18	12	6	28	15
Klamath	1,338	268	20	47	18	35	16
Menomini1	396	274	20	80	29	6	3
Mohave	479	46	10	0	0	0	0
Mohawk	1,154	129	11	68	53	2	3
Navajo	20,000	178	1	15	8	0	0
Nez Perce	1,761	132	7	34	26	6	3
Okanagan	575	101	18	28	28	10	14
Omaha	1,182	125	11	18	14	0	0
Oneida	2,304	250	11	64	26	6	3
Onondaga	551	75	14	6	8	36	52
Osage	1,781	124	7	37	30	3	3
Ottawa	170	127	75	24	19	4	4
Paiute	1,409	217	15	4	2	0	0
Pawnee	650	88	14	5	6	0	0
Piegan	2,085	122	6	56	46	3	5
Pitt River	581	24	4	8	33	7	44
Ponca	566	83	15	11	13	1	1
Potawatomi	2,580	30	1	13	43	7	41
Pueblo	8,183	43	1	0	0	0	0
Puyallup	1,600	134	8	29	22	21	20
Quillayute	229	35	15	0	0	1	3
Seneca	3,146	115	4	62	54	4	8
Shawnee	693	24	3	7	29	8	47
Sioux	27,613	1,441	5	275	19	38	3
Spokane	665	18	3	8	44	2	20
Tonkawa	59	44	75	0	0	0	0
Tuscarora	378	87	23	18	21	19	28
Umatilla	183	50	27	1	2	2	4
Umpqua	88	21	24	5	24	9	56
Ute	1,795	126	7	9	7	15	13
Walla Walla	528	30	6	26	87	0	0
Wichita	428	37	9	1	3	0	0
Winnebago	2,581	199	8	61	31	7	5
Yakima	2,309	57	2	4	7	10	19
Yuki	290	67	23	12	18	1	2
Yuma	634	27	4	0	0	2	7
Total	214,153	9,207		1,941		433	

been available as spouses. Or one might argue, especially for some northern tribes, that the fur trade had caused rates of intermarriage to increase in the ethnohistorical period, since French *voyageurs*, especially, became desirable spouses because of their trading connections.

Nonetheless, there are at least two hypotheses concerning Indian-Indian marriage that seem to be supported by the Boas data set. First, it seems clear that Indian people in the period represented by the sample, the nineteenth and the late eighteenth centuries, boldly married across significant political, ethnic, and linguistic boundaries. Of the 471 intertribal marriages represented in the data set, 302 were consummated between persons who represented tribes that were both contiguous to each other and represented the same language family. But 125 marriages represented unions between spouses who represented tribes contiguous but of a different language family, and 27 marriages represented tribes that were not contiguous but of the same language family. There were 17 marriages between spouses who represented populations that were neither contiguous to each other nor in the same language family. We should note that even tribes in the sample that were of the same language family most often spoke languages that were not mutually intelligible.[10]

These empirical databases—for Cheyennes and other Plains Indians, for Mvskoke Creeks, and for the tribes surveyed by Boas—fly in the face of cladistic theories about how societies are supposed to evolve. Instead of exhibiting patterns of isolated, exclusive evolution, these data show a continual, significant movement of people, and hence their genes, language, and culture, from society to society across hundreds and thousands of miles of territory. While the historical period under consideration—several hundred years—seems a long time from the perspective of written history, it constitutes a mere instant of evolutionary time. If we take the entire life span of the human species to be 120,000 years, then 400 years is merely 0.3 percent of the total. If something like the rates of intermarriage for small-scale societies indicated in these data sets, 6 percent per generation, have been maintained in all continents for the whole period of human evolution, then this is a strong argument for the maintenance of relative homogeneity in the human species. It is an argument for the "multiregional" hypothesis because it shows how genes can migrate quickly across continents without the necessity of the massive and traumatic long-distance migrations that are required by the competing "replacement" hypothesis (Wolpoff 1989).

MODELING MARRIAGE

Some of the reasons for far-flung marriages among tribal societies in North America are transparent, explicit, and well known to ethnohistorians. Many such marriages on the Plains were public, ceremonial affairs intended to cement political or trade alliances among chiefs of different tribes, one or both of whom would send a son to the other chief's camp to create a matrilocal marriage with the other chief's daughter (Albers 1993). Marriage as political alliance was also explicit among the Mvskokes of the Southeast, who not only married between their tribal towns to create and sustain political alliances, but also made strategic marriages with Europeans. At one point, the leaders of the Alabama towns encouraged their young women to marry French soldiers (Corkran 1967:179).

The so-called mixed-blood faction among the Creeks has its origins in the marriages between English-speaking, usually Scots-Irish, traders and the daughters of Mvskoke chiefs in the eighteenth century. The Spanish, too, are represented in Creek society by a group still known as the "Spanish Clan." But these marriages with Europeans account for only a small part of the large number of marriages observed in the historical records and databases discussed here. The Indian-Indian marriages, and especially those arranged among ordinary or low-ranking citizens, must be explained by a more subtle method that depends on understanding how the marriage system works, and especially on understanding the relationship between kin systems and demography.

The fields of kinship, demography, and population genetics have had separate developments within anthropology, to the detriment of all three fields and to the disadvantage of anyone who wants to take a synthetic approach to the study of human evolution (Hammel and Howell 1987). Ethnologists have tended to study kinship systems as symbolic systems, with little attention paid to how the age and sex structure of a society—its demography—might restrict marriage choices or might explain certain special features of the kin system. For example, it is clear that the existence of such institutions as the levirate, the sororate, and polygyny depend on high fertility and the existence of large sibships. Otherwise there would be no siblings to marry the spouses of dead brothers or sisters. But seldom are these demographic factors mentioned in discussions of these kin institutions (Greenhalgh 1990).

Conversely, studies of tribal demography have tended to ignore the consequences of kin classification and marriage choice for fertility rates and consequently for the distributions by age and sex observed in tribal populations. At the extreme, population geneticists, as a professional dictum, claim to be disinterested in the difference between marriage and mating, as if marriage and its derived social institutions had no consequences for the phenomena they study. I will suggest here, however, by reference to marriage rules and the notion of "marriage pool," that the concern of ethnologists with rules and beliefs is quite relevant to issues of genetic diversity and gene flow. I will suggest that these factors tend to "push" potential marriage partners from their home band or village, resulting in the high rates of intermarriage shown in the data presented earlier and thus resulting in greater genetic diversity and more gene flow.[11]

I begin with a simple model that shows how marriage choices are limited in any small band, even under ideal demographic conditions. That is, even if we assume optimum demographic conditions, this model band will nonetheless very quickly reach a point at which it has a marriage pool of zero and must look elsewhere for spouses. To begin the life of this ideal band, we will select 8 unrelated persons, 4 males and 4 females. We will assume population stability, and to that end, we will require each woman to obligingly produce 1 son and 1 daughter. We will assume the simplest rule of incest, the one embraced by the Cheyennes and many other small-scale societies, that no one may marry a person with whom one is known to share an ancestor.

Figure 3.2
Marriage through Three Generations of an Indian Band

First Generation

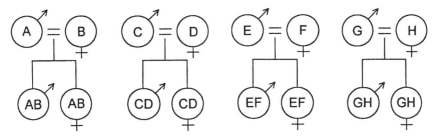

Second Generation

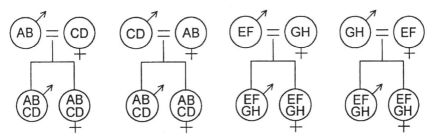

Third Generation

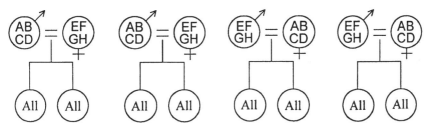

As shown in Figure 3.2, the first generation of this model band can reproduce to create 8 persons in the second generation representing four types of ancestry—AB, CD, EF, and GH. These persons in turn select spouses with whom they do not share a known ancestor and create only two types of descendants in the next generation—ABCD and EFGH—and these in turn marry each other to form the last generation, all of whom are ABCDEFGH, labeled "all" on the figure. Because they all share ancestors at this point, no further marriage is possible after three generations of intragroup or endogamous marriage, which create a band of 24 living persons after the death of the first generation.

Marriage can proceed for one more generation in the group if we double the size of unrelated founders, making it 16 instead of 8, which gives a band size of 48 persons for the last three generations, assuming here that the first two generations have died. If we want to go a step farther, we can once again double the number of unrelated founders to 32, and thus the band members can marry endogamously for an additional, sixth, generation, and we get 96 as the population comprising the last three generations, assuming that the first three generations have died.[12] By reference to this ideal model, then, we can see that even a large-sized band soon reaches the limits of possibility for endogamous marriage, even with an ideal sexual balance and complete sibship balance of two offspring per mother within the band.

If we allow births to be distributed randomly by sex in our model band, however, we see that the limit of endogamy is reached much sooner. Assuming still that each woman has exactly two children, but assigning sex by chance, we get Alpha Group (Figure 3.3) from a first simulation run.[13] Because of the imbalance between the sexes, four women are left over in the second generation, women who are unable to find a spouse in their own band. (We have so far assumed no polygyny.) In the third generation, two more women are left over, since only one male was born from the two couples in the second generation who were able to marry.

Beta Group (Figure 3.4) represents the results of a second simulation run with the same assumptions as the first run. Here we find two men left over in the second generation, and two women in the third. Gamma Group (Figure 3.5), the third run, is highly imbalanced toward males, with two left over in the second generation and two more in the third.

To simulate a pattern of exogamy among such small groups, let us assume that Alpha, Beta, and Gamma groups coexist and are arranged geographically from west to east, so that excess males or females who cannot find spouses in their own groups can attempt to find spouses in neighboring groups. Let us assume that males move geographically instead of females, as is common among real human societies. In this case, Alpha Group must recruit males to provide husbands for the four excess women in the second generation. Fortunately, it can recruit two of them from Beta Group, and two more from Gamma Group.

In the next generation, Beta Group cannot help Alpha Group with husbands because it, like Alpha, also has two excess females, but Gamma Group can supply two males either to Alpha or to Beta. In addition to the descendants shown in the third generation, additional spouses will be generated by the marriages arranged in the second generation among Alpha, Beta, and Gamma.

Finding spouses in neighboring bands is complicated by the fact that previous generations might have married into these same bands. Therefore, marriage choices in a neighboring band must exclude the descendants of relatives pre-

Figure 3.3
Possible Marriages within Alpha Group, with Sex Determined by Chance

First Generation

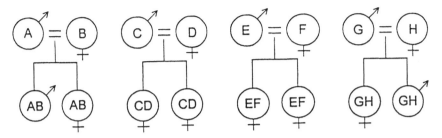

Second Generation

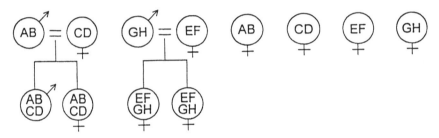

Third Generation

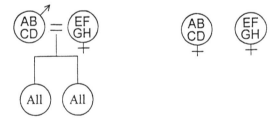

viously married in, people with whom one would share an ancestor. The more previous intermarriages there have been, and the farther back in time these marriages took place, the more restricted the marriage pool will be in a neighboring band.

Uneven sibships in one's home band, the normal condition of real human groups, also restrict marriage choices within the band and encourage exogamy. If some women in a group have no children while others have six or seven, the

Figure 3.4
Possible Marriages within Beta Group, with Sex Determined by Chance

First Generation

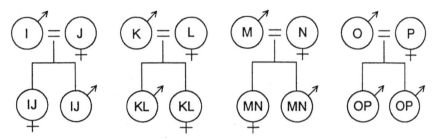

Second Generation

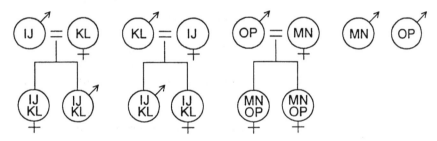

Third Generation

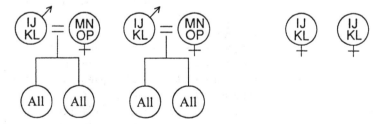

limits of endogamy are reached much sooner. Large sibships of one's relatives in neighboring bands also accelerate the production of people one cannot marry, so that after a few generations it might be hard to find a spouse anywhere in the vicinity. Polygyny also complicates the picture; someone like the Cheyenne chiefs Black Kettle and White Antelope would have large numbers of descendants in nearly every band.

In this discussion so far, we have not even mentioned mate selection and the

Figure 3.5
Possible Marriages within Gamma Group, with Sex Determined by Chance

First Generation

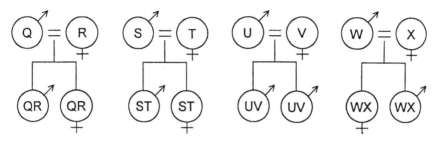

Second Generation

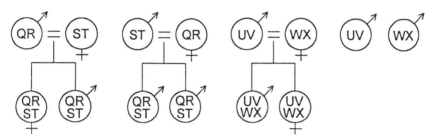

Third Generation

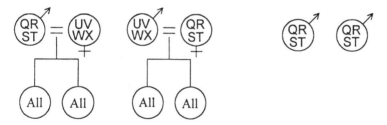

fact that an individual might require a pool of seven or eight potential spouses before one can be found who is suitable for reasons of health, appearance, or compatibility. Different assumptions can be made about the significance of these factors, giving different results, but the unavoidable conclusion from all of this is that small-scale societies ordinarily must marry out at considerable distances to avoid incest and find suitable mates. But how far away must they marry, in geographical terms?

For most human collecting societies, ecological factors determine population density, band size, and hence the distance separating contiguous bands. For the Plains Indians, bands of about 150 persons were separated by about 80 to 150 miles. If a spouse came from a contiguous band, then that would represent a distance of approximately 100 miles, say between Alpha and Beta groups in our example. But if the spouse came from Gamma to Alpha, that would be approximately 200 miles. Cheyenne ethnohistory shows that this range of marriage is not unusual. In the early nineteenth century, a group of 20 young Blackfeet men was reported to have traveled over 800 miles to the Cheyennes to find wives. Many of the intermarriages recorded in the Boas data were between tribes located hundreds of miles apart (Grinnell 1962, vol. 1:39–40).

The demographic factors discussed here all conspire to make marriage with foreigners a reasonable alternative, especially for bands on the edge of the range of their ethnic or linguistic group. For them, an appropriate spouse speaking the same language might be 300 miles away, but a spouse of different language only next door. Also, the nature of marriage in collecting societies makes foreign spouses more acceptable. A man, for example, is not necessarily looking for a nearly constant companion and intimate lover, as in a middle-class American family, but someone who will mind the camp with other women, work independently, and oversee the children. The relationship does not require a lot of conversation. For a woman, too, her constant friends and companions are other women, especially her mother and sisters if they live in the same band, not necessarily her husband (Albers and Medicine 1983).

Both with Cheyenne bands and Creek tribal towns, where there is one foreign spouse present in a group, there are usually several more, most often siblings or cousins to one another. If they are women, they might create a bilingual camp such as those recorded for the Wotapio, Hotamhetaneo, and Masikota bands among the Cheyennes, and all or nearly all the towns of foreign origin among the Mvskoke Creeks (Burton, Dyson, and Ardener 1994). Also, there come to be traditions of intermarriage between pairs of bands that are foreigners to each other, ethnically and linguistically, but that are intermarried over many generations. When spouses join a foreign band at marriage, it may well be a band that already houses one set of their grandparents and probably some "hybrid" aunts, uncles, and cousins as well.

Looking next at Creek society in the ethnohistorical period, we should note that many of the sociological contrasts between them and the Cheyennes were based on differences in ecology. The Creeks were horticultural and sedentary, not nomadic, and lived in about 50 semipermanent villages of about 500 to 1,000 persons each.[14] Although there were upwards of 20 matrilineal clans altogether among the Creeks, each village ordinarily comprised only 5 to 8. The clans often occupied a particular neighborhood in the village, and each clan usually constituted about the same number of persons as a Cheyenne band, about 80 to 150 persons.

The clans of a Mvskoke tribal town, as their members married and reproduced each generation, were subject to the same stochastic distributions of sex as illustrated in figures 3.2 to 3.5, as well as stochastic differences in the size of sibships. Each generation, there could be surplus potential brides or grooms in a clan who could not find spouses from other clans in the same town. Consequently, they had to look in neighboring towns for spouses, where they must avoid marrying members of their own clan, just as Cheyenne spouses had to avoid marrying the descendants of their kin who had previously married into a nearby band.

While the presence of clans in Mvskoke society tended to increase the size of the marriage pool in each town, it did not eliminate the need to marry outside the town, and especially the need to marry foreigners.[15] Pressures for exogamy in this case devolved not only from stochastic distributions of sex and size of sibship, but from the operation of a demographic version of the Sewall Wright effect.[16] Even though the names of clan ancestors are usually forgotten after a few generations, nevertheless clan membership continues through time, and ultimately one clan will come to dominate other clans in number, so that half or more of the citizens of a town might be of the same clan (Swanton 1928:153–158). The older the town, the more difficult this situation will become. In fact, one can argue theoretically that single-clan towns are the inevitable result of this process, given enough time.

CONCLUSION

As a graphic representation of their theories of human evolution, cladistic theorists have promoted the symbol of the branching tree, a device used by Darwin and Lamarck, among others, to show biological speciation through time. The evidence presented here, however, suggests that as a representation of evolutionary processes within the human species, even at the biological level, this device is inappropriate. The North American data suggest that our evolution is not best characterized by the independent development of small, diverging populations, but by a constant flow of people, and hence their genes, language, and culture, across the fuzzy boundaries of tribes and nations, spreading within a region such as the Plains or the Southeast within a few generations, and across the continent in a few more. That this is not a new process is attested in North America, biologically, by the fact that the same mitochondrial DNA lineages occur among Native Americans from Alaska to Chile, and that language families like Algonquian and Siouan are spread over thousands of miles of territory (Santos et al. 1996).

The distribution of genes resulting from tribal intermarriage is better represented, I believe, not by the analogy of the tree, but by the analogy of a tapestry, in which multicolored threads of wool, linen, or even gold, which we can see as representing human diversity, are distributed all across the warp and weft of our global habitat. In tapestries, each kind of thread is distributed independently, joining with others in strategic places to create images or abstract designs. The threads can be short or long, or even absent on some parts of the tapestry.

By definition, a tapestry must tell a story, and historic sagas are related in famous tapestries such as the Bayeux tapestry, where a series of panels 70 meters long tells the story of the Norman invasion of England and their victory at the Battle of Hastings in 1066 (Grape 1994). Similarly, other European tapestries record the stories of "The Defeat of the Spanish Armada" and "The Entry of Louis XIV into Dunkirk" (Thomson 1980:105, 107). By analogy, if we take the global distribution of human genes to represent the threads and textures of a genetic tapestry, there is also a story to be read in the pattern that we find, if we could but read it. At this stage in the development of science, we do not yet entirely know what the pattern on the genetic tapestry looks like, or what momentous past events might be represented there.

We do know, however, that genetic threads are distributed independently of one another across the globe. All the reds (representing, say, skin color) will not congregate with the blues (skull shape) or the greens (body form) or the yellows (hair type) (see Cavalli-Sforza, Menozzi, and Piazza 1994). That is the simpleminded design suggested by racist theories, and we already know that the story of our species is much more complicated than that.

If we take the distribution of threads in our tapestry to represent human language, we might well expect that a language tapestry of the globe would exhibit a mosaic design, because languages by definition are mutually unintelligible. But in real human societies, we know that these mosaics overlap, because multilingual people are not rare in small-scale societies, they are common (Owen 1965; Sharrock 1974; Wurm 1972:33f.). If we take the tapestry of language to be historical, like the Bayeux tapestry, we should be able to see languages and language families changing through time from left to right, blending together, melding occasionally into creoles, pidgins, and mixed languages, and always borrowing from one another.

The tapestry of human evolution is most complex at the cultural level. People seem to change religions and political forms as often as they change clothing, despite their continual, emotional allegiances to particular nationhoods and prophets. But as anthropologists, we know already that one cannot predict a person's religion or political affiliation on the basis of his or her language, or his or her genetic structure either. In American cities, there are people of African ancestry who speak English and practice Islam. In Ethiopia, there are black Jews who speak Amharic.[17]

Nevertheless, we cannot say at this point that the search for transcendent regularities among biology, language, and culture in the human species should be abandoned. We can only say that the relationships among these aspects of human life are not nearly as simple as the cladistic and racial theorists seem to think that they are. Having rejected the claims of cladists, however, I believe that we are obliged to suggest alternative hypotheses. In this chapter, I have tried to describe some structural regularities that underlie distributions of biological, linguistic, and cultural phenomena in aboriginal North America.

NOTES

1. My thanks to David Meltzer for suggesting the word "package."

2. Exceptions to this generalization are the interest in the Ghost Dance as a millenarian movement and scholarly interest in "acculturation." See Mooney 1965 and Linton 1940.

3. In biology, these views are represented in the notion of "punctuated equilibrium" (Eldredge 1985); in political economy, such views are generally Marxist (Marx 1970).

4. The standard sources for tribal movements and band names are Hodge 1907–1910; Clark 1982; and Schoolcraft 1860.

5. The "ethnohistorical period" is when aboriginal peoples were observed by travelers and traders, not by trained ethnographers, and for which there are only sketchy historical records.

6. The Mvskoke term *etvlwa* is usually translated as "tribal town" and refers to the politically independent towns of whatever ethnicity that were members of the Mvskokullke Etvlwa Etelaketa, or Creek confederacy. Strictly speaking, "Mvskoke" refers to language or ethnicity, "Creek" refers to any member of the confederacy, no matter of what ethnicity. See Moore 1988.

7. I understand from colleagues that such results are not unusual when genealogies of societies with unilineal clans are analyzed.

8. Under an NSF grant entitled "Demographic Adaptation under Stress: The Mvskoke Confederacy, 1780–1910," I have compiled 1,826 names of tribal towns from historical narratives and maps.

9. *Human Biology* 67(3), *Special Issue on the Population Biology of Late Nineteenth-Century Native North Americans and Siberians: Analyses of Boas's Data*, edited by Richard L. Jantz.

10. Ideally, languages are mutually unintelligible, while dialects of a language are intelligible. In practice, there is a great deal of disagreement among native speakers about which are languages and which are dialects.

11. I have data concerning the consequences of kinship for exogamy that must wait one more year for publication because of a contractual arrangement with a Native American group.

12. In general, the survey of band societies entitled *Man, the Hunter* characterized collecting groups as comprising "35–75 individuals"; see Lee and De Vore 1968:127, 332–333.

13. I flipped a coin to determine sex.

14. I call the villages "semipermanent" because they had to be moved periodically as arable land played out and local resources such as firewood were exhausted. Loosely, the Creeks might be called "swidden" or "slash-and-burn" farmers, depending on exactly what one means by these terms.

15. Different towns had different rules about the propriety of marrying into father's parents' clans.

16. See Kauffman's discussion of Sewall Wright's theories in Kauffman 1993:33f. Because small clans are more vulnerable to extinction than large clans, ultimately one

clan will comprise an entire society. Sewall Wright applied this phenomenon to genetics, saying that one allele will ultimately displace all the others, given enough time.

17. To get some sense of the lack of fit among biology, language, and culture, browse through *Ethnologue* (Grimes 1992) or the Soviet atlas of minorities and languages, listed here as Brook and Apenchenko 1964.

REFERENCES

Albers, Patricia
1993 Symbiosis, Merger and War. In *The Political Economy of North American Indians*. John H. Moore, ed. Pp. 94–132. Norman: University of Oklahoma Press.
Albers, Patricia, and Beatrice Medicine
1983 *The Hidden Half*. Washington, DC: University Press of America.
Bartram, William
1980 *Travels through North and South Carolina, Georgia, East and West Florida*. Charlottesville: University Press of Virginia (orig. 1792).
Bellwood, Peter
1996 Phylogeny vs reticulation in prehistory. *Antiquity* 70:881–890.
Brook, S. E., and V. S. Apenchenko
1964 *Atlas narodov mira*. Moscow: USSR Academy of Science.
Burton, Pauline, Ketaki K. Dyson, and Shirley Ardener, eds.
1994 *Bilingual Women*. Oxford: Berg.
Cavalli-Sforza, L. L., P. Menozzi, and A. Piazza
1994 *The History and Geography of Human Genes*. Princeton, NJ: Princeton University Press.
Clark, William
1982 *The Indian Sign Language*. Lincoln: University of Nebraska Press (orig. 1884).
Corkran, David H.
1967 *The Creek Frontier, 1540–1783*. Norman: University of Oklahoma Press.
Eldredge, Niles
1985 *Time Frames: The Rethinking of Darwinian Evolution and the Theory of Punctuated Equilibrium*. New York: Simon and Schuster.
Grape, Wolfgang
1994 *The Bayeux Tapestry*. Munich: Prestel.
Greenhalgh, Susan
1990 Toward a Political Economy of Fertility: Anthropological Contributions. *Population and Development Review* 16(1):85–106.
Grimes, Barbara F., ed.
1992 *Ethnologue*. 12th ed. Dallas, TX: Summer Institute of Linguistics.
Grinnell, George B.
1962 *The Cheyenne Indians*. 2 vols. New York: Cooper Square Publishers.
Hammel, Eugene A., and Nancy Howell
1987 Research in Population and Culture: An Evolutionary Framework. *Current Anthropology* 28(2):141–160.
Harris, Marvin
1968 *The Rise of Anthropological Theory*. New York: Thomas Crowell.

Hawkins, Benjamin
1982 *A Sketch of the Creek Country in the Years 1798 and 1799, and Letters of Benjamin Hawkins, 1796–1806*. Spartanburg, SC: Reprint Co. (orig. 1848).

Hill, Jonathan D., ed.
1996 *History, Power, and Identity: Ethnogenesis in the Americas, 1492–1992*. Iowa City: University of Iowa Press.

Hodge, Frederick W., ed.
1907–1910 *Handbook of American Indians North of Mexico*. Bulletin 30, Bureau of American Ethnology. Washington, DC: Government Printing Office.

Jantz, Richard, ed.
1995 *Special Issue on the Population Biology of Late Nineteenth-Century Native North Americans and Siberians: Analyses of Boas's Data. Human Biology* 67(3).

Jorgensen, Joseph
1972 *The Sun Dance Religion*. Chicago: University of Chicago Press.

Kauffman, Stuart A.
1993 *The Origins of Order*. Oxford: Oxford University Press.

Kroeber, Alfred
1923 *Anthropology*. New York: Harcourt, Brace, and Co.

Lee, Richard, and Irven DeVore, eds.
1968 *Man the Hunter*. Chicago: Aldine.

Linton, Ralph
1940 *Acculturation in Seven American Indian Tribes*. New York: D. Appleton-Century Co.

Lowie, Robert H.
1963 *Indians of the Plains*. New York: American Museum Science Books.

Marx, Karl
1970 *A Contribution to the Critique of Political Economy*. New York: International Publishers.

Mielke, James H., and Alan C. Swedlund
1993 Historical Demography and Population Structure. In *Research Strategies in Human Biology: Field and Survey Studies*. Pp. 140–185. G. W. Lasker and C.G.N. Mascie-Taylor, eds. Cambridge: Cambridge University Press.

Mooney, James
1965 *The Ghost-Dance Religion and the Sioux Outbreak of 1890*. Chicago: University of Chicago Press (orig. 1896).

Moore, John H.
1987 *The Cheyenne Nation*. Lincoln: University of Nebraska Press.
1988 The Mvskoke National Question in Oklahoma. *Science and Society* 52(2):163–190.
1994 Putting Anthropology Back Together Again: The Ethnogenetic Critique of Cladistic Theory. *American Anthropologist* 96(4):925–948.
1996 *The Cheyenne*. Cambridge and Oxford: Blackwell.

Moore, John H., and Janis E. Campbell
1995 Blood Quantum and Ethnic Intermarriage in the Boas Data Set. *Human Biology* 67:499–516.

Owen, Roger
1965 The Patrilocal Band: A Linguistically and Culturally Hybrid Social Unit. *American Anthropologist* 67:675–690.

Santos, Sidney, et al.
1996 Multiple Founder Haplotypes of Mitochondrial DNA in Amerindians Revealed by
       RFLP and Sequencing. *Annals of Human Genetics* 60(4):305–319.
Schoolcraft, Henry R.
1860 *Information Respecting the History, Condition, and Prospects of the Indian Tribes
       of the United States*. Philadelphia: Lippincott.
Sharrock, Susan R.
1974 Crees, Cree-Assiniboines, and Assiniboines: Interethnic Social Organization on the
       Far Northern Plains. *Ethnohistory* 21:95–122.
Swanton, John R.
1928 Social Organization and Social Usages of the Creek Confederacy, In *42nd Annual
       Report of the Bureau of American Ethnology*. Pp. 23–472. Washington, DC: Gov-
       ernment Printing Office.
Thomson, Francis P.
1980 *Tapestry*. New York: Crown Publishers.
Wolpoff, Milford H.
1989 Multiregional Evolution: The Fossil Alternatives to Eden. In *The Human Revolu-
       tion*. Paul Mellars and Chris Stringer, eds. Pp. 62–108. Edinburgh: Edinburgh
       University Press.
Wurm, S. A.
1972 *Languages of Australia and Tasmania*. The Hague: Mouton.

4

Soviet Ethnogenetic Theory and the Interpretation of the Past
Richard W. Lindstrom

Soviet concepts of ethnogenesis have been heralded by some as sophisticated alternatives to approaches to culture history used in the West. Research in the former Soviet Union, however, has been shaped by specific
political and historical circumstances. Theorists there may talk about the
autonomy of race, language, and culture, but in practice, Soviet understand-
ings of ethnogenesis have taken it as axiomatic that ethnic groups are stable
configurations, and that prehistoric culture change came about through the
movements of established groups marked off from one another by specific
and enduring traits.—Editor

The breakup of the Soviet Union has provided a wealth of opportunities for
researchers in both the former Soviet Union (FSU) and the West. Reduced gov-
ernmental control has removed a major barrier to collaborative research with
Soviet scientists (Milisauskas 1990). Former Soviet researchers are now publishing and attending conferences in the West, and Western scholars are traveling
to the countries of the FSU to teach and conduct research. Western scholars
newly introduced to the anthropology of the FSU are often surprised by its
sophistication in many areas and have been quick to adopt concepts and theories
that seem more developed than their counterparts in the West. This has happened
at a time in the West when there has been increasing interest in theories of
ethnicity and ethnogenesis.

Researchers such as John Moore (1994a) have seen Soviet ethnogenetic theory as an alternative to traditional culture-historical approaches to human history. But Moore and perhaps others as well have shown significant

misunderstandings about the nature of Soviet *ethnos* theory and its role in interpreting the past.[1] My analysis of Soviet ethnogenetic theory illustrates the way in which political and historical circumstances in the first half of this century have shaped this body of ideas and have influenced its application in Soviet archaeology. While showing why Soviet ethnogenetic theory does not satisfy expectations for the interpretation of the past, I also try to identify specific elements of that theory that are potentially productive for prehistorians.

THEORIES OF ETHNICITY

In the latter half of the twentieth century, Western anthropology has shown growing interest in ethnicity, arising from dissatisfaction with the concept of "race" as an analytical category and a desire to distance the discipline from the excesses of a race-based anthropology that had such disastrous results in Nazi Germany (Arnold 1990; Tonkin, McDonald, and Chapman 1996; Trigger 1989; Veit 1989). Though current theories of ethnicity cover a very wide range of forms, recent evaluations of ethnicity (Banks 1996; Hutchinson and Smith 1996) have adopted a generally bipolar view of the dominant theories. At one pole are primordialist theories that assume that ethnicity is a given in social life, pervasive and permanent. At the other pole are instrumentalist theories of ethnicity that see ethnicity as a social tool, adopted when needed, and mutable to suit an individual's or group's current social and cultural circumstances. Recently Moore (1994b) has touched on this dichotomy of theory as related to the interpretation of human history, labeling the two poles as cladistic and ethnogenetic. Many shades exist between and within these classes of theory, but the duality is a helpful way of understanding the major issues. Encompassed in the primordialist/instrumentalist dichotomy are critical issues about the relationships between ethnicity and material culture, as well as language and biology (human genetic variability).

Primordialist theories generally view language, biology (usually in the form of "race"), and material culture as expressions of an underlying and enduring "ethnic identity." Particular aspects of material culture are commonly interpreted as direct indexes of ethnic identity. Because ethnicity is seen as innate and unchanging, ethnospecific markers are also considered to be relatively stable (though more mutable than ethnicity itself; see Nash 1996). Language is usually considered to be the most ethnospecific of all cultural attributes, making the "linguistic group" roughly the equivalent to the "ethnic group." Ethnicity is tied to biology by the assumption that members of an ethnic group share a common genetic descent, preserved by ethnic endogamy. In a somewhat circular fashion, common descent is often seen as the foundation for the development of common ethnic identity.

Instrumentalist theories have a very different understanding of the relationships between ethnicity and these other attributes. The relationships are held to be much more tenuous, with little correlation among them. Since ethnicity is held to be contextual rather than innate, the material trappings of ethnicity are thought to be readily adopted, modified, and discarded as needed. Shared language is often thought of as a key requirement for membership in an ethnic group, but language choice is viewed as more personal and dependent on context. Instrumentalist theories concentrate on the importance of a perceived shared origin rather than a biological one. The inclusive nature of many ethnic groups and the ability of individuals to belong to one or more groups in a lifetime are thought to blur or erase the genetic homogeneity of ethnic groups (see Moore, this volume).

Though ethnogenetic theory has primarily developed in the context of ethnography, it has played an important role in the interpretation of the archaeological record. Archaeologists, lacking data on such important attributes as language and group self-awareness, have relied on ethnography (and ethnoarchaeology) to provide theoretical support for the association of material remains with social units in the form of ethnic groups. While this theoretical basis for interpreting the past is invaluable, differences in theory can have major repercussions in archaeological reconstructions of human history.

Cladistic and ethnogenetic theories have specific consequences when they are adopted by prehistorians. Those subscribing to the cladistic view are likely to feel that by tracing elements in the archaeological record (e.g., ceramic forms or ornamentation), they can follow the histories of particular ethnic groups. Archaeological cultures are seen as the material expression of ethnic groups that are roughly equivalent to different demes, or breeding populations. Such a culture-historical framework is typical of research on Indo-European origins and dispersals that looks to the archaeological (and biological) record for evidence to support various hypotheses regarding linguistic relationships and development. Elsewhere in the world, studies of the spread of the Polynesian (Rouse 1986) and Numic (Madsen and Rhode 1994) languages also rely heavily on cladistic approaches to human history.

Alternatively, scholars favoring ethnogenetic models are less disposed to equate archaeological cultures or populations with identifiable ethnic groups. Their argument is that the fleeting nature of ethnic groups and their variable association with language, material culture, and biology make them a difficult target for study in prehistory. They generally see archaeological cultures as the material expressions of social interactions between ephemeral social units, speaking any number of languages that may or may not be known historically.

Moore (1994a), in developing an ethnogenetic alternative to cladistic theory, cites the example of ethnogenetic studies in the Soviet Union as a successful application of this theoretical framework. He sees the Soviet attention to the definition of *ethnos*, the disjunction of changes in language, biology, and material culture, and the recognition of the instability of ethnic boundaries as particularly valuable. These interpretations were derived exclusively from the study of ethnogenetic theory in Soviet ethnography. However, a broader view of Soviet anthropology suggests that the usage of ethnogenetic theory in archaeology has strayed from this model, becoming strongly cladistic in application.[2]

SOVIET APPROACHES TO ETHNICITY

The primary unit of inquiry in Soviet ethnography is the *ethnos*, which Iulian Bromlei and Viktor Kozlov (Bromlei 1975:11, cited in Dragadze 1980:162) define as "a firm aggregate of people, historically established on a given territory, possessing in common relatively stable particularities of language and culture, and also recognizing their unity and difference from other similar formations (self awareness) and expressing this in a self-appointed name (ethnonym)." Other Soviet definitions similarly and almost universally see an *ethnos* as a group of people sharing a common territory, material culture, degree of biological homogeneity, and, most importantly, a common language (Arutiunov 1983). Stability is another characteristic that is frequently stressed (Bromlei 1974:56; Cheboksarov 1970:131; Vainshtein 1980:7). The *ethnos* is more stable than nations or societies, and though its specific character may change, it nonetheless can be traced through history (Dragadze 1980).

Ethnogenetic studies are considered an integral part of Soviet bioanthropology, counted as one of its three branches (along with studies of human origins and human morphology), and defining its main task as "the study of the history of nations" (Debets 1961:3). Mikhail M. Gerasimov, one of the leading Soviet bioanthropologists for more than a generation, considers ethnicity to be crucial to any historical studies in bioanthropology. Gerasimov prefaces his work (Gerasimov, Rud', and Iablonskij 1987:3) by noting that "use of anthropological material as a historical source is a tradition in the work of Soviet anthropologists. The methodological basis of Soviet historical anthropology is the concept of the grouping of races, cultures, and languages in independent societies."

Based on this perceived grouping of ethnicity and biology, Soviet bioanthropologists played a role in the determination of the ethnic origins of the Soviet peoples. Studies followed one of a number of paths: They estimated the proportions of various "races" that mixed to create the physical type of a modern ethnic group; or they compared archaeological materials with modern groups to determine if a modern ethnic group migrated into a region and when; or they compared linguistic relationships with the distributions of racial types to decide whether significant migration had taken place when the modern language was adopted in a region. Each of these methods makes the basic assumption that language and genetics (as expressed in racial type) should be linked together within the *ethnos*. It also makes the implicit assumptions that the ethnic group is homogeneous, both racially and linguistically, and that the group is stable.

ETHNICITY IN SOVIET ARCHAEOLOGY

Ethnogenetic theory plays a significant role in Soviet archaeology as well. Archaeologists, trained primarily as historians in the FSU, are introduced to the concept of ethnicity in two ways: in narrative texts describing the history of ethnic groups, where the ethnic group is the unit of analysis; and through readings of ethnographic literature, where material culture is often treated as a defining feature of the ethnic group. From these sources, archaeologists adopt a concept of ethnicity that suits their source of data. Ethnic groups become defined based on specific items of material culture, and objects are considered to be markers of ethnic identity. Once ethnicity is established, archaeologists adopt a narrative historical approach and follow these ethnic groups (in the form of archaeological cultures) through time and space, altering the ethnic indicators if necessary, but always sure that they are following a group of people who are linguistically, ethnically, and biologically related. The model of choice for archaeologists tends to be a strictly cladistic branching history for an ethnic group, despite the options supplied by ethnogenetic theory (Arutiunov 1994). Integrative origins of an *ethnos* (considered by Moore as one of the primary attractions of ethnogenetic theory) are stigmatized and virtually ignored by archaeologists. Pëtr N. Tret'iakov (1963:10) argued that "in our literature we find virtually no cases in which the formation of a new cultural-ethnic community was validly regarded as the result of integration of two or more related communities, or of a process of assimilation of certain tribes by others, with retention of substrate elements." Soviet archaeologists employing ethnogenetic theory are not interpreting the past in the flexible way that Moore envisioned based on ethnogenetic theory as conceptualized in Soviet ethnography. Rather, branching culture-historical, cladistic interpretations dominate.

Because of its binding of language, material culture, and biology within the *ethnos*, Soviet ethnicity theory is characterized as being among the most strongly primordial (Banks 1996:18; Sokolovskii and Tishkov 1996:191; Tishkov 1992: 372), insisting as it does that "ethnoses exist objectively, independently of consciousness, as definable entities" (Bromlei 1974:56). Soviet ethnography, archaeology, and biological anthropology all consider the *ethnos* to be a basic unit of study, and ethnogenesis an important field of research (for examples, see Bromley 1974; Debets, Levin, and Trofimova 1952; and Tret'iakov 1963, respectively). Ethnographers search for the particular cultural traits that define ethnic groups, and they reconstruct histories of the ethnogenetic events that led to their creation. Archaeologists view archaeological cultures as the material remains of specific ethnic groups. Biological anthropologists also focus on ethnogenesis, reconstructing constituent ethnic elements in a population based on genetic traits and morphological similarities to other groups (prehistoric, historic, and modern). Ethnic groups are traced through time and space in an effort to create ethnic histories. The net result is the unification of biology, language, and material culture within the *ethnos*, such that "ethnogenesis includes formation of the dominant physical type for a given people, as well as its language and the principal features of its spiritual and material culture" (Arutiunov 1994:84). In all cases, Soviet ethnogenetic theory, with its strong primordialist leaning, informs and guides anthropological research in the FSU.

THEORY AND PRACTICE

The picture of Soviet ethnogenetic theory that emerges from a broad survey of Soviet anthropological scholarship is very different from that envisioned by Moore. At each of the points that he cites as being valuable in Soviet theory, the actual application of theory to the study of human history is virtually the opposite of what he anticipates, creating a strongly cladistic view of the past. By defining ethnicity in terms of biology, material culture, and language, bioanthropologists, archaeologists, and linguists made the *ethnos* a real, material subject of study. Rather than a theory that emphasizes the disjunction of material culture, biology, and language, Soviet anthropology unites these within the concept of *ethnos*. Where Moore saw the Soviets focusing on the instability of ethnic boundaries, there is actually a tendency to assume that ethnic boundaries are stable and traceable in the past. Though the particular traits used to define the boundaries of the *ethnos* shift through time (and interpretation), the idea that such boundaries persist is never lost. Ethnogenetic studies of the past become recipes for the formation of modern ethnic groups, combining various cultural, linguistic, and biological elements from "known" ethnic groups into modern *ethnoses*.

Ethnogenetic theory and practice in the Soviet Union are clearly disjointed. While theorists deny links between biology and ethnicity (Bromlei 1974:62), bioanthropologists take such links as fundamental to their research. Theorists caution against tracing ethnicity in the archaeological record (Arutiunov 1994), while archaeologists continue to ascribe ethnicity to archaeological cultures. To understand why such a rift exists between theory and practice, we need to consider how and why ethnogenesis came to play such an important role in Soviet anthropology. To a great degree, political control of anthropology, crises arising from the Great October Revolution, and the rise of fascist Germany had profound and lasting effects on Soviet anthropology and the study of prehistory.

Prior to and immediately following the Great October Revolution, Russian archaeology was on a course very similar to that of its contemporary counterparts in the West, with a primary focus on culture history. Archaeology, as a branch of history, was very important to the new Marxist government, and from the very beginning, political influence was felt. Vladimir Il'ich Lenin himself created by decree the Russian (later State) Academy for the History of Material Culture (R[G]AIMK), which was headed by Nikolai Ia. Marr until 1934 (Lebedev 1992; Mongait 1959). The GAIMK immediately became the foremost academic institution for archaeological research in the USSR, and Marr the most prominent and powerful administrator.

Marr was a Near Eastern philologist by training and one of the Bolsheviks' staunchest supporters (Barber 1981:14). Marr was a "fiery patriot" (Editors 1950a:11), the only Communist member of the Russian Academy of Sciences for a decade following the revolution (Byrnes 1990:21), and was not particularly popular with his "bourgeois" colleagues. In his attempt to create a truly Marxist historical science, Marr developed a "theory of stages," or stadial theory, relying heavily on linguistics and Friedrich Engels' (1884) theories of cultural development. In this theory, the stage of economic development of a culture essentially determined all other aspects of the culture, including material culture, language, and sometimes even "race" (Bulkin, Klejn, and Lebedev 1982). In the stadial theory, cultures inevitably passed through specific well-defined socioeconomic stages in their progression toward communism. By formalizing the theory of stages for linguistics and archaeology, "Marr saw not only the opportunity to find in archaeological materials support for conclusions based on linguistic materials, but also the stimulus for development of archaeology itself as a real historical science" (Artamonov 1949:4).

While Marr's theory was decidedly noncladistic, assigning cultural and linguistic similarities to shared levels of development rather than shared origins, its effect on archaeological interpretation was certainly to reinforce notions of stability and continuity of ethnic groups through time. As Bruce Trigger (1989: 225) notes, "[Marr's] theory of linguistic change encouraged archaeologists . . . to interpret the archaeological sequence for each region from the earliest times to the present as stages in the history of a single people." Migration and diffusion were dismissed as possible forces for culture change. "The most ancient population of each region became an immovable autochthonous mass that from time to time experienced incredible transformations in culture and language in response to changes in technology" (Bulkin, Klejn, and Lebedev 1982:275). By forcing archaeologists to focus on historical development rather than interaction, Marr's theory predisposed archaeologists to assume cultural continuity through time.

This early disassociation of ethnicity from material culture did have a significant positive impact on Soviet archaeology. By stressing the interpretation of the archaeological record in socioeconomic terms rather than focusing on typology and description, as Western archaeologists of the period were doing (Trigger 1989), Soviet archaeologists were among the first to study social questions in prehistory, shying away from diffusionist theories that were frequently used to explain cultural development (Sal'nikov 1952:7). The Marxist focus on social structures in archaeology was potentially very productive, but in ethnography it was much more limiting.

Under the stadial theory, the search for ethnic origins was almost completely dismissed in the years before the "Cultural Revolution" of 1934–1939 (Artsikhovskij 1954:14). Under the guidelines of Marr's theory, archaeological cultures were expressions of peoples at a particular stage of economic development. Through time, their material culture, their language, and sometimes even their physical type would change as their economic development progressed. Because ethnicity was thought to be essentially an "effect" of economic development, there was no point in trying to establish the historical path and relationships of an ethnic group.

Ethnogenetic studies in the Soviet Union before World War II were pursued for the most part without an explicit theory of ethnicity. Soviet ethnography suffered greatly under Iosef Stalin, being virtually abolished by 1931, the casualty of a wave of Marxist scholars bringing scholarship in line with Marxist theory (Slezkin 1993; Slezkine 1991). Economic organization, law, politics, or interethnic relations of native peoples were considered the realm of the Soviet state and were politically too controversial to approach (Humphrey 1984). Soviet ethnography instead focused on the culture (ethnicity) of ethnic groups rather than their sociopolitical structure. Ethnic groups were studied in terms of what made them unique, and what differentiated them from other groups. The concept of *ethnos* was formulated to include material culture, language, and biology. Ethnicity and ethnogenesis had played a central role in anthropological research and theory in the Soviet Union as early as 1923, as exemplified in the work of Sergei Shirokogorov (though it was published in exile; see Skalnik 1986). Through the 1950s, tight political control of scholarship kept ethnography from explicitly pursuing the study of ethnicity, but when it reemerged under the patronage of Bromlei after World War II, it was continuing a tradition that had never disappeared from practice.

In a political environment that strictly limited the interpretation of cultural development, social (and thus synchronic) questions came to the fore. Despite the emphasis on history, Soviet ethnography has been characterized as primarily synchronic (Gellner 1977) and classificatory (Dunn and Dunn 1974), focusing on defining the distinctive characteristics of groups at a single time and place and describing social institutions. Such studies were given the requisite "historical" content by placing them within the framework of socioeconomic stages. The evolutionary frameworks of Karl Marx and Engels (and then of Marr) provided the diachronic structure, and it was unwise to challenge these politically mandated frameworks with contradictory evidence. Illuminating instances of cultural influence or migration were politically embarrassing, as they contradicted Marr's officially accepted theory of cultural evolution. However, beginning in the early 1930s, the Soviet government was faced with a menace that required a restructuring of research and interpretation of ethnicity and archaeology to respond to a growing ideological, political, and later physical threat from Germany.

RISE OF FASCISM

In Germany, archaeologists were firmly convinced that the role of archaeology was to trace the history of culture (Arnold 1990; Trigger 1989). Archaeological cultures were believed to be the material expressions of distinct ethnic groups.

The link between archaeological culture and ethnicity, always quietly assumed, became ever tighter under the influence of Gustaf Kossinna. Kossinna's *Kultur-kreis* theory, formulated before World War I, was founded on the belief that "sharply defined archaeological culture areas correspond unquestionably with the areas of particular peoples or tribes" (Veit 1989:37). Kossinna, originally a linguist, like Marr, developed the theory to parallel linguistic theories for the dispersal of Indo-European languages. A strident patriot, Kossinna saw the German people (and their ancestors) as genetically, linguistically, and culturally superior to other peoples, expanding and spreading their high culture and language to others.

The political goals of Germany in the 1930s were well served by Kossinna's work and were strongly reflected in archaeological research. German archaeologists were tracing the history of Germanic peoples (as a linguistic and ethnic group) as far back as the Mesolithic (Trigger 1989:166) and demonstrating how Germanic expansions had influenced the development of "lesser" peoples such as the Slavs. Throughout the 1930s, German archaeologists became ever bolder in their ethnic interpretations of archaeological materials, and the German state increasingly used archaeological research to support its goals (Arnold 1990).

Bioanthropology in Germany also played a crucial role in supporting the nationalist regime. In the mid-1920s, physical anthropology in Germany adopted human genetics into its study of human racial differences. *Rassenkunde* (racial research) saw in Mendelian genetics support for a biological basis to many human behaviors and dispositions. Behavioral traits were wedded with the notion of race, as well as a "natural" inequality of the races, and therefore inequality in culture and achievement. Nazi programs of forced sterilization, denial of jobs to Jews and other peoples of "mixed blood," and ultimately the incarceration and extermination of millions all rested to some degree on a foundation of bioanthropological/racial research (Proctor 1988).

The USSR under Stalin was not blind to the increasing nationalist and expansionist fervor in Germany or to the value of archaeological and bioanthropological research in its propaganda. The government, faced with numerous internal problems, needed to develop a sense of nationalism quickly to prepare the country for impending conflict. Bulkin, Klejn, and Lebedev note that "Soviet scholarship responded vigorously to the resulting growth of national self-consciousness, the expression of national pride and the fostering of the best indigenous traditions. This led Soviet researchers to examine carefully the problems of ethnogenesis" (1982:276). Ethnogenetic research, officially discouraged by Marr's stadial theory throughout the 1920s, was seen as a way to establish the historical importance of modern ethnic groups and develop a sense of national pride. It legitimized historical claims to territory and fostered nationalism by emphasizing the Slavic role in the development of European culture. Shortly after the war, Mikhail I. Artamonov wrote that "a critical role in the success in our science in terms of ethnogenetic problems, was played by the Great Patriotic war. As ideological preparation for war for world supremacy, fascism, as is known, widely used racial theories and legends of German people as the chosen, and of their primordial supremacy over all other peoples, and most of all over Slavic peoples. Soviet science drew the task of struggling against the fascist 'historical constructions' " (1949:4). Archaeological research into social structures suddenly was criticized as "unproductive sociology" and was abandoned. In its place, "direction from the leaders of party organs helped correct the situation" by focusing research on ethnogenesis (Artamonov 1949:3).

Suddenly endorsed by the Soviet government, ethnogenetic studies developed rapidly. Encouraged partly by the interest of incorporating the "small peoples" into the USSR, and partly as a direct response to German historical propaganda, archaeologists and others were sent out to trace the histories and origins of the peoples of the USSR, and in particular the history of the Slavs. The political importance of their work was not lost on archaeologists. John Barber notes that "Soviet historical scholarship in the late 1920s and early 1930s was dominated by the consciousness of the political relevance of the past, by the search for historical analogies to contemporary political issues, and by the continual appeal to history in support of current policies" (1981:vii).

Increasing political control of archaeology was smoothed through changes in membership among Soviet archaeologists. In the early 1930s, a new generation of idealistic Marxist archaeologists, including Vladislav I. Ravdonikas and Mikhail I. Artamonov, was coming to prominence in the USSR, replacing virtually all prerevolutionary scholars. These politically informed archaeologists recognized that "if archaeological material allows several various interpretations, then it follows to choose from them that which is more patriotic" (S. N. Bykovskij, cited in Shnirel'man 1993:56). Ideological struggles came to dominate the academic scene, and tolerance for alternative views gave way to dogmatic orthodoxy (Barber 1981; Byrnes 1990; Lebedev 1992; Slezkine 1991). As ethnogenetic studies developed and grew more valuable for political uses, they became more similar to those of Kossinna and other Germans (Trigger 1989: 230). The relationship between ethnicity and archaeological culture (or even individual material traits) was strengthened, and ethnic history, like linguistic history, was constructed as a branching tree (in many cases, with Slavs at the roots). Archaeological cultures as distant as the Paleolithic were described as clearly Slavic (Derzhavin 1944:7), and the highly publicized history of their expansion and influence on other cultures rivaled German propagandists' histories of the Germanic peoples.

The transition in bioanthropological research to politically mandated ethnogenetics did not come easily. It required considerable reorientation within Soviet bioanthropology. As Iakov Ia. Roginskij and Maksim G. Levin optimistically portrayed it, the "theoretical reworking of questions of the correspondence of anthropological types with ethnic and linguistic groups of mankind allowed the use of concrete anthropological material as a historical source for the study of problems of origins of various people" (1978:36). Despite warnings to the contrary from ethnography, biological types identified within modern groups were traced through space and time to construct the history of an ethnic group. These studies, particularly those in Siberia and Soviet Central Asia (Asimov 1981) were used to establish the administrative divisions of the newly expanded Soviet Union (Humphrey 1984).

After World War II, physical anthropology and archaeology continued to be dominated by ethnogenetic studies. The elimination of the threat of German national anthropology did not end the need to consolidate the Soviet government's power over newly acquired territories. Ethnogenetic studies had proved so politically successful that they were expanded. Teams of ethnographers, linguists, archaeologists, and bioanthropologists were dispatched throughout the USSR to study the ethnic histories and origins of the various ethnic groups within the union. Archaeologists and bioanthropologists were specifically tasked with determining the traits, biological or material, that defined particular ethnic groups, past and present.

The multidisciplinary research teams that were dispatched after the war helped crystallize the form of ethnogenetic studies. The addition of ethnogenetics to bioanthropology and archaeology reinforced the unifying concept of *ethnos*. It came to be the standard unit for research in ethnography, archaeology, and bioanthropology, allowing the history of an *ethnos* to be traced by the distribution of material culture or "racial" types.

BRONZE AGE CULTURES

A substantial rift exists between recent theories of ethnogenetics (with assertions of the separation of "race" and ethnicity, the independence of linguistic and ethnic development, and the "rhizotic" nature of ethnogenesis) and the Soviet practice of ethnogenetic research since the 1930s (with a unification of biology, language, and material culture within a stable, ever-dividing *ethnos*). Such a gap between theory and practice is lamented, but altogether too common in Soviet sciences. Theory is often separated from practice, both by the educational system and by the government's interest in practical (read "political") applications of all sciences (Graham 1993). While Soviet ethnogenetic theory is attractive in many ways, it is the practice that is most problematic. This is most clear in archaeology, where ethnogenetic studies have led to cladistic interpretations of human history that take the errors of Soviet ethnogenetics to the extreme. Studies of the Bronze Age Eurasian steppe are an excellent example: though they are developed in a framework of ethnogenetic theory, they are decidedly culture-historical in their interpretations of the past. They should serve as a caution to archaeologists eager to follow Soviet examples.

Archaeological studies of the Southern Trans-Urals are a stunning example of the influence of Soviet ethnogenetic theory on the interpretation of prehistory. Research in this area demonstrates how Soviet archaeology has subsumed the study of language, race, and material culture within the concept of the *ethnos*.

As the *ethnos* has become the dominant focus for research in each of these areas, the concept has thoroughly undermined other interpretations of data. Such key processes as culture change and variation are hidden under the idea of a stable *ethnos*. Language formation, transmission, and expansion all become ciphers for the formation and migration of ethnic groups, despite the difficulties of associating language with ethnicity (Haarmann 1986) or material culture (Ehret 1988). A wealth of biological variation, containing information on intermarriage and migration, all disappears under a blanket of ethnicity. In Andronovo studies, archaeological data have become so inextricably linked to the concept of *ethnos* that prehistory cannot be interpreted in any other terms.

The Andronovo "culture-historical community" is the most extensive and best-represented archaeological phenomenon of the Bronze Age of the Eurasian steppe zone (Map 4.1). Stretching from the Ural Mountains to the Yenisei River in Siberia, it has been a focus of archaeological studies since the first descriptions early in the twentieth century (Teploukhov 1927). Since that time, understanding of the archaeological record has expanded greatly, with the identification of numerous distinct archaeological subcultures within what has been interpreted as Andronovo. These various subgroups partition the Andronovo community into chronological, geographic, and "ethnic" units.

From early in the history of Andronovo research, the ethnogenetic focus has been clear: prehistory has been interpreted within the framework of the *ethnos*, and archaeologists have attempted to trace these ethnic groups through time, eventually relating the prehistoric to historic ethnolinguistic groups (Asimov 1981:50). While theory explicitly recognizes that archaeological cultures and ethnic groups are not identical (Tret'iakov 1963), in practice, certain indicators or assemblages are considered to be "quite reliable ethnocultural indicators, allowing us to trace the movements of groups of peoples of interest to us" (Ol'khovskij 1992:31). The equation of archaeological culture with an ethnic group allows the archaeologist to consider the history of material culture as the ethnic history of a people. Prominent Soviet prehistorians are of the opinion that "the archaeological culture reflects the culture of one ethnos, representing a social unit" and "should be characterized by a single language among its bearers" (Kuz'mina 1994:59). This view of an archaeological culture is also favored by Soviet bioanthropologists and linguists.

Elena Kuz'mina (1981) defines specific criteria that must be met to link an archaeological culture with an attested ethnic group, including the following:

1. There must be "genetic links" between the attested and ancestral cultures.

2. The ethnicity of the prehistoric group must be verified through linguistic paleontology.

3. The distribution of the archaeological culture must correlate with toponyms that will reveal the previous extent of a linguistic group.

To these, she later (1994) adds:

Map 4.1
Approximate Extent of Andronovo Culture

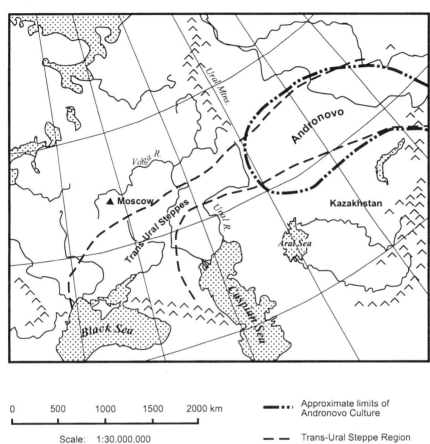

0	500	1000	1500	2000 km

Scale: 1:30,000,000

■ ▪ ▪ ▪ Approximate limits of Andronovo Culture

— — Trans-Ural Steppe Region

4. There must be verification of the ethnic attribution using bioanthropological material.

Kuz'mina has applied these criteria to her analysis of Indo-Iranian origins in relation to Andronovo cultures (Kuz'mina 1981, 1986, 1988, 1994; Smirnov and Kuz'mina 1977). These criteria, echoed by Arutiunov (1994:84) and widely applied by Soviet archaeologists, clearly demonstrate the assumption that language, biology, and culture are linked together within the *ethnos*.

Using criteria such as these, Soviet (and FSU) archaeologists have "demonstrated" the cultural (and ethnic and linguistic) continuity of Andronovo cultures with attested Indo-Iranian–speaking groups, the Sarmatians and Scythians. Traits used to make such links vary from individual elements (e.g., mortuary ritual, cult of fire, handmade pot production, ornament, and so on) to assemblages that are composed of any number of these elements. In fact, the attributes selected for ethnic identification vary in number and specifics from author to author and case to case depending on the point being argued. When the "genetic" ties between the archaeological and historical cultures have been established, the next phase of interpretation is to project ethnicity and language into the past, assigning language and ethnicity to given archaeological cultures. Thus, depending on the researcher, various Andronovo cultural groups have been described as Indo-European, Indo-Iranian, Finno-Ugric, and Indo-Aryan speakers, with cultural, ethnic, and biological identities to match.

Though the tendency to equate archaeological, linguistic, and ethnic units had been present since before the revolution, in the Trans-Urals the unification of ethnolinguistic and archaeological groups has become marked. In 1977, Vladimir F. Gening published his article "Mogil'nik Sintashta i problema rannikh Indoiranskikh plemën (The Sintashta cemetery and the problem of the early Indo-Iranian tribes)." In this article, Gening correlates elements of mortuary ritual expressed in individual burials at Sintashta with verses describing mortuary ritual in the Rigveda and Avesta (early Aryan and Iranian sacred writings) and concludes that these elements are expressions of Indo-Iranian ethnicity. Gening's students, currently the leading archaeologists in this region, quickly adopted Gening's interpretation and began to expand it to other archaeological cultures. Research has focused on ever more conjectural arguments for the ethnolinguistic identities of the peoples represented and has drifted ever further from the specific analysis of the archaeological and biological record. Linguistic reconstructions and ethnic attributions so strongly dominate the field that often the data are forced into schemes that are created based on ethnicity, rather than allowing the archaeological material to be interpreted in its own light. Arguments now frequently arise over which sites represent the earliest or purest Indo-Iranian ethnic groups, arguments that are well illustrated by contributions to a recent symposium (see Zdanovich, Ivanova, and Tairov 1995).

The attributions of a particular ethnicity to Andronovo cultural groups are seldom unanimous, though the equation of archaeological culture with ethnicity is universal. Valerij N. Chernetsov (1973), recognizing the heterogeneous nature of Andronovo cultures, hypothesized that Andronovo did not represent a single ethnolinguistic group, but rather an Ugric substrate, to which he attributed the Fedorov culture, and an intrusive Indo-Iranian element, the Alakul' culture. Vladimir S. Stokolos (1972), Mikhail F. Kosarev (1965), and others have shared this view. The extent to which such attributions of ethnicity can be carried is seen in recent studies of the Sintashta and Petrov cultures. Though the differentiating features of these two cultures have yet to be made clear, Gennadij B. Zdanovich (1990) has gone so far as to hypothesize that the Sintashta culture was Indo-Aryan, while the Petrov was Indo-Iranian. Such a hypothesis can do little but confuse an already-difficult situation for archaeologists who are now virtually required to assign archaeological cultures to attested ethnolinguistic groups.

The archaeological studies of the Bronze Age cultures east of the Urals can be classified as cladistic or culture-historical. Modern ethnolinguistic groups are projected into the past, archaeological cultures are interpreted as ethnic units, and the members of these ethnic units are expected to be physically different from one another (to be different "races" or "physical types"). Archaeological culture change is interpreted in terms of the movement of ethnic groups, carrying with them their culture, biology, and language. The culture history of the steppe zone, as reconstructed by Soviet scholars, was not developed as culture history per se, but rather is the result of an ethnogenetic theoretical framework. For Western prehistorians interested in ethnogenetic theory as an alternative to traditional culture history, it is imperative that we understand why this happened, and especially how to avoid such a transmutation of ethnogenetic interpretation in our own research.

NEW DIRECTIONS

While ethnogenetic theory is thought to be a valuable alternative to culture history, Soviet ethnogenetic studies provide extreme examples of the reification of the language/culture/biology trinity and the projection of ethnicity into the past. While Moore stresses the ephemeral nature of ethnicity (as, paradoxically, did Marr), Soviet ethnogenetic studies have instead emphasized the stability of ethnic groups. The definition of the *ethnos* became expansive and all-encompassing. Though there has perhaps been a general trend in archaeology away from ethnogenetic studies in the last decade, there is still a well-defined and influential school of "archaeological ethnogenetics" that equates archaeological cultures unequivocally with specific, stable ethnic groups (Bulkin, Klejn, and Lebedev 1982).

Soviet ethnogenetic theory was developed, to a great extent, to serve nationalist goals of Stalin and the Soviet government. These goals were best served by a theory of ethnicity that was strongly primordialist, linking biology, material culture, and language within an innate, stable *ethnos*. The political will behind this emphasis on *ethnos* theory in prehistory was clearly played out on the pages of the *Vestnik drevnej istorii* [Bulletin of ancient history], where in one issue Marr is acclaimed for his contributions to the study of ethnogenesis (Editors 1950a) and in the next is denounced by Stalin for the harm his theories had done to the study of the past (Editors 1950b; Stalin 1950). Though Soviet theorists in ethnography rigorously deny the rigidity of the *ethnos*, in practice the opposite has been the rule in the interpretation of prehistory.

What can Soviet ethnogenetic theory offer to a new theory of ethnogenesis? The emphasis on classification and typology in Soviet ethnography has done very well in demonstrating that ethnicity is a complex concept. From the beginning, the Soviets have had an interest in the classification of ethnic units, defining features that delimit ethnic groups and the principles that crosscut ethnic groups. An example of this ethnic typology is seen in the article of É. Khershak and J. Kumpes (1993), "Dva tipa étnichnosti (Khorvatskij i Serbskij primery)" (Two types of ethnicity [The Croatian and Serbian example]), in which the authors define a "Jewish" ethnic type (based on shared religion) and a "French" ethnic type (based on shared territory and political unity). They, like most Soviet anthropologists, consider *ethnoses* as "objective real formations, at the foundation of which lie historical continuity and specific configurations of socioanthropological traits" (1993:29). Though this definition is distinctly "primordialist," their analysis emphasizes that ethnicity can have very different bases.

Soviet ethnogenetic theory is also strong on the hierarchical classification of ethnic units. Ethnic units can exist on many different levels, from family groups to nations. When we are seeking ethnogenetic events, we must consider precisely what level of ethnicity we are exploring. Are we looking at the formation of a national ethnicity, ethnolinguistic group, or tribe? At what level are ethnogenetic processes operating, and what are the expectations for material culture, biology, and language at the particular level of interest? Clearly the ethnic groups used by Luigi L. Cavalli-Sforza, Paolo Menozzi, and Alberto Piazza (1994) in their genetic research are not the same as those recognized by and important to individuals within a village, and ethnogenetic processes involving each will be very different. By focusing on particular levels of ethnicity, we can better formulate models of behavior for the many factors involved.

Other Soviet studies focus on the relationship between ethnicity and political or other structural entities. Sergei A. Arutiunov (1983) classifies such relationships into three categories: (1) ethnic boundaries coincide with political boundaries; (2) the ethnic group is not politically independent, but forms an autonomous local unit within the political structure; (3) the ethnic group is not politically independent, and its ethnicity is expressed in nonmaterial ways. It should be noted that such a typology closely reflects the political organization of ethnic groups within the USSR. The relationship of ethnicity to political power is a common focus of research in instrumentalist constructions of ethnicity. In the Soviet Union, rather than being an important element of theory, it has reflected political realities of the administration of the Soviet Union.

Moore's emphasis on the coalescent nature of ethnogenesis is greatly lost in Soviet ethnogenetic research outside of ethnography, but needs to play a prominent role in the developing theory. Ethnic history is very likely to be intertwining or "rhizotic"—that is, "an incessantly drawn-out net woven from the threads of individual ethnohistorical processes that converge from various directions and diverge in various directions in the knots of ethnogenesis" (Arutiunov 1994:80). Linguistic, biological, and cultural history will also follow a pattern of occasional branching and frequent horizontal transmission, but rarely in a pattern to match that of ethnic history.

Transitional events, the innovations that define or divide cultures, are also vital to ethnogenetic studies. The particular events that cause an ethnic group to develop must be a focus of research. However, we must keep in mind that ethnicity is multifaceted and exists on many levels. If an event is identified (e.g., the adoption of mound burial), this may or may not correspond to the creation of an ethnic (or linguistic) group. Soviet ethnographers have evolved complex classifications and rankings of the ethnic unit, but ethnicity is used fairly indiscriminately by archaeologists. A theory of ethnogenesis must allow us to identify transitional events and to establish on what level they are taking place. Archaeologists must consider events within their cultural context and then decide if it is reasonable to consider them "ethnogenetic."

Ethnicity is complex and variable. It can change from generation to generation, and even within the lifetime of the individual. Ethnic self-identification can vary with context and levels of interaction, from interpersonal relationships to national entities. The relationship of ethnicity to material culture is problematic. While certain elements of material culture can be used as indexes of membership (dress, mortuary ritual, and so on), the indexes are highly sensitive to context and may not be the same for all individuals who consider themselves members of a particular ethnic group. In different contexts, indexes of different levels of ethnicity may dominate or be completely absent. Using material culture as an index of ethnicity through time is even more problematic. Changes in material culture are unlikely to be adopted evenly by all individuals and groups in a society, depending on sociopolitical context.

The relationship of biology and ethnicity has been deservedly criticized. Moore's chapter in this volume provides abundant evidence of the degree of biological mixing that occurs among ethnic groups (whether through intermarriage, raiding for wives, or adoption). Any definition of ethnicity that includes biology or common biological descent or suggests that ethnic affiliation may be determined using biological data must be viewed with great caution.

Language, after self-identification, is the most common element used in definitions of ethnicity. However, language use is highly plastic. While linguistic differences may limit interaction between individuals or groups, bilingualism develops quickly and facilitates interaction, sometimes to the point where a new common language is formed. By defining the ethnic group in terms of language, material culture, and biology, highly variable, context sensitive, and virtually independent variables are confounded. The *ethnos* defined in this way can be only the most tenuous reflection of the real, complex, evolving situation. By making the *ethnos* the focus of research (archaeological, bioanthropological, or linguistic), variation and nuance can be lost to the researcher.

While it is clear that the traditional cladistic approach to human history is insufficient, ethnogenetic theory, particularly in its Soviet form, cannot be seen as a perfect substitute. Occasionally an ethnic group may appear in which language, biology, and culture come into alignment, and this may persist for some period of time. But often language, biology, and material culture will vary in ways that cannot be accommodated by the concept of *ethnos*. Events may affect one, several, or all of these spheres, but rarely will they all react in the same way. A new theory of ethnogenesis for the study of human history must combine elements of Soviet ethnogenetic theory with a better understanding of the relationship of language, culture, and biology. The practical application of Soviet ethnogenetic theory must be taken as a caution to be kept in mind as ethnogenetic studies become emphasized in the West.

NOTES

1. The Russian term *ethnos* embodies a sense of stability and innateness. In this chapter, *ethnos* is used only where it is meant in this way.
2. "Anthropology" is used here to denote a broad social science, rather than as a direct translation of the Russian *antropologiia*, which is translated as "bioanthropology."

REFERENCES

Arnold, Bettina
1990 The Past as Propaganda: Totalitarian Archaeology in Nazi Germany. *Antiquity* 64: 464–478.
Artamonov, Mikhail I.
1949 K Voprosu ob Étnogeneze v Sovetskoj Arkheologii. *Kratkie Soobshcheniia, Institut Istorii Material'noj Kul'tury AN SSSR* 29:3–16.
Artsikhovskij, A. V.
1954 *Osnovy Arkheologii.* Moscow: Gosudarstvennoe Izdatel'stvo Politicheskoj Literatury.
Arutiunov, Sergei A.
1983 Processes and Regularities of the Incorporation of Innovations into the Culture of an Ethnos. *Soviet Anthropology and Archeology* 21(4):3–28.
1994 Ethnogenesis: Its Forms and Rules. *Anthropology and Archeology of Eurasia* 33(1): 79–93.
Asimov, M. S.
1981 Ethnic History of Central Asia in the 2nd Millennium B.C.: Soviet Studies. In *Ethnic Problems of the History of Central Asia in the Early Period (Second Millennium B.C.).* M. S. Asimov, ed. Pp. 44–52. Moscow: Nauka.
Banks, Marcus
1996 *Ethnicity: Anthropological Constructions.* London: Routledge.
Barber, John
1981 *Soviet Historians in Crisis, 1928–1932.* New York: Holmes & Meier.
Bromlei, Iulian V.
1974 Ethnos and Endogamy. *Soviet Anthropology and Archeology* 13(1):55–69.
Bromlei, Iulian V., ed.
1975 *Sovremennye Étnicheskie Protsessy v SSSR.* Moscow: Nauka.
Bromley, Julian, ed.
1974 *Soviet Ethnology and Anthropology Today.* The Hague: Mouton.

Bulkin, V. A., Leo S. Klejn, and Gleb S. Lebedev
1982 Attainments and Problems of Soviet Archaeology. *World Archaeology* 13(3):272–295.

Byrnes, Robert F.
1990 *Creating the Soviet Historical Profession, 1917–1934.* Hoover Institution Working Papers in International Studies, I-90-32. Stanford, CA: Hoover Institution, Stanford University.

Cavalli-Sforza, Luigi L., Paolo Menozzi, and Alberto Piazza
1994 *The History and Geography of Human Genes.* Princeton: Princeton University Press.

Cheboksarov, Nikolaj N.
1970 Problems of the Typology of Ethnic Units in the Works of Soviet Scholars. *Soviet Anthropology and Archeology* 9(2):127–153.

Chernetsov, Valerij N.
1973 Étno-kul'turnye Arealy v Lesnoj i Subarkticheskoj Zonakh Evrazii v Épokhu Neolita. In *Problemy Arkheologii Urala i Sibiri.* A. P. Smirnov, ed. Pp. 10–17. Moscow: Nauka.

Debets, Georgij F.
1961 Forty Years of Soviet Anthropology. Jerusalem: *Israel Program for Scientific Translations.* PST cat. no. 228.

Debets, Georgij F., Maksim G. Levin, and Tat'iana A. Trofimova
1952 Antropologicheskij Material kak Istochnik Izucheniia Voprosov Étnogeneza. *Sovetskaia Étnografiia* (1):22–35.

Derzhavin, Nikolaj S.
1944 *Proiskhozhdenie Russkogo Naroda.* Moscow: Sovetskaia Nauka.

Dragadze, Tamara
1980 The Place of "Ethnos" Theory in Soviet Anthropology. In *Soviet and Western Anthropology.* E. Gellner, ed. Pp. 161–170. New York: Columbia University Press.

Dunn, Stephen P., and Ethel Dunn
1974 The Intellectual Tradition of Soviet Ethnography. In *Introduction to Soviet Ethnography.* S. P. Dunn and E. Dunn, eds. Vol. 1, pp. 1–53. Berkeley, CA: Highgate Road Social Science Research Station.

Editors
1950a N. Ia. Marr i Izuchenie Drevnej Istorii. *Vestnik Drevnej Istorii* (1):3–11.

Editors
1950b Ot Redaktsii. *Vestnik Drevnej Istorii* (2):25–27.

Ehret, Christopher
1988 Language Change and the Material Correlates of Language and Ethnic Shift. *Antiquity* 62:564–574.

Engels, Friedrich
1884 *The Origin of the Family, Private Property, and the State.* Aylesbury: Penguin Books, 1986.

Gellner, Ernest
1977 Ethnicity and Anthropology in the Soviet Union. *Archives européennes de sociologie* 18(2):201–220.

Gening, Vladimir F.
1977 Mogil'nik Sintashta i Problema Rannikh Indoiranskikh Plemën. *Sovetskaia Arkheologiia* 3:53–73.
Gerasimov, Mikhail M., N. M. Rud', and Leonid T. Iablonskij
1987 *Antropologiia Antichnogo i Srednevekovogo Naseleniia Vostochnoj Evropy.* Moscow: Nauka.
Graham, Loren R.
1993 *Science in Russia and the Soviet Union: A Short History.* Cambridge: Cambridge University Press.
Haarmann, Harald
1986 *Language in Ethnicity: A View of Basic Ecological Relations.* Contributions to the Sociology of Language, 44. Berlin: Mouton de Gruyter.
Humphrey, Caroline
1984 Some Recent Developments in Ethnography in the USSR. *Man*, n.s., 19:310–320.
Hutchinson, John, and Anthony D. Smith, eds.
1996 *Ethnicity.* Oxford: Oxford University Press.
Khershak, É., and J. Kumpes
1993 Dva Tipa Étnichnosti (Khorvatskij i Serbskij Primery). *Étnograficheskoe Obozrenie* (4):29–40.
Kosarev, Mikhail F.
1965 O Kul'turakh Andronovskogo Vremeni v Zapadnoj Sibiri. *Sovetskaia Arkheologiia* (2):242–246.
Kuz'mina, Elena E.
1981 Proiskhozhdenie Indoirantsev v Svete Novejshikh Arkheologicheskikh Dannykh. In *Ethnic Problems of the History of Central Asia in the Early Period (Second Millennium B.C.).* M. S. Asimov, ed. Pp. 101–125. Moscow: Nauka.
1986 *Drevnejshie Skotovody ot Urala do Tian'-Shania.* Frunze: Ilim.
1988 Kul'turnaia i Étnicheskaia Atributsiia Pastusheskikh Plemën Kazakhstana i Srednej Azii Épokhi Bronzy. *Vestnik Drevnej Istorii* 1988 (2):35–60.
1994 *Otkuda Prishli Indoarii?* Moscow: Rossijskaia Akademiia Nauk.
Lebedev, Gleb S.
1992 *Istoriia Otechestvennoj Arkheologii: 1700–1917 gg.* St. Petersburg: Izd. S.-Peterburgskogo Universiteta.
Madsen, David B., and David Rhode, eds.
1994 *Across the West: Human Population Movement and the Expansion of the Numa.* Salt Lake City: University of Utah Press.
Milisauskas, Sarunas
1990 People's Revolutions of 1989 and Archaeology in Eastern Europe. *Antiquity* 64: 283–285.
Mongait, Alexander
1959 *Archaeology in the USSR.* David Skvirsky, transl. Moscow: Foreign Languages Publishing House.
Moore, John H.
1994a Ethnogenetic Theory. *National Geographic Research and Exploration* 10(1):10–23.
1994b Putting Anthropology Back Together Again: The Ethnogenetic Critique of Cladistic Theory. *American Anthropologist* 96(4):925–948.

Nash, Manning
1996 The Core Elements of Ethnicity. In *Ethnicity*. J. Hutchinson and A. D. Smith, eds. Pp. 24–28. Oxford: Oxford University Press.

Ol'khovskij, Valerij S.
1992 Ob Arkheologicheskikh Sledov Migratsii v Épokhu Bronzovogo i Rannego Metalla. In *Margulanovskie Chteniia 1990*. Z. S. Samashev, V. S. Ol'khovskij, E. A. Smagulov, K. M. Bajpakov, M. K. Shakenov, and R. L. Nauryzbaeva, eds. Pp. 30–32. Moscow: Institut Arkheologiia, AN Respubliki Kazakhstan.

Proctor, Robert
1988 From *Anthropologie* to *Rassenkunde* in the German Anthropological Tradition. In *Bones, Bodies, Behavior: Essays on Biological Anthropology*. G. W. Stocking, Jr., ed. Pp. 138–179. History of Anthropology, vol. 5. Madison: University of Wisconsin Press.

Roginskij, Iakov Ia., and Maksim G. Levin
1978 *Antropologiia*. Moscow: Vysshaia Shkola.

Rouse, Irving
1986 *Migrations in Prehistory*. New Haven, CT: Yale University Press.

Sal'nikov, Konstantin V.
1952 *Drevnejshie Pamiatniki Istorii Urala*. Sverdlovsk: Sverdlovskoe Oblastnoe Gosudarstvennoe Izdatel'stvo.

Shnirel'man, Viktor A.
1993 Zlokliucheniia Odnoj Nauki: Étnogeneticheskie Issledovaniia i Stalinskaia Natsional'naia Politika. *Étnograficheskoe Obozrenie* (3):52–68.

Skalnik, Peter
1986 Towards an Understanding of Soviet *Étnos* Theory. *South African Journal of Ethnology* 9(4):157–166.

Slezkin, Iuri
1993 Sovetskaia Étnografiia v Nokdaune: 1928–1938. *Étnograficheskoe Obozrenie*. (2): 113–125.

Slezkine, Yuri
1991 The Fall of Soviet Ethnography, 1928–38. *Current Anthropology* 32(4):476–484.

Smirnov, Konstantin F., and Elena E. Kuz'mina
1977 *Proiskhozhdenie Indoirantsev v Svete Novejshikh Arkheologicheskikh Otkrytij*. Moscow: Nauka.

Sokolovskii, Sergey, and Valery Tishkov
1996 Ethnicity. In *Encyclopedia of Social and Cultural Anthropology*. A. Barnard and J. Spencer, eds. Pp. 190–193. London and New York: Routledge.

Stalin, Iosef
1950 Otnositel'no Marksizma v Iazykoznanii. *Vestnik Drevnej Istorii* (2):3–19.

Stokolos, Vladimir S.
1972 *Kul'tura Naseleniia Bronzovogo Veka Iuzhnogo Zaural'ia: Khronologiia i Periodizatsiia*. Moscow: Nauka.

Teploukhov, S. A.
1927 Drevnie Pogrebeniia v Minusinskom Krae. *Materialy po Étnografii* 3(2):57–112.

Tishkov, Valery A.
1992 The Crisis in Soviet Ethnography. *Current Anthropology* 33(4):371–394.

Tonkin, Elisabeth, Maryon McDonald, and Malcolm Chapman
1996 History and Ethnicity. In *Ethnicity*. J. Hutchinson and A. D. Smith, eds. Pp. 18–
     24. Oxford: Oxford University Press.
Tret'iakov, Pëtr N.
1963 The Ethnogenetic Process and Archeology. *Soviet Anthropology and Archeology*
     1(4):3–13.
Trigger, Bruce G.
1989 *A History of Archaeological Thought*. Cambridge: Cambridge University Press.
Vainshtein, Sev'ian I.
1980 *Nomads of South Siberia: The Pastoral Economies of Tuva*. Michael Colenso,
     transl. Cambridge: Cambridge University Press.
Veit, Ulrich
1989 Ethnic Concepts in German Prehistory: A Case Study on the Relationship between
     Cultural Identity and Archaeological Objectivity. In *Archaeological Approaches
     to Cultural Identity*. S. Shennan, ed. Pp. 35–56. One World Archaeology, 10.
     London: Unwin Hyman.
Zdanovich, Gennadij B.
1990 Arkaim. In *Rifej, 1990: Uralskij Kraevedcheskij Sbornik*. A. P. Moiseev, ed.
     Pp. 229–243. Cheliabinsk: Iuzhno-Uralskoe Knizhnoe Izdatel'stvo.
Zdanovich, Gennadij B., Nad'ia O. Ivanova, and Aleksandr D. Tairov, eds.
1995 *Kul'tury Drevnikh Narodov Stepnoj Evrazii i Fenomen Protogorodskoj Tsivilizatsii
     Iuzhnogo Urala*. Vol. 5(1–2). Cheliabinsk: Cheliabinskij Gosudarstvennyj Univ-
     ersitet.

5

Setting the Boundaries: Linguistics, Ethnicity, Colonialism, and Archaeology South of Lake Chad

Scott MacEachern

Archaeologists working in Africa commonly assume that language relationships are a sign of ancient cultural and ethnic affiliations. In and around the northern Mandara Mountains of Cameroon and Nigeria, however, European colonial administrators adapted poorly understood sociolinguistic boundaries between communities and regions to divide up their administrative territories into "tribal" groupings practical for governing and taxation. Thus a social milieu that was actually characterized by multilingualism, dialectal variation, and constant interchanges between communities was transformed during the colonial era into a static set of "ethnic groups" that could be located on maps of Africa. Archaeologists have, in turn, used these largely artificial constructs to "read" the ethnicity of ancient artifacts by ethnographic analogy, thereby colonializing not only the African present but also the past.—Editor

Archaeologists working in Africa often use reconstructions derived from historical linguistics as a supplement to research, and especially in the production of models of ancient societies. This is not surprising, since one of archaeologists' main objectives is the delineation of ancient human groups analogous to those seen in the world today. One of the central elements in any human society is language: mother tongues and linguae francae, languages spoken well and badly, the shifting borderlands between dialect and language, and the relationships between multilingualism and cultural interchange. Language plays a central part in most definitions of ethnicity, mediating common cultural elements, claims of common origin, and the relationships of identification that act reflexively between the individual and the collective (Fishman 1989:22–65). Linguistic research can yield information about social relationships and cultural institutions otherwise difficult for archaeologists to obtain. These are powerful attractions, and it is not surprising that archaeologists have tried to establish links between prehistoric traditions and protolanguages established through historical linguistic research.

Archaeologists have, unfortunately, used outdated concepts of African societies and language groups as the bases of their models of the African past, concepts that implicitly treat human groups as static, homogeneous, monolithic entities—"tribes," as usually rendered (MacEachern 1998). A corrective was long overdue to these earlier views of traditional societies, and this is now being absorbed into research on the continent (Astuti 1995; David et al. 1991; Dietler and Herbich 1994; Marliac and Langlois 1996; McIntosh 1998; Stahl 1991). At the same time, there remains a tendency to exempt linguistic analyses from this corrective. Manipulating the linguistic affiliation of a group of people seems to be more difficult than establishing districts for purposes of taxation and rule by administrative fiat. Presumably the patterning of language use and affiliation across a region would preserve elements of precolonial social and cultural relationships into the colonial period. So persuaded, archaeologists continue to use linguistic distributions as stand-ins for primordial human systems of relationship.

There are dangers in this, and they involve the ways in which people use language as a criterion for the charting of social and political worlds. First, archaeologists often conceive of language distributions simply as substitutes for the "tribal" distributions that they now accept as obsolete. Geolinguistic examination of dialect boundaries has led to critiques of the isogloss concept similar to anthropological critiques of fixed group boundaries (Trudgill 1984:46–51; Chambers and Trudgill 1980). If we take into account the complexities of language use across Africa, it becomes obvious that interpreting people's use of language in the past will be just as complicated as interpreting other components of human ethnic variability. Second, language identities were consciously manipulated through time by various groups in Africa, especially but not uniquely in the European-African encounter. Colonialists needed to acquire or impose vehicular languages so that they could control local groups, but their ignorance of local conditions afforded Africans opportunities for the manipulation of that unfamiliarity for their own ends (Dorward 1974; Fabian 1986; MacEachern 1993a). This included the propagation of specific languages and dialects and the disparagement of others as "debased" or "uncivilized" (Fabian 1983; Harries 1991; Ranger 1991; Jewsiewicki 1991). Missionization and colonial education played a central role in such cases, as the project of establishing standardized speech and reified ethnicities supported the remodeling of Africa in a colonial image.

In this chapter, I examine some of these relationships between ethnic, linguistic, and archaeological entities around the northern Mandara Mountains. I will try to show how internal and external forces have over the past few hundred years affected linguistic affiliations and interactions in this area as these present themselves to local people and to foreigners both African and Euro-American. In the course of this work, I refer to the small-scale units within which Mandara populations live as *territorial lineage groups* (this term is discussed later) and more generally as *communities*, while using the terms *ethnic groups* and *tribes* as, respectively, the modern and traditional ethnographic designations for large-scale, stable, and somewhat-monolithic ethnolinguistic units, the existence of which I dispute in this area in the precolonial period.

THE MANDARA MOUNTAINS: HISTORICAL AND CULTURAL CONTEXTS

Ethnic Contexts

The environment of the northern Mandara massif and of the plains and in-selbergs surrounding it has been described in other publications (e.g., Boutrais et al. 1984). The geographical and especially cultural dichotomies between mountains and plains, at present and in the historical period, are extremely striking (Map 5.1). Small, non-Muslim communities, which ethnographers have traditionally divided up into "tribes," occupy the northern massif, in places at some of the highest population densities in rural Africa. Over the last two decades, these "tribes" have been increasingly referred to as ethnic groups, but little has changed beyond the terminology, since these ethnic groups (Map 5.2) retain the same boundaries and features as did the "tribes" before them. These ethnic groups are defined on the basis of complex and varied combinations of cultural and linguistic characteristics, to a great extent modified by colonial intervention (this will be discussed later; see also MacEachern 1990, 1998). They vary greatly in size and are built up out of varying numbers of patrilineages. These latter are best thought of as political/territorial units and invariably incorporate groups of people who are not recognized as members of the descent group. I denominate them as territorial lineage groups, and they would under most circumstances have probably been the precolonial units of primary individual identification (with all of the implications for ethnicity that the term implies [Barth 1969:13–14]) for montagnard people. The geographic focus of these territorial lineage groups is usually a defensible terrain feature, in many cases a prominence, ridge line, or internal plateau.

European colonization of this area took place at the beginning of the twentieth century, when the plains had for the most part been under the control of centralized, literate, Islamic polities for some hundreds of years. Along the northern peripheries of the mountains, the Wandala state has been of central importance in the political history of the region. The Wandala display ample evidence of cultural elements shared with massif communities, including language, lineage and probably caste systems, origin traditions, rituals and beliefs in the supernatural, and political systems (MacEachern 1990:65–74; Bourges 1996:18–40). It is probably best to conceive of the Wandala as a people of heterogeneous

Map 5.1
The Northern Mandara Mountains, with Wandala Communities

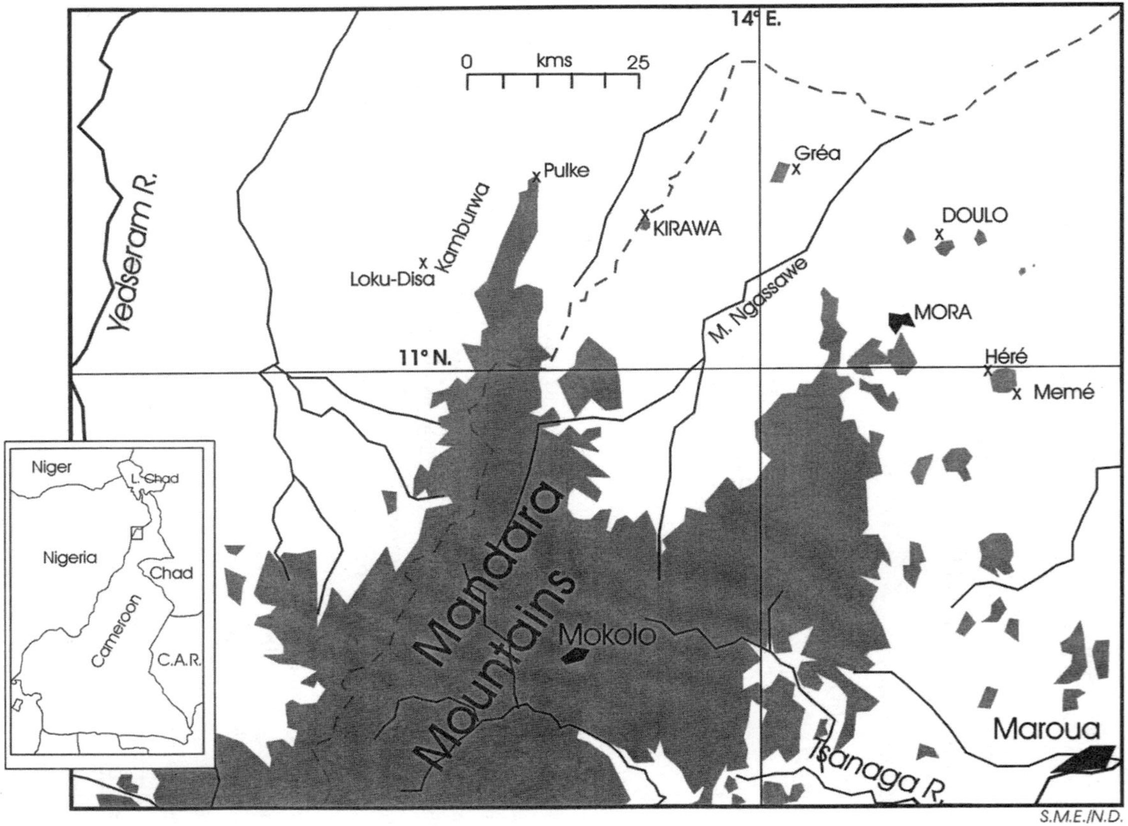

Map 5.2
"Ethnic Groups" in and around the Northern Mandara Mountains

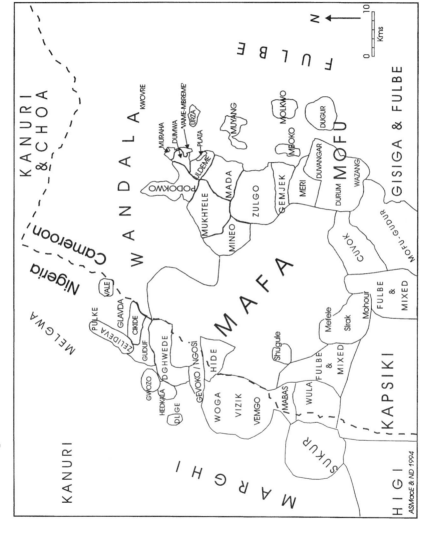

Note: The outlined areas indicate the extent of the massif. Ethnic boundaries are approximate.

origins who were able to obtain the military resources necessary for domination of the plains immediately north of the Mandara massif. From that plains focus, the accoutrements of a Sudanic state—urbanism, literacy, Islam, bureaucracy, and so on—eventually followed (Barkindo 1989; Forkl 1986, 1989; MacEachern 1990, 1993c; Morrissey 1984).

Montagnard and Wandala communities existed within a web of paradoxical relationships, with intermarriage, trade, and warfare coexisting at short distances and at very short notice. The mountains furnished the Wandala state with resources necessary for its survival: iron and slaves for internal use and external trade, and defensive positions when more powerful forces approached in the plains. Iron and defensive positions could, however, be obtained only through negotiation and trading, while raiding and kidnapping were the primary mechanisms used to obtain slaves. Montagnards depended upon their Wandala neighbors for resources that were in chronically short supply in the mountains— primarily salt and protein—and in some cases were able to prevail upon the Wandala to intervene in the frequent conflicts that occurred between different territorial lineage groups within the massif.

Linguistic Contexts

The languages spoken throughout the Mandara Mountains and in the plains around the mountains (Map 5.3) belong primarily to the Biu-Mandara branch of Chadic. The important exceptions are Fulfulde (West Atlantic), Kanuri (Saharan), Arab (Semitic), and Hausa (Western Chadic), all spoken by regionally important Muslim populations. The Biu-Mandara languages in this region are in turn divided into two subgroups. The Wandala languages are spoken along the northern and western edges of the mountains. Wandala is the only one of these languages spoken to any significant degree on the plains, by the Wandala themselves and by the Melgwa, a non-Muslim group. Other dialects of Wandala are spoken by Muraha, Kwovré, Pulke, some Zelideva, and other montagnards, who live alongside the Wandala around the traditional capitals of Kirawa, Doulo, and Mora (Maps 5.2 and 5.3). The other languages of the Wandala group are spoken in the montagnard communities along the northern and western peripheries of the massif. Speakers of the Mafa languages, the second coordinate group of Biu-Mandara, occupy most of the eastern and all of the southern part of the area. The northeastern and northwestern extremities of the massif exhibit a great deal of linguistic fragmentation, with most montagnard languages in these areas spoken by between 1,000 and 10,000 people, while in the interior plateau and along the southern boundaries of the massif, language communities are often considerably larger. Thus the five dialects of the Pelasla language, found near the northeastern extremity of the massif, are spoken by a total of about 3,000 speakers, while further to the south the three Mafa dialects are spoken by over 140,000 people.

Map 5.3
Languages in and around the Northern Mandara Mountains

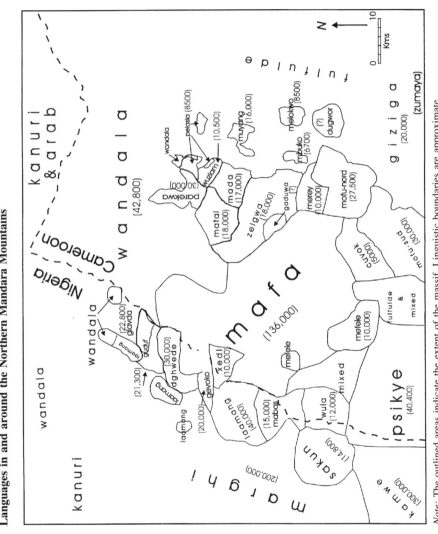

Note: The outlined areas indicate the extent of the massif. Linguistic boundaries are approximate.

Archaeological and Historical Contexts

Systematic archaeological research has been undertaken in and around the northern Mandara Mountains since the early 1980s (David and Sterner 1989; MacEachern 1996a). We have now excavated a number of sites dating primarily to the last 2,000 years, the period since which iron technologies became firmly entrenched in the region. Available data indicate a considerable degree of cultural continuity through time and across space for the peripheries of the northern mountains throughout this time period (MacEachern 1993b, 1994, 1996a). Material produced in these areas over the last 2,000 years is recognizably ancestral to pottery produced in the same areas today, and indeed we can trace the roots of some present-day ceramics traditions to these early plains occupations. For present purposes, there are two significant characteristics of the archaeological record in this area. First, we have little archaeological evidence of occupation of the northern Mandara Mountains before 500 years ago (David 1998:60; MacEachern 1990, 1996b). This indicates an important shift in the population balance in and around the massif as people living on the plains moved up into the mountains, clearing and terracing the hillsides and establishing the present configuration of montagnard territorial lineage groups. These events were probably tied to the emergence of the Wandala state. Second, both ancient and modern ceramic traditions are found over areas much larger than the ethnic groups that are demarcated in the area today; in fact, the analysis of material culture in general would in this area render such groups quite invisible (MacEachern 1998). We might expect that this would drastically lessen the utility of archaeological research, but it appears that in this case the ethnographic reconstructions, and not the archaeological ones, may be at fault.

PRECONTACT RELATIONS: THE WANDALA AND THE MONTAGNARDS

The ascent to regional power of the Wandala state from the fifteenth to the nineteenth centuries was also a process of differentiation of the Wandala from the Chadic-speaking societies that surrounded them. Wandala of 500 years ago appears to have been a small chiefdom, little different from others that bordered it along the northwestern edges of the Mandara massif (MacEachern 1990:92–122, 319–323). Over the next centuries, Wandala social and political systems changed drastically, probably in large part because of Wandala control of trade routes to the Kanuri capital of Birni Ngazargamo. This change involved an expansion of Wandala territory to the east and southeast and the development of a cavalry force similar to that of other plains groups. It eventually entailed an increase in the power of the royal lineage and of the *tlikse*, the head of that lineage and ruler, the integration of Wandala society into regional economic and social systems, conversion to Islam, and the development of a literate class of bureaucrats. This process of reinvention and differentiation could not have failed to impinge upon the other societies of the region. Indeed, it largely created the montagnard population, since the Wandala expansion was fueled by the conquest of neighboring territories and the export of slaves to the Kanuri, and montagnards appear to be in great part the descendants of refugees from these activities.

It would be a mistake to try to examine the relationships between Wandala and montagnards as if these relations were invariant through space and time. I shall concern myself primarily with these relationships when the Wandala state attained its largest extent, through the last half of the eighteenth and the nineteenth centuries. During this period, the Wandala elite in their capitals at Doulo and Mora claimed a somewhat-theoretical suzerainty over a large area of the plains around the Mandara Mountains. Even in the core area of the Wandala state, between the Loku-Disa inselbergs in the west and Héré and Memé in the east, the important communities at Kamburwa, Kirawa, and Gréa appear to have retained a considerable degree of autonomy (Bourges 1996; MacEachern 1996b). This autonomy is reflected in the wide variation within the Wandala language, in which different dialects for Kamburwa, Kirawa, Gréa, the Mora-Doulo area, and areas south of Mora exist (Summer Institute of Linguistics 1996). This situation ended in the middle of the nineteenth century when *tlikse* Bukar Anarbana broke the powers of the local leaders and split the state into smaller units, more dependent upon the central power (Forkl 1986:6–7; 1989: 542–543).

The Wandala influence upon neighboring montagnards was quite variable. Ethnohistorical data (MacEachern 1990:67–68) indicate differences in montagnard perceptions of the Wandala living in neighboring communities and those living in the capital: trade and peaceful contacts originated with Wandala neighbors, while the slave raids and kidnappings came from Wandala living further away. Neighbors of the Wandala had to evolve accommodations to life near the centers of power, while montagnard communities at a further remove retained more independence but correspondingly were more frequently engaged in active conflict with the Wandala. We may thus expect different processes of differentiation between populations along the northeastern and northwestern extremities of the massif, where montagnards and plains dwellers have interacted at close quarters for centuries, and in the intervening areas away from the capitals.

We know little about the mechanisms of administration that the Wandala attempted to deploy in montagnard territories. These appear to have generally followed the Kanuri pattern, with the Wandala ruler appointing local men as *chetima* and/or *makaji* and giving them the responsibility of controlling and extracting tribute and cooperation. The limited data available indicate that the Wandala were knowledgeable about the variety of montagnard communities (MacEachern 1990:190), but the effectiveness of these local representatives appears often to have been almost nil. Wandala rule probably had little effect upon the ethnic and linguistic milieu in areas at some distance from the centers of state power. This was not the case, however, around the Wandala capitals and their territories. In these areas, ethnic and linguistic variation is highest, and cultural diversity occurs at the smallest of geographical scales. The Muraha community at Mora, the Kwovré at Doulo, the Geblege and Valé around Kirawa, and the Pulke, Warrabe, and Kiva communities in the mountains south of Pulke speak dialects of Wandala (MacEachern, field notes 1993; Müller-Kosack 1999). Distributional and ethnohistorical data indicate that Wandala was not the original language of most of these people, and this is thus the only region of the northern Mandara Mountains where mountain communities have adopted the language of an Islamic, plains-based state as a mother tongue. This testifies to a significant linguistic impingement, probably resulting from centuries of close contact between Wandala centers and the montagnard communities that participated in the day-to-day life of the state, intermarrying with the Wandala, supplying them with iron, provisions, and shelter, taking their part in wars and in raiding expeditions against other groups, and supplying blacksmiths and other ritual experts as necessity demanded.

In these central areas, the distinction between local montagnard communities and a Wandala peasantry only sketchily committed to Islam even in the early twentieth century often would not have been great. Intermarriage between montagnard and Wandala communities continued to be significant even after the Wandala elite converted to Islam. In the late nineteenth century, the *tlikse* of the Wandala had numerous montagnard wives and concubines, and some of his children by these women held important offices. After the Wandala last sought refuge in the mountains during the Muslim military leader Rabih az-Zubayr's campaigns in 1894, some Wandala women from the capital at Doulo refused to return to the town, converted to traditional religions, and married Muraha men (MacEachern, field notes 1996). Such degrees of intermarriage would have been especially important linguistically, contributing to the common heritage of mountain and plains communities.

The degree of linguistic and ethnic fragmentation in these areas of the northwestern and northeastern massif may well also be related to Wandala practices. Montagnard people from Urza, Muyan/Palbara, Doulo, and Gwoza speak of the threat of Wandala slave raids and kidnappings to travelers on the plains and piedmonts that separate lineage-group territories in a number of regions. Communication in such areas was possible but not to be attempted lightly, so that marriage on inselbergs, for example, would in most cases be with families living on the same mountain. Such isolation might also encourage dialect development and correspondingly retard the development of wider social and political affiliations between montagnard communities.

The Wandala were never a colonial power in the sense that their successors, the English, French, and Germans, would be. Their ability to influence events in the mountains by force was minimal, and they worked within a shifting network of alliances and feuds that encompassed both montagnard communities and Wandala factions (Morrissey 1984:179; Rohlfs 1875:35, 53). Their ties with mountain communities, through intermarriage, alliance, and even enslavement and warfare, meant that the Wandala did not operate as much in the context of ignorance, prior assumption, and oversimplification that would characterize European colonial administrations. Wandala effects on the montagnard ethnic and linguistic milieu did not involve the manipulation of languages or the imposition of new types of boundaries between communities, but were side effects of more general relations between different political and social systems.

THE COLONIAL AND POSTCOLONIAL ENCOUNTERS: EUROPEANS AND INDIGENOUS PEOPLES

The Beginnings of the Colonial Relationship

The area around the Mandara Mountains was brought under German rule in 1902, and after World War I, Great Britain and France administered the captured territory under a League of Nations mandate. European administration began in profound ignorance of Mandara societies. A few European travelers had visited the area during the nineteenth century, and so the new colonialists had at least some useful descriptions of the Wandala and neighboring plains polities, including the Kanuri state of Bornu and the Fulbé chieftaincies of Adamawa. The first detailed map of the peripheries of the massif was produced as an annex to the German-British border agreement of 1906 (Moisel 1906) and was followed by successive surveys and reports on the plains and mountain peripheries. The mountains, however, remained to a great extent unknown until well after World War I.

When the first colonial officers arrived in the area, they found Wandala and other Muslim leaders who cooperated, made useful auxiliaries, and were eager to use European forces to quell "troublemakers" in their territories (Goodridge 1997; Lembezat 1949; MacEachern 1993a; Salamone 1985). Colonial rule was focused around occupation of the capitals of indigenous states, while montagnards were difficult to reach, spoke a multitude of strange languages, and often actively resisted contact with outsiders. The populations of Wandala and neighboring states, and especially their elites, were Muslims, with habits and outlooks that were, if not always congenial, at least familiar to Europeans. Montagnards, on the other hand, were adherents to local religions and local cultural norms. They went about naked, ate unspeakable foods—locusts, dogs, "rotted" meat— and often appeared drunk and truculent. They reacted violently to attempts at taxation—not surprisingly, given the population densities and strains upon available resources in different parts of the massif. The most prevalent view throughout the German, and into the French and British, period of administration was that montagnards were naturally backward, rebellious, and hostile to their control, and European reactions to real or imagined montagnard outrages were often devastating (AOM [Archives d'Outre-Mer]), A.E.F. Série 2D39/8866; Beauvilain 1989:316–339; Lembezat 1949, 1950).

Wandala control over European contact with montagnards broke down gradually over the early twentieth century, with a slow growth in the knowledge of

European officers about the areas they worked in and the people who lived there. Colonial taxation systems forced men from montagnard communities to travel outside their own territories to work, bringing increasing contact with Europeans and creating a pool of indigenous translators and intermediaries. This is not to say that Europeans and montagnards came to any sort of rapprochement, but simply that the Europeans learned of the disadvantages of using Wandala and Fulbe intermediaries (Beauvilain 1989:327). It became obvious with the progress of French administration in Cameroon that the Wandala state could not in fact collect taxes, furnish security, or generally administer according to European norms.

Administration and Control

From about 1916 until 1926 and the appointment of Paul Marchand as governor, French control of the montagnards in Cameroon was essentially military and oriented toward the extraction of taxes and punishment for disorder. Punitive columns were led by Wandala guides through the hills to accomplish military objectives, and to many montagnards, the new occupiers were probably not very different from the old. Eventually, however, the French administrators realized that civil control of the region was essential if colonization was to move beyond raid and counterraid. By the mid-1920s, the rhetoric of governance changed from one of "punishment" and "control" to one of "taming" and "education" (Beauvilain 1989:352–358; AOM Série Géographique 932/9267). Accompanying this was a gradual removal of responsibility for montagnard communities from the hands of Wandala and other Muslim chiefs, and its placement in the hands of local leaders. This process was slow; most of the northern massif was still under military (and to some extent Wandala) administration in 1936, and the creation and modification of administrative divisions was an ongoing colonial project from that time until Cameroon became independent in 1960.

Before the mid-1920s, the rather haphazard nature of French interaction with montagnards meant that administrative units around the mountains could be large, and indeed the three initial military divisions, centered upon the towns of Mora, Mokolo, and Maroua, took in the entire northern Mandara massif. The boundaries between these units were based primarily on the limits of the mountains. The names of different montagnard "tribes" were well known, but they appear to have been distinguished primarily upon the defensibility of the heights that they occupied and the trouble that they gave to officers on their rounds. Civilian administration and pacification demanded considerably more sophisticated partitioning of administrative and fiscal responsibility among the different regions. First, local leaders had to be found to take up that responsibility—no easy task in areas where political power was traditionally as decentralized as in many parts of the northern Mandara massif. Second, coherent administrative districts had to be carved out of the zones of influence of Wandala (and in the south, Fulbé) centers, their boundaries demarcated, and their relationships to one another agreed upon.

In some areas, such demarcation was simple. Within the plains areas still controlled by the Wandala state, the division of cantons and *chefferies* ("chief-ships") followed the limits of Wandala administrative districts. The inselbergs that dotted the plains around the massif had historically sheltered montagnard communities and in some cases were also associated with a Wandala community colocated at the foot of the mountains for purposes of defense and resource extraction. In these cases, montagnard groups were included within relevant Wandala *chefferies*: the Mafa at Gréa within Kolofata (established to administer Gréa in the eighteenth century, since the spirits of the inselberg made it fatal for the Wandala chief to live at Gréa itself), the Valé at Keroua within Keroua canton, the Kwovré at Doulo within Doulo canton, and so on. The Muraha living on the massif above the Wandala capital at Mora were made part of Mora-Massif canton, and the chiefship of that canton was given to the traditional representative of the Muraha at the Wandala court, the *tli-mura*. On the other hand, small, scattered groups that had been important in the history of the area around the massif—the Maya, predecessors to the Wandala, or the Mungur blacksmiths (Seignobos 1986, 1991), for example—became administratively in-visible, since their numbers in any one canton were quite small.

As noted earlier, the relationships between Wandala and montagnard groups were often quite close, and in many cases there was little change in administra-tive identifications. One exception was on Urza inselberg. Here, montagnard territorial lineage groups of diverse origins, most but not all speaking Pelasla (Mouchet 1947; MacEachern, field notes, 1986, 1996) and with a good deal of independence from the Wandala community at Mémé, were nevertheless brought as a single unit under the administrative control of that town. The same process occurred within the inselbergs along the eastern side of the massif, including Muyan-Palbara and Molkwo: the limits of the physical features became the boundaries of the administrative units, and montagnard communities were grouped with nearby Wandala communities. As with Urza, there was a consid-erable degree of cultural and linguistic diversity in each of these territories (Richard 1977:36–42).

The delimitation of administrative units was more difficult within the massif, where the relationship between physical features and montagnard occupation was not as clear-cut. In some areas, demarcation of cantons was relatively easy. Mada lineage groups occupied a coherent block of terrain, for the most part claimed descent from one ancestor, spoke one language, and had an obvious chief in Tcavay, a man of Ngirmayo lineage group who had become familiar to French authorities from the late 1930s (MacEachern, field notes 1986; Richard 1977:43). Similarly, the limits of Ouldemé canton to the north of Mada were relatively easy to determine, although the origins of the Uldemé territorial line-age groups are more complicated than are those of the Mada.

In other areas, the matter was more difficult. Perhaps the best illustration of this is the way in which the territorial lineage groups speaking the various dialects of Pelasla were treated. The different Urza lineage groups were, as noted, somewhat isolated on their inselberg. The distribution of the speakers of the other four dialects was more complicated. The Plata, speakers of the Platla dialect, live on the same area of the massif as do the much more numerous Uldemé (Wuzlam speakers) and were included within Ouldemé canton. They became known to colonial administrators and anthropologists as the Gwéndélé lineage of Uldemé "ethnic group"—this despite the fact that they speak a different language, are distinct in many different technological and cultural elements, and consider themselves a group distinct from the Uldemé (MacEachern 1990:252–261).

A number of independent territorial lineage groups living to the north of the Plata, including the Zulé, Ndrémé, Mbremé, Afam, and Mabar, speakers of two other dialects of Pelasla, were lumped together within the Wandala canton of Ouarba as an entirely fictitious montagnard ethnic group, the "Vamé-Mbremé." Consideration of this "ethnicity" persisted in the literature of the area until the mid-1980s (Boulet, Beauvilain, and Gubry 1984), despite its lack of cultural and historical reality (Nyssens 1986). The three Dumwa territorial lineage groups, speaking the fifth, Dumwa, dialect of Pelasla, were apportioned between the "Vamé-Mbremé" to the south and the Muraha to the north, although these groups considered themselves to be closely enough related for lineage exogamy to be invoked. The result of colonial cantonal demarcation was in this case the reinforcement of one ethnic division (Urza speakers as representative of all montagnards at Urza), the administrative disappearance of other groups (the Plata and Dumwa territorial lineage groups), and the manufacture of an ethnic group where none had existed before (the "Vamé-Mbremé").

In Muktelé territory, territorial lineage groups of diverse origins were in precolonial times for the most part speakers of the Matal language. The creation of two cantons of very different sizes in this area was due to the varying availability of cantonal leaders (Juillerat 1971:21), but these canton boundaries swept up a number of small communities speaking neighboring languages. These "Muktelé" cantons thus became constellations of Matal, Parekwa, Mada, and Zelgwa speakers, with the latter three on the peripheries of the districts. Similarly, three cantons were carved out of the territory of the Podokwo lineage groups, their boundaries depending on the physical configuration of the massif, the availability of men of high prestige to be canton chiefs, and some of the highest rural population densities in Africa (Lembezat 1952; Siran n.d.). Again, the origins, histories, and cultural affiliations of the Podokwo were quite diverse. In this case, informants suggest that some Podokwo territorial lineage groups incorporated speakers of other languages, including Matal, Wandala (Muraha montagnards and not Wandala themselves), and Wuzlam, instead of the dominant Parekwa (MacEachern, field notes 1986, against Siran n.d.). Further to the south, a set of communities of widely varying cultural, linguistic, and political characteristics (including Gudur, Dugur, Duvangar, Wazan, Mikiri, Mowosl, Gayam, Tseré, and Tsaki-Chebé) were swept up under the appellation "Mofu" in the cantons of Meri arrondissement, and colonial officers and other Europeans were soon talking of "the Mofu" as a distinct ethnic unit (Vincent 1991:48–56).

The demarcation of cantonal/*chefferie* boundaries along the northern edge of the massif by the French colonial administration was predicated on a number of intersecting factors. These included linguistic and historical relationships between communities, but the configuration of geographical features, proximity to Wandala centers and inclusion within traditional Wandala units, and the availability of local people suitable for chiefship were all also important. Overriding all else, however, was the necessity for defining administrative units that would be clearly demarcated and unambiguous for the purposes of taxation, judicial control, and other administrative functions. The primary effect of all of this boundary making was simplification, the creation of a view of ethnic and linguistic diversity in and around the massif that was essentially a somewhat-variant version of the cultural situation in metropolitan France. In order to "tame" and "educate" the "natives," the colonial government had to deliver to them some of the results of European culture, bureaucratized, organized, and compartmentalized as it was. In order to do that, Mandara populations had to be grouped appropriately, and this implicitly demanded the imposition of European concepts of acceptable ethnic variation. "Education" in its widest sense was not only to be delivered as a European cultural good, it had to be delivered in a European fashion—and, most importantly, to people organized in a European manner.

Missionaries and Teachers

The effects of these divisions were immediate. Inclusion within a particular canton/*chefferie* made one subject to some extent to the power of the chief of that district, and the use and misuse of judicial and taxation powers by those chiefs, Wandala and montagnard, forms a constant theme in the histories of the region. Incorporation within a larger administrative unit would have an effect upon the ethnic identifications of particular communities as groups within a district were treated as one, as good or poor administration affected them in similar ways, and as their responses to the outside world were correspondingly homogenized. I have noted (MacEachern 1990:261–263) that being the target of a lawsuit initiated by Wandala outsiders had increased the sense of solidarity evident among the Pelasla- and Wuzlam-speaking groups of Ouldemé canton. People who described themselves as Plata in 1986 were more ready to call themselves Uldemé after the lawsuit had been successfully—and communally—resisted in 1989. We may multiply such processes many times through the last 50 years in and around the massif.

Eventually other, more direct sorts of outside influence followed the new administrative initiatives. Most important has been the provision for missions and schools in and around the massif; mission work in this area, primarily for montagnard "animist" groups, began in earnest in the 1950s. Religion and education have in many cases gone together, with Catholic schools remaining a dominant mode of education into the 1960s. These innovations have had a number of effects upon linguistic and cultural identifications. Education was provided by canton, and usually in the dominant language of that canton, although in some cases local vehicular languages, *Wandala* or *Fulfulde*, would be used instead. This contributed to the homogenization of language use within any canton, since children speaking minority languages would have no choice but to use the dominant languages in school. Smaller language groups within each canton tend to disappear within that area, while languages that are not predominant in any canton are in danger of disappearing completely.

The provision of education has for the last 40 years also been used by colonial and national governments as one incentive to entice montagnards to emigrate from their homes in the massif to settlements on the plains below. In these new communities, they can be more easily controlled and integrated into the new, Westernized political and social systems of a modern African state. The success of this policy has varied widely in different parts of the massif, and the provision of schooling has never been the most successful feature within it. People from certain areas, for example, Mada and Zulgo territories, have moved onto the plains in large numbers and at long distances from their original homes, and these people now dominate many of the new villages created to the east and northeast of the massif. Other groups like the "Vamé-Mbrémé" and Podokwo ethnic groups have also moved, but much more locally, while Muktélé people, for example, have to a greater extent been content to remain in the massif.

Western educational systems have had two different effects upon cultural and linguistic affiliations around the massif. The first has been the tendency of more advanced students to learn one of the vehicular languages, to convert to Islam, and to move to one of the villages or towns in the area, where they enter either the traditional Islamic or modern national economic/political systems (Boutrais 1984:290). This has always been one potential avenue of advancement for montagnards, but it has become more attractive as people have moved onto the plains. The extent to which montagnards have accepted Christianity as a viable alternative to both local religions and Islam has varied from one part of the massif to another. More recently, mission work and the development of regional networks of affinity based upon education and proselytization have helped to foster some consciousness of a regional montagnard identity among converts, who defiantly adopt the derogatory Islamic identification of *kirdi* ("pagan") to distinguish themselves from Muslims.

Ethnographers and Archaeologists

Foreign observers have been misrepresenting the Mandara Mountains to the outside world since the early nineteenth century, when Dixon Denham's illustrations of the massif made it look like the Swiss Alps. The tradition continued in the twentieth century, first with the spate of works written about World War I campaigns in the area and then with the anthropological and popular works written by French administrators. Needless to say, the latter reflected the administrative decisions and "tribal" demarcations made by these same officials in the colonial government between the 1920s and 1960. Many anthropologists working in the area from the 1950s onward used these same groupings. It was obvious to most anthropologists that the human milieu in the mountains was intensely complicated, but the ethnographic requirements for linguistic competency and long-term study in a small area led to a common result: researchers described the cultural complexity within their own study areas, but remained content to use the colonial terminology for other areas. This allowed the universe of ethnonyms to remain manageable for the massif as a whole and simplified dealing with local bureaucrats. The result was the reproduction of colonial administrative divisions within the anthropological literature.

Researchers affiliated with the Mandara Archaeological Project (David and Sterner 1989) began work in the region in 1984. When we began, our view of cultural variation in the area mirrored what we read on ethnographic maps. We assumed that the mountains were occupied by a constellation of different ethnic groups, with boundaries that we could use as one of the bases of an archaeological survey strategy. We further assumed that late prehistoric cultural variation in the area, in the plains and on the mountains, would be similar to that found today. Ethnic-group boundaries would have existed; marriage, trade, and taphonomy might transcend or obscure them, but they would be meaningful cultural divisions through an appreciable amount of time and would approximate in scale modern ethnic groups in the area.

Our research made it obvious that some of our assumptions did not address the complexity of the northern Mandara Mountains. Ethnoarchaeology sits on the boundary between archaeological and ethnographic research in a number of ways. It confronts researchers with data about present-day peoples on a significantly different geographical scale than does conventional ethnographic research. Such research must often move across social boundaries as investigators seek to understand the sorts of social relationships that may bring archaeological distributions into being. It became clear that the montagnard communities of the region did not behave like well-behaved components of traditional ethnic groups. People married, traded, and fought within and across "ethnic" frontiers, they moved from place to place, they negotiated social and political relationships of appalling complexity, and they took their languages with them wherever they went. The "ethnic groups"—or "tribes"—that colonial administrators tried to create and that archaeologists hope to locate in prehistory hardly exist in the area today, and we cannot assume that they existed there in ancient times.

CONCLUSIONS

It would be convenient for archaeologists if human communities came as a packaged set, with language, social relations, cultural traditions, and ethnic identifications covarying so that they could confidently use one as a stand-in for all of the others. To be able to infer, say, language use or ethnic boundaries from ceramic distributions would make their lives much easier. It would be still more convenient if such monoliths possessed enough historical stability to be detectable archaeologically. The problem is that such stable monoliths are outside our own experience: the convolutions of human action and affiliation are messy and contradictory today, even on a planet of sharp boundaries and identity cards. It appears, on the other hand, that ancient communities and "traditional" societies in different parts of the world did indeed work that way—in any case, that is often how they are described in anthropological and archaeological texts.

In and around the Mandara Mountains, we see the production of such "traditional" societies, undertaken by dominating forces both indigenous and foreign. Wandala influence was limited and relatively nondeliberate. The Wandala had to command certain areas, and that domination had cultural effects. European control was different: administrators after the mid-1920s were engaged in an attempt to "tame" and "educate" Mandara groups that they saw more or less as savages. That "taming" required that people be localized both in geographic and cultural space, their birthplaces noted, their social affiliations made clear, and (eventually) their customs described through the objective eye of the ethnographer (see also Dozon 1985; Ravenhill 1996). There were two reasons for this. In the first place, it is obvious that the bureaucratic structures established by the French required such unambiguous identifications. At the same time, the European colonial world of the nineteenth and twentieth centuries was one obsessed by identities, both on the practical level of learning the toponymy of the new cultural spaces now controlled and more generally because of the ways that European nationalities were themselves being described. The permutations of blood, folk, and culture, so important in the various forms of European nationalism through this period, led to a conception of traditional nationalities as being culturally stable and monolithic, and this conception was then exported to Africa and elsewhere.

It does not appear that precolonial communities in northern Cameroon much resembled these European models of human variation. Traditions indicate that extraordinarily complex and dynamic sociocultural relations within and between communities characterized this region. Migration was common, at varying geographical and human scales, and people maintained important social and ritual links at long distances. Ethnic identifications were statistical and contingent, situationally variable. Multilingualism and trade languages, used with varying degrees of proficiency, mediated interactions across language boundaries. Group identities shifted quickly; oral traditions are filled with the names of groups that no longer exist, having been dispersed or submerged within other communities. These processes did not occur within the monoliths perceived by colonial officers, ethnographers, and archaeologists.

Our archaeological research on ethnic variation in this area has been hobbled by a false definition of ethnicity, one that in many ways resembles European nationalism writ small. More realistic definitions hold in common a sense of identifications that are multivariate, dynamic, and often ambivalent, residing in psychological states and changing social relations rather than in immutable givens. These elements are not especially suitable targets for archaeological research. Our strengths lie above and below the level of ethnicity, in the everyday lives of households and communities and in the regional interactions that have been a continuing part of existence in and around the massif. It may be time to decolonize the prehistory of the northern Mandara Mountains by recognizing the colonial imprint in the models of human existence that we accept as normal and by attempting to derive models that are both more humane and more suitable for the region.

NOTE

I want to thank John Terrell for his editorial work on this publication and on the symposium that preceded it, and Bruce Mannheim for acting as discussant at that symposium. I would like to thank Genevieve LeMoine, Nicholas David, and Lelia DeAndrade for their comments on earlier drafts of this chapter. I have not followed all of their suggestions, but they were very much appreciated. The research behind this chapter has been carried out through grants from the Social Sciences and Humanities Research Council of Canada (grants 410-83-0819, 410-85-1040, 410-88-0361, 410-92-1860, and 410-95-0379), the National Geographic Society, and Bowdoin College.

REFERENCES

Archives d'Outre-Mer
1919–1923 Documents on Government in Northern Cameroon. CAOM/AEF /Série D, 2D29/doss. 39/ no. 8866, and CAOM/AEF/Série Géographique/cart. 30/doss. 258. Aix-en-Provence: Centre des Archives d'Outre-Mer.
Astuti, R.
1995 "The Vezo Are Not a Kind of People": Identity, Difference, and "Ethnicity" among a Fishing People of Western Madagascar. *American Ethnologist* 22(3):464–482.
Barkindo, B. M.
1989 *The Sultanate of Mandara to 1902.* Stuttgart: Franz Steiner Verlag.
Barth, F.
1969 Introduction. In *Ethnic Groups and Boundaries: The Social Organization of Culture Difference.* F. Barth, ed. Pp. 9–38. Boston: Little, Brown.
Beauvilain, A.
1989 *Nord-Cameroun: Crises et peuplement.* Paris: published privately.
Boulet, J., A. Beauvilain, and P. Gubry
1984 Les groupes humains. In *Le Nord du Cameroun: Des hommes, une région.* J. Boutrais et al., eds. Pp. 103–157. Collections mémoires 102. Paris: Editions de l'ORSTOM.
Bourges, C.
1996 Ceramic Ethnoarchaeology and Historical Process: The Case of Gréa, North Cameroon. M.A. thesis, University of Calgary.

Boutrais, J.
1984 Les tendances de l'évolution actuelle. In *Le Nord du Cameroun: Des hommes, une région*. J. Boutrais et al., eds. Pp. 281–301. Collections mémoires 102. Paris: Editions de l'ORSTOM.

Boutrais, J., et al.
1984 *Le Nord du Cameroun: Des hommes, une région*. Collections mémoires 102. Paris: Editions de l'ORSTOM.

Chambers, J., and P. Trudgill
1980 *Dialectology*. Cambridge: Cambridge University Press.

David, N.
1998 The Ethnoarchaeology and Field Archaeology of Grinding at Sukur, Adamawa State, Nigeria. *African Archaeological Review* 15(1):13–64.

David, N., K. Gavua, S. MacEachern, and J. Sterner
1991 Ethnicity and Material Culture in North Cameroon. *Canadian Journal of Archaeology* 15:171–178.

David, N., and J. Sterner
1989 The Mandara Archaeological Project, 1988–89. *Nyame Akuma* 32:5–9.
1995 Constructing an Historical Ethnography of Sukur (Adamawa State). I. Demystification. *Nigerian Heritage* 4:11–33.

Dietler, M., and I. Herbich
1994 Ceramics and Ethnic Identity: Ethnoarchaeological Observations on the Distribution of Pottery Style and the Relationship between the Social Contexts of Production and Consumption. In *Terre cuite et société*. Pp. 459–472. Juan-les-Pins: Editions APDCA.

Dorward, D.
1974 Ethnography and Administration: A Study of Anglo-Tiv "Working Misunderstanding." *Journal of African History* 15:457–477.

Dozon, J.-P.
1985 Les Beté: Une création coloniale. In *Au coeur de l'ethnie: ethnies, tribalisme, et état en Afrique*. J.-L. Amselle and E. M'bokolo, eds. Pp. 49–85. Paris: Editions la Découverte.

Fabian, J.
1983 Missions and the Colonization of African Languages: Developments in the Former Belgian Congo. *Canadian Journal of African Studies* 17(2):165–187.
1986 *Language and Colonial Power*. Berkeley: University of California Press.

Fishman, J.
1989 *Language and Ethnicity in Minority Sociolinguistic Perspective*. Multilingual Matters 45. Clevedon: Multilingual Matters.

Forkl, H.
1986 Sozial- und Religionsgeschichte der Wandalá in Nordkamerun. Manuscript on file with the author.
1989 The Development of Urban Structures with Reference to Political Evolution in the Wandala Kingdom (17th to 19th Century, Northern Cameroon). In *Households and Communities*. S. MacEachern, D. Archer, and R. Garvin, eds. Pp. 542–550. Calgary: Archaeological Association, University of Calgary.

Goodridge, R.
1997 Slavery, Abolition, and Political Reform in Northern Cameroon to 1937. Paper presented at the SSHRC/UNESCO Summer Institute "Identifying Enslaved Af-

ricans, the 'Nigerian' Hinterland, and the Diaspora." York University, Toronto, July 1997.

Harries, P.

1991 Exclusion, Classification, and Internal Colonialism: The Emergence of Ethnicity among the Tsonga-Speakers of South Africa. In *The Creation of Tribalism in Southern Africa*, L. Vail, ed. Pp. 82–117. Berkeley: University of California Press.

Jewsiewicki, B.

1991 Formation of the Political Culture of Ethnicity in the Belgian Congo, 1920–1959. In *The Creation of Tribalism in Southern Africa*. L. Vail, ed. Pp. 324–349. Berkeley: University of California Press.

Juillerat, B.

1971 *Les bases de l'organisation sociale chez les Mouktélé (Nord-Cameroun)*. Paris: Institut d'Ethnologie.

Lembezat, B.

1949 *Administration des primitifs du Nord-Cameroun*. Centre des Hautes Etudes d'Administration Musulmane dossier no. 366. Aix-en-Provence: Archives d'Outre-Mer.

1950 *Kirdi—les populations païennes du Nord-Cameroun*. Mémoires de l'IFAN, Centre du Cameroun, sér. pop. 3. Yaoundé: IFAN.

1952 *Mukuléhé, un clan montagnard du Nord-Cameroun*. Paris: Berger-Levrault.

MacEachern, S.

1990 Du Kunde: Processes of Montagnard Ethnogenesis in the Northern Mandara Mountains of Cameroon. Ph.D. dissertation. University of Calgary.

1993a Indigenous States, Ethnographic Knowledge, and Military Operations in the Western Sudan. Paper presented at the Alberta Anthropology Graduate Students' Conference, Calgary, February 1993.

1993b Archaeological Research in Northern Cameroon, 1992: The Project Maya-Wandala. *Nyame Akuma* 39: 7–13.

1993c Selling the Iron for Their Shackles: Wandala-Montagnard Interactions in Northern Cameroon. *Journal of African History* 43(2): 247–270.

1996a Iron Age Beginnings North of the Mandara Mountains, Cameroon and Nigeria. In *Aspects of African Archaeology: Papers from the 10th Congress of the PanAfrican Association for Prehistory and Related Studies*. Gilbert Pwiti and Robert Soper, eds. Pp. 489–496. Harare: University of Zimbabwe Publications.

1996b Political Complexity around the Mandara Mountains: Archaeological and Ethnohistorical Perspectives. Paper presented at the biennial conference of the Society of Africanist Archaeologists, Posnan, September 1996.

1998 Scale, Style, and Cultural Variation: Technological Traditions in the Northern Mandara Mountains. In *The Archaeology of Social Boundaries*. Miriam Stark, ed. Pp. 107–131. Washington, DC: Smithsonian Institution Press.

MacEachern, S., and A. Garba

1994 Preliminary Results of Research by the Projet Maya-Wandala, Nigeria, 1993. *Nyame Akuma* 41:48–55.

Marliac, A., and O. Langlois

1996 Les civilisations de l'Âge du Fer au Diamaré (Cameroun septentrional): Des cultures aux ethnies. *Anthropologie* 100(2/3): 420–456.

McIntosh, R.

1998 *The Peoples of the Middle Niger: The Island of Gold*. Oxford: Blackwell.

Moisel, M.

1906 *Das deutsch-englische Grenzgebiet zwischen Yola un dem Tschad, auf Grundlage der astronomischen und geodätschen Arbeiten der deutsch-englischen Grenzexpedition (1903–1904).* 1:250,000. Berlin, Foreign Office archives dossier FO 93/ 96/55 (MFQ 289).

Morrissey, S.

1984 Clients and Slaves in the Development of the Mandara Elite. Ph.D. dissertation, Boston University. Ann Arbor: University Microfilms International.

Mouchet, J.-J.

1947 Prospection ethnologique sommaire de quelques massifs du Mandara: Massif Hurza. *Bulletin de la Société d'Études Camerounaises* 17–18:111–124.

Müller-Kosack, G.

1999 Homepage of the northern Mandaras (http://www.gmk.clara.net/).

Nyssens, O.

1986 Tradition orale et pouvoir rituel chez les Vamé du Nord-Cameroun. Paper presented at the conference "Relations Inter-Ethniques et Cultures Materielles dans le Bassin du Tchad (3ème Colloque Mega-Tchad)," Paris, 11–12 September 1986.

Ranger, T.

1991 Missionaries, Migrants, and the Manyika: The Invention of Ethnicity in Zimbabwe. In *The Creation of Tribalism in Southern Africa.* L. Vail, ed. Pp. 118–150. Berkeley: University of California Press.

Ravenhill, P.

1996 The Passive Object and the Tribal Paradigm: Colonial Museography in French West Africa. In *African Material Culture.* M. J. Arnoldi, C. Geary, and K. Hardin, eds. Pp. 265–282. Bloomington: Indiana University Press.

Richard, M.

1977 *Traditions et coutumes matrimoniales chez les Mada et les Mouyeng, Nord-Cameroun.* St. Augustin: Anthropos-Institut, Haus Volker und Kulturen.

Rohlfs, G.

1875 *Quer durch Afrika: Reise vom Mittelmeer nach dem Tschad-See und zum Golf von Guinea.* Leipzig: F. A. Brockhaus.

Salamone, F.

1985 Colonialism and the Emergence of Fulani Identity. *Journal of Asian and African Studies* 20(3–4):193–202.

Seignobos, C.

1986 Les Zumaya ou l'ethnie prohibée. Paper presented at the conference "Relations Inter-Ethniques et Cultures Materielles dans le Bassin du Tchad (3ème Colloque Mega-Tchad)," Paris, 11–12 September 1986.

1991 Les Murgur ou l'identification ethnique par la forge (Nord Cameroun). In *Forge et forgerons*, Y. Monino, ed. Pp. 42–225. Paris: Éditions de l'ORSTOM.

Siran, J.-L.

n.d. Premières notes Podokwo. Manuscript on file with the author.

Stahl, A.

1991 Ethnic Style and Ethnic Boundaries: A Diachronic Case Study from West-central Ghana. *Ethnohistory* 38(3):250–275.

Summer Institute of Linguistics

1996 *Ethnologue: List of the World's Languages* (http://www.sil.org/ethnologue).

Trudgill, P.
1984 *On Dialect: Social and Geographical Perspectives*. Oxford: Blackwell.
Vincent, J.-F.
1991 *Princes montagnards du Nord-Cameroun: Les Mofu-Diamaré et le pouvoir politique*. Paris: Editions l'Harmattan.

6

Manchu-Tungusic and Culture Change among Manchu-Tungusic Peoples

Lindsay J. Whaley

Proponents of "family-tree" models of human history say that much of our contemporary variation in biology, language, and culture is a byproduct of large-scale human migrations in the past. While the diversity of the languages spoken by the Manchu-Tungusic peoples of Siberia and northern China can be epitomized as a family tree, such a portrayal masks the actual (and decidedly complex) historical relationships among these tongues that have been discovered by linguists using standard comparative techniques.— Editor

A spate of books have appeared in recent years that attempt to account for the modern demographic mosaic of our globe by re-creating past episodes of human prehistory (Cavalli-Sforza, Menozzi, and Piazza 1994; Diamond 1997; Gamble 1994; and Ruhlen 1994, to name some widely read examples). These works, though differing in emphases and objectives, agree on one fundamental issue: present-day variation among humans, whether it be examined linguistically, culturally, or genetically, is best seen as a byproduct of large-scale migrations that have occurred over the past 100,000 years. The sequences and effects of such migratory activity are uniformly understood to follow a phylogenetic pattern, in which similarity between populations is presupposed to derive from shared ancestry, and differentiation between populations is presupposed to result from isolation as one group moves apart from another.

In this chapter, I examine a set of facts about a language family, Manchu-Tungusic, that do not fit comfortably within a phylogenetic understanding of linguistic and cultural change. I begin by reviewing Manchu-Tungusic language classification to underscore that both the internal constituency of this language family and its proposed position within a larger macrofamily are controversial. The intended lesson from this review is that the presentation of the Manchu-Tungusic languages in a tree-structure format, while convenient and conventional, masks the actual relationships that have been determined using standard comparative techniques. Therefore, the dendritic diagram can hardly be taken to represent an underlying phylogenetic reality. Next, I make some simple observations about the known history of various Manchu-Tungusic groups that challenge the phylogenetically based view that language and culture covary closely, even if not perfectly. Among these observations are remarks about language obsolescence within Manchu-Tungusic that run counter to many commonsense assumptions about patterns of contact-induced language change. Such assumptions have played a role in many accounts of prehistory, so the Manchu-Tungusic facts serve as a useful reminder that we should take care not to generalize across geographic and temporal boundaries without good reason to do so. Before moving to the case study of Manchu-Tungusic, however, I provide a slightly elaborated theoretical context for the discussion in the following sections.

MICRO- VERSUS MACROVIEWS ON CULTURE CHANGE

After many decades spent lurking in the shadow of synchronically based approaches to language structure, historical-comparative linguistics has re-emerged as a vibrant area of language research. The renewed interest in the history of languages, both within the field of linguistics proper and in related disciplines, has been sparked by a number of factors, not the least of which have been hotly contested proposals about distant relationships that hold between language families. Among these, one would have to recognize Greenberg's work on Amerind (1987), Illich-Svitych (1971–1984) and Dolgopolsky (1989) on Nostratic, and Starostin (1984) and Bengtson (1992) on Dene-Caucasian.

Indeed, even though such proposals have been criticized on methodological grounds by many historical linguists, they continue to be promoted by a devoted minority, and many are still optimistic that spatial, temporal, and processual correlations between such linguistic macrofamilies with archaeological and genetic evidence—what Colin Renfrew (1987) has called the "emerging synthesis"—are painting a reasonably accurate picture of major demographic transformations that have occurred around the globe in the distant past. These migrations are understood to splinter existing populations that were relatively uniform and localized. The result is that a migrating group will maintain commonalities with the homeland population whence it sprung, yet develop innovations that set it apart.

Such an outlook neatly accords with the branching model found in traditional classifications of languages and with the model furnished by Cavalli-Sforza, Menozzi, and Piazza (1994) in their work on the geography of human genes. Because the divergence of an erstwhile-uniform population into two related, yet now-distinct, groups involves the actual displacement of individuals, one expects genetic differentiation to correlate strongly with linguistic and cultural differentiation. As populations expanded out of their ancient homelands, they brought their genes and aspects of their material culture with them, thereby accounting for correspondences in the distribution of linguistic, archaeological, and genetic data. The correspondences are never exact, of course, partly because of the natural tendency toward divergence among isolated communities over time, and partly because of substratum effects that arise from indigenous populations swallowed up in the path of the migrations.

Variation has been explained alternatively with a rhizotic (Moore 1994) or reticulate model by scholars examining specific areas of the world at a finer-grained level of detail (e.g., Atkinson 1989; Dewar 1995; Terrell 1986; and many chapters in this volume). The assumption of the reticulate model is that concentrated interaction between human groups is and has been the norm such that the similarities between groups are just as likely to be a function of borrowing and convergence as of shared ancestry. Genes get spatially displaced because of intermarriage; material artifacts are passed from region to region due to commercial and intellectual exchange; linguistic forms enter a speech community as a result of contact with other communities. The nature of these processes is such that language, genes, and culture traits can be passed from one group to another independently. Consequently, there is no expectation that genetic variation should correspond closely to cultural or linguistic variation (though it could). This expectation places the reticulate model at odds with a phylogenetic account.

One approach to harmonizing these two conflicting perspectives has been to relegate them to different levels of explanation. To one degree or another, each of the works mentioned at the outset of this chapter takes this tack. It is perhaps nowhere better articulated than in an article by Peter Bellwood (1996). He suggests (1996: 883) that the reticulate models "can explain some situations of small-scale ethnogenesis perfectly well, but on large geographic scales beyond the range within which human groups can be expected to interact directly they fall short as sufficient explanations for the totality of human variation." Consequently, the dendritic model is exclusively (or at least primarily) to be employed in reconstructing distant eras of human prehistory that presumably are marked by mass migrations across, and colonization of, vast regions of territory. It is these events that are responsible for producing the phylogenetic structure revealed by tree diagrams of language families and genetic families. The reticulate model, in contrast, is better applied at a much more detailed level of observation. Of course, such a level of detail is generally unavailable for reconstructing the distant past anyway, so by dint of necessity the reticulate model will, under Bellwood's view, usually be appropriate only for fairly recent instances of ethnogenesis. The effect of reticulate processes, however, might still be observable in the "noise" that necessarily accompanies proposals about events far removed in time.

The evident strength of Bellwood's proposal is that it avoids what he has called elsewhere a "uniformitarian viewpoint" (Bellwood 1995:272), one that places all instances of genetic, cultural, and language change into a single framework. The roles Bellwood assigns to the dendritic and reticulate models, however, are questionable. In essence, by consigning the reticulate model to recent "small-scale ethnogenesis," he is requiring one to frame most questions about prehistory, especially questions dealing with more temporally distant events, in a phylogenetic perspective. It is no wonder, then, that he considers large-scale migrations—which go part and parcel with the dendritic approach—to explain the peopling of the earth. His methodological design forces him to do so.

Whatever the merits of the phylogenetic framework, it must be stressed that the claims it makes operate only at a remarkably general level. A multiplicity of details, many of which do not align with the larger picture, arises at a finer level of investigation. These details also require some account if we are to have any confidence in our claims about the composition of macrofamilies of languages, population expansions, and the transmission of material culture in prehistory. Of course, one may treat such details as theoretical noise that can safely be ignored at macrolevel views of prehistory, but another possibility is that these details are in fact the more telling feature of the language family, regional population, or culture complex being investigated. Unfortunately, because of the nature of the evidence for such things, most of these details are elusive and may be so permanently. The risk, then, is that the very general explanations that are assumed to be based on large-scale population movements are co-opted as all-purpose explanations for the spread of genes and language and other cultural artifacts in ancient times. That is, the risk is that the phylogenetic model is assumed to be more accurate because explicit reticulate accounts are confounded by a lack of necessary information.

In the following sections, I use case studies drawn from Manchu-Tungusic peoples of Siberia and northern China to revisit some of the theoretical issues mentioned here in more concrete terms. The choice of Manchu-Tungusic is particularly instructive because on a superficial level the language family seems consistent with a phylogenetic model: the languages are spatially ordered such that they radiate out from a region of high language density (the Amur River basin), and their geographic distribution is roughly consistent with some tree diagrams used to capture the genetic affiliations among the languages (e.g., Ruhlen 1991). However, as will be shown, the Manchu-Tungusic situation, even when it is observed in general terms, is not as neat as one would hope using a phylogenetic model. I also examine aspects of the groups who use these languages that highlight the complexity of the correlations that may hold between communities, language, culture, and genes.

MANCHU-TUNGUSIC

The Manchu-Tungusic family consists of roughly twelve languages spanning a huge geographical range in central and northeastern Asia. Concentrated groups of speakers are found as far south as the Hingan Mountains of China and as far north as the Arctic Circle. To the west, Manchu-Tungusic–speaking peoples inhabit areas of Xinjiang province in China. To the east, there are communities in the Kamchatka Peninsula (see Map 6.1).

Most Manchu-Tungusic–speaking groups traditionally lived a nomadic existence as reindeer herders and hunters or a more sedentary existence as fishers. The bulk of communities have forsaken these ways of life, as well as their languages, only recently under the pressures of tsarist and Soviet Russia and Communist China, though one can identify instances of cultural transformation that predate the modern era.[1] The greatest density of Tungusic languages is found in the Amur River basin (Nanai, Udige, Negidal, Oroch). However, the oral history of these groups and the information that can be gleaned from Chinese texts suggests that this distribution has arisen, not because the Amur basin was the homeland of a Proto-Tungus people, but because many of these groups discovered the richness of food supply in this region. The homeland for the speakers of Proto–Manchu-Tungusic, which is best taken as a cover term for a set of closely related dialects and languages,[2] has been located by some in Manchuria (Schmidt 1923; Shirokogorov 1929). Others believe the homeland to be somewhere around Lake Baikal (Janhunen 1983 proposes the eastern shore) or to the west of Baikal (Levin 1960). However, given the nomadic nature of Tungusic clans and the vast geographical range their seasonal migrations can cover, it may be misleading to present too restricted an area as a homeland.

Traditional classification of Manchu-Tungusic separates the languages into at least two major groups, the Northern and the Southern. One representative scheme is provided in Figure 6.1.[3] Only Manchu and Jurchen have writing systems that predate the twentieth century. Therefore, the bulk of classification has rested on observing similarities and differences in contemporary Tungusic varieties. While the supposed time depths that correlate to splits in the family are rarely made explicit, the family as a whole probably has a time depth roughly equivalent to that of Indo-European.

The twofold division between a Northern and a Southern branch found in Figure 6.1 was a central tenet of all early work on Manchu-Tungusic classification (Grunzel 1894; Patkanov 1906; Schmidt 1915; Cincius 1949; Benzing 1956). However, since that time, this classification has been repeatedly attacked on the grounds that the Southeastern branch is better described as a transitional group between the Northern and Southern branches than as being wholly contained in the latter (Sunik 1959; Vasilevich 1960; Avrorin 1960; Menges 1968; Doerfer 1978). An example of a classification scheme based on this notion is provided in Figure 6.2.

Though there has been widespread agreement that a trinary branching structure better captures the formal relationships within the family, the precise connections among the three branches have been a point of controversy. Avrorin (1960), Poppe (1965), and Menges (1968) all accept the need to segregate Manchu but still hold that it is genetically closer to the Transitional branch than to the Northern branch. Just the opposite position is taken by Sunik (1959), Doerfer

Map 6.1
The Distribution of Tungusic Languages

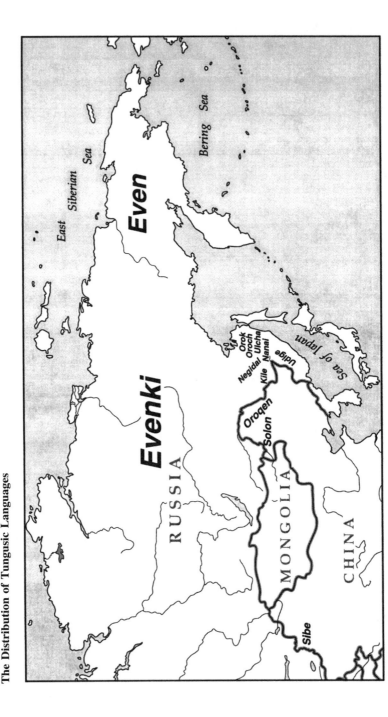

Figure 6.1
Manchu-Tungusic Classification

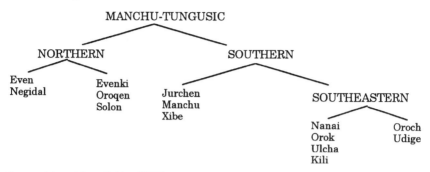

Source: Adapted from Ruhlen (1991).

(1971, 1978), and Vovin (1993). Yet another possibility has been presented by Ikegami (1974), who recategorizes the Transitional aggregate of languages into two distinct branches, one (containing Udige and Oroch) that is closer to the Northern cluster and a second (containing Nanai, Ulcha, and Orok) that is closer to the Manchu group.[4]

No matter which one of these revised dendritic structures is adopted, there remain serious anomalies that cast doubt on the usefulness of these models to capture the genetic relationships within Manchu-Tungusic. Consider just one example, the reflexes of Proto-Tungusic *p in word-initial position, which are often used as a major criterion in determining the status of languages in Manchu-Tungusic classification (e.g., Poppe 1965:25–26 employs it as one of five mor-phophonological characteristics for his treatment of Manchu-Tungusic). In broad terms, *p- > f- in Manchu, and *p- > x- in the Transitional branch (the erstwhile Southeastern branch). The Northern branch manifests three patterns: *p- > ∅ (Oroqen, Solon, at least one dialect of Even, some dialects of Evenki), *p- > x- (Negidal, some dialects of Evenki), and *p- > h- (Even, some dialects of Evenki). For this feature, then, the Transitional branch patterns more closely to the Northern branch since both carry the x- reflex. However, at a slightly more detailed level of inquiry, this general account runs into some problems. Nanai and Ulcha maintain word-initial p-, with some dialects using f-. Rather than using x- as the other Transitional branch languages do, they have a feature that affiliates them more closely to Manchu. At least one Nanai dialect (Hezhe; see Zhang, Li, and Zhang 1989) has both f- and h-, which means that it simulta-neously patterns like Manchu and like the Northern branch. Some Kili dialects have x- and others f-. For this feature, then, some Kili dialects pattern akin to the Northern branch, while others are like Manchu. Within the Northern branch alone, Even and Negidal dialects manifest different realizations of *p- against expectations given the scheme in Figure 6.2. Certain Evenki dialects are like Negidal, others are like Even, and others are like Oroqen and Solon.

Figure 6.2
Doerfer's (1978) Classification of Manchu-Tungusic Languages

NORTHERN	TRANSITIONAL	SOUTHERN
Northeastern	Central-Eastern	-Manchu/Xibe
-Even	-Oroch	-Jurchen
	-Udege	
Northwestern	Central-Western	
-Evenki (incl. Oroqen)	-Kili	
-Solon (incl. Oroqen)	-Nanai	
-Negidal	-Ulchi	
	-Orok	

Even allowing for identical, yet independent, innovations for certain languages, there is no obvious way to fit all these facts into a phylogenetic pattern. Clearly, the distribution of this linguistic feature in Tungusic languages is at least partly due to mutual influences on particular languages and dialects. If this were an isolated instance of a linguistic detail that does not adhere to a well-established dendritic classification, we could easily dismiss its significance. However, a similar messiness accompanies the mapping of nearly every linguistic feature in Tungusic languages. It is largely for this reason that Tungusologists cannot agree on the most basic divisions within the language family.

As might be expected, there is even greater disagreement on finer levels of branching distinctions. As just one example, Menges (1968) places Solon and Negidal into the Transitional group (see Figure 6.2). Others, such as Cincius (1949), see these two languages as dialectal variants of Evenki. Vovin (1993) follows Cincius in the conviction that Solon and Negidal are very similar to Evenki but considers Even no closer to Evenki-Solon-Negidal-Oroqen than to the Transitional branch.

Part of the irresolution of the Manchu-Tungusic classificatory picture can be attributed to lack of information. Comparative work on these languages has been uneven, with Manchu and Evenki, for example, receiving a relatively high degree of attention (though very little compared to, say, any Indo-European language), and languages such as Ulcha and Oroqen relatively little. For this reason alone, definitive relationships about certain languages and dialects are hard to establish. The bigger problem, however, is that the known facts do not allow for the sort of phylogenetic approach to classification that has been used with success for other language families.

In the case of Manchu-Tungusic, this state of affairs perhaps should not be unexpected since the language demographics have for some time been typical of a linguistic convergence area (a region in which linguistic features are passed easily, even among languages that are not genetically related). First, there is a significant degree of diversification within these "languages" that a conventional branching scheme like that in Figures 6.1 and 6.2 obscures. Evenki is said to have over fifty distinct dialects with varying degrees of mutual intelligibility (Bulatova 1994). The dialects have been influenced by contact with each other, with other Tungusic groups, and, most importantly, with some combination of unrelated languages including Yakut, Buryat, Dolgan, Nenets, Ket, Mongolian, Dagur, Mandarin Chinese, and Russian. The contact has included extensive lexical borrowing and structural changes to Evenki, though the latter process has not been examined systematically.

Contact among languages has been fostered by the traditional nomadism of speakers of Tungusic languages, which lasted in some areas into the 1950s. Particularly in Siberia, the seasonal movement of some groups led them to traverse huge distances and interact with a variety of other Tungusic speakers, as well as speakers of unrelated languages. Significantly, the "contact" between linguistic varieties has not only been a byproduct of interaction between people or groups speaking different languages or dialects; it has occurred because multilingualism within communities was typical (being replaced only recently with monolingualism in Mandarin Chinese or Russian). The result is that we now find a number of shared linguistic characteristics that may be genetic, may be typological, or may be areal.

While these facts make it arduous at best and misguided at worst to determine a phylogenetic structure within Manchu-Tungusic, they pose the same problems for extracting the relationship between Manchu-Tungusic and other language families. Manchu-Tungusic languages do possess many structural similarities to those found in Mongolian and Turkic language families, a fact that has led many to accept their inclusion into a larger macrofamily, Altaic (e.g., Miller 1971). The evidence from cognates, which would furnish more conclusive evidence for the distant relationship, has been evasive, so much so that some linguists (e.g., Unger 1990) now suppose Manchu-Tungusic to be unrelated to the other two families or at least to be unrelated to Turkic (e.g., Janhunen 1996). Nichols (1992:4) phrases the resulting theoretical problem well:

But the disturbing fact remains that the pronominal roots [of Altaic languages] are just too similar, in both the consonantism and the patterns of suppletion, to be the product of chance. As long as relatedness and the family tree are the only theoretical constructs available to historical linguistics, we face a dilemma: either "Altaic" languages are genetically related (in which case they must be quite closely related, for the pronoun similarities are comparable to those that obtain with a single branch of Indo-European such as Germanic or Balto-Slavic; yet the lexical stock proves to offer very few good cognates, much unlike the situation in Germanic or Balto-Slavic) or they are not (in which case the pronominal similarities are due to chance, which seems highly unlikely).

Rather than holding fast to a traditional dendritic view of Altaic (and Manchu-Tungusic), it is preferable to explore other theoretical constructs.[5]

To this point, my discussion has been aimed at demonstrating that the dendritic structure given to Manchu-Tungusic in most classificatory accounts is a function of presentation, not reality. Though such a depiction is a convenient way to express rough degrees of structural similarities, one cannot actually determine paths of descent from shared ancestry. Rather, the details of Manchu-Tungusic suggest that the current linguistic diversity in the family has been arrived at through a reticulate process involving interaction among Tungusic languages and non-Tungusic languages. In this way, these languages present a challenge to Bellwood's view that a phylogenetic model is preferable for macroviews of linguistic and cultural change because phylogenetic structures are observable at this level of generality.

PATTERNS IN CULTURE CHANGE AND LANGUAGE LOSS

In proposing the phylogenetic relationships of populations, it is often suggested that it is the convergence of independent findings from linguistics and archaeology (as well as genetics) that provides the best evidence. Therefore, one might salvage the questionable family-tree structure of Manchu-Tungusic languages by demonstrating that certain culture traits correspond to the proposed branches. I use this section, however, to demonstrate that no such corroboration is found. I do this in two ways. First, I point out that dominant cultural characteristics run counter to the predictions of the tree structure standardly imposed on the language family and, second, that patterns of interaction between Manchu-Tungusic speakers and larger cultures run contrary to assumptions usually made in phylogenetic approaches.

It is worth noting that the next century will see the disappearance of nearly all, if not all, of the Manchu-Tungusic languages as well as the obsolescence of most aspects of their traditional culture: building techniques, hunting styles, religion, dress, medicine, and so on. All of the Manchu-Tungusic groups either have assimilated or are assimilating into the larger Russian and Chinese cultures that engulf them. This assimilation is largely a result of national policies directed toward minority groups in tsarist and Soviet Russia and in China. Prior to Russian expansion into Siberia and Chinese industrialization of its northern frontiers, the Tungusic communities were no more affected by these nations than by other minority groups. Even after sustained contact and the opportunity to observe the ostensible benefits of assimilating into these "more advanced" societies, Tungusic groups (the Manchu have a very different history, to be discussed later) tended toward strong conservation of their heritage. It was only after forced settlement and forced curtailment of traditional activities that rapid assimilation occurred.

Of course, on a broad scale, the story of the Manchu-Tungusic peoples looks hauntingly familiar and seems to fit well with the basic assumptions of the population-dispersal model that has become a popular perspective on prehistory. A migration of a technologically dominant people (the Russians and the Chinese in our case) brings about a corresponding movement of language and other cultural artifacts into a new region, swallowing up any subordinate communities (the Tungus). However, at a finer level of detail lie some intriguing facts that underscore the tremendous complexity that one finds in tracking the correlation between language, people, and culture.

1. *Cultural differences among various Manchu-Tungusic groups commonly do not correlate with branches within the language family.* A great number of examples might be adduced to support this observation, but I will limit the discussion here to just one: the utilization of domestic reindeer. Perhaps more than anything else, the reindeer has come to serve as a symbol of the Tungus[6] for outsiders, so I find this particular example well suited to drive home the point that macrolevel generalizations, which may be useful in understanding the correlation between language and culture in the broadest of terms, often fit problematically with the facts.

The employment of domesticated reindeer as a pack animal, means of conveyance, ceremonial sacrifice, or food source[7] is a characteristic of the cultural history of all Tungusic groups. Only some groups, however, entered into large-scale herding, such as the Evenki of central Siberia, and some abandoned the use of domestic reindeer altogether. The Oroqen (Heilongjiang and Inner Mongolia, China), for example, appear only to have enlisted the reindeer as mounts for hunting and as beasts of burden for carrying the meat of slain quarry. Eventually, even in these limited functions, the reindeer was replaced by the horse, perhaps as late as the seventeenth century (Qiu 1983). The removal of the reindeer from Oroqen culture has been so complete that the absence of reindeer has become one of the ways in which Oroqens differentiate themselves from other Tungus groups.[8] The Evenki, on the other hand, had begun herding reindeer before the time they were encountered by the Russians in the sixteenth century (Forsyth 1992), a practice that continues to this day among some Evenki (though the practice has been greatly affected by past Soviet attempts to collectivize the herds and integrate the Evenki into the Communist industrial state). Beyond the significance of reindeer to the Evenki local economy, the animal plays an important role in Evenki lore, traditional religion, and other vital aspects of Evenki culture.

Most significant for our purposes is that the cultural divergence between the Evenki and the Oroqen, which must be recognized as a substantial one, does not correlate at all with linguistic divergence, for the Oroqen and Evenki languages are quite closely related by all accounts. In fact, most linguists working outside of China consider them to be dialects of the same language and to be mutually intelligible to a high degree.[9] Thus the Evenki share reindeer herding with other Tungusic groups (such as some Even communities) that are linguistically more distant than Oroqen, but they do not share this characteristic with the Oroqen. Here, then, is an instance where a basic cultural trait (domestic reindeer use) has varied freely and independently of language.

The historical factors that underlie the relinquishment of domestic reindeer by the Oroqen are instructive. In the seventeenth century, the Oroqen had increased contact with the Mongols, who had already reaped the benefits of the domesticated horse for many centuries. No doubt the Oroqen would have quickly recognized the benefits of horses over reindeer for hunting both in the horse's superior speed and its greater load-bearing capacity. Given the geographic proximity of the Oroqen to the Mongols, the possibility of acquiring horses arose, either through raids or through trade. In addition, Qiu (1983) notes that at the point in Oroqen history when they arrived at the Hingan Mountains, a plague decimated the reindeer population. Such an event would have accelerated the process of adapting horse-riding technology into Oroqen culture.

One finds, then, that the spread of domesticated-horse use to the Oroqen did not come about as a result of a more advanced culture expanding into Oroqen territory, but just the opposite. The Oroqen, by virtue of their nomadic style of life, moved into contact with a culture that possessed a desirable technology. Notably, the Oroqen did not assimilate into Mongolian culture. They managed to keep their cultural distance, so to speak, despite their spatial proximity and their willingness to take on a certain alien cultural characteristic as their own. Indeed, this pattern of interaction with other cultures appears to be the norm among Tungus groups: Aspects of other cultures are borrowed readily, but the bulk of the traditional culture is left intact, thereby maintaining distinctiveness.

It is of some interest that even in cases of heavy borrowing of cultural traits from neighboring societies, Tungus groups have tended to maintain their languages. For instance, the Manyagir and Birar (both groups live[d] to the southeast of Lake Baikal) appropriated a series of Mongolian practices including cattle rearing and horse riding. In addition, they replaced their traditional dress and dwellings with those of the Mongolians (Forsyth 1992). Despite incorporating specific Mongolian culture traits in these ways, they remained distinctively Tungus, both in their own perception and the perception of outsiders, in no small measure because they continued using a Tungusic language. Similarly, the Even who settled along the Okhotsk Sea adopted the house-building technology of the Korak and Chucki, but preserved, among other things, their traditional costume and language, thus ensuring that their cultural uniqueness remained (Forsyth 1992).

This being the case, we must recognize that one prevalent property of the Tungusic peoples, at least over the last 500 years, has been a willingness to adopt a subset of the practices of their neighbors while preserving language use. In reconstructing the history of the Tungus, then, the linguistic relationships among Tungusic languages are not only unreliable guides to the cultural relationships, they are often misleading.

2. *The size and prestige of Manchu-Tungusic cultures has not served as an accurate predictor of their persistence through time.* At a macrolevel of generalization, it can be observed that cultures with superior technology tend to expand, often as a function of political will. In the process, the language of the expanding culture (as well as many other cultural characteristics) is taken on quite rapidly by any communities that come into contact with or are engulfed by the expanding group. In those cases where the expansion is accompanied by

the actual physical displacement of a population into a new territory, the spread of language and material culture will be accompanied by a gene flow as well. Hence this scenario nicely accommodates the view that language, material culture, and genes translate through space in tandem. If this is so, then tracing the movement of any one of them over time should act as a relatively reliable guide to the movement of the other two.

Once again, however, the known history of Manchu-Tungusic peoples supplies a striking counterexample to these basic generalizations. The case of the Manchu is particularly noteworthy. Ethnic Manchus currently number well over four million. This is around 200 times greater than the next largest Tungusic group, the Evenkis. Besides their unequaled numbers, the Manchus developed an economic and political structure that ultimately allowed them to establish one of the largest empires in history. Between its large numbers and its political superiority over surrounding powers (most notably the Mongolians and the Chinese), the Manchu nation possessed attributes that should have at least protected significant portions of traditional Manchu culture, if not spread that culture into the areas they conquered.

On the contrary, those of Manchu descent have so thoroughly integrated into greater Chinese society that "Manchu culture" no longer exists except as a matter of historical record. The language is on the brink of extinction.[10] Unique aspects of Manchu society such as arranged marriages and burial practices are no longer employed. Perhaps most significant, there is little evidence of any sort of unifying "ethnic consciousness" among Manchus, a fact discovered by the Japanese in the 1930s when they unsuccessfully attempted to flame ethnic passions among the Manchus in order to encourage separatist feelings in Manchuria.

The loss of an independent Manchu identity is all the more surprising when one considers some of the details surrounding their rise to dynastic power. The Jurchen, who were the direct historical antecedents to the Manchus, developed metallurgy, engaged in productive farming techniques, and manufactured arms, practices that made them quite different from other Tungusic cultures. It was their unfortunate lot, however, to live sandwiched between a Chinese population expanding from the south and the Mongolians, who were coming down into China to conquer it from the north. Despite the external pressures that encompassed them, several Jurchen tribes actively resisted subjugation and assimilation into the Chinese and Mongolian cultures. At a later date, the Jurchen were united under the charismatic leadership of Nurhachi (1559–1626). Eventually, these unified tribes, who renamed themselves Manchus, conquered most of Mongolia and China, establishing the Qing dynasty (1644–1911). In the conquest of China alone, the Manchus defeated a population that was at least 50 times more numerous and was superior by technological standards.

Perhaps as a result of their own near conquest at the hands of the Mongolians and the Chinese, the early Manchu leaders actively sought to remain distinct from the people they conquered. Nurhachi had two of his court experts devise a writing system based on Mongolian script so that state business might be carried out in Manchu.[11] Not surprisingly, the Manchu language attained a high degree of prestige, enough so that it remained the language used for diplomatic purposes with Russia well into the nineteenth century, long after it had been replaced by Mandarin Chinese as the primary language spoken by the Manchus.

The Manchus, following the Tungusic pattern of cultural contact noted previously, readily adopted some aspects of Chinese culture while seeking to buttress their own ethnic identity in other ways: The Manchu homeland was closed to Chinese immigration, a policy that was enforced physically by a massive trench lined by willows; intermarriage between Chinese and Manchus was proscribed; the traditional shamanistic religious system was maintained; and there was in general a conscious effort "to foster differences of custom between the two groups" (Fairbank 1992:148).

Given this history, it is astounding that the Manchus, the only Manchu-Tungusic group to have achieved a level of power on a global scale, are also the only group known to have been completely eliminated due to assimilation. With their vast numbers, the prestige attached to their language, the development of a writing system, and an explicit attempt to maintain some cultural purity, one would have expected them at least to persist longer than any of the Tungusic groups.

In light of Jared Diamond's treatise on the rise of human societies, *Guns, Germs, and Steel* (1997), one might wonder, in fact, why a good deal of eastern Asia does not now speak and write Manchu. Diamond dedicates an entire chapter of his book to explaining "How China Became Chinese," yet in the reasoning he provides for the spread of Chinese culture and language, the absence of Manchu influence is truly mystifying. He proposes that Chinese food production led to technical innovations such as metallurgy, gunpowder, and writing, to name a few. The technology, coupled with political unity, led to rapid Sinicization of the less technologically equipped ethnic groups as the Chinese population expanded.

Of course, nearly all the same characteristics could be attributed to the Manchus starting in the late 1600s. They were militarily stronger than their neighbors (including the Chinese Ming dynasty); they were politically unified; they had farming technology and metallurgy. By Diamond's formula, they were in a strong position to steamroll north through Siberia and east into Korea. The larger populations of Chinese to the south and Mongolians to the west might have served as a barrier to conquest; ironically, it was only these two regions that the Manchus bothered to subjugate.

Incredibly, nowhere in his discussion does Diamond make reference to the Manchus. Indeed, he makes several assertions that suggest that he is largely unaware of their existence. To wit, he claims that China's languages fall into four families (Sino-Tibetan, Austroasiatic, Tai-Kadai, Miao-Yao), thereby omitting Mongolian, Turkic, and most significantly for present purposes, Manchu-Tungusic. At several points in his book, and again in the chapter cited, he avers, "China developed just a single well-attested writing system" (1997:331), yet the

Manchus and their ethnic antecedents, the Jurchen, both of whom were in China, developed writing systems. The former was used for official state business in the Qing dynasty for hundreds of years. The fact that Chinese has had expanding influence while Manchu language and culture have all but disappeared is a useful reminder that the typical patterns of cultural influence and decline that are assumed by most reconstructions of prehistory have crucial exceptions that can only be understood at a geographically and temporally specific level.[12]

3. *Rates of obsolescence among Tungusic languages are often the opposite of what one would expect.* To this point, I have been treating Tungusic groups as if they were mostly alike, differing only on the basis of a few cultural variables. This is not the case at all. One can observe differences at many levels, but most significantly for our purposes, the groups have not behaved uniformly in their response to external pressures. One area in which this is clearly evidenced is in rates of language obsolescence. While all the Tungusic languages are seriously endangered, they have been approaching extinction at different rates.

On the one hand, this is not a surprising fact. After all, some groups inhabit more isolated regions than others, the patterns of contact with other cultures have differed for historical reasons, and demographic variables such as population size are rarely fully equivalent. What is surprising, though, is that expectations about the relative rates of language obsolescence are just the opposite of what has actually occurred in some cases.

Compare, for instance, the Evenki and the Oroqen. Russian traders and trappers encroached in large numbers into Evenki territory at the beginning of the seventeenth century. Although the Evenki offered staunch resistance to Russian attempts at subjugation, they were colonized by the end of the century for all practical purposes. Thus they were under obligation to pay tribute to the Russians (in the form of sable and fox furs), and their lands were constantly being appropriated for use by Russians (Forsyth 1992).

The Russian policies toward the native peoples of Siberia prompted migrations by many Evenkis to more remote regions of Siberia.[13] Even so, they were unable to escape subjugation, and the tribute requirements were sufficient to distract their energies from reindeer herding to hunting and trapping for furs. The end result was an economic reliance on the Russians. The powerful external strain on Evenki culture was a constant force toward assimilation. While the strain was severe under the tsars, it increased under Soviet rule. Among other things, the Soviets collectivized Evenki reindeer herding, sought to settle the nomadic Evenkis, promoted literacy in Russian, and instituted a boarding-school system for nomadic peoples that effectively removed children from their homes as early as age one (Grenoble and Whaley 1999).

The combined effect of three centuries of heavy pressure to Russify native populations has by and large succeeded. With respect to language use, only about 30 percent of ethnic Evenkis (out of a population of 30,000) considered Evenki to be their primary language by 1989 (Bulatova 1994:69). In addition, the vast majority of Evenki speakers are bilingual, if not multilingual (with Yakut commonly being spoken), and there is a clear tendency for Evenki to fall into disuse in favor of the other two languages.

While these facts predict a dire future for Evenki, the language has disappeared less rapidly than Oroqen. In 1982, only 54 percent of ethnic Oroqens claimed to speak Oroqen at all, and estimates of fluent Oroqen speakers are usually around 30 percent (e.g., Zhang 1995), almost all of whom are over 50 years of age. Although the current estimates of the percentage of fluent Evenki and Oroqen speakers are equivalent, the recalcitrant fact is that the obsolescence of Oroqen appears to have taken place in the course of a single generation, whereas the process of Evenki obsolescence has been occurring for several hundred years. Such an anomaly can only be addressed at a microlevel, where specific variables in culture-contact situations can be isolated and compared.

The existence of the Oroqen on the northern frontier of China in remote areas allowed the Oroqen to maintain traditional lifestyles without much interference from the Qing rulers (1644–1911), the Yuan dictatorship (1912–1916), the warlords (1916–1927), or the centralized powers that followed them. It was not until the 1950s, under Mao's "Great Leap Forward," an attempt at economic revitalization in China, that the Oroqen clashed with the dictates of a national government. The Great Leap Forward involved the rapid expansion of infrastructure and increased exploitation of natural resources. As the railways pushed northward, the Oroqen were brought into sustained contact with industrial China for the first time. Observing the primitive lifestyle of these nomads, Mao's regime conceived of a better way of life for the Oroqen, one that would literally take them out of the woods and give them access to a series of promised material and social benefits—economic opportunity, free health care, and education. In the name of modernization, the Oroqen were compelled to denounce their traditional hunter-gatherer activities in favor of communal living with other minorities and the Han majority. At some point between the Communist conception of a new Oroqen culture and its actual creation, disaster struck. Diseases brought north by the massive migration of Han people decimated the Oroqen population. Their hunting grounds were turned over to a swelling forestry industry and to collective farming. Local animal populations declined seriously. The Oroqen quickly became persecuted and socially marginalized. Fueled by serious social problems brought on by this turn of events, the Oroqen dropped the traditional stricture on exogamy. The norm in interethnic unions was for children not to speak Oroqen.

In the 1960s, it was recognized that the government's policies toward minorities had created not an improved way of life but alienation and poverty. There was renewed interest in providing better living accommodations, education, and opportunities for minorities. Special dispensations were offered minority groups: they were exempted from the "one child per family" limit imposed on the Han majority; they were given money to school their children; some were appointed to local ruling bodies; and so on. The impulse behind the policy shift appeared pure, but the expected response did not occur, at least for the Oroqen. Rather than bolstering Oroqen culture, the government action led to an explosion in the number of Han who married Oroqen, in part so that their children might gain the privileges of minority status. The dramatic increase in intermarriage meant an even more rapid dissipation of traditional Oroqen ways. Rather than undergoing any sort of natural transformation, the culture is simply being eliminated.

A comparison between the Oroqen and the Evenki reveals several significant differences in the pattern of contact that the two groups had with expanding macrocultures. In the case of the Evenki, their subjugation began long before they lost numerical superiority in the areas in which they lived. In contrast, the Oroqen were forced to settle among other ethnic groups.[14] The combination of a rapidly growing Han population and the presence of other minorities (Mongolians and Dagurs, in particular) left the Oroqen as a tiny percentage of the populations of individual settlements. Second, the Oroqen, because of their overall small numbers (around 2,000 to 3,000 at the time of settlement) were forced into exogamy as a matter of survival almost immediately. The rate of Evenki intermarriage with other groups proceeded over a much longer interval of time. Finally, many of the Oroqen were compelled to pursue occupations far removed from their traditional hunting activities both because of pressure from the government to do so and because the supply of game did not lend itself to continued hunting on the level needed for subsistence.[15] The Evenki continue to engage in reindeer herding, albeit of a much different nature than before collectivization. Though other lines of difference between the Evenki and the Oroqen might be pursued (see Grenoble and Whaley 1999), the discussion here is sufficient to establish the point that ostensibly counterintuitive patterns of contact-induced change of cultures are explicable only at a microlevel, a level that makes reference to specific situational features and specific culture traits.

CONCLUSION

In making the preceding set of observations about Manchu-Tungusic languages and cultures, I have put forth evidence to support the position that culture and language are not tightly linked in their diachronic transformations. The ubiquitous contact between Manchu-Tungusic societies and unrelated peoples, a function both of geographic accident and widespread nomadism, has been a continual source of innovation in the Manchu-Tungusic languages and traditions, as has multilingualism. Simultaneously, there has been a conscious effort on the part of most Manchu-Tungusic communities to maintain distinctive qualities. The resultant situation is one of a counterbalance between integration with surrounding cultures and divergence from them in order to remain different. Only in the twentieth century, with the advent of the full colonization and centralized administration of Siberia and northern China, was this balance destroyed.

Though the dynamics that underlie the recent history of Manchu-Tungusic groups may not be universal, there is plenty of evidence that they are not specific to this region (for example, see Terrell, chapter 10 in this volume, for similar observations about patterns of language contact along the Sepik coast of New Guinea). For this reason, accounts of culture and language history must be pliable enough to capture the processes of negotiation between borrowing and conservatism that have characterized some regions of the world for the long periods of time.

Of course, it is possible that the sorts of malleability in Manchu-Tungusic cultural and linguistic systems that have resulted from contact are only microlevel phenomena. Bellwood (1995:272) articulates a version of this position: "If one looks at the ethnographic world on the scale of neighboring groups of communities (i.e., the micro-scale) one sees the results of reticulate interaction everywhere. . . . But a different viewpoint must emerge, in part, if one thinks carefully about the historical significance of language families or phyla on the scales of Indo-European or Austronesian." However, this seems to be a dangerous division of labor for the interpreter of prehistory. It is premature to assume that a model of population dispersal is largely preferable for explaining the distribution of language phyla, whereas a significantly more complex model of culture interaction is operative in accounting for the distribution of language branches and individual languages. The major lesson from microlevel research is that communities are not uniform in their circumstances, and this lack of uniformity translates into divergent patterns of evolution and transformation, even at the level of phyla. Rather than take phylogenetic models as the standard for any reconstruction of prehistoric demographic shifts and reticulate models as the norm for recent ethnogenesis, a more fruitful approach would be to accept that either model is potentially useful for certain regions of the world in certain time periods.

NOTES

The content and style of this chapter have been greatly improved by the suggestions of many individuals: Fengxiang Li, Todd Vanden Berg, Hoyt Alverson, John Edward Terrell, William Scott, Lenore Grenoble, and two anonymous reviewers.

1. The Manchus and Xibe were somewhat exceptional in this regard, having long ago inherited a very different social structure from their cultural ancestors, the Jurchen.

2. Miller (1994) summarizes a proposal by Janhunen (1983) that takes the Proto-Tungus to be eleven communities that had undergone independent development for several thousand years. Miller goes on to point out that Janhunen never presents the evidence he used to develop this position.

3. I have maintained the same branching structure as that given by Ruhlen. However, I have altered the spelling of some names, and I have not included four of the languages he lists. In four instances (Akani, Birar, Manegir, Samagir), the names he gives are ethnonyms that have been used for certain Tungusic groups, though it has never been established that the languages of these groups are sufficiently unique to treat them as distinct from other Tungusic tongues shown in Map 6.1. I have also used Nanai in place of Ruhlen's Gold since this label is rarely used by contemporary Tungusologists. Ruhlen

bases his classification on Benzing (1956). This work is largely a reiteration of Cincius (1949). Both classifications have been substantially revised in the last 40 years.

4. Grenoble and Whaley (1997) and Whaley, Grenoble, and Li (1999) provide a more detailed discussion of problems in Manchu-Tungusic classification.

5. Nichols proposes a model called population typology. At its core, population typology provides a way to analyze morphosyntactic diversity among languages. Her goal is to establish which kinds of diversity are universal, which are geographical, and which are due to shared ancestry.

6. The term "Tungus" is potentially misleading. It has in the past been used as a synonym for Evenki. I am using this term in a broader sense as a label for the set of ethnic groups that have traditionally spoken any one of the Tungusic languages. In this way, it is intended to exclude the Manchu, Xibe, and Jurchen.

7. Domestic reindeer were typically not killed for their meat, but does were milked.

8. Ramsey (1987) echoes the popular etymology of the appellation Oroqen as "reindeer people" (oron, "reindeer," plus a possessive suffix). Most contemporary Oroqen reject this suggestion, arguing instead that the name derives from a form of the word oro, "mountain" (thus giving "mountain people"), an etymology noted by Shirokogorov (1929). The Oroqen are quick to point out that only the latter proposal is consistent with their traditions. It is their understanding that they were originally hunters who dwelled in the mountains. At some point in the remote past, certain clans left the mountains and took up reindeer herding (these became the Evenki), while they maintained their original hunting heritage.

9. The linguistic difference is more pronounced than has previously been imagined. See Grenoble and Whaley (1997) and Whaley, Grenoble, and Li (1999).

10. The 1982 census in China listed 70 speakers of the language. During fieldwork carried out with Fengxiang Li in China during the summers of 1996, 1997, and 1998, we were told that there are less than a dozen speakers left. The Xibe language, which may have as many as 15,000 speakers, developed from a Manchu garrison established in Xinjiang in 1765.

11. The move toward literacy may also have been prompted by the fact that their Jurchen ancestors had also developed a writing system, this one borrowed from the Khitan, a people whom the Jurchen overthrew in the twelfth century.

12. The impetus for the decline of the Qing dynasty and the rapid dissipation of a distinct Manchu identity has always been a matter of debate. It is likely that the Chinese-style political structure established by the Manchu rulers and a dependence on Confucianism played a large role. It is also significant that from the outset there was diversity within those who were of Manchu ethnicity (Crossley 1990).

13. There are instances of official policy measures in the seventeenth to nineteenth centuries that were intended to protect the rights of the northern minorities of Russia. Vakhtin (1992:9) writes of the Code of Indigenous Administration (1822), which was meant to protect the legal rights of native populations and "showed a sincere desire to preserve the native economy against Russian capitalism." Vakhtin goes on to note, however, that official policy frequently failed to translate into official action.

14. It should be noted that in certain cases, an isolation of sorts was maintained. For instance, in Wulubutie, the Oroqen "hunters' village" (a series of government-built brick houses) lies a kilometer away from the rest of the town. The high rate of intermarriage, however, is rapidly removing any actual physical isolation that might have existed at the time of settlement.

15. In January 1996, hunting was banned in the Oroqen Autonomous Banner, Inner Mongolia. The official rationale was concern over a number of endangered species in the region that were being hunted (and forested) into extinction. In effect, this is the final nail in the coffin of Oroqen traditional culture.

REFERENCES

Atkinson, R.
1989 The evolution of Ethnicity among the Acholi of Uganda: The Precolonial Phase. *Ethnohistory* 36:19–43.

Avrorin, V. A.
1960 O klassifikacii tunguso-manchzhurskix jazykov. *XXV mezhdunarodnyj kongress vostokovedov, Doklady delegacii SSSR*. Moscow: Izd. XXV Vsemirnogo kongressa orientalistov.

Bellwood, Peter
1995 Language Families and Human Dispersal. *Cambridge Archaeological Journal* 5: 271–274.
1996 Phylogeny vs Reticulation in Prehistory. *Antiquity* 70:881–890.

Bengtson, John D.
1992 Notes on Sino-Caucasian. In *Nostratic, Dene-Caucasian, Austric and Amerind Cultures*. V. Shevoroshkin, ed. Pp. 334–341. Bochum: Brockmeyer.

Benzing, Johannes
1956 Die tungusischen Sprachen: Versuch einer vergleichenden Grammatik. *Abhandlungen der geistes- und sozialwissenschaftlichen Klasse, Akademie der Wissenschaften und der Literatur*, Heft 11, pp. 949–1099. Wiesbaden: Verlag der Akademie der Wissenschaften und der Literatur in Mainz.

Bulatova, Nadezhda Ja
1994 Evenkijskij jazyk. In *Kransnaja kniga jazykov narodov Rossii: Enciklopedicheskij slovar'-spravochnik*. Pp. 68–70. Moscow: Academia.

Cavalli-Sforza, L. Luca, Paolo Menozzi, and Alberto Piazza
1994 *The History and Geography of Human Genes*. Princeton: Princeton University Press.

Cincius, Vera I.
1949 *Sravnitel'naja fonetika tunguso-man'chzhurskix jazykov*. Leningrad: Uchpedgiz.

Crossley, Pamela
1990 *Orphan Warriors*. Princeton: Princeton University Press.

Dewar, Robert E.
1995 Of Nets and Trees: Untangling the Reticulate and Dendritic in Madagascar's Prehistory. *World Archaeology* 26:301–18.

Diamond, Jared
1997 *Guns, Germs, and Steel*. New York: W. W. Norton.

Doerfer, Gerhard
1971 Bemerkungen zur linguistischen Klassifikation. *Indogermanische Forschungen* 76: 1–14.
1978 Classification Problems of Tungus. In *Tungusica*, Band 1, pp. 1–26. Wiesbaden: Otto Harrassowitz.

Dolgopolsky, A. B.
1989 Problems of Nostratic Comparative Phonology. In *Reconstructing Languages and Cultures*. V. Shevoroshkin, ed. Pp. 90–98. Bochum: Brockmeyer.

Fairbank, John King
1992 *China: A New History*. Cambridge, MA: Belknap Press of Harvard University Press.

Forsyth, James
1992 *A History of the Peoples of Siberia*. Cambridge: Cambridge University Press.

Gamble, Clive
1994 *Timewalkers: The Prehistory of Global Colonization*. Cambridge, MA: Harvard University Press.

Greenberg, Joseph H.
1987 *Language in the Americas*. Stanford, CA: Stanford University Press.

Grenoble, Lenore, and Lindsay Whaley
1997 Evenki Language-Dialect Continuum: A First Round. Paper presented at the Tenth Biennial NSL Conference, University of Chicago.
1999 Language Policy and the Loss of Tungusic Languages. *Language and Communication* 19:373–386.

Grunzel, J.
1894 *Entwurf einer vergleichenden Grammatik der altaischen Sprachen*. Leipzig.

Ikegami, Jiro
1974 Versuch einer Klassifikation der Tungusischen Sprachen. In G. Hazai and P. Zieme, eds. *Sprache, Geschichte und Kultur der Altaischen Volker*. G. Hazai, ed. Pp. 271–272. Berlin: Akademie-Verlag.

Illich-Svitych, V. M.
1971–1984 *Opyt sravnenija nostraticheskix jazykov*. 3 vols. Moscow: Nauka.

Janhunen, J.
1983 Kita-Ajia no minzoku to gengo no bunrui. *Gekkan Gengo* 112:46–53.
1996 *Manchuria*. Helsinki: Finno-Ugrian Society.

Levin, M. G.
1960 On the Ethnogenesis of the Tungus. In *XXV International Congress of Orientalists*. Moscow: Oriental Literature Publishing House.

Menges, Karl H.
1968 Die tungusischen Sprachen. *Handbuch der Orientalistik, Tungusologie*. Leiden: E. J. Brill.

Miller, Roy Andrew
1971 *Japanese and the Other Altaic Languages*. Chicago: University of Chicago Press.
1994 The Original Geographic Distribution of the Tungus Languages. In *Non-Slavic Languages of the U.S.S.R.* H. I. Aronson, ed. Pp. 272–297. Columbus, OH: Slavica Publishers.

Moore, John H.
1994 Putting Anthropology Back Together Again: The Ethnogenetic Critique of Cladistic Theory. *American Anthropologist* 96:925–948.

Nichols, Johanna
1992 *Linguistic Diversity in Space and Time*. Chicago: University of Chicago Press.

Patkanov, S.
1906 Opyt geografii i statistiki tungusskix plemën Sibiri. *Zapiski Imperatskago russkago geograficheskago obshchestva* 31/1.

Poppe, Nikolai
1965 *Introduction to Altaic Linguistics*. Wiesbaden: Otto Harrassowitz.
Qiu, Pu
1983 *The Oroqens: China's Nomadic Hunters*. Beijing: Foreign Languages Press.
Ramsey, S. Robert
1987 *The Languages of China*. Princeton: Princeton University Press.
Renfrew, Colin
1987 *Archaeology and Language: The Puzzle of Indo-European Origins*. London: Jonathan Cape.
Ruhlen, Merritt
1991 *A Guide to the World's Languages*. Stanford, CA: Stanford University Press.
1994 *The Origin of Language*. New York: John Wiley & Sons.
Schmidt, P.
1915 *Etnografiia Dal'nego Vostoka*. Vladivostok: Sbornik.
1923 The Language of the Olchas. *Acta Universitatis Latviensis* 8:231–288.
Shirokogorov, S. M.
1929 *Social Organization of the Northern Tungus*. Shanghai: Commercial Press.
Starostin, Sergei
1984 Gipoteza o geneticheskix svjazjax sino-tibetskix jazykov s enisejskimi i severno-kavkazskimi jazykami. *Lingvisticheskaja rekonstruktsija i drevnejshaja istorija vostoka* 4:19–38.
Sunik, O.
1959 Tunguso-man'chzhurskie jazyki. In *Mlado-pis'mennye jazyki narodov SSSR*. Pp. 318–351. Moscow and Leningrad: Izdatel'stvo Akademii Nauk SSSR.
Terrell, John Edward
1986 *Prehistory in the Pacific Islands*. Cambridge: Cambridge University Press.
Unger, J. Marshall
1990 Summary Report from the Altaic Panel. In *Linguistic Change and Reconstruction Methodology*. P. Baldi, ed. Pp. 479–482. Trends in Linguistics: Studies and Monographs, 45. Berlin: Mouton de Gruyter.
Vakhtin, Nikolai
1992 *Native Peoples of the Russian Far North*. London: Minority Rights Group.
Vasilevich, G. M.
1960 K voprosu o klassifikacii tunguso-man'chzhurskix jazykov. *Voprosy jazykoznanija* 2:43–49.
Vovin, Alexander
1993 Towards a New Classification of Tungusic Languages. *Ural-Altaische Jahrbücher* 65:99–113.
Whaley, Lindsay J., Lenore A. Grenoble, and Fengxiang Li
1999 Revisiting Tungusic Classification from the Bottom Up: A Comparison of Evenki and Oroqen. *Language* 75:286–321.
Zhang, Yang-chang, Bing Li, and Xi Zhang
1989 *The Hezhen Language*. Changchun: Jilin University Press.
Zhang, Xi
1995 Vowel Harmony in Oroqen. Paper presented at the annual meeting of the Linguistic Society of America, New Orleans.

7

Recognizing Ethnic Identity in the Upper Pleistocene: The Case of the African Middle Stone Age/ Middle Palaeolithic

Pamela R. Willoughby

Prehistorians have argued that the appearance of biologically modern human beings in Europe 30,000 to 40,000 years ago is marked archaeologically by the elaboration of regional differences in tool assemblages signaling that people had at last acquired the linguistic and cultural abilities needed to express their ethnicity through material culture. Anatomically modern humans, however, had evolved long before then in Africa, where no distinguishable correlation has been found between the biological appearance of *Homo sapiens* and the use of stylistically advanced tools and other kinds of "modern" technological developments. Africa currently offers little support for the assumption that biological change and cultural innovation go hand in hand in the archaeological record.—Editor

Over the last decade, specialists in human evolution or palaeoanthropology have become increasingly concerned with the issue of the origin of our own species, *Homo sapiens*, something that remains surprisingly difficult to understand (G. A. Clark 1999). Evidence drawn from a variety of sources (human genetics, archaeological sites, hominid fossils, and new dating techniques) points to the continent of Africa as the source of the earliest anatomically modern humans, and to a speciation event that produced our direct ancestors there sometime prior to 100,000 years ago (Cann, Stoneking, and Wilson 1987; Stoneking 1993; Vigilant et al. 1991). Geneticists count the number of DNA base changes in segments of mitochondrial or nuclear DNA. These changes are due to neutral mutation and do not affect an organism's development or reproductive success. Such segments are useful for historical studies and plot patterns of genetic relationships over time. Mitochondrial DNA sequences do not vary greatly within and between human populations. This is in stark contrast to the pattern in our closest living relatives, the African apes (Gagneux et al. 1999), implying that humans have a recent common ancestry and/or a significant bottleneck in our past.

The out-of-Africa or replacement model proposes that modern humans evolved exclusively in Africa, and that their descendants subsequently migrated into Eurasia, replacing or interbreeding with the indigenous populations between 30,000 and 40,000 years ago (Stringer and Andrews 1988). An alternative to this model is the multiregional or continuity perspective. Its supporters see modern populations developing out of local groups throughout Eurasia and Africa around the same time, with some gene flow between separate regions (Frayer et al. 1993; Thorne and Wolpoff 1992; Wolpoff 1989). It is assumed that the global distribution of human populations observed was established quite early in human evolution, and that subsequent migrations and gene flow have not disrupted the original pattern.

While later Pleistocene hominid evolution seems to be clearer as a result of recent work, new problems arise when we try to compare observed biological changes with technological and cultural developments. Palaeolithic archaeologists study the development of human technology and cultural adaptation from the origins of stone-tool manufacture to the end of the Pleistocene, while human palaeontologists study the fossil remains of the hominids who produced Palaeolithic tools. It is traditionally argued that the technology of the earliest European modern *Homo sapiens*, the Upper Palaeolithic, represents the first sign of modern behavior, produced by people with an intellectual capacity and cultural system comparable to our own (Mellars 1991; Klein 1992, 1999).

Modernity is expressed in a number of ways in the European Upper Palaeolithic. One is in innovation in stone-tool production, as long, parallel-sided blanks (blades or bladelets) become the basic artifact form, what J. Grahame Clark (1977:23) calls mode 4 technology (Figure 7.1). While the method of manufacture is now standardized (using conical or cylindrical prismatic cores), there is also an increase in the variety and complexity of tools. New materials are employed for their manufacture, including bone, ivory, and antler. Objects used for personal adornment (pendants, jewelry made from bored animal teeth and carved beads), portable art (Venus and animal figurines), and eventually parietal (cave) art also appear sometime after 40,000 years ago (Mellars 1989, 1991). The first fired clay objects, animal and human figurines from sites such as Dolní Věstonice in the Czech Republic, are also of Upper Palaeolithic age (Soffer et al. 1992). At the same time, studies of animal bones in these sites reveal the development of specialization in hunting strategies. Fewer species are preyed upon, and, rather than young and elderly individuals, increasingly dangerous adult animals are hunted, which would have required more planning and cooperation than previously seen (Klein 1989, 1992, 1996; Klein and Cruz-Uribe 1996). The Upper Palaeolithic may see the beginnings of intentional burial (Gar-

Figure 7.1
J. Grahame Clark's Modes of Technology

Mode	Description	African archaeological industries	European archaeological industries
Mode 5 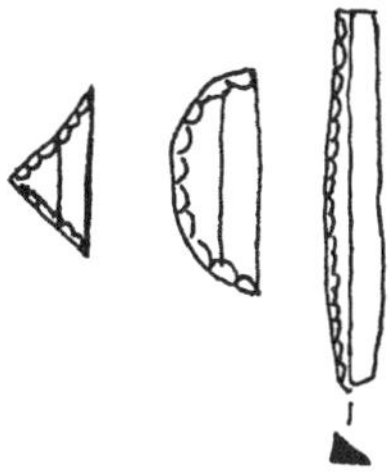	geometric pieces, especially microliths; composite tools, backed bladelets	Epipalaeolithic (North Africa); Later Stone Age or LSA (sub-Saharan Africa); Howieson's poort (South Africa)	Epipalaeolithic and Mesolithic
Mode 4 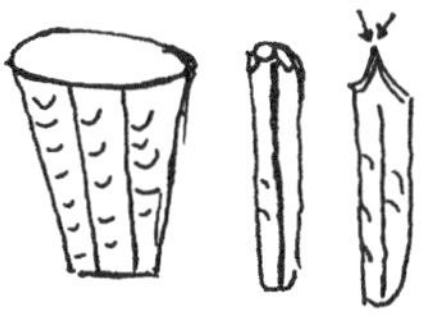	blade tools produced on prismatic cores	Upper Palaeolithic and Epipalaeolithic (North Africa); Middle Stone Age in South Africa?	Upper Palaeolithic
Mode 3 	flake tools from prepared (Levallois) or from radial cores	Middle Palaeolithic (North Africa); Middle Stone Age or MSA (sub-Saharan Africa)	Middle Palaeolithic

Source: J. Grahame Clark (1977:23).

gett 1989, 1999); if one accepts that Middle Palaeolithic Europeans, the neandertals, had burials, the Upper Palaeolithic ones remain qualitatively more complex in grave goods and conception.

In the Upper Palaeolithic, there also seem to be increased regional and temporal differences in tool types and assemblages; this is interpreted as the first expression of an ethnic marker in the prehistoric record. As the chapters in this volume illustrate, ethnicity is sometimes difficult to recognize in material culture. An ethnic group is self-defined; people áre linked by culture, place of origin, language, religion, òr other shared attributes. Since the nineteenth century, when archaeologists began to explore the prehistoric record, it was assumed that similarities in artifact design and decoration reflect common social identity. People learned to manufacture material items from their parents or relatives; individual groups or families would have preferences for certain design elements or styles. Distinctive artifacts could be identified; these *fossiles directeurs* or index fossils allowed the recognition or discovery of archaeological cultures in time and space. These types are the bane of students of prehistory, as they must be identified and placed in their proper culture-historical position. But can similar things be recognized when technology and culture are reflected in stone, and not in more malleable materials?

For stone tools, traits that reflect choice among functionally equivalent options are interpreted as the material remains of a single human group, one whose members learned to manufacture items in the same way. On some classes of retouched tools, it is relatively easy to identify these isochrestic (Sackett 1982) characteristics. For example, a projectile point has some functional constraints (size, shape, symmetry, and having a pointed business end so that it will penetrate the intended target). But other features, such as shaping the base for the purpose of hafting a point onto a handle, have much scope for individual variation. The more similar decisions taken in tool production, the more closely related the people who manufactured them are likely to have been. In this way, shared methods of manufacture and style of stone tools can be used to identify areas of interaction and social contact in the remote past.

The relatively sudden and synchronous appearance of the Upper Palaeolithic throughout Europe has been called the creative explosion (Pfeiffer 1982). It is interpreted as the archaeological sign of what divided the ancients from moderns (Stringer and Gamble 1993), people with the same mental and cultural capacities as ourselves. But with the new evidence derived from genetics, geochronology, and palaeontology, it is clear that people who were anatomically modern *Homo sapiens* appear in the fossil record well before the beginnings of the Upper Palaeolithic. For once, biological and cultural change did not occur simultaneously, something that traditional models used by Palaeolithic archaeologists were unable to explain. In addition, defenders of Middle Palaeolithic hominids have proposed that key elements of Upper Palaeolithic modernity may have been invented independently by both neandertals and moderns (d'Errico et al. 1998; Zilhão and d'Errico 1999). The possibility that these groups interbred has also recently resurfaced with regard to a 28,000-year-old modern child skeleton from the Lager Velho site in Portugal (Duarte et al. 1999) and redating of neandertals from level G_1 at Vindija Cave in Croatia (Smith et al. 1999).

HOW HAVE TECHNOLOGICAL CHANGE AND VARIATION BEEN INTERPRETED BY PALAEOLITHIC ARCHAEOLOGISTS?

Ever since the first Palaeolithic sites were recognized as products of human behavior, early in the nineteenth century, archaeologists have insisted that increasingly complex cultural systems evolved in a regular, unilinear manner over the course of the Pleistocene. Sequences of development were mapped using site stratigraphy and faunal correlation, and retouched stone tools characteristic of each named period were defined. Often, single tool types could be used as indicative of an entire period (such as bifacial handaxes for the Acheulean), thereby becoming index fossils analogous to those defined by palaeontologists. In the absence of more reliable dating techniques, these *fossiles directeurs* took on the role of chronological and even population markers. These diagnostic tool types were often the only items collected in the field for future study.

The discovery of different species of hominids associated with each major stage of the Palaeolithic (*Homo erectus* and archaic *Homo sapiens* with the Acheulean, the neandertals with the European Middle Palaeolithic or Mousterian, moderns with the Upper Palaeolithic) reinforced the assumption that biological change had to be accompanied by cultural innovation. Many archaeologists saw technological or behavioral change as the cause (or effect) of biological change. In other words, some kind of feedback system was initiated with the first stone-artifact manufacture, and from then on, biology and culture were inseparable, each influencing the other in a systemic fashion (for a recent example of the same kind of thinking, see Foley's 1987 attempt to use cladistics in order to classify stone-tool assemblages and their manufacturers). The reason for the parallel development of anatomy and culture was the subject of much speculation. Most explanations focused on population or racial differences, as it was assumed that each group had its own unique way of doing things. Even developments that may span hundreds of thousands of years, such as the flake and handaxe industries of the Lower Palaeolithic, were interpreted as the material record of two separate, parallel groups (Sackett 1981). If both kinds of tools were found in the same sites, this meant racial mixing of flake and handaxe peoples. Rather than groups of hunter-gatherers being primitive isolates, each with its own unique adaptation and technology, archaeologists assumed that they were in direct contact with each other over vast reaches of time and space. How else could they have come up with the same types time and again? One possible alternative explanation is technological. There are only a certain number of ways to fracture cryptocrystalline silica rocks. What changed could have been the preliminary stage of production alone. If one learned to break large flakes off of cores, retouching these flakes bifacially could result in similar handaxe forms, as was initially suggested by Glynn Isaac (1972:397–398). Shaping stone pebbles in a circular or radial fashion could lead to the invention of Levallois prepared core methods and to the bulk of forms found in the Middle Palaeolithic.

Developing prismatic cores meant a switch from amorphous flakes to standardized blade preforms, making Upper Palaeolithic assemblages appear to be more refined or evolved than earlier tool kits.

While Franz Boas and his followers succeeded in separating race, language, and culture in anthropology, the continuing insistence on parallelism in human biological and cultural evolution harkens back to the biological determinism of the nineteenth century. No one talks about savagery, barbarism, and civilization anymore, but many Palaeolithic archaeologists continue to describe the stages of biocultural development in the Palaeolithic and later periods using the progress models of earlier anthropologists (Bowler 1989). While the tempo and mode of biological and cultural changes in our remote past still seem remarkably similar, culture could have been the prime mover, or, most likely, some external factor affected both (such as the regular global climatic cycling between cold glacial and warm interglacial phases characteristic of the Pleistocene) (Foley 1989; McBrearty 1993; Willoughby 1993a).

The expectation that change in populations or species is accompanied by technological innovation is one of the main reasons that modern human origins have become of such concern in the last ten years. For the first time, sites beyond the radiocarbon barrier of 40,000 years ago could now be chronometrically dated using methods such as electron spin resonance (ESR) of mammal teeth and/or thermoluminescence (Tl) of sediments or burned flint artifacts (Aitken, Stringer, and Mellars 1993). But the dates produced by these methods were a surprise. At least two groups (or possibly species) of humans, neandertals (*Homo neanderthalensis*) and modern *Homo sapiens*, were responsible for very similar archaeological industries in the Near East, the Tabun B and C variants of Middle Palaeolithic or Mousterian (Bar-Yosef 1989; Lieberman and Shea 1994; Akazawa, Aoki, and Bar-Yosef 1998). Redating sites in Africa confirmed that modern humans existed there during the Middle Palaeolithic or Middle Stone Age (MSA), possibly as early as the end of the Acheulean around 200,000 years ago. So it appears that the evolution of anatomically modern humans was not directly linked with the creative explosion of the subsequent Upper Palaeolithic or its sub-Saharan African analogue, the Later Stone Age (LSA). Worse yet, it might not have been associated with any sign of technological change or innovation at all. In order to understand the process of modern human origins, archaeologists now have to shift their attention to periods before the Upper Palaeolithic and to regions outside of Western Europe.

STYLE, LANGUAGE, ETHNICITY, AND THE MIDDLE-UPPER PALAEOLITHIC TRANSITION

Most ideas about the tempo and mode of Palaeolithic change have been developed using data from Western Europe. Here the appearance of modern humans is associated with the archaeological shift from the Middle to the Upper Palaeolithic, between 30,000 and 40,000 years ago (Mellars 1989). Modern humans, bringing with them a lithic technology based on production of prismatic blades, replaced earlier hominids, neandertals, whose technology centered on supposedly unstandardized mode 3 flake tools (Figure 7.1). While neandertals might have locally evolved into moderns, new data show that both groups overlap in time as well as in space (Klein 1992; Lévêque, Backer, and Guilbaud 1993; Smith et al. 1999; Zilhão and d'Errico 1999). The recent successful extraction of mitochondrial DNA from the original Neander Valley hominid skeleton suggests that neandertals share a common ancestor with living humans prior to 500,000 years ago, but no more recently (Krings et al. 1997, 1999). As a result, they most likely represent a separate human species.

If modern humans were already present well before the beginning of the Upper Palaeolithic, then what was responsible for its technological innovations? The most popular explanation to date is that true symbolically based language and culture developed at this time (Milo and Quiatt 1993; Schepartz 1993; see alternative views in Lindly and Clark 1990, 1991). When hominids developed the same mental capacities as ours, they became able to express their ethnic identity in material culture. What actually happened is unclear, as there is no apparent biological change after the appearance of modern anatomy over 100,000 years ago. Richard Klein (1996), for one, has suggested that some rewiring of the human brain suddenly occurred. Since this process is completely undetectable, he suggests that we will never know the real reason for the Middle/Upper Palaeolithic transition. But, for the first time, differences in material culture would be understandable in terms of ethnic or cultural affiliation. A clear break with the world of the ancients had occurred.

What has failed to be recognized by most archaeologists is that the symbolic model preserves the traditional explanation for the Middle/Upper Palaeolithic transition. Earlier hominids could continue to be seen as culturally and technologically indistinguishable from neandertals, regardless of how advanced they appeared to be anatomically. The old ideas of neandertals being behaviorally clueless, randomly walking periglacial Eurasia in search of a meal and a shelter, have been revived in recent discourse (see an assessment in Willoughby in press). But if this is the case, since their African modern counterparts were doing much the same things, they were just as intellectually challenged by their environment as the neandertals were.

If the earliest Upper Palaeolithic industry associated with modern humans in Europe is the Aurignacian, then the process of technological change is quite straightforward. "[I]ts remarkable uniformity and synchroneity over a vast area clearly suggest that it was the product of a rapidly expanding population" (Klein 1992:8) rather than a local, restricted development. Its distinctive stone (steeply retouched nosed and carinated scrapers, strangled blades, small bladelets) and bone tools (split-based and biconical points) represent a break with the transitional industries of the Middle/Upper Palaeolithic boundary, such as the Ulluzian of Italy (Mussi 1990), the Châtelperronian of France (Harrold 1989), and the Szeletian of central Europe (Allsworth-Jones 1990). These seem to have more

in common with the final Mousterian than with later phases of the Upper Palaeolithic, so the discovery of neandertal skeletal remains with Châtelperronian
artifacts at two French sites, Saint-Césaire and Arcy-sur-Cure (Lévêque, Backer,
and Guilbaud 1993; Zilhão and d'Errico 1999) was inevitable.

Archaeologists use the term *style* to refer to features of artifacts and assemblages that reflect social relationships between groups. People who employ the
same styles learned to manufacture and use items in similar ways; due to socialization, they consistently made the same decisions out of a range of functionally equivalent (isochrestic) choices (Sackett 1982). As a result, similar kinds
of artifacts and assemblages reflect common, shared, experiences. These can be
emblematic, signaling membership in the same social or ethnic group, or can
provide a means of information exchange within and between groups (Sackett
1977, 1982; Conkey 1978; Wiessner 1983; Wobst 1977). According to the standard interpretation of Palaeolithic variability, it is only when modern symbolically based language and culture are created that people can express their shared
identity. If this is so, then locally specific archaeological industries should have
appeared early in the Upper Palaeolithic. But the Aurignacian does not fit this
expectation either. Its diagnostic elements appear over a wide region almost
simultaneously, perhaps signaling the absence of social boundaries between
groups. A number of researchers (Jochim 1987; Soffer 1987) have suggested
that it would be more adaptive for immigrants to maintain flexible, open, social
networks in a new environment where resource predictability would be low. It
would only be when people settled down in a region that local variation would
reappear. Such a pattern has been suggested for the Aurignacian, Perigordian,
and Magdalenian, all phases of the European Upper Palaeolithic, as well as for
the Palaeo-Indian period in North America (Goodyear 1989). If the Upper Palaeolithic represents the beginning of modern symbolically based cultural systems, researchers generally agree that Middle Palaeolithic assemblages reflect
only functional or technological concerns (Binford 1973; Binford and Binford
1966, 1968). This could be due to raw-material availability and abundance or
tool life histories (of manufacture, use, and reuse) (Rolland and Dibble 1990).
But it could not be representative of culture-historical differences, as was originally proposed by François Bordes (1973, 1981).

Using ethnographic data, Lewis Binford has created models of hunter-gatherer
mobility and adaptation that contrast more sedentary collectors with mobile foragers (Binford 1980, 1989; Kelly 1992). Collectors stay in more or less
permanent base camps and send work parties out for special tasks in resource
procurement; in other words, they move resources to people. Foragers set up
temporary camps near food sources and move frequently when these are de-
pleted, thereby moving people to resources. An archaeologist would expect collectors to have more curated or maintained technology, more caches, and more
complex sites, in which much effort has been expended, while foragers would
concentrate on expedient tool manufacture (made at the place of use and then
immediately discarded—a sort of make it, use it, then lose it mentality). The

pattern of tool manufacture and discard over space can be used to determine which pattern existed.

While these constructs were initially applied only to recent prehistoric hunter-gatherer populations, as Binford clearly intended, he later used them to explain why there were major differences between the Middle and Upper Palaeolithic (Binford 1989). This is perhaps surprising given that in their initial studies of Mousterian industries, Sally and Lewis Binford had emphasized the behavioral similarities of neandertals and modern humans (Binford and Binford 1966:291; 1968:78). But now Lewis Binford (1989) was arguing that neandertals had not even reached the behavioral capacity of modern foragers. Their technology was expedient; variation between their assemblages was only functional. Neandertals also soon became incapable of planning cooperative hunting (even hunting at all?) or of long-term planning (Binford 1989:33–35; Stringer and Gamble 1993). In a review, Brian Hayden (1993) points out that many archaeologists have consciously or unconsciously returned to the state of dehumanizing neandertals characteristic of their nineteenth-century predecessors. But even Hayden does not suggest an obvious way to address and to resolve the problem of neandertal cultural capacity. One way might be to look at what non-neandertal, Middle Palaeolithic hominids were doing at the same time. If there are similarities in adaptation, biological and behavioral differences between neandertals and modern humans cannot account for them.

THE AFRICAN EVIDENCE FOR MODERN HUMAN ORIGINS

For a number of researchers working in Eurasia, but especially in Africa, the idea of a single African origin of modern humans fits the available evidence quite well (Aiello 1993; Allsworth-Jones 1993; Bar-Yosef 1989; Bräuer 1989; J. Desmond Clark 1988, 1993; Foley 1989; Hublin 1992; Klein 1989, 1999; Lahr 1996; Rightmire 1989; Stringer 1990; Stringer and Andrews 1988). In sub-Saharan Africa, skeletal remains of early modern humans are often found in association with Middle Stone Age (MSA) tool assemblages (Goodwin 1928; J. Desmond Clark 1988; Willoughby 1993b). Examples include Border Cave (Beaumont, de Villiers, and Vogel 1978) and Klasies River Mouth (Singer and Wymer 1982; Deacon 1989; Klein 1989; Rightmire and Deacon 1991; Thackeray 1992; Volman 1984) in South Africa, the Kibish Formation at the Omo River in southern Ethiopia, the Ndutu Beds at Olduvai Gorge, the Ngaloba Beds at Laetoli, and near Lake Eyasi in northern Tanzania (Bräuer 1989; Mehlman 1987, 1991; Rightmire 1989). In North Africa, hominids are also found in Middle Palaeolithic contexts at sites like Dar es Soltan (with Aterian artifacts) and Jebel Irhoud, Morocco (with Mousterian ones) (Hublin 1992). Many of these finds are single fossil specimens, fragmentary, or from insecure contexts, leading some researchers to question the whole notion of early modern humans in Africa (Frayer et al. 1993). But the evidence is strong enough to point to a pattern of association of both archaic *Homo sapiens* (sometimes referred to as *Homo hei-delbergensis*) and anatomically modern humans with the MSA and/or Middle Palaeolithic (between 200,000 and 30,000 B.P.). There can be no doubt that modern humans developed in Africa during this period. Whether or not these early moderns are ancestral to all living humans is another question entirely.

MSA assemblages are typical mode 3 (figure 7.1), composed of retouched flake tools (scrapers and points) produced from more or less round (discoidal or biconical) cores worked radially around their equators. Levallois prepared core techniques are also employed in variable amounts. In both cases, the goal was to produce more standardized flakes than previous reduction systems. Since North African assemblages are closer to European ones in their artifact types and percentage frequency, they are likewise referred to as Middle Palaeolithic. Sub-Saharan sites have their own features and are labeled Middle Stone Age or MSA after the sequence developed by A.J.H. Goodwin (1928) for South Africa. For Goodwin, the MSA was composed of all industries not of Early (ESA) or Later Stone Age (LSA) form, but stratified between them (Thackeray 1992:388–389). Both Levallois and the other methods of flake production used during the African Middle Palaeolithic/MSA were developed during the preceding (mode 2) Acheulean, but the large core and flake tools (bifacial handaxes and cleavers) characteristic of that period no longer occur in any appreciable numbers. Within the MSA, the degree of blade production varies from region to region, but is extremely high in southern Africa (Thackeray 1989, 1992; Volman 1984). However, most of these are referred to as flake-blade industries, since they are made using a variety of prepared core methods similar to Levallois. Even Acheulean assemblages with blades are known, within the Kapthurin Formation at Lake Baringo, Kenya (McBrearty, Bishop, and Kingston 1996), and in the pre-Aurignacian from Tabun Cave and Yabrud I rockshelter in the Middle East (Bar-Yosef and Kuhn 1999).

There are regional differences in African MSA assemblages. Some have a higher percentage of blades than others, while others show the same tool types over broad regions. What this variability represents (ethnicity/style, function, raw-material contingencies) is vigorously debated (Ambrose and Lorenz 1990; J. Desmond Clark 1988; Klein 1992, 1996). Once established, the local pattern of MSA tool types and frequencies seems to have undergone very little change until around 30,000 years ago. At this point, attention turns to the production of blades, bladelets, and geometric segments, which can be microlithic or not, J. Grahame Clark's (1977:23) mode 5. This new technology, referred to as Later Stone Age (LSA) in sub-Saharan Africa (Brooks and Robertshaw 1990; Wadley 1993), is the temporal equivalent of the Eurasian Upper Palaeolithic but the technological equivalent of the Epipalaeolithic or Mesolithic. It was originally defined by Goodwin and Van Riet Lowe "as several stone industries and/or cultures that included nonlithic items, such as ostrich-eggshell beads and worked bone implements, and excluded MSA stone tools, except as recycled manuports" (in Wadley 1993:244).

Initially, the discovery of modern human skeletal material in association with Middle Palaeolithic/MSA artifacts was used to show how far behind Africa was from the supposedly contemporary Upper Palaeolithic (J. Grahame Clark 1977: 210, 219). In his 1970 synthesis *The Prehistory of Africa*, J. Desmond Clark wrote that in the Upper Pleistocene the older prepared core techniques of the Middle Palaeolithic persisted in many parts of Africa. "In the past, this fact has been construed to mean that after the end of the Middle Pleistocene, Africa received more cultural stimulus from outside its boundaries than it transmitted. It has been interpreted also as showing the extreme conservatism of African culture and its populations" (J. Desmond Clark 1970:124). A year later, Karl Butzer concluded that "equally intriguing is the more subtle, geographically significant appearance of new population centers in Eurasia, the continent that had eclipsed the African heartland by the Late Pleistocene. If tool workmanship be an index of cultural progressiveness, and site tool density an index of population size, then Africa would probably qualify as the major center of population and cultural innovation of Early and Middle Pleistocene times. But during the last interglacial, tool craftsmanship found a new focus in Europe, at least judging by the artful handaxes of the final Acheulean or the fine flaking techniques of the Mousterian. Population density, insofar as can be inferred from the evidence, achieved a new high during the European Late Pleistocene. By this time, Africa may have become a cultural backwater" (Butzer 1971:462). In other words, while in Europe modern humans were developing blade-tool assemblages, bone and antler technology, portable and parietal art, and complex social systems, their African counterparts were continuing to wallow in the Middle Palaeolithic mode 3 doldrums.

With the redating of critical sites in Africa and the Levant (Bar-Yosef 1989; Akazawa, Aoki, and Bar-Yosef 1998), this relationship took on new meaning. The fact that early moderns could be associated with Middle Palaeolithic assemblages was due to the extreme antiquity of both. Since it appeared that, in Africa at least, hominids were biologically precocious while apparently maintaining neandertal-like Middle Palaeolithic technologies, a new problem arose. Why did the archaeological assemblages show no marked change when modern humans appeared? When anatomy changed, the archaeological record should also have shifted in a significant fashion, signaling the onset of an Upper Palaeolithic adaptation, one that expressed ethnicity and social recognition. But this did not seem to happen in Africa (Foley and Lahr 1997). Could there have been modern humans with archaic minds in Africa, as has been suggested for sites in Israel where neandertals act like collectors (at Kebara Cave), while proto–Cro-Magnons or early moderns seem to be foragers (at Jebel Qafzeh) (Lieberman and Shea 1994)? Is it possible that at least some African MSA people were fully modern in all respects, not just anatomically? Or is it that, as Stanley Ambrose and Karl Lorenz (1990:28) have suggested, "perhaps early Upper Pleistocene man (in Africa) had modern biological hardware, but simply lacked the software—the cumulative body of knowledge and tradition—required to make effective use of a technology not yet invented"?

THE AFRICAN MIDDLE STONE AGE/MIDDLE PALAEOLITHIC AND THE TRANSITION TO THE LATER STONE AGE/UPPER PALAEOLITHIC

Debates about modern human origins, both biological and cultural, have usually focused on evidence from Europe and the Middle East. Even those archaeological studies dealing with symbolism that have appeared since the replacement model was first proposed ignore other regions. However, if the first anatomically modern humans are African, it is necessary to examine the development of their technologies if the question of cultural origins is to be addressed. What kind of cultural developments were initiated in the African MSA? Is there evidence here for the kind of behavioral shift that takes place in Europe at the Middle/Upper Palaeolithic transition? If not, why not? Are there archaeological changes within the MSA, and do they help us understand the emergence of modern human behavior?

A number of review articles have explored aspects of African Middle Palaeolithic/MSA patterning since the out-of-Africa model was first proposed (Allsworth-Jones 1993; J. Desmond Clark 1988; Klein 1992, 1996; Marks 1992; Thackeray 1992; Willoughby 1993b). Most stress the lack of great cultural change when these early modern humans first appear. If MSA is used for assemblages between 200,000 and 30,000 to 40,000 years old, we are dealing with an enormous time span on a vast continent for which "we have a staggering paucity of post-Acheulean data points either through time or across space" (Mehlman 1989:8). Those that exist look remarkably similar, so attempts to subdivide this period temporally and spatially in Africa have met with limited success. The first MSA industries are really late Acheulean in character, reproducing the same kinds of flake tools but lacking the diagnostic bifacial handaxes and cleavers. In East Africa, for example, the earliest MSA is the Sangoan Industry. Named for the type site of Sango Bay, Uganda, the Sangoan is marked by the presence of core axes, picks, and other heavy-duty tools. It was initially felt to represent the first adaptation of hominids to tropical forest environments, as it is found in areas that have such conditions today (J. Desmond Clark 1988: 281). But most Sangoan artifacts came from surface collections or selected assemblages. Sally McBrearty's (1988, 1991, 1993) work at Muguruk and Simbi in western Kenya points to a different picture. At Simbi, faunal remains, predominantly of grazers, and stable-carbon-isotope analysis of soil carbonates both point to savanna conditions during the Sangoan occupation, and many small artifacts were excavated (McBrearty 1991, 1993).

Early MSA or transitional ESA/MSA sites are associated with full glacial open conditions, rather than with the tropical environments of interglacials and the present. During the last glacial maximum (LGM) between 22,000 and 18,000 years ago, a drop of $4 \pm 2°C$ (Bonnefille, Roeland, and Guiot 1990:349) led to major climatic changes, to a widespread disruption of human settlement, and perhaps to the complete abandonment of large regions such as North Africa

(Close 1986:175). Drier, cooler climates resulted in desert and semiarid steppe conditions in some parts of Africa, and in the reduction or elimination of tropical forests in equatorial zones (Foley 1989; McBrearty 1993; Roberts 1984; Willoughby 1993a, 1993b). Robert Foley (1989:306) suggests that cycling between increasing forests during interglacials and increasing savannas during glacials could have led to the isolation of some archaic *Homo sapiens* populations and to the speciation event that produced modern humans. But it does not seem to have affected their technology until much later.

What does the African archaeological evidence show about cultural developments during this period? In North Africa, the earliest Middle Palaeolithic is Mousterian, with Levallois and other regional features (Map 7.1). In the Maghreb, Mousterian assemblages contain many sidescrapers, points, denticulates, backed flakes, and Levallois elements (J. Desmond Clark 1980:548), along with some tanged pieces (Ferring 1975:113). They are often stratified under Aterian levels. First identified at the site of Bir el Ater in eastern Algeria, the Aterian is a Mousterian industry with varying (but significant) percentages of tanged tools and bifacial foliates, ranging from at least 60,000 B.P. to as recently as 30,000 B.P. Upper Palaeolithic elements such as endscrapers, borers, and burins are also present. The Aterian is found throughout North Africa, from the Atlantic coast to Egypt, but not in the Nile Valley (Ferring 1975:113; J. Desmond Clark 1980:547; Van Peer 1998; Cremaschi et al. 1998). In most of North Africa, there is a hiatus in occupation from the end of the Aterian (around 30,000 to 40,000 B.P.) to the beginning of the Epipalaeolithic after 18,000 years ago (Ferring 1975:119, 121). This could be a product of worsening environmental conditions brought on by the last glacial maximum, which forced hominids to leave. "It seems somewhat unfashionable to suggest that most of North Africa was completely depopulated for a period of 10 or possibly even 20 millennia, but nevertheless, that is the model that provides the best fit for the data at present available" (Close 1986:175).

One of the few archaeological sites with a record spanning this period is the Haua Fteah on the Mediterranean coast of Libya (McBurney 1967). It shows a Levalloiso-Mousterian mode 3 industry present by at least 60,000 B.P. followed by the Libyan pre-Aurignacian, characterized by parallel-sided blades from prismatic cores, of mode 4 or Upper Palaeolithic form. After this, there is a return to the Levalloiso-Mousterian until about 40,000 B.P., at which time the Dabban appears. The Dabban is a fully Upper Palaeolithic mode 4 industry composed of backed blades, endscrapers, and burins, said to be related to coeval industries in the Levant (Phillipson 1993:94). But whether it was produced by immigrants from the Near East or vice versa is not clear (Marks 1992:239). Another site with the possibility of a continuous sequence is Sodmein Cave on the Red Sea in Egypt (Van Peer et al. 1996).

Elsewhere in northeast Africa, Mousterian industries are commonly followed by Aterian ones (J. Desmond Clark 1980:549). Sites in Egypt and the Sudan show Middle Palaeolithic links with other groups in the same area, but there

Map 7.1
African Technological Development in the Middle Palaeolithic/Middle Stone Age

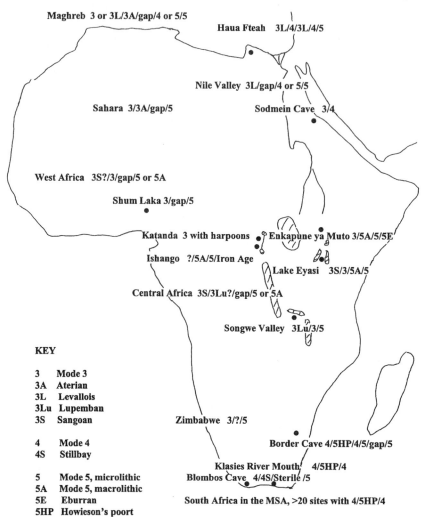

Maghreb 3 or 3L/3A/gap/4 or 5/5

Haua Fteah   3L/4/3L/4/5

Nile Valley 3L/gap/4 or 5/5

Sahara 3/3A/gap/5

Sodmein Cave 3/4

West Africa 3S?/3/gap/5 or 5A

Shum Laka 3/gap/5

Katanda 3 with harpoons

Enkapune ya Muto 3/5A/5/5E

Ishango   ?/5A/5/Iron Age

Lake Eyasi   3S/3/5A/5

Central Africa 3S/3Lu?/gap/5 or 5A

Songwe Valley 3Lu/3/5

KEY

3	Mode 3
3A	Aterian
3L	Levallois
3Lu	Lupemban
3S	Sangoan
4	Mode 4
4S	Stillbay
5	Mode 5, microlithic
5A	Mode 5, macrolithic
5E	Eburran
5HP	Howieson's poort

Zimbabwe 3/?/5

Border Cave 4/5HP/4/5/gap/5

Klasies River Mouth 4/5HP/4
Blombos Cave 4/4S/Sterile /5

South Africa in the MSA, >20 sites with 4/5HP/4

are no specific similarities with the Levant. If there was a population movement of modern humans out of Africa during the Middle Palaeolithic, there is no archaeological sign of it (Marks 1992:239, 244–245). Philip Van Peer (1998) proposes that a sudden change toward blade technology may have occurred here around 40,000 years ago, prompting the expansion out of Africa.

In West Africa, little is known of the MSA except from surface finds. Allsworth-Jones (1986:166) has reported on sites in Nigeria and Cameroon and stresses similarities with the North African Middle Palaeolithic. But West African material also has parallels with the technologies of eastern and southern Africa where prepared cores and flakes were shaped to produce points and scrapers (Phillipson 1993:87). As in North Africa, there is usually a gap from the end of the MSA until after the last glacial maximum, as is seen at sites like Shum Laka in Cameroon (Cornelissen 1996, 1997). Therefore, it is impossible to describe the actual process of technological change from the MSA to the LSA. Within areas covered today by equatorial rainforest, there are find spots and possible MSA sites being reported (Mercader and Marti 1999), but it is not clear if these areas were forested at the time of human occupation.

It is from eastern and southern Africa that the bulk of our knowledge about the MSA comes, but long cultural-historical sequences are known only from a handful of sites. The most detailed sequences come from a series of sites around Lake Eyasi and from nearby Olduvai Gorge, both in northern Tanzania. Michael Mehlman (1987, 1989, 1991) examined archaeological material from Mumba rockshelter (Mumba Höhle), from the lakeshore near Lake Eyasi (both initially excavated by Ludwig Kohl-Larsen in the 1930s), and from Nasera rockshelter (Apis Rock), 90 kilometers to the north. One of the two transitional industries here, the Mumba, is a combination of MSA and LSA elements and shows a gradual transition from one to the other. Over time, the number of retouched points decreases, and the numbers of backed tools increase (the opposite is the case in the second transitional industry, referred to as the Nasera). The Mumba Industry's mixture of mode 3 and mode 5 elements (crescents, backed knives, points, thumbnail scrapers, Levallois flakes and cores, and numerous bipolar cores) is reminiscent of the South African Howieson's poort (Mehlman 1991: 178). Sibel Barut Kusimba (1999) has recently reexamined LSA sites from Lukenya Hill, a large inselberg in southern Kenya. Tracing the movement of lithic materials across space, she proposes that prior to the last glacial maximum, people were less mobile, following a collector pattern of moving resources from special work sites to home bases. But during the LGM, increasing dry and cool conditions made it necessary to spend less time at individual settlements.

In other regions of East Africa, many finds of MSA flake tools have been made. At Enkapune ya Muto, Stanley Ambrose excavated one of the earliest LSA industries, one that was stratified above an MSA level and dated to over 40,000 years ago. Ostrich-eggshell beads are present in assemblages dated to the same period (Ambrose 1998; Robbins 1997). At Kalambo Falls in northern Zambia, a sequence from Acheulean to Sangoan to MSA is known (J. Desmond Clark 1988). Just to the north in southwestern Tanzania, both Sangoan and flake-dominated MSA sites were located during a preliminary survey of the Lake Rukwa rift valley in 1990 (Willoughby 1992, 1993b, 1996a, 1996b). These are made in a wide variety of fine raw materials, such as cryptocrystalline silica, volcanic rocks, and quartz and quartzite, and are remarkably different from the following LSA, which is microlithic and quartz dominated. A Pleistocene and Holocene LSA sequence with no radical change in technology was excavated by the author in July 1997 at IdIu22, a collapsed volcanic rockshelter in the

Songwe River valley. Further west, in central Africa, Sangoan industries are followed by Lupemban ones, with heavy-duty core tools such as axes, rare foliate pieces, and lanceolates (J. Desmond Clark 1988:244–245). Following the Lupemban, there is usually a hiatus in occupation; then microlithic quartz LSA mode 5 assemblages appear (Cornelissen 1997).

It is only in South Africa that the MSA is well known. The best archaeological sequence comes from Klasies River Mouth near Cape Town (Singer and Wymer 1982; Deacon 1989; Thackeray 1989, 1992; Thackeray and Kelly 1988). Excavations in 1967 and 1968 by Ronald Singer and John Wymer produced a sequence of four MSA levels, labeled I to IV, with a distinctive macrolithic mode 5 industry, the Howieson's poort, sandwiched in the middle (Singer and Wymer 1982). The MSA levels contain long, thin flake-blades (blades made from prepared cores rather than prismatic ones), manufactured on local quartzite. In the Howieson's poort, the dominant forms are backed and geometric pieces (crescents, trapezes). They are often on finer materials than the MSA ones (such as quartz, hornfels, chalcedony, and silcrete) and range in size from about 10 to 60 millimeters in maximum dimension (Thackeray 1992:390). In all but their size and age, they are typically LSA. The Howieson's poort takes its name from a site north of Klasies where this material was first excavated. The discovery of LSA-like assemblages here led to the Howieson's poort being labeled a transitional industry between the MSA and LSA. But its presence between MSA levels at Klasies and a number of other sites (such as Border Cave, Rose Cottage Cave, Apollo 11 Cave in Namibia, and possibly at Die Kelders), below MSA levels (at Sehongong and other sites in Lesotho, Montagu Cave, and elsewhere) or above them (at Nelson Bay Cave, Cave of Hearths) (Thackeray 1992:396; Wadley et al. 1997) clearly shows a reoccurring regional pattern of MSA affiliation. It is unclear how old the Howieson's poort is. Various dates have been suggested, averaging between 60,000 and 40,000 B.P. (Thackeray 1992:403; Parkington 1990), but it is possible that it is significantly older yet.

As is the case elsewhere, there are very few South African sites showing an unbroken archaeological sequence spanning the MSA/LSA transition. The earliest LSA comes from levels 1WA and 1BS.LR at Border Cave and may date to around 39,000 B.P. (Wadley 1993:260). It exhibits few formal tools or bladelets. Many *pièces esquillées* (scalar pieces) occur, showing a heavy reliance on bipolar flaking techniques. Ground bone points and ostrich-eggshell beads appear for the first time (Wadley 1993:260). Ostrich-eggshell beads are also known from White Paintings Rockshelter in the Tsodilo Hills of Botswana in levels dated to over 30,000 years ago (Robbins 1999). More pieces of worked shell are found here than finished beads. Such beads are a major product of some populations of !Kung San, where they formed the nucleus of the *hxaro* system of reciprocal exchange between partners in different ecological zones (Wiessner 1977, 1982; Ambrose 1998; Robbins 1999).

One site, with a transitional sequence dated to around 20,000 years ago, is Rose Cottage Cave in the Orange Free State (Wadley et al. 1997; A.M.B. Clark

1999). Here LSA assemblages were grafted onto an MSA root that already contained a few bladelets and other LSA hallmarks (Clark 1999). But generally, Lyn Wadley (1993:260) concludes that there are very few South African sites between 40,000 and 19,000 B.P. Those that exist either fall into a transitional category or are nonmicrolithic, with few bladelets, and most of the latter are in the range of 18,000 to 22,000 years old.

THE PLACE OF THE AFRICAN RECORD IN UNDERSTANDING THE ORIGINS OF SYMBOLIC BEHAVIOR

When the African MSA/Middle Palaeolithic and later record is reviewed, it is clear that only a few sites have been intensively examined, so any comparisons must therefore be tentative. Very few sites show a continuous sequence over the MSA/LSA boundary. Those that do show that a very early transition occurred more than 30,000 years ago (e.g., Border Cave, Matupi Cave in eastern Congo, Enkapune ya Muto in Kenya). Elsewhere, there is little sign of the change. It is possible that the cool, dry climate of the last glacial maximum prevented human occupation of large parts of Africa, thereby accounting for the lack of a transitional record or any archaeological record at all. As a result, most researchers who discuss the transition and its significance for the onset of modern behavior are comparing evidence over 30,000 years old with that from less than 18,000 years ago. It is not surprising, therefore, that profound differences are seen. In the few places where a record can be seen, there is no sudden replacement of flakes by blade technology, as both are major components of the MSA. The few sites that show continuity with the LSA show a gradual change, with the addition of new mode 5 technological elements (geometric pieces, bladelets). It is obviously premature to conclude that the Middle Palaeolithic/ MSA in Africa was qualitatively different from the Upper Palaeolithic/LSA.

There are obvious anomalies in the African Upper Pleistocene record when it is compared to Western Europe. L. B. Vishnyatsky (1994) has reviewed Palaeolithic industries that run ahead of time, in other words, those that are technologically precocious. Two of the anomalies he describes are African—the Libyan pre-Aurignacian of Haua Fteah and the Howieson's poort of South Africa (Vishnyatsky 1994:136–137). In both, the range of tool types is more like that of the succeeding periods than like coeval developments. While the former is only known from one site, the latter is widespread in southern Africa. Geometric segments and blade technology are common in some MSA assemblages; in other areas, flake technology (with or without Levallois) predominates. Both the Aterian and the Howieson's poort are best understood as exhibiting stylistic similarities, ethnic affiliation, and/or information exchange over a large geographic space, in a modern fashion. Other signs of Upper Palaeolithic–like technology are beginning to be reported. One is the early appearance of bone harpoons and fish bones in the MSA of Katanda, in eastern Congo, as well as ostrich-eggshell beads dated through amino-acid racemization to between 40,000 and 90,000 B.P. (Brooks et al. 1995; Yellen et al. 1995; Yellen 1998). Both are common in the LSA of nearby Ishango, but unexpected in MSA contexts. At Blomblos Cave in South Africa, Christopher Henshilwood and Judith Sealy (1997) have found bone tools, evidence of fishing, and bifacially pressure-flaked leaf-shaped silcrete points, all from a MSA (Stillbay) level. The tanged pieces of the Aterian represent the development of hafting technology, as well as a shared cultural or technological system. In other areas, evidence of hafting during the MSA is more circumstantial and amounts to basal thinning or notching of points and scrapers (Willoughby 1996a).

Philip Chase and Harold Dibble (Chase 1991; Chase and Dibble 1987) reviewed the evidence of symbolic behavior in pre–Upper Palaeolithic contexts in Europe. They looked for evidence of lithic-assemblage variability, burials, other rituals, and art and concluded that no Middle Palaeolithic hominid could show any modern cultural tendencies. This is not the case for Africa, but if this problem is ever to be solved, one must investigate the few sites that span the transition into the Upper Palaeolithic/LSA. It is only at such places that the cultural capacity of MSA people can be compared to that of LSA ones. It is possible that the transition between the two was gradual, more in keeping with the scenarios of modern human biological development in Africa. Where continuous sequences should be found, such as in North Africa, environmental change may have resulted in a hiatus in settlement and a breakdown of a long-standing cultural system. Perhaps the worst-case scenario is the possibility that modern symbolically based behavior evolved and left no apparent archaeological sign. As is the case in the Middle East, it is very likely that there were anatomically modern Africans with archaic minds.

According to J. Desmond Clark (1988:238), "the MSA was a time of several very important innovations, a more structured social organization that might be deduced from a pattern of regular transhumance and reoccupation of key localities and the hafting of stone working parts in traditional ways to form simple composite tools." For him and other researchers (e.g., Deacon 1989), modern human culture is probably an MSA invention. But as has become apparent in this discussion, it is not easy to create a culture-historical sequence for the African Upper Pleistocene, given the state of our knowledge. Little is known about adaptation beyond the range of lithic materials. Faunal remains, when present, have been used primarily as palaeoenvironmental indicators; Richard Klein (1989; Klein and Cruz-Uribe 1996) and Curtis Marean (1997) are among the few who have tried to compare MSA and LSA subsistence strategies.

It is even more difficult to evaluate the evidence for the emergence of modern human behavior, ethnic markers, and symbolism, given that basic culture-historical work remains to be done in many parts of the continent. It is likely that modern human anatomy developed in Africa, but the fossil evidence for this is fragmentary and often controversial. But it is a mistake to look for the origins of modern human culture using only European models. Modern human adaptations apparently developed during the African MSA without major technological changes.

This chapter has been an attempt to evaluate the African evidence in the light of Western European models of ethnicity, symbolic origins, and technological evolution in the Palaeolithic. It is believed by many that the beginnings of self-identification, ethnicity, and culture itself can be seen in the European Upper Palaeolithic. Even with the limited data available to us concerning what changed between the MSA and the LSA, it is clear that such models do not explain what happened in Africa in the LSA/Upper Palaeolithic or even earlier. Evidence outside of Europe must not be ignored if we ever expect to answer the question of how and why modern human behavior began. In turn, we should not be surprised (or dismayed) if the path of Upper Pleistocene biocultural evolution took more than a single direction.

NOTE

My research on East African Upper Pleistocene archaeology has been supported by the Social Sciences and Humanities Research Council of Canada (SSHRCC), the L.S.B. Leakey Foundation, the Association of Commonwealth Universities, the Boise Fund of Oxford University, and the Support for the Advancement of Scholarship Fund and the Social Sciences Research Fund, both at the University of Alberta. Field research in Tanzania has been conducted under permits from the Department of Antiquities, Ministry of Education and Culture, as well as from the Tanzania Commission on Science and Technology (COSTECH). I thank the former director of the Department of Antiquities, Dr. Simon Waane, for his assistance and encouragement. I would like to dedicate this chapter to J. Desmond Clark, who has led the way in the interpretation of the African Stone Age, and to James Sackett, who introduced me to issues about modern human origins, style, and symbolism, albeit from a Western European Palaeolithic perspective.

REFERENCES

Aiello, Leslie
1993 Fossil Evidence for Modern Human Origins in Africa: A Revised View. *American Anthropologist* 95(1):73–96.
Aitken, Martin J., Christopher B. Stringer, and Paul Mellars, eds.
1993 *The Origin of Modern Humans and the Impact of Chronometric Dating*, Princeton: Princeton University Press.
Akazawa, Takeru, Kenichi Aoki, and Ofer Bar-Yosef, eds.
1998 *Neandertals and Modern Humans in Western Asia*. New York: Plenum Press.
Allsworth-Jones, Philip
1986 Middle Stone Age and Middle Palaeolithic: The Evidence from Nigeria and Cameroun. In *Stone Age Prehistory*. Geoff N. Bailey and Paul Callow, eds. Pp. 153–168. Cambridge: Cambridge University Press.
1990 The Szeletian and the Stratigraphic Succession in Central Europe and Adjacent Areas: Main Trends, Recent Results, and Problems for Resolution. In *The Emer-

gence of Modern Humans. P. Mellars, ed. Pp. 160–242. Ithaca, NY: Cornell University Press.

1993 The Archaeology of Archaic and Early Modern *Homo sapiens*: An African Perspective. *Cambridge Archaeological Journal* 3(1):21–39.

Ambrose, Stanley H.

1998 Chronology of the Later Stone Age and Food Production in East Africa. *Journal of Archaeological Science* 25(4):377–392.

Ambrose, Stanley H., and Karl G. Lorenz

1990 Social and Ecological Models for the Middle Stone Age in Southern Africa. In *The Emergence of Modern Humans.* Paul Mellars, ed. Pp. 3–33. Ithaca, NY: Cornell University Press.

Barham, Lawrence

1998 Possible Early Pigment Use in South-central Africa. *Current Anthropology* 39(5): 703–710.

Bar-Yosef, Ofer

1989 Geochronology of the Levantine Middle Palaeolithic. In *The Human Revolution.* Paul Mellars and Christopher Stringer, eds. Pp. 589–610. Princeton: Princeton University Press.

Bar-Yosef, Ofer, and Steven Kuhn

1999 The Big Deal about Blades: Laminar Technologies and Human Evolution. *American Anthropologist* 101(2):322–338.

Beaumont, P. B., H. de Villiers, and J. C. Vogel

1978 Modern Man in Sub-Saharan Africa prior to 49,000 years B.P.: A Review and Evaluation with Particular Reference to Border Cave. *South African Journal of Science* 74(11):409–419.

Binford, Lewis R.

1973 Interassemblage Variability: The Mousterian and the "Functional" Argument. In *The Explanation of Culture Change: Models in Prehistory.* Colin Renfrew, ed. Pp. 227–254. London: Duckworth.

1980 Willow Smoke and Dogs' Tails: Hunter-Gatherer Settlement Systems and Archaeological Site Formation. *American Antiquity* 45(1):4–20.

1989 Isolating the Transition to Cultural Adaptations: An Organizational Approach. In *The Emergence of Modern Humans.* Erik Trinkaus, ed. Pp. 18–41. Cambridge: Cambridge University Press.

Binford, Lewis R., and Sally R. Binford

1966 A Preliminary Analysis of Functional Variability in the Mousterian of Levallois Facies. In *Recent Studies in Palaeoanthropology.* Theme issue. *American Anthropologist* 68(2)(2):238–295.

Binford, Sally R., and Lewis R. Binford

1968 Stone Tools and Human Behavior. *Scientific American* 220(8):70–84.

Bonnefille, Raymonde, J. C. Roeland, and J. Guiot

1990 Temperature and Rainfall Estimates for the Past 40,000 Years in Equatorial Africa. *Nature* 346(6282):347–349.

Bordes, François

1973 On the Chronology and Contemporaneity of Different Palaeolithic Cultures in France. In *The Explanation of Culture Change: Models in Prehistory.* Colin Renfrew, ed. Pp. 217–226. London: Duckworth.

1981 Vingt-cinq ans après: Le complexe moustérien revisité. *Bulletin de la Société Préhistorique Française* 78(3):77–87.

Bowler, Peter
1989 *The Invention of Progress: The Victorians and the Past.* Oxford:Basil Blackwell.

Bräuer, Gunter
1989 The Evolution of Modern Humans: A Comparison of the African and Non-African Evidence. In *The Human Revolution.* Paul Mellars and Christopher Stringer, eds. Pp. 123–154. Princeton: Princeton University Press.

Brooks, Alison, David M. Helgren, Jon S. Cramer, Alan Franklin, William Hornyak, Jody M. Keating, Richard G. Klein, William J. Rink, Henry Schwarcz, J. N. Leith Smith, Kathlyn Stewart, Nancy E. Todd, Jacques Verniers, and John E. Yellen
1995 Dating and Context of Three Middle Stone Age Sites with Bone Points in the Upper Semliki Valley, Zaire. *Science* 268(5210):548–553.

Brooks, Alison, and Peter Robertshaw
1990 The Glacial Maximum in Tropical Africa. In *The World at 18,000 B.P.: Low Latitudes.* Clive Gamble and Olga Soffer, eds. Pp. 121–169. London: Unwin Hyman.

Butzer, Karl W.
1971 *Environment and Archeology: An Ecological Approach to Prehistory.* 2nd ed. Chicago: Aldine Atherton.

Cann, Rebecca L., Mark Stoneking, and Alan C. Wilson
1987 Mitochondrial DNA and Human Evolution. *Nature* 325(6099):31–36.

Chase, Philip
1991 Symbols and Paleolithic Artifacts: Style, Standardization, and the Imposition of Arbitrary Form. *Journal of Anthropological Archaeology* 10(3):193–214.

Chase, Philip, and Harold L. Dibble
1987 Middle Paleolithic Symbolism: A Review of Current Evidence and Interpretations. *Journal of Anthropological Archaeology* 6(3):263–296.

Clark, Amelia M. B.
1999 Late Pleistocene Technology at Rose Cottage Cave: A Search for Modern Behavior in an MSA Context. *African Archaeological Review* 16(2):93–119.

Clark, Geoffrey A.
1999 Highly Visible, Curiously Intangible. *Science* 283(5410):2029–2032.

Clark, Geoffrey A., and Catherine A. Willermet, eds.
1997 *Conceptual Issues in Modern Human Origins Research.* Hawthorne, NY: Aldine de Gruyter.

Clark, J. Desmond
1970 *The Prehistory of Africa.* London: Thames and Hudson.
1980 Human Populations and Cultural Adaptations in the Sahara and Nile during Prehistoric Times. In *The Sahara and the Nile.* Martin Williams and Hugues Faure, eds. Pp. 527–582. Rotterdam: Balkema.
1988 The Middle Stone Age of East Africa and the Beginnings of Regional Identity. *Journal of World Prehistory* 2(3):235–305.
1993 African and Asian Perspectives on the Origins of Modern Humans. In *The Origin of Modern Humans and the Impact of Chronometric Dating.* Martin J. Aitken, Christopher Stringer, and Paul Mellars, eds. Pp. 148–178. Princeton: Princeton University Press.

Clark, J. Grahame D.
1977 *World Prehistory in New Perspective*. 3rd ed. Cambridge: Cambridge University Press.

Close, Angela E.
1986 The Place of the Haua Fteah in the Late Palaeolithic of North Africa. In *Stone Age Prehistory*. Geoff N. Bailey and Paul Callow, eds. Pp. 169–180. Cambridge: Cambridge University Press.

Conkey, Margaret W.
1978 Style and Information in Cultural Evolution: Toward a Predictive Model for the Paleolithic. In *Social Archaeology: Beyond Subsistence and Dating*. Charles L. Redman, Mary Jane Berman, Edward V. Curtin, William T. Langhorne, Jr., Nina W. Versaggi, and Jeffrey C. Wanser, eds. Pp. 61–85. New York: Academic Press.

Cornelissen, Els
1996 Shum Laka (Cameroon): Late Pleistocene and Early Holocene Deposits. In *Aspects of African Archaeology*. Gilbert Pwiti and Robert Soper, eds. Pp. 257–263. Harare: University of Zimbabwe Publications.

1997 Central African Transitional Cultures. In *Encyclopedia of Precolonial Africa*. Joseph O. Vogel, ed. Pp. 312–320. Walnut Creek, CA: Altamira Press.

Cremaschi, Mauro, Savino di Lernia, and Elena A. A. Garcea
1998 Some Insights on the Aterian in the Libyan Sahara: Chronology, Environment, and Archaeology. *African Archaeological Review* 15(4):261–286.

Deacon, Hilary J.
1989 Late Pleistocene Palaeoecology and Archaeology in the Southern Cape, South Africa. In *The Human Revolution*. Paul Mellars and Christopher Stringer, eds. Pp. 547–564. Princeton: Princeton University Press.

In press Modern Human Emergence: An African Archaeological Perspective. Proceedings of the Dual Congress, Sun City, South Africa.

Débénath, André
1994 L'Atérien du nord de l'Afrique et du Sahara. *Sahara* 6:21–30.

D'Errico, Francisco, João Zilhão, Michèle Julien, Dominique Baffier, and Jacques Pelegrin
1998 Neanderthal Acculturation in Western Europe? A Critical Review of the Evidence and Its Interpretation. *Current Anthropology* 39:S1–S44.

Duarte, Cidalia, João Mauricio, Paul B. Pettitt, Pedro Souto, Erik Trinkaus, Hans van der Plicht, and João Zilhão
1999 The Early Upper Paleolithic Human Skeleton from the Abrigo do Lagar Velho (Portugal) and Modern Human Emergence in Iberia. *Proceedings of the National Academy of Sciences* 96(13):7604–7609.

Ferring, C. Reid
1975 The Aterian in North African Prehistory. In *Problems in Prehistory: North Africa and the Levant*. Fred Wendorf and Anthony E. Marks, eds. Pp. 113–126. Dallas: Southern Methodist University Press.

Foley, Robert
1987 Hominid Species and Stone-Tool Assemblages: How Are They Related? *Antiquity* 61(233):380–392.

1989 The Ecological Conditions of Speciation: A Comparative Approach to the Origins of Anatomically-Modern Humans. In *The Human Revolution*. Paul Mellars and Christopher Stringer, eds. Pp. 298–318. Princeton: Princeton University Press.

Foley, Robert, and Marta M. Lahr
1997 Mode 3 Technologies and the Evolution of Modern Humans. *Cambridge Archaeological Journal* 7(1):3–36.

Frayer, David W., Milford H. Wolpoff, Alan G. Thorne, Fred H. Smith, and Geoffrey Pope
1993 Theories of Modern Human Origins: The Paleontological Test. *American Anthropologist* 95(1):14–50.

Gagneux, Pascal, Christopher Willis, Ulrike Gerloff, Diethard Tautz, Phillip A. Morin, Christophe Boesch, Barbara Fruth, Gottfried Hohmann, Oliver A. Tyder, and David S. Woodruff
1999 Mitochondrial Sequences Show Diverse Evolutionary Histories of African Hominoids. *Proceedings of the National Academy of Sciences* 96(9):5077–5082.

Gargett, Robert H.
1989 Grave Shortcomings: The Evidence for Neandertal Burial. *Current Anthropology* 30(2):157–190.
1999 Middle Palaeolithic Burial Is Not a Dead Issue: The View from Qafzeh, Saint-Césaire, Kebara, Amud, and Dederiyeh. *Journal of Human Evolution* 37(1):27–90.

Goodwin, A.J.H.
1928 An Introduction to the Middle Stone Age in South Africa. *South African Journal of Science* 25:410–418.

Goodyear, Albert C.
1989 A Hypothesis for the Use of Cryptocrystalline Raw Materials among Paleoindian Groups of North America. In *Eastern Paleoindian Lithic Resource Use*. Christopher J. Ellis and Jonathan C. Lothrop, eds. Pp. 1–9. Boulder, CO: Westview Press.

Harrold, Francis
1989 Mousterian, Châtelperronian, and Early Aurignacian in Western Europe: Continuity or Discontinuity? In *The Human Revolution*. Paul Mellars and Christopher Stringer, eds. Pp. 677–713. Princeton: Princeton University Press.

Hayden, Brian
1993 The Cultural Capacities of Neandertals: A Review and Re-evaluation. *Journal of Human Evolution* 24(2):113–146.

Henshilwood, Christopher S., and Judith Sealy
1997 Bone Artefacts from the Middle Stone Age at Blombos Cave, Southern Cape, South Africa. *Current Anthropology* 38(5):890–895.

Hublin, Jean-Jacques
1992 Recent Human Evolution in Northwestern Africa. *Philosophical Transactions of the Royal Society* 337B(1280):185–191.

Isaac, Glyn Llwelyn
1972 Chronology and the Tempo of Cultural Change during the Pleistocene. In *Calibration of Hominoid Evolution*. Walter W. Bishop and John A. Miller, eds. Pp. 381–403. Edinburgh: Scottish Academic Press.

Jochim, Michael
1987 Late Pleistocene Refugia in Europe. In *The Pleistocene Old World*. Olga Soffer, ed. Pp. 317–331. New York: Plenum.

Kelly, Robert L.
1992 Mobility/Sedentism: Concepts, Archaeological Measures, and Effects. *Annual Review of Anthropology* 21:43–66.

Klein, Richard G.
1989 Biological and Behavioral Perspectives on Modern Human Origins in Southern
    Africa. In *The Human Revolution* Paul Mellars and Christopher Stringer, eds.
    Pp. 529–546. Princeton: Princeton University Press.
1992 The Archaeology of Modern Human Origins. *Evolutionary Anthropology* 1(1):5–
    14.
1996 Anatomy, Behavior, and Modern Human Origins. *Journal of World Prehistory* 9(2):
    167–198.
1999 *The Human Career*. 2nd ed. Chicago: University of Chicago Press.
Klein, Richard G., and Kathryn Cruz-Uribe
1996 Exploitation of Large Bovids and Seals at Middle and Later Stone Age Sites in
    South Africa. *Journal of Human Evolution* 31(4):315–334.
Krings, Matthias, Helga Geisert, Ralf W. Schmitz, Heike Krainitzki, and Svante Pääbo
1999 DNA Sequence of the Mitochondrial Hypervariable Region II from the Neandertal
    Type Specimen. *Proceedings of the National Academy of Sciences* 96(10):5581–
    5585.
Krings, Matthias, Anne Stone, Ralf W. Schmitz, Heike Krainitzki, Mark Stoneking, and
    Svante Pääbo
1997 Neandertal DNA Sequences and the Origin of Modern Humans. *Cell* 90(1):19–30.
Kusimba, Sibel Barut
1999 Hunter-Gatherer Land Use Patterns in Later Stone Age East Africa. *Journal of
    Anthropological Archaeology* 18(2):165–200.
Lahr, Marta M.
1996 *The Evolution of Modern Human Diversity: A Study on Cranial Variation*. Cam-
    bridge: Cambridge University Press.
Lévêque, F., A. M. Backer, and M. Guilbaud, eds.
1993 *Context of a Late Neandertal*. Monographs in World Archaeology 16. Madison,
    WI: Prehistory Press.
Lieberman, Daniel E., and John Shea
1994 Behavioral Differences between Archaic and Modern Humans in the Levantine
    Mousterian. *American Anthropologist* 96(2):300–332.
Lindly, John M., and Geoffrey A. Clark
1990 Symbolism and Modern Human Origins. *Current Anthropology* 31(3):233–261.
Marean, Curtis W.
1997 Hunter-Gatherer Foraging Strategies in Tropical Grasslands: Model Building and
    Testing in the East African Middle and Later Stone Age. *Journal of Anthropo-
    logical Archaeology* 16(3):189–225.
Marks, Anthony E.
1992 Upper Pleistocene Archaeology and the Origins of Modern Man: A View from the
    Levant and Adjacent Areas. In *The Evolution and Dispersal of Modern Humans
    in Asia*. Takeru Akazawa, Kenichi Aoki, and Tasuku Kimura, eds. Pp. 229–251.
    Tokyo: Hokusen-sha Publishing Company.
McBrearty, Sally
1988 The Sangoan-Lupemban and Middle Stone Age Sequence at the Muguruk Site,
    Western Kenya. *World Archaeology* 19(3):388–420.
1991 Recent Research in Western Kenya and Its Implications for the Status of the San-
    goan Industry. In *Cultural Beginnings*. J. Desmond Clark, ed. Pp. 159–176. Bonn:
    Dr. Rudolf Habelt GMBH.

1993 Reconstructing the Environmental Conditions Surrounding the Appearance of Modern Humans in East Africa. In *Culture and Environment: A Fragile Coexistence*. Ross W. Jamieson, Sylvia Abonyi, and Neil Mirau, eds. Pp. 145–154. Calgary: Chacmool Archaeological Association.

McBrearty, Sally M., Laura Bishop, and John Kingston
1996 Variability in Traces of Middle Pleistocene Hominid Behavior in the Kapthurin Formation, Baringo, Kenya. *Journal of Human Evolution* 30(6):563–579.

McBurney, Charles B. M.
1967 *The Haua Fteah (Cyrenaica) and the Stone Age of the South-East Mediterranean*. Cambridge: Cambridge University Press.

Mehlman, M.
1987 Provenience, Age, and Associations of Archaic *Homo sapiens* Crania from Lake Eyasi, Tanzania. *Journal of Archaeological Science* 14(2):133–162.
1989 Later Quaternary Archaeological Sequences in Northern Tanzania. Ph.D. dissertation, University of Illinois, Urbana-Champaign.
1991 Context for the Emergence of Modern Man in Eastern Africa: Some New Tanzanian Evidence. In *Cultural Beginnings*. J. Desmond Clark, ed. Pp. 177–196. Bonn: Dr. Rudolf Habelt GMBH.

Mellars, Paul
1989 Technological Changes at the Middle-Upper Palaeolithic Transition: Economic, Social, and Cognitive Perspectives. In *The Human Revolution*. Paul Mellars and Christopher Stringer, eds. Pp. 338–365. Princeton: Princeton University Press.
1991 Cognitive Changes and the Emergence of Modern Humans in Europe. *Cambridge Archaeological Journal* 1(1):63–76.

Mercader, Julio, and Raquel Marti
1999 Middle Stone Age Site in the Tropical Forests of Equatorial Guinea. *Nyame Akuma* 51:14–24.

Milo, Richard, and Duane Quiatt
1993 Glottogenesis and Anatomically Modern *Homo sapiens*: The Evidence for and Implications of a Late Origin of Vocal Language. *Current Anthropology* 34(5): 569–598.

Mussi, Margherita
1990 Le peuplement de l'Italie à la fin du Paléolithique moyen et au début du Paléolithique supérieur. In *Paléolithique moyen récent et Paléolithique supérieur ancien en Europe*. Catherine Farizy, ed. *Mémoires du Musée de Préhistorie d'Ile de France* 3:251–262.

Parkington, John
1990 A Critique of the Consensus View on the Age of Howieson's Poort Assemblages in South Africa. In *The Emergence of Modern Humans*. Paul Mellars, ed. Pp. 34–55. Ithaca, NY: Cornell University Press.

Pfeiffer, John E.
1982 *The Creative Explosion*. New York: Harper and Row.

Phillipson, David
1993 *African Archaeology*. 2nd ed. Cambridge: Cambridge University Press.

Rightmire, G. Philip
1989 Middle Stone Age Humans from Eastern and Southern Africa. In *The Human Revolution*. Paul Mellars and Christopher Stringer, eds. Pp. 109–122. Princeton: Princeton University Press.

Rightmire, G. Philip, and Hilary Deacon
1991 Comparative Studies of Late Pleistocene Human Remains from Klasies River
    Mouth, South Africa. *Journal of Human Evolution* 20(2):131–156.
Robbins, Lawrence R.
1997 Eastern African Advanced Foragers. In *Encyclopedia of Precolonial Africa*. Joseph
    O. Vogel, ed. Pp. 335–340. Walnut Creek, CA: Altamira Press.
1999 Direct Dating of Worked Ostrich Eggshell in the Kalahari. *Nyame Akuma* 52:11–
    16.
Roberts, Neil
1984 Pleistocene Environments in Time and Space. In *Hominid Evolution and Com-
    munity Ecology*. Robert Foley, ed. Pp. 25–53. London: Academic Press.
Rolland, Nicholas, and Harold L. Dibble
1990 A New Synthesis of Middle Palaeolithic Variability. *American Antiquity* 55(3):
    480–499.
Sackett, James R.
1977 The Meaning of Style in Archaeology. *American Antiquity* 42:369–380.
1981 From de Mortillet to Bordes: A Century of French Palaeolithic Research. In *To-
    wards a History of Archaeology*. Glyn Daniel, ed. Pp. 85–99. London: Thames
    and Hudson.
1982 Approaches to Style in Lithic Archaeology. *Journal of Anthropological Archae-
    ology* 1:59–112.
Schepartz, Lynn A.
1993 Language and Modern Human Origins. *Yearbook of Physical Anthropology* 36:91–
    126.
Singer, Ronald, and John Wymer
1982 *The Middle Stone Age at Klasies River Mouth in South Africa*, Chicago: University
    of Chicago Press.
Smith, Fred H., Erik Trinkaus, Paul B. Pettitt, Ivor Karavanic, and Maja Paunovic
1999 Direct Radiocarbon Dates for Vindija G_1 and Velika Pećina Late Pleistocene Hominid
    Remains. *Proceedings of the National Academy of Sciences* 96(22):12281–12286.
Soffer, Olga
1987 Upper Paleolithic Connubia, Refugia, and the Archaeological Record from Eastern
    Europe. In *The Pleistocene Old World*. Olga Soffer, ed. Pp. 333–348. New York:
    Plenum.
Soffer, Olga, Pamela Vandiver, Bohuslav Klima, and Jiri Svoboda
1992 The Pyrotechnology of Performance Art: Moravian Venuses and Wolverines. In
    Before Lascaux. Heidi Knecht, Anne Pike-Tay, and Randall White, eds. Pp. 259–
    275. Boca Raton, FL: CRC Press.
Stoneking, Mark
1993 DNA and Recent Human Evolution. *Evolutionary Anthropology* 2(2):60–73.
Stringer, Christopher B.
1990 The Emergence of Modern Humans. *Scientific American* 263(6):98–104.
Stringer, Christopher B., and Peter Andrews
1988 Genetic and Fossil Evidence for the Origin of Modern Humans. *Science* 239(4845):
    1263–1268.
Stringer, Christopher B., and Clive Gamble
1993 *In Search of the Neanderthals*. London: Thames and Hudson.

Tattersall, Ian, and Jeffrey H. Schwartz
1999 Hominids and Hybrids: The Place of Neanderthals in Human Evolution. *Proceedings of the National Academy of Sciences* 96(13):7117–7119.
Thackeray, Anne I.
1989 Changing Fashions in the Middle Stone Age: The Stone Artefact Sequence from Klasies River Main Site, South Africa. *African Archaeological Review* 7:33–57.
1992 The Middle Stone Age South of the Limpopo River. *Journal of World Prehistory* 6(4):385–440.
Thackeray, Anne I., and Alison J. Kelly
1988 A Technological and Typological Analysis of Middle Stone Age Assemblages Antecedent to the Howieson's Poort at Klasies River Main Site. *South African Archaeological Bulletin* 43(147):15–26.
Thorne, Alan G., and Milford H. Wolpoff
1992 The Multiregional Evolution of Humans. *Scientific American* 266(4):76–83.
Van Peer, Philip
1998 The Nile Corridor and the Out-of-Africa Model: An Examination of the Archaeological Record. *Current Anthropology* 39:S115–S140.
Van Peer, Philip, Pierre M. Vermeersch, Jan Moeyersons, and Wim Van Neer
1996 Palaeolithic Sequence of Sodmein Cave, Red Sea Mountains, Egypt. In *Aspects of African Archaeology*. Gilbert Pwiti and Robert Soper, eds. Pp. 149–156. Harare: University of Zimbabwe Publications.
Vigilant, Linda, Mark Stoneking, Henry Harpending, Kristen Hawkes, and Alan C. Wilson
1991 African Populations and the Evolution of Human Mitochondrial DNA. *Science* 253(5027):1503–1507.
Vishnyatsky, L. B.
1994 "Running Ahead of Time" in the Development of Palaeolithic Industries. *Antiquity* 68(258):134–140.
Volman, Thomas
1984 Early Prehistory of Southern Africa. In *Southern African Prehistory and Paleoenvironments*. Richard Klein, ed. Pp. 169–220. Rotterdam: Balkema.
Wadley, Lyn
1993 The Pleistocene Later Stone Age South of the Limpopo River. *Journal of World Prehistory* 7(3):243–296.
Wadley, Lyn, D. Margaret Avery, Amelia M. B. Clark, B. S. Williamson, Carolyn R. Thorpe, P.T.N. Harper, S. Woodburne, J. C. Vogel, and Johan Binneman
1997 Excavations at Rose Cottage Cave. *South African Journal of Science* 93(10):439–482.
Wiessner, Polly
1977 Hxaro: A Regional System of Reciprocity for Reducing Risk among the !Kung San. Ph.D. dissertation, University of Michigan.
1982 Risk, Reciprocity, and Social Influence on !Kung San Economies. In *Politics and History in Band Societies*. Eleanor Leacock and Richard B. Lee, eds. Pp. 61–84. Cambridge: Cambridge University Press.
1983 Style and Social Information in Kalahari San Projectile Points. *American Antiquity* 49(2):253–276.

Willoughby, Pamela R.

1992 An Archaeological Survey of the Songwe River Valley, Lake Rukwa Basin, Southwestern Tanzania. *Nyame Akuma* 37:28–35.

1993a Culture, Environment, and the Emergence of *Homo sapiens* in East Africa. In *Culture and Environment: A Fragile Coexistence.* Ross W. Jamieson, Sylvia Abonyi, and Neil Mirau, eds. Pp. 135–143. Calgary: Chacmool Archaeological Association.

1993b The Middle Stone Age in East Africa and Modern Human Origins. *African Archaeological Review* 11:3–20.

1996a The Middle Stone Age in Southwestern Tanzania. *Kaupia/Darmstädter Beiträge zur Naturgeschichte* 6:57–69.

1996b Middle Stone Age Technology and Adaptation in Southwestern Tanzania. In *Aspects of African Archaeology.* Gilbert Pwiti and Robert Soper, eds. Pp. 171–190. Harare: University of Zimbabwe Publications.

In press Archaeologists, Palaeoanthropologists, and the People without Culture. For *The Entangled Past: Integrating History and Archaeology.* Calgary: Chacmool Archaeological Association.

Wilson, Allan C., and Rebecca L. Cann

1992 The Recent African Genesis of Humans. *Scientific American* 266(4):68–73.

Wobst, H. Martin

1977 Stylistic Behavior and Information Exchange. In *For the Director: Research Essays in Honor of James B. Griffin.* Charles E. Cleland, ed. *Anthropological Papers of the University of Michigan Museum of Anthropology* 61:317–342.

Wolpoff, Milford H.

1989 Multiregional Evolution: The Fossil Alternative to Eden. In *The Human Revolution.* Paul Mellars and Christopher Stringer, eds. Pp. 62–108. Princeton: Princeton University Press.

Yellen, John E.

1998 Barbed Bone Points: Tradition and Continuity in Saharan and Sub-Saharan Africa. *African Archaeological Review* 15(3):173–198.

Yellen, John E., Alison S. Brooks, Els Cornelissen, Michael J. Mehlman, and Kathlyn Stewart

1995 A Middle Stone Age Worked Bone Industry from Katanda, Upper Semliki Valley, Zaire. *Science* 268(5210):553–555.

Zilhão, João, and Francesco d'Errico

1999 The Chronology and Taphonomy of the Earliest Aurignacian and Its Implications for the Understanding of Neandertal Extinction. *Journal of World Prehistory* 13(1):1–68.

8

Demography, Ethnography, and Archaeolinguistic Evidence: A Study of Celtic and Germanic from Prehistory into the Early Historical Period

John Hines

Between about 1000 B.C. and A.D. 1000, much of Europe was dominated by two linguistic traditions, Celtic and Germanic. Writing the history of ese language groups is difficult, since little is known for certain. The evidence we have suggests that the linguistic map of northern and western Europe was remarkably homogeneous until early historic times, when geography began to play a detectable role in the development of greater linguistic diversity across the face of Europe. But geography alone does not explain what happened.—Editor

In the period that begins archaeologically with the Iron Age and ends in the historical Early Middle Ages, western Europe, northern Europe, and some of central Europe were dominated by two linguistic entities, the Celtic and the Germanic. Both of these linguistic groups can be associated with distinctive culture groups in the later centuries of the first millennium B.C. It is clear enough that the La Tène styles of the final centuries B.C. were the prestigious mode among most Celtic-speaking peoples in western Europe, that is, among members of a society with a social elite whose roots can reasonably be traced back into the princely burials of the preceding Hallstatt Culture (Hatt 1970:61–136; Pauli 1980, esp. 16–36; Maps 8.1 and 8.2). The earliest distribution of the Germanic language group as we know it coincides clearly and substantially with the Iron Age Jastorf Culture of northern Europe (Häßler 1991:193–199; Map 8.1). A complex of more distinctive and prestigious Germanic art styles had developed by the fifth century A.D. and was widely distributed through Europe in a process that can in very broad terms be correlated with the impact and power of

Map 8.1
Location of the La Tène and Jastorf Cultures in Europe

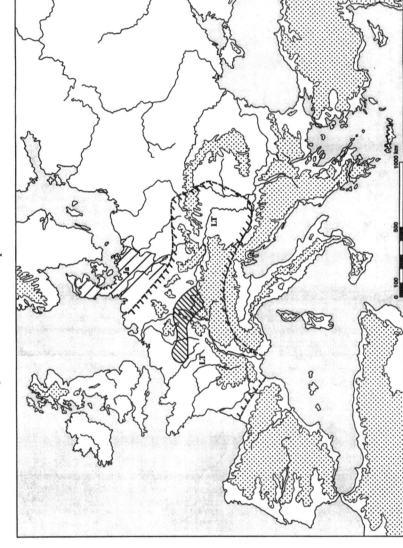

Note: LT designates area conventionally identified as the La Tène culture zone (after Powell 1980:115); the starred area is the area of origin of La Tène style. Ja designates the area conventionally identified as the Jastorf culture zone.

Germanic-speaking groups in Europe in the immediately post–Roman-period centuries, a period commonly referred to as the Germanic migration period (Haseloff 1981). In none of these cases, however, can there be any suggestion that the language group and the culture group were coterminous, nor that either of the language groups was entirely contained within the culture group with which it is associated, or vice versa.

Specific and apparently general ethnic labels for the peoples who used these distinctive cultural and linguistic varieties are found only in external, classical sources. The people associated with the Celtic–La Tène complex were referred to as Κελτοί, Γαλάτοι, Galli, and Galatae (e.g., Herodotus, Polybius, Strabo, Diodorus Siculus, Caesar, and Livy; Rankin 1987). The name Γερμάνιοι occurs, presumably coincidentally, in Herodotus (1.125), where it refers to a Persian γένος, before the terms Γερμανοί and Germani appear regularly for a mass of northern European peoples, mostly in Latin sources, from the first century B.C. onwards (e.g., Strabo, Caesar, and Livy). These ethnographic terms are never explicitly linked with references to uniform language and culture within the groups thus identified; indeed, whenever the authors go into ethnographical detail, it is usually to assert linguistic and cultural differences within these broad groups (e.g., Diodorus Siculus 5.32; Strabo 4.1.1; Caesar 1.1; Tacitus 28–46). From our point of view, then, as group identities, the terms *Celtic* and *Germanic* can have no primary meaning other than to refer to Celtic- and Germanic-speaking peoples. However, this does not exclude the possibility of there having been distinctive cultural developments within these language groups that affected, in turn, the subsequent history of the language itself. One may indeed argue that, rather than the capricious smiles and frowns of Fortune, such cultural explanations are the most satisfactory way of explaining the history of the decline of the one language group and the advance of the other within the same territory in the period under review.

Traditional philology identifies Celtic and Germanic as branches of the Indo-European (IE) family tree and reconstructs Common Celtic and Germanic stages in the evolution of this language family. Apparently distinctive similarities between these and other protolanguages of equivalent status posit an early European linguistic continuum in which Italic lies close to Celtic, Celtic, in turn, close to Germanic, and Germanic to Balto-Slavic (e.g., Meillet 1908; Dillon and Chadwick 1967:210–212; Mallory 1989:107–109). Subdivisions are then traced in Common Celtic and Germanic (as in the other protolanguages, of course). The major division in Celtic is perceived to be that between *p*- and *q*-Celtic, linguistic branches in which reconstructed Proto-Indo-European (PIE) $*k^w$ appears as *p* or *q*, respectively, a division that is particularly well represented by the Brythonic and Goidelic languages of the British Isles (i.e., within Insular Celtic). Unless a Gaulish substrate underlies Breton, all of the Continental Celtic languages, none of which have complete replacement of IE $*k^w$ by *p*, died out, probably by the middle of the first millennium A.D. Three principal branches of Germanic are postulated, West, North, and East, and while their interrelationship remains the subject of dispute, it is most commonly held that at a certain stage a unified North-West Germanic stood distinct from East Germanic (Nielsen 1989). The "eastern" group of the Germanic languages is now extinct.

Much the same types of evidence for geographical distribution are available for both of these language groups across the period of this survey. The earliest evidence is mostly in the form of personal, group, or place names recorded in classical sources, while in some cases archaic Celtic place names can still be recognized in modern forms (Rix 1954; Map 8.2). The earliest texts in both language groups are inscriptions—in Continental Celtic in a variety of scripts from the late third century B.C. onwards, and in Germanic in the runic script from the second century A.D. (Eska and Evans 1993; Odenstedt 1991). Some areas of the historical-distribution map can then be filled in by extrapolation from later sources, as, perhaps most significantly, in the case of the q-Celtic Irish language.

In the case of both language groups, there is good reason to infer certain phases of expansion of the geographical range of the language family during the period under review. The evidence of early Celtic names and inscriptions points consistently to the area of Europe west of the Rhine and northwest and southwest of the Alps, including much of Iberia and the British Isles, as a Celtic-language territory of the pre-Roman Iron Age (Rix 1954); for Herodotus, indeed, the Celts were the most westerly of the peoples of Europe in the fifth century B.C. (4.49). Diverse traditions recorded by ancient historiographers imply the invasion, conquest, and apparently the settlement, too, of parts of Britain, Iberia, and northern Italy by Celtic groups, though they do not thereby explicitly postulate the introduction of the Celtic language *de novo* in these regions (e.g., Polybius 2.17; Livy, esp. 5.33–38; Strabo 1.3.21). A scatter of apparently Celtic place names runs east across Europe, more or less along the line of the Danube toward the Black Sea and the Aegean (see Map 8.2), and further traditions record conquering Celtic groups establishing themselves as far east as Galatia in eastern Anatolia (Strabo 4.4.2; 12.5.1). Evidence for substantial linguistic expansion and change in the wake of these eastern movements is, however, very thin: the most extraordinary is St. Jerome's statement in the preface to the second book of his commentary on Paul's Epistle to the Galatians (*Patrologiae Latinae* 26, cols. 307–438, at col. 357), that at the end of the fourth century A.D. the language of the Galatians was still recognizably similar to the native language around Trier in the Rhineland.

In a valuable passage at the beginning of his well-known *Commentaries on the Gallic Wars*, Julius Caesar describes the mass migration of the presumably Celtic-speaking Helvetii (Caesar 1, esp. 2–6). This group, Caesar asserts, was in a state of virtually constant warfare with its Germanic neighbors, but, he would have us believe, migrated not under pressure from the north but because the situation of their territory offered them too little scope for warfare and plunder. Our distribution map of the Continental Celtic languages suggests that the Celtic language may to some extent have yielded territory to Germanic around the

Map 8.2
Place Names of Celtic Character in Europe and Anatolia

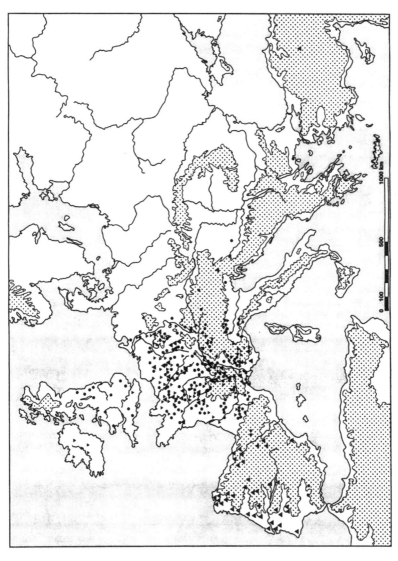

Note: Only securely located examples are shown. Circles indicate names in -*dūnum*; larger standing triangles, names in -*briga*; smaller pendant triangles, names in -*magus*.

Source: After Rix (1954).

Rhineland, in Belgium, and in southern Germany, but Continental Celtic seems mostly to have given way to Romance (Vulgar Latin) languages within the Roman Empire rather than to Germanic. A period of extensive conquests and colonization by Germanic peoples coincided with the collapse of the empire between the fourth and sixth centuries A.D. With varying success, Germanic kingdoms were established in Iberia, Gaul, Italy, and Britain, but only in the latter case, in what became England, do we know that a territorially large-scale and effectively permanent language shift was the result. A smaller-scale but essentially similar change may have been the establishment of the Breton-speaking community by refugees from Britain at this time. We can thus see that there were linguistic consequences of population movement, but in most cases it is impossible for us to be sure how deep or thorough such effects of immigration were, and for how long they lasted. In the case of the Germanic and Celtic language groups, large-scale territorial language shift as a result of migration seems to have been exceptional.

The history, real and reconstructed, of relationships between varieties within the Celtic and Germanic language groups is of special interest and significance in the present context. Inevitably, the real evidence for the situation in the earlier phases is far less adequate than one would wish. In the case of Celtic, the earliest evidence comes from the Continent. The general tenor of early Celtic philology has been to assume that there was prehistoric dialectal variance within Continental Celtic and to try to identify it—attempts that, as D. Ellis Evans has it, have been "hardly conclusive" (1979:536). As a corollary to this supposition, one can ask whether, conversely, a high level of Continental Celtic homogeneity is thereby implied. The quality of the evidence is hardly any more conclusive in support of this proposition either, although consideration of the question makes some interesting points.

For practical reasons, sound changes have always commanded the lion's share of attention in comparative historical linguistics and philological reconstruction. Phonologically, the major cleft attributable to an early stage of Celtic is that between q and p as the reflexes of IE $*k^w$. As noted earlier, the q-form is consistently retained only in the Gaelic languages, while the innovation $p < *k^w$ is general in Brythonic and predominant in the other branches of Continental Celtic (i.e., Gaulish, Hispano-Celtic, and Lepontic). The distribution of this opposition in Insular Celtic coincides with that of em/en versus am/an as the reflexes of the IE syllabic nasals $m̥$ and $n̥$, but, contrary to authoritative views that this too represents an ancient cleft among the Celtic languages, it seems simply to be the result of a later raising of the vowel in am/an in Irish (McCone 1996:50–51). The q/p opposition is largely allophonic rather than phonemic, and altogether these phonological differences hardly amount to a sharp linguistic distinction. A further dialectal difference of effectively the same level of magnitude is apparently the development of dental affricates from dental clusters in Gaulish (the so-called *tau gallicum*) (Schmoll 1959; Lewis and Pedersen 1961;

Bachellery 1972:40–49; Evans 1979; Eska and Evans 1993; McCone 1996; Villar 1997).

Morphological differences may have been more pervasive, although here the paucity and uncertainty of surviving records put substantial limitations on reconstruction. Nothing useful can be said about verbal paradigms, for instance. Hispano-Celtic appears to have had several peculiar noun inflections, either unusually archaic forms or unexpected innovations (Schmoll 1959; Bachellery 1972:49–52). In Insular Celtic, the q/p division is substantially reinforced by the disappearance of all noun case distinctions in the prehistoric period in Brythonic, while a system of five cases survives in Gaelic to the present day. The quantity of data is, of course, far too small for serious lexical comparisons. In respect of syntax, however, it has been inferred that subject-object-verb (SOV) and subject-verb-object (SVO) orders predominate in Continental Celtic, in contrast to the V-initial basic pattern of later Insular Celtic; again, a preference for SOV distinguishes the apparently more conservative Hispano-Celtic (Eska and Evans 1993).

Distributionally and philologically, it appears that the q/p split in Celtic was a primary one, with the q-Celtic-speaking group either making its way to or surviving in the western margins of Europe, in particular in Ireland (Schmidt 1993; cf. McCone 1996:67–68). The most plausible scenario is that the p-form arose as an innovation in either Continental or Brythonic Celtic and spread like a wave through that language group, stopping short of Ireland and not, indeed, appearing as a complete change in Gaulish and Hispano-Celtic. From both archaeological and historical evidence it is quite clear that Brythonic would have been open to influence from Continental Celtic (and vice versa) for most of the Iron Age, especially in the final centuries B.C., and could indeed have been affected by colonization from the Continent. In interpreting sound change and the division it created, however, we should note that the clearly parallel change of IE $*g^w > b$ is regular throughout Celtic (and also in Greek), and that $*k^w > p$ can be found in neighboring language groups too, for example, in Latin *lupus* ($< *ulpus$) and Gothic *wulfs* (cf. Lithuanian *vilkas*, Polish/Russian *wilk*/ВОЛК, and Greek λύκος; Bammesberger 1984:72). Assuming that p did emerge from $*k^w$ as a diachronic sound change, it is no doubt possible for the shift to have occurred independently in more than one language variety. The fact that it is found so widely in what are independently identified as closely related areas of a linguistic continuum could be explained by the mutual inheritance of some suprasegmental features that governed the change. Some special explanation, however, would then appear to be needed for the selective and coherent geographical range within which this change actually took place. To whatever chronological stratum we choose to assign the shared features, the result is a widespread *Sprachbund* in respect of the distribution of instances of the $p <$ $*k^w$ form.

A unitary linguistic situation is more strikingly in evidence in the best reconstruction we can make of the Germanic language group in its earliest stages. A written version of the East Germanic Gothic language is known from fourth-century Bible translations, and this testifies to a few distinctive phonological developments from what is postulated as Common Germanic, namely, the raising of the vowels *e, *o, and *ē and minor consonantal modifications, none of them unique to Gothic (Wright 1954, esp. 26–39 and 70–83). Otherwise, the majority of the relevant early evidence that we have is from southern Scandinavia, an area that is the eventual homeland of the North Germanic branch, but that up to the sixth century A.D. appears to have been a strikingly conservative area linguistically, preserving the Common Germanic phonological and morphological system almost intact. Frustratingly, none of the runic inscriptions datable from the second to the sixth centuries A.D. from here gives us clear evidence of the phonological situation in relation to the earliest sound changes we would expect in this area. Meanwhile, however, innovations appear to have been gathering pace in the West Germanic area, especially as a distinctive English language developed after the introduction of Germanic language and culture to lowland Britain in the fifth and earlier sixth centuries (Hines 1995). Along the North Sea continental littoral, the Frisian dialect followed suit, sharing in several of the innovations found in English and apparently maintaining a North-West Germanic continuum by adjusting to an intermediary place between its western neighbor (Old English) and its eastern (Old Saxon). From the late sixth and seventh centuries onwards, attestable innovations gathered pace in North Germanic.

Any attempt to write a summary review of linguistic history like this is unsatisfactory, not because the points made are inaccurate or unjustified, but because so little can be known for certain, and the general picture has to be based on tiny scraps of evidence, the careful individual recognition and evaluation of which cannot be included within a survey of this kind. It can nonetheless be stated that not only our comparative philological reconstructions but also our small store of empirical evidence point to an unusually homogeneous linguistic map of late Iron Age northern and western Europe—compared, for instance, with practically every other regional case study discussed in this volume—and indicate that linguistic branching and divergence become observable here as a persistent phenomenon only in historical circumstances. Thus Brythonic yields modern Welsh, Cornish, and Breton; Goidelic yields Irish, Scots Gaelic, and (somehow) Manx; West Germanic yields English, Frisian, and Low and High German, the first and last of which appear in many dialects; North Germanic yields Icelandic, Faroese, and in mainland Scandinavia what is essentially a diversified dialect continuum hidden beneath, though of course now influenced by, the standardized national languages Danish, Norwegian, and Swedish. It is quite clear that geographical separation must have been a significant factor in these divergent courses of development. Thus Brythonic in Wales, Cornwall, and Brittany became separated by stretches of sea in the same way, probably, as the Celtic of Ireland was cut off from the innovations of Continental and

Brythonic Celtic. West Germanic diversified as it expanded into Britain and was probably reintroduced into Frisia.[1] The deepest split in North Germanic is the one that developed between the Atlantic islands of Iceland, the Faroes, and probably the now-extinct Orkney and Shetland Norn, and the Scandinavian mainland.

Substantial problems arise, however, if one invokes separation alone as the explanation—rather than just the context—of linguistic divergence. To begin with, we have been required to postulate a high degree of linguistic similarity, including innovations shared over large geographical ranges, and indeed across seaways, particularly within the Celtic language group in the preceding pre- and protohistorical epochs. In the case of North-West Germanic, developments in English and Frisian point at the very least to the maintenance of a continuum, and more likely to its re-creation, after the old, notionally unitary phase of West Germanic had been broken; yet divergence within these language groups continued through the Middle Ages while and despite the fact that the level of contact around the North Sea, as reflected in both archaeological and historical evidence, increased. In these circumstances, then, contact and linguistic convergence appear to have been in inverse proportion. As a possible explanation of this curious situation, I have suggested (Hines 1995) that in the earlier cultural circumstances, contact may have tended to lead to linguistic convergence, while the later divergence of the Germanic languages can be correlated with its known historical context, in particular with the (slow) emergence and definition of national groups and states, which demonstrably included political attempts to appropriate the power of a sense of ethnic unity and the ability of both language and material culture to symbolize that identity—the net result of which was a form of "nationalization" of language and the deliberate cultivation of linguistic boundaries.

Although, as shown by the dominant tenor of Celtic philology noted earlier, comparative historical linguistics gives preferential attention to differential sound changes and branching, *Sprachbunde* are familiar phenomena that are known from many historical, geographical, and cultural contexts. A pertinent and valid question to consider is whether convergent tendencies may not have been especially strong in the context of the European Iron Age, quite contrary to the implications of the family-tree model. Such a situation would certainly fit nicely with the observable and inferable similarities among languages in Europe of this horizon, where the "common" protolanguage stage often lies in or just behind the threshold of recorded history. Of course, we can have no real idea of how representative our factual evidence is, and thus of how similar varieties of spoken language actually were over wide areas of Europe between approximately 1000 B.C. and A.D. 500. There were linguistic differences, which, indeed, our ancient authorities are sometimes at pains to emphasize (e.g., Diodorus Siculus 5.32; Caesar 1.1). The crucial point is the apparent ability of common linguistic forms to be maintained and of innovations to spread over a wide range so as, cumulatively, to produce the high levels of linguistic similarity over large areas in late pre- and protohistorical Europe postulated by comparative philology and supported by the little empirical evidence we have.

Culturally and socially, a profoundly assimilatory situation of this kind has a number of significant historical sociolinguistic implications. One of the primary functions of language—perhaps *the* primary function—is communication. In cultural circumstances in which the pragmatic communicative function of language is dominant, the maintenance of a high level of linguistic similarity is easy to understand. Whether this function alone could explain the levels of regularity apparently found over such wide areas in Iron Age Europe is open to question. For a more satisfactory historical model, we undoubtedly need to consider the symbolic, identificatory function of language too.

The linkage of language and identity is too often and too readily conceived of in basically contrastive terms—as gang A, for instance, asserts its internal solidarity and its difference from its social context by using its own peculiar argot. In many cultural circumstances, especially those with a stable but largely subsistence-level economy, the critical option for group/ethnic identity is not which out of a series of alternative groups one belongs to (*a, b,* or *c,* and so on), but whether or not one is within and acts in harmony with the only available group. Like other common features of material culture such as building styles, domestic pottery types, and so on—features that may not be ostentatiously symbolic but that are nevertheless regularized—language is a medium of expression that can unite and define the social community. Unless, then, there are particular circumstances in which cultural differentiation serves a purpose, the dominant trend should be assimilatory as far as not only language but also other cultural media are concerned. Even when cultural differentiation does have a functional role to play, such demands may be satisfied by any one or any combination of the media of cultural expression, and not all such media need be employed as special symbolic modes.

Our historical perception also requires us to build into our reconstruction the possible dissemination of prestigious cultural forms—material and linguistic— by a dominant social group. This phenomenon has already been noted as a likely factor in the diffusion of "Celtic" features across eastern Europe and can reciprocally be observed in the adoption of Hellenistic modes by the "Celtic" community in Galatia. Yet at the same time as we recognize the potential importance of social relations of this kind in the diffusion of cultural norms, we must also acknowledge the fact that a social elite cannot always monopolize or retain perfect control over what may have arisen as its own distinctive features, and that these can be appropriated by the population at large (cf. Sahlins and Service 1960:87–92; Miller 1982). This is a useful principle, for it provides a basis upon which new cultural norms can both be dispersed rapidly and generalized throughout the population over a wide geographical range.

It would thus in theory be possible for the unity of, say, "Common Germanic" to have been recently achieved in the early centuries A.D., rather than being an inheritance from time immemorial, just as it remains possible that many of the shared features of the *p*-Celtic language varieties were of recent origins in the late centuries B.C. As far as the general hypothesis is concerned, the essential process or cultural-linguistic mechanism is the same whether the time scale is very long, very short, or something in between. In this case, indeed, the time scale must explicitly be categorized as unknowable, precisely because we are here at the distant fringe of the protohistorical threshold between prehistory, where we are totally dependent upon reconstructions, and the historical period, with its observable linguistic data.

In sum, a comparison of the historical linguistic evidence with what we can infer with varying degrees of confidence for the protohistorical and prehistoric stages of the languages concerned implies that in Iron Age northern and western Europe, a strong link between language variety and a conscious identity, and in consequence the cultivation of linguistic distinctiveness to express a special group attachment, was an innovation that arose with the Germanic language group. Whether this was in direct imitation of Roman culture or not does not concern us here. If the process is correctly identified, it got under way at the same time that Germanic political units were being substantially re-formed into major confederacies (e.g., the Goths, Franks, Saxons, Danes, and Langobards) that functioned as aggressive military entities around the time of the fall of the Roman Empire and throughout the migration period.

This implies, in turn, an especially demotic view of linguistic development in the earlier Iron Age in western and northern Europe. In this view, language in the Celtic and Germanic areas can be regarded as having been a property of the people as a whole and thus in a real sense shared between them wherever they belonged within wide areas, in a way significantly similar to that in which they shared their biological needs and naturally governed habits and many common aspects of basic material culture. The distinctive assertion of a special ethnic identity is itself a special cultural development that, it is hereby argued, became more widespread as either an imposed or a developed property of general culture as the first millennium A.D. progressed.

Of course, the objection can be made that this is groundless speculation because, as has repeatedly been noted, we can really know very little about the linguistic situation in the last few centuries B.C. and the early centuries A.D. across most of western and northern Europe. Actually, this is not that significant a problem. The crucial point is that very little of the linguistic variety of modern Europe can be explained on the basis of prehistoric linguistic difference—only, in fact, the difference between the great language families. If the late prehistoric "homogeneity" we have accepted as the implication of reliable comparative linguistic reconstruction in the protohistoric field is real, we are justified in proposing an explanation in the demotic terms just outlined. If it is an illusion, we have to explain how its appearance was achieved, and then to find a place either for the rapid (and invisible) convergence of the postulated earlier linguistic varieties in the first millennium A.D. or for the equally invisible extinction of these postulated varieties in a phase of extraordinary and comprehensive language shift. In other words, the essence of the assimilatory model must stand in any case; only the time scale can vary.

Even in the Germanic world, however, this does not imply that the connection between group formation and material-cultural symbolism was direct, simple, and ubiquitous, nor does it imply any connections between either of these phenomena and linguistic differentiation. Indeed, careful analysis of the probable chronology of developments delivers to us one sequence of group formation as represented in historical records; a different chorological and chronological sequence in the development and expansion of material-cultural symbolism of group identity; and yet another order for the adoption of language as a mode of expression for the same basic purpose. Nor is the harnessing of potentially symbolic cultural media to the process of identification essentially Germanic in any way; within the range of this case study, it was a phenomenon that apparently was first adopted within the Germanic-speaking area and then spread not only through that area but also into other language groups.

The history of literacy within the Germanic language group seems to reflect this enculturation of language in a very clear way. The Germanic languages as a family stand in an exceptional place in the history of vernacular literacy in the early Middle Ages, rivaled only (interestingly) by Irish. According to Anglo-Saxon historical records, the English language was used for a written law code as early as around A.D. 600, while vernacular religious poetry and other religious texts were appearing in both Germany and England before the end of the seventh century, and more substantial corpora of written ethical poetry—religious and heroic—can be traced back to at least the eighth century (Godden and Lapidge 1991; Bostock 1974). In addition to what can be inferred for Anglo-Saxon England (Hines 1995), aspects of a persistent, joint vernacular Latin *Sprachpolitik* can be traced in the acts of Merovingian and Carolingian kings and emperors on the Continent. The most substantial surviving vernacular product of this is the corpus of Old Saxon religious poetry of the ninth century (see Doane 1991).

It is possible to identify a range of points of significant contrast in culture within the Celtic language area. Many of the older, simple generalizations about Celtic society are rightly challenged now (see Arnold and Gibson 1995), but we can still be confident that socially and economically, pre-Roman Celtic-speaking Europe was not very different from late Iron Age Germanic-speaking Europe (cf. Strabo 4.4.2, where the ancient geographer emphasizes the similarity of the two groups). Very broadly, these areas were occupied by what are conventionally referred to as chiefdom societies, within which the kin group was a major social entity, but with an important "heroic" warrior aristocracy attached to the chieftain (see Earle 1991, esp. 1–118). Larger-scale confederations that resemble embryonic states seem intermittently to have formed but never to have proved durable before the late Roman period. Economic surpluses, in the form of production or manpower, allowed the elite, in particular, to engage in some long-distance trade in materially or prestigiously valuable goods. Distinct peoples (often referred to in the literature as "tribes") were recognized and were strongly associated with particular territories. Politically, however, it is striking how widely Celtic-speaking groups appear to have adhered to a system of division of power and a habitual resistance to centralization. Thus in early Ireland, we see a plethora of tiny kingdoms, and there appear to have been succession rules that militated against and at least delayed the onset of a single, "permanent" monarchical line (Charles-Edwards 1993:89–111). Historical evidence for ancient Galatia (Strabo 12.5.1) and early medieval Wales and Brittany (Davies 1990:44–155; Galliou and Jones 1991:148–74), reveals that even these small Celtic territories were divided into segments and only rarely, if ever, truly unified under single political authority. Romantic notions of an innate Celtic "love of freedom" may thus contain just a smidgen of reality in respect of an ancient tradition of social stability maintained through divisive and (in relative terms) meritocratic and egalitarian political structures. This, perhaps, is what Caesar recognized in his insistence upon the "factionalism" of the Gallic Celts (Caesar 6.11). In such circumstances, the existence of superordinate Celtic institutions such as that of the druidic priesthood in Gaul is particularly intriguing (Caesar 6.13).

It is eventually possible to trace the growing crystallization of a sense of integrated political and ethnic identity within Celtic-speaking populations under intense pressure from expanding Germanic groups in the Middle Ages, that is, the English and the Franks, and later the Vikings and the Normans (though see Patterson 1995 for a strong argument of the case that internal change was a factor too). Once again, even a summary comparison of early vernacular textual culture in England, Wales, and Ireland may provide us with a valuable insight into the place of language in these developments. It is, for instance, tempting to suggest that the appearance of vernacular "institutional" texts such as laws and religious poetry in Irish from approximately the same dates as those in Old English is essentially related to the marked and persistent Irish difference within the Celtic world (Williams 1958). Meanwhile, one can, in this light, attribute even greater significance to the limited status of the Welsh language as a literary medium before the ninth or tenth centuries than Thomas Charles-Edwards has in his discussion of the topic (1995). It is not until these dates that religious lyrics and written law are known in Welsh, despite the fact that a tradition of Welsh vernacular heroic literature and panegyric has a history traceable back to the early seventh century.

Elsewhere (Hines 1996), I have attempted to summarize both the reasons why attempts should be made to integrate linguistic, historical, and archaeological evidence in order to further our understanding of the human past and present, and the problems facing any such endeavor. I used the term "archaeolinguistics" to designate this area of inquiry. It was chosen to signal the desirability of a genuine merger of the study of the separable topics of language, culture, and history in both theoretical and empirical terms, while I also argued that this branch of study should concern itself with historical contexts as well as prehistory. This was to stand in contrast to the usual conjunction of archaeology and historical linguistics only in respect of linguistic prehistory, which is overwhelmingly concerned with the exploration of possible scenarios of linguistic, cultural, and demographic diffusion based on comparative linguistic reconstruction, genetic maps, and the archaeological record.

In practice, the interpretation of the past in relation to linguistic history and prehistory has also been deeply affected by the role assigned to language in more recent times. Modern scholarship tends to construct the past in the same way as modern people construct a role and meaning for their languages. It is not implied that such constructions are intrinsically or necessarily false in their entirety. Indeed, the unmasking and criticism of such subjective interpretations is so familiar at present that the reciprocal point—the extent to which our intellectual present has in fact been constructed and is constrained by the facts of even the deep past—merits special emphasis in turn. From the case study examined in this chapter, however, it can be argued that a scrutiny of the past of which we are the direct linguistic and cultural heirs delivers a clear warning to us against being tempted to believe that we can know further than we can see, despite the reconstructability of ancestral grammatical systems.

The range and variety of the whole field may be represented by identifying six "stages" within it, stages that differ in their real or notional chronological position and in the nature of their evidence and the philosophical questions that this reasonably poses. The value of this descriptive scheme lies in making clear the differences between the stages, and with that, the different possibilities for culture-historical understanding that each one offers. In some cases, one can argue that the understanding of one stage can be enhanced from the perspective of another, but it cannot be suggested that the same things can or should be done with archaeology and language in every context.

The six stages of archaeolinguistics are outlined in the article referred to earlier (Hines 1996) and will be summarized very briefly here (Table 8.1). A point of particular interest in the present context is the way in which scholarly perception of the identificatory properties of language changes silently but radically as we move across the range. In the lowest stages, interpretation is predominantly demographic. The reconstructed prehistory of language is discussed in terms of the evolution and geographical spread of biologically modern humans (cf. Willoughby, this volume). By the prehistoric stage, this has given way to the association of linguistic distribution with cultural complexes, either in a very broad way, in terms, for instance, of Neolithic agriculturalism, or in narrower terms of particular cultures defined by symbolic features such as the Beaker or Kurgan cultures (Mallory 1989, esp. 164–185). By the protohistoric stage, the terms are predominantly ethnolinguistic—Greeks, Celts, Slavs, Balts, Germani, and so on—and the scope for misalignment between cultural habits on the one hand and linguistic affinity and ethnic identity on the other is widely emphasized (e.g., Renfrew 1987:2–3, 24, 211–249; Trigger 1989:161–163; Shennan 1989). In the historical and contemporary stages, political and socioeco-

Table 8.1
The Six Stages of Archaeolinguistics: A Descriptive Summary

Stage	Linguistic data	Current principal linguistic foci	Current interpretive range
CONTEMPORARY	Corpora. Infinitely expandable.	Dialectal, sociolectal, and idiolectal variation. Language contact, shift, and interference.	Sociology (sociolinguistics): class, gender, cultural, or ethnic group links.
HISTORICAL	Literary and documentary corpora. Some sound recordings/phonetic transcripts. Copious.	Language definition and change (normally in autonomous terms); standardization. Dialectal variation. Language contact and expansion; pidginization and creolization.	Socioeconomic dominance of nations or social groups. Long-distance trade and colonization. Language politics.
PROTOHISTORICAL	Sparse inscriptions or records in other languages. Mostly reconstructed. Linguistically, chronologically, and geographically reliable.	Reconstruction of parent languages; linguistic genealogy.	Correlation with culture and ethnic groups (often not differentiated).
PREHISTORIC	Totally reconstructed. Grammatically substantial. Chronology and geography uncertain.	Grammatical reconstruction of proto-languages in phonological, morphological, and lexical terms.	Correlation with cultural and demographic prehistory.
MACROPHYLA	Constructed from reconstructions. Grammatically sparse; linguistic coincidences may be statistically insignificant.	Reconstruction of proto-forms in phonological and lexical terms.	Correlation with demographic prehistory.
GENESIS		Reconstruction of original lexemes.	Correlation with evolution and dispersal of *Homo sapiens sapiens*.

nomic groupings claim virtually all attention. Analyses are made of the linguistic consequences of historical invasions and colonization, the development of worldwide trading contacts, and the forced migration of slaves. Modern sociolinguistics is focused largely on fine-scale differences within society, and it is difficult to discern any serious interest in, for instance, the sociolinguistics of middle-class speakers of a standardized language.[2]

All of this could, of course, be explained as the simple and necessary change of focus and perspective as the scope for detailed analysis and interpretation is lost as we move further into the past. But this defense comes very close to making explicit an assumption about the consistency and simplicity of the identificatory properties of language throughout history and prehistory that would be hard to maintain in any simple form if it were debated as a matter of principle. It remains clear just how selective interpretational approaches to language in history or prehistory can be. The real danger lurking in the selective focus in any one stage is not so much that it denies the possibility of the excluded factors having played any role in that context as that it implies that they are effectively insignificant there. This standpoint is quite untenable in respect to the highly significant phase of European linguistic development reviewed in the case study here.

The case study of the Celtic- and Germanic-speaking groups in the period from around 1000 B.C. to A.D. 1000 has necessarily maintained a clear view of the increasingly hypothetical character of the linguistic situation and its contexts as we move away from historical ancient and medieval Europe through the proto-and telehistorical fringes into the realms of prehistory that are only tentatively illuminated by archaeology and comparative linguistic reconstruction and extrapolation. The perspective adopted in this case study was quite strictly "protohistorical" in the sense that it accepted standard comparative philology as a valid basis for discussion, at least in respect of the near, protohistorical phase. This perspective implies that there were strong assimilatory tendencies and extensive *Sprachbunde* within the Celtic and Germanic linguistic areas up to and within this horizon. In the early historical period, there was then a marked shift toward divergence.

The most awkward problem that the model of early assimilation apparently faces emerges when we place it within the broader context of archaeolinguistics. We need to reconcile this proposition with the fact of the differentiation of families—a term I prefer to "branching"—within the Indo-European group of the prehistoric stage. In fact, even if all of the Indo-European language groups of Europe (e.g., Baltic, Celtic, Germanic, Greek, Romance, Slavonic) did derive historically from what was once a single, uniform parent language, Proto-Indo-European, there is no insurmountable incompatibility of process. Over such a large geographical area we could only expect a continuum of linguistic variation, not uniformity, and it would not be surprising if more distinctive varieties within the "family" were able to crystallize around foci that were able to rise to positions of eminence and influence such as we know very well have existed in Europe since Neolithic times (cf. the druidical system in late pre-Roman Gaul, referred to earlier).

While we have been careful here to talk about cultural norms "within" the Germanic and Celtic culture groups rather than presuming that the cultural and linguistic groups are coterminous, the evidence reviewed here implies that cultural traditions and language groups did coincide to a significant extent. It appears likely, therefore, that cultural norms—particularly social ideals that were crucial in governing both the history of language in medieval and modern Europe and the popular and intellectual perception of language at the same time—were essentially disseminated within the distinct linguistic groups, thus catalyzing the growing together of language, culture, and identity.

In our protohistorical case study, we have identified a situation in which reconstructed linguistic history has essentially demographic implications at a highly significant level, referred to earlier as the "demotic" view of linguistic development in the earlier Iron Age. At the same time, some significant connections between linguistic variety and culture group can be detected, from which the transition to linguistic history strongly constrained by ethnopolitical factors appears a simple, though not an inevitable, one. There appears in fact to be no reason, either theoretical or empirical, why variation between these factors should follow a regular life cycle; the dominance of one rather than the other should, however, be explicable in terms of the axiom that linguistic history is part of general cultural history. Thus within the protohistorical phase—the linguistic evidence for which we must either accept as reliable or condemn all reconstructions of even earlier stages as idle dreams—we find the same range of variability in the people-culture-language relationship that conventional archaeology and language separate and disperse across a complete evolutionary scheme.

The past has seen profound variability in the pragmatic and symbolic employment of language. People in the past were able to treat and develop language in many different and even superficially contradictory ways, precisely because language is a cultural variable. One can therefore have little confidence in the reality of models built upon mere coincidences between cultural features and linguistic distributions for phases in which, linguistically, we cannot actually see what was happening.

NOTES

1. The demographic history of Frisia from the later Roman period into the early Middle Ages has long been obscure. The latest archaeological interpretation, however (Heidinga 1999; Gerrets 1999), posits the virtual abandonment of the area by about the fourth century A.D., followed by repopulation in the fifth and sixth centuries. This is an attractive though radical hypothesis that certainly helps to make sense of the whole culture-historical record in this area.

2. A perfect illustration of this point arrived just as I was completing this chapter. In the first circular for the 4th International Conference of the European Society for the Study of English at Debrecen, Hungary, September 1997, a seminar entitled "Discovering Historical Sociolinguistics" was advertised. The abstract for the session begins: "The seminar explores new ways of understanding the history of the English language by combining modern sociolinguistic approaches and research into social history. An entirely new perspective can be put on long-term variation and change in English when these processes are approached in terms of their social embedding, including social stratification and mobility, gender and the family" (*European English Messenger* 5[2] [1996]:71).

REFERENCES

Arnold, Bettina, and D. Blair Gibson, eds.
1995 *Celtic Chiefdom, Celtic State.* Cambridge: Cambridge University Press.
Bachellery, Édouard
1972 Le Celtique Continental. *Études Celtiques* 13:29–60.
Ball, Martin J., and James Fife, eds.
1993 *The Celtic Languages.* London: Routledge.
Bammesberger, Alfred
1984 *Lateinische Sprachwissenschaft.* Regensburg: Pustet.
Bostock, J. K.
1974 *A Handbook on Old High German Literature.* 2nd ed., rev. K. C. King and D. R. McLintock. Oxford: Clarendon Press.
Caesar, Julius
1986 *The Gallic War.* H. J. Edwards, ed. and trans. London: Heinemann.
Charles-Edwards, Thomas
1993 *Early Irish and Welsh Kinship.* Oxford: Clarendon Press.
1995 Language and Society amongst the Insular Celts, AD 400–1000. In *The Celtic World.* Miranda Green, ed. Pp. 703–736. London: Routledge.
Davies, John
1990 *Hanes Cymru.* London: Allen Lane. Published in English as *A History of Wales.* 1993. London: Allen Lane.
Dillon, Myles, and Nora K. Chadwick
1967 *The Celtic Realms.* London: Weidenfeld and Nicolson.
Diodorus Siculus
1933–1967 *Diodorus of Sicily.* 12 vols. Various eds. and trans. London: Heinemann.
Doane, Alger
1991 *The Saxon Genesis.* Madison: University of Wisconsin Press.
Earle, Timothy, ed.
1991 *Chiefdoms: Power, Economy, and Ideology.* Cambridge: Cambridge University Press.
Eska, Joseph F., and D. Ellis Evans
1993 Continental Celtic. In Ball and Fife 1993:26–63.
Evans, D. Ellis
1979 The Labyrinth of Continental Celtic. *Proceedings of the British Academy* 65:497–538.
Galliou, Patrick, and Michael Jones
1991 *The Bretons.* Oxford: Blackwell.
Gerrets, Danny
1999 Evidence of Political Centralization in Westergo: The Excavations at Wijnaldum in a (Supra-)regional Perspective. *Anglo-Saxon Studies in Archaeology and History* 10:119–26.
Godden, Malcolm, and Michael Lapidge, eds.
1991 *The Cambridge Companion to Old English Literature.* Cambridge: Cambridge University Press.
Haseloff, Günther
1981 *Die germanische Tierornamentik der Völkerwanderungszeit.* Berlin: De Gruyter.

Häßler, Hans-Jürgen, ed.
1991 *Ur- und Frühgeschichte in Niedersachsen*. Stuttgart: Theiss.

Hatt, Jean-Jacques
1970 *Celts and Gallo-Romans*. James Hogarth, trans. London: Barrie and Jenkins.

Heidinga, Anthonie
1999 The Frisian Achievement in the First Millennium AD. *Anglo-Saxon Studies in Archaeology and History* 10:11–16.

Herodotus
1920–1924 *Herodotus*. A. D. Godley, ed. and trans. 4 vols. London: Heinemann.

Hines, John
1995 Focus and Boundary in Linguistic Varieties in the Late North-West Germanic Continuum. In *Friesische Studien II*. V. F. Faltings, A.G.H. Walker, and O. Wilts, eds. Pp. 35–62. Odense: Odense University Press.
1996 Language and Culture in an Archaeological Perspective. *Archaeologia Polona* 34: 183–197.

Lewis, Henry, and Holger Pedersen
1961 *A Concise Comparative Celtic Grammar*. 3rd ed. Göttingen: Vandenhoeck und Ruprecht.

Livy
1922–1959 *Livy*. 14 vols. Various eds. and trans. London: Heinemann.

Mallory, James P.
1989 *In Search of the Indo-Europeans*. London: Thames and Hudson.

McCone, Kim
1996 *Towards a Relative Chronology of Ancient and Medieval Celtic Sound Change*. Maynooth: Depart of Old and Middle Irish, St. Patrick's College.

Meillet, Antoine
1908 *Les dialectes indo-européens*. Paris: Société de Linguistique de Paris. Published in English as *The Indo-European Dialects*. Tuscaloosa: University of Alabama Press, 1967.

Miller, Daniel
1982 Structures and Strategies: An Aspect of the Relationship between Social Hierarchy and Cultural Change. In *Symbolic and Structural Archaeology*. I. Hodder, ed. Pp. 89–98. Cambridge: Cambridge University Press.

Nielsen, Hans Frede
1989 *The Germanic Languages: Origins and Early Dialectal Interrelations*. Tuscaloosa: University of Alabama Press.

Odenstedt, Bengt
1991 *On the Origin and Early History of the Runic Script*. Stockholm: Almqvist and Wiksell.

Patterson, Nerys Thomas
1995 Clans Are Not Primordial: Pre-Viking Irish Society and the Modelling of Pre-Roman Societies in Northern Europe. In Arnold and Gibson 1995:129–136.

Pauli, Ludwig, ed.
1980 *Die Kelten in Mitteleuropa: Kultur, Kunst, Wirtschaft*. Salzburg: Amt der Salzburger Landesregierung.

Polybius
1922–1927 *The Histories*. W. R. Paton, ed. and trans. London: Heinemann.

Powell, Thomas G. E.
1980 *The Celts*. 2nd ed. London: Thames and Hudson.
Rankin, Herbert D.
1987 *Celts and the Classical World*. London: Routledge.
Renfrew, Colin
1987 *Archaeology and Language: The Puzzle of Indo-European Origins*. London: Cape.
Rix, Helmut
1954 Zur Verbreitung und Chronologie einiger keltischer Ortsnamentypen. In *Festschrift für Peter Goessler*. Pp. 99–107. Stuttgart: Kohlhammer.
Sahlins, Marshall D., and Elman R. Service, eds.
1960 *Evolution and Culture*. Ann Arbor: University of Michigan Press.
Schmidt, Karl Horst
1993 Insular Celtic: p and q Celtic. In Ball and Fife 1993:64–99.
Schmoll, Ulrich
1959 *Die Sprachen der vorkeltischen Indogermanen Hispaniens und das Keltiberische*. Wiesbaden: Harrassowitz.
Shennan, Stephen J.
1989 Introduction: Archaeological Approaches to Cultural Identity. In *Archaeological Approaches to Cultural Identity*. Stephen J. Shennan, ed. Pp. 1–32. London: Unwin Hyman.
Strabo
1917–1932 *The Geography of Strabo*. 8 vols. H. L. Jones, ed. and trans. London: Heinemann.
Tacitus
1920 *Germania*. M. Hutton, ed. and trans. In *Tacitus: Dialogus, Agricola, Germania*. London: Heinemann.
Trigger, Bruce G.
1989 *A History of Archaeological Thought*. Cambridge: Cambridge University Press.
Villar, Francisco
1997 The Celtiberian Language. *Zeitschrift für celtische Philologie* 49–50:898–949.
Williams, John Ellis Caerwyn
1958 *Traddodiad Llenyddol Iwerddon*. Published in English as *The Irish Literary Tradition*. P. K. Ford, trans. Cardiff: University of Wales Press, 1992.
Wright, Joseph
1954 *Grammar of the Gothic Language*. 2nd ed. Oxford: Clarendon Press.

9

Contexts of Change in Holocene Britain: Genes, Language, and Archaeology

Martin Paul Evison

> While there is little reason to think that the associations between the bio-
> logical, cultural, and linguistic traits that people embody are entirely ran-
> dom, there is also no reason to believe that people always transmit their
> distinguishing traits to the next generation as a fixed set of predetermined
> characteristics. How likely they are to do so depends on history, and the
> British archaeological record reveals how fortuitous our ethnic characteris-
> tics can be.—Editor

I write here in the belief that humans are not disembodied: that the dimensions
of biology, language, culture, and mind do not exist in complete independence.
Conversely, as Franz Boas indicated more than half a century ago (Boas 1940),
genetic, linguistic, and cultural patterns cannot be "equated" with coidentifying
groups of people (ethnic groups). Rather, these dimensions exist, and presumably existed in the past, in complex and contingent interrelationships that de-
mand explanation by anthropologists.

I would like to consider the Holocene history of Britain in the light of these
assumptions, beginning with the Early Mesolithic, which followed the onset of
the present interglacial period; the Late Mesolithic, incorporating the transitions
to agriculture; and the Early Medieval period, which, occurring several millennia
later in time, provides relatively detailed evidence of ethnic change occurring
regionally in Britain at that time. This experimental analysis is inevitably selective and generalized, but I believe that it illustrates the dynamic, interactive, and
contingent nature of the processes likely to have constantly restructured the
genetic, linguistic, and cultural patterns and ethnic identities of people in the

Map 9.1
Britain and Northwest Europe, Showing Extent of Maximum Ice during the Last
Glacial Advance (circa 16,000 B.P.) and the Land Bridge connecting Britain to
the Continent (at circa 9,000 B.P.)

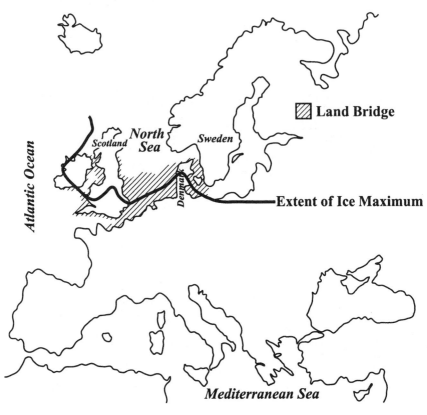

past. Furthermore, I believe that it leads to a consideration of the important role
aspects of self-identity and choice played, consciously or unconsciously, directly
or indirectly, in these processes.

Britain and northwestern Europe offer a useful platform from which to study
both Holocene prehistory and variation of ethnic identity, material culture, language, and biology. A significant amount of genetic and palaeoecological evidence accumulated during the twentieth century, and models derived from
archaeology, historical linguistics, and historical texts extend even further back.
The close proximity of continental Europe allows events there to be compared
and contrasted with developments in Britain from a time when the island was
still part of the continental land mass and largely covered by ice sheets (Map
9.1).

Variations in language, culture, and biology in northwestern Europe are already the subject of consideration in genetics (Cavalli-Sforza, Menozzi, and Piazza 1994) and archaeology (Renfrew 1987). The models used by these authors are essentially coevolutionary, in the sense that they assume that cotransmission of genes, language, and culture is the norm, and variations from this pattern are treated as exceptions that in some way "prove the rule." As Boas has already shown, however, the theoretical basis of Renfrew and Cavalli-Sforza's interpretations is questionable. My departure from Renfrew and Cavalli-Sforza is that I reject the covariation narrative in favor of historical contingency—that is, dependence on social, economic, and environmental circumstances and choice. I believe that there is no fundamental reason why a fixed set of gene frequencies, language, and cultural traits must be transmitted together from one generation to the next in any community. Equally, however, there is no reason why they should not. It depends on history.

A HISTORICAL MODEL OF BIOLOGICAL AND CULTURAL TRAITS

It was an intrinsic feature of racial anthropology to equate race, language, and ethnicity in Britain (Beddoe 1885) and in Europe (Coon 1939). Although modern archaeologists and geneticists are unanimous in their rejection of scientific racism, the equation of biology, language, and culture is retained in those contemporary models of European prehistory that do attempt to address archaeological, linguistic, and genetic evidence (Ammerman and Cavalli-Sforza 1984; Cavalli-Sforza, Menozzi, and Piazza 1994; Renfrew 1987).

Genes, language, and culture are "properties of the body"—genes are encoded in the DNA, linguistic and cultural constructs are encoded in memory in the brain—and as communities are composed of a number of individuals, they can be ascribed gene frequencies or linguistic and cultural patterns. But why should gene distributions, language, and cultural traits be bound together? While a propensity for language of some sort is evidently innate in humans, the form of that language is culturally determined and can, like other cultural traits, be spread without a dispersal of people of equal magnitude. Linguistic and cultural behaviors can be abandoned, amended, or supplemented during the life of the individual. Genes cannot change during life, and only the transmission of genes implicitly requires the movement of people—a very broad concept. Gene distributions are also affected by natural selection due to environmental factors such as climate and disease, and by "sexual selection" for genetically encoded traits sought in a mate.

It is my aim here to demonstrate that genetic, linguistic, and cultural traits can be regarded as independently variable attributes of communities. I intend to show that one need not tie gene frequencies, ethnic groups, material culture, and languages together into discrete bundles simply in order to follow the geographic and temporal progress of each package through history. Instead of trying to pursue a kind of "law of cotransmission," I would like to adopt a historically based paradigm in which the cultural and linguistic traits of individuals and the cultural, linguistic, and genetic traits of communities are independent. Rather than equating these factors, I would like to examine how these variables are likely to have behaved given what is known of prevailing historical circumstances during three discrete archaeological periods. How could the relationships between these variables have changed and why? How may each individual variable have been reconstituted through time? In what way can we begin to envisage how the actions of individuals and groups influenced or controlled these processes?

Early Mesolithic (c. 10,000–7,500 B.P.)

The Early Mesolithic of northwestern Europe was a period of climatic amelioration following the last glaciation that had enormous ecological impact enabling substantial demographic change. Can palaeoecological and archaeological evidence be used to constrain a historical description of cultural and demographic restructuring? Can genetic evidence be used to make further inferences about such a distant period? Is it possible to avoid making simple equations of genes and culture?

The rate of warming at the beginning of the current interglacial was rapid in northwestern Europe, and although both climatic and ecological changes were regional in nature, huge areas of formerly cold open tundra landscape became much more hospitable to local communities. Although larger game species were superseded by smaller fauna as shrubs and light woodland developed, hunting opportunities remained considerable. Throughout the Mesolithic, coastal and inland aquatic environments provided people with fish, shellfish, crustaceans, waterfowl, and aquatic mammals (Simmons, Dimbleby, and Grigson 1981; Jones and Keen 1993:208–274). The North Sea periphery in the Early Mesolithic can be seen as a rapidly expanding ecosystem.

There is much archaeological evidence of Late Upper Palaeolithic and Early Mesolithic activity in the southern part of the North Sea periphery, including Britain (Megaw and Simpson 1979:24–76). Although the Late Upper Palaeolithic material culture of Britain is sometimes seen as an indigenous development, its presence is often explained, somewhat contradictorily, as the consequence of seasonal visits of small groups of hunters from the "continent." Britain was still part of the continent during the Early Mesolithic, connected by a substantial land bridge extending from southern England to northern France in the west and across to Denmark in the east. The propensity of Pleistocene groups for "opportunistic" activity in British periglacial areas throughout the Upper Palaeolithic (Wymer 1981:80) calls for incursions of increased frequency and duration from the beginning of the current interglacial proper, about 10,000 B.P. Social and technological organization developed during the Late Upper Palaeolithic may have enabled communities already active along the coasts of the North Sea periphery to exploit increasingly productive areas of what had formerly been marginal parts of their existing territories. Schmitt (1995) suggests that such a process can be detected in the archaeological record of southern Sweden, and there is evidence that formerly marginal coastal areas of the North Sea periphery may have been settled within a relatively short period of time following the climatic amelioration (Bjerck 1995:139).

The beginning of the Mesolithic is likely to have been a critical phase in the development of the first substantial communities in Britain. Social conventions that may have evolved during the Palaeolithic serving to regulate population numbers or govern access to resources may have been maintained less forcefully as greater catchments became available following the climatic amelioration, but geographical remoteness and changing environments may have threatened the viability of some communities. From modern ethnographic evidence, we know that social conventions that promote outside marriage often evolve in isolated groups of small numbers—in Mbuti and Thule communities, for example (Cavalli-Sforza and Cavalli-Sforza 1995:19–20). Such arrangements are likely to have developed during the Early Mesolithic as communities spread out into sparsely occupied territory. This would have offered the added benefit of access to resources in the territory of kin and potentially have been important in the resolution and avoidance of conflict between communities.

As the Early Mesolithic progressed, increasing interactions with rising numbers of people from different communities are likely to have been important factors in a dynamic process. The zones of relatively sharp genetic change detectable in Europe occur almost exclusively at topographic barriers (Map 9.2), and it is likely that traditions of intermarriage or community mobility across the North Sea basin would have facilitated gene flow between communities in Britain and those to the south and southeast. Although population geneticists disagree on the size of the contribution of in situ Mesolithic ancestors to the modern European gene pool (Richards et al. 1996; Cavalli-Sforza, Menozzi, and Piazza 1994:108, 255–301; Ammerman and Cavalli-Sforza 1984), all accept that a contribution of some size is detectable throughout Europe. If Early Mesolithic populations had been both low and sparse (as Ammerman and Cavalli-Sforza suggest), founder effects and genetic drift would have contributed to genetic heterogeneity as relatively isolated communities became established (Cavalli-Sforza, Menozzi, and Piazza 1994:15), a process compounded by the development of the English Channel and the North and Baltic seas.

Archaeological evidence such as the antler frontlets found at Star Carr, Biesdorf, and Hohen Viecheln together with other less obviously symbolic items (Megaw and Simpson 1979:59–60; Gendel 1987:69; Schmitt 1995:163–165) indicate a degree of homogeneity in material culture. On the basis of similar evidence of a wide distribution of Venus figurines in Europe prior to the last glacial maximum, Renfrew has postulated a degree of linguistic unity in Palaeolithic Europe as well (Renfrew 1991:8).

The palaeoecological evidence summarized here indicates that there would have been little environmental constraint on geographic and demographic ex-

Map 9.2
Location of 33 Zones of Sharp Genetic Change in Europe

Source: Barbujani and Sokal (1990). Reprinted with permission.

pansion during the Early Mesolithic, and the limited archaeological evidence suggests an unusual degree of mobility accompanied by detectable homogeneity in material culture (Table 9.1). Small and vulnerable populations are likely to be "flexible in their attitudes and actions, as well as mutually supportive and mutually dependent on each other" (Terrell 1986:182). The exchange and alliance of ideas and practices and of living members of communities would implicitly have eroded boundaries of interethnic identity—and may have been seen to do so at the time. Intentionally or unintentionally, such strategies would have enhanced benefits accrued from ecological and climatic changes occurring during the early Holocene. The employment of such strategies can be seen in the ethnographic record to benefit sparsely distributed communities in central Africa, the Arctic (Cavalli-Sforza and Cavalli-Sforza 1995:19–20), and Micronesia (Terrell 1986:181–182). There would have been extensive regional and temporal variation in these processes that is difficult to detect with the present state of

Table 9.1
Summary of Genetic, Linguistic, and Cultural Processes Postulated for Key Phases of Holocene Prehistory in Britain

Period	Genes	Language	Artifact	Mind
Early Mesolithic	Reduced regional heterogeneity. Growing communities.	Linguistic diversity continues.	Homogeneity of material culture.	Marrying out extended. Settlement of marginal territories. Increased contact and exchange.
Late Mesolithic	Large and homogeneous population. Geography forming barrier to gene flow.	Employed in negotiation of ethnic boundaries. Overtaken by Indo-European *lingua franca*.	Heterogeneity of technical and ritual material culture. Employment of material culture to delineate ethnic boundaries.	Increasing competition and heterogeneity of economic and social practices. Development of mechanisms to deal with or ameliorate conflict. Use of landscape to validate territorial claims.
Early Medieval	Influx and admixture. Effects of geographical barriers reduced.	Borrowing and language shifts due to settlement. Change due to social pressures or choices.	Interchange of symbolic and technical material culture. Use of material culture to build and transcend ethnic boundaries.	Movement of communities, conflict, and accommodation. Negotiation of boundaries using culture/language and marriage.

knowledge. Supporting linguistic evidence is nonexistent, and the archaeological and genetic evidence is, overall, sparse and ambiguous. Nevertheless, an alternative hypothesis proposing the independent development of genetically and culturally isolated regional "peoples" is without significant support; genetic admixture is more in keeping with the evidence.

Late Mesolithic (c. 7,500–3,000 B.P.)

The climatic amelioration that began with the early Holocene stabilized during the course of the Mesolithic. In many parts of northwestern Europe, the amount of available territory was progressively reduced by inundation with sea water. In contrast to the Early Mesolithic, palaeological evidence indicates considerable constraint on demographic expansion. Is it possible to assess the demographic and socioeconomic consequences of these constraints in historical terms?

The transition to agriculture had begun by the Late Mesolithic. Can the introduction of farming be attributed to indigenous developments, or is it necessary to postulate the arrival of a new and distinct "people"? To what extent does the genetic evidence allow us to distinguish between the two hypotheses? Is there a historical alternative to these paradigmatic extremes?

Climate continued to improve throughout the Mesolithic, and the North Sea basin was rapidly inundated between approximately 9,000 and 8,000 B.P. Although occasional local events may have appeared catastrophic, the rise in sea level would have been barely perceptible on a day-to-day basis (see Simmons, Dimbleby, and Grigson 1981:84–86). In some coastal areas, such as western Scotland and parts of Scandinavia (Fischer 1995), the land level was gradually rising as well. Although marine resources shifted in location, they continued to be available, and there is substantial evidence for their exploitation throughout the Mesolithic (Fischer 1995). Inland lacustrine environments may not have been affected adversely. A warmer climate and increased rainfall may have raised the density of some resources, but there is some accompanying evidence for peat accumulation and soil degradation even in this early period. Many game animals, clearly an important part of the Early Mesolithic diet in Britain, dwindled in numbers or disappeared as a consequence of shrinking habitats or pressure from hunting. By about 7,500 B.P., inundation of the North Sea basin was complete.

The likely demographic consequences of a shrinking land area are critical to an assessment of the competing hypotheses explaining the transition to agriculture following the Mesolithic period. A sparse population might have allowed migrating farmers originating from the Near East to spread unhindered into northwestern Europe (Ammerman and Cavalli-Sforza 1984), but a thriving population implies indigenous communities capable of resisting intrusive settlement who may have fostered agriculture independently (Zvelebil 1986; Thomas 1988, 1991; Tilley 1994).

The fundamental changes in climatic and ecological circumstances indicate that many social, economic, and technological practices developed early in the

Mesolithic would not have remained ecologically tenable as the period progressed. To use an evolutionary analogy, they would have ceased to be viable or "adaptive." Changes to these practices were necessary if population numbers were to be maintained or grow as the Mesolithic progressed. Shifts in what we categorize as economic or technological activities are likely to have been accompanied by changing social and ritual practices occurring in Mesolithic communities, since these must have operated within a cosmological framework or system of beliefs. The nature of these practices would have depended on choice, within a prevailing political context, and clearly those practices that were seen as good for the community would have prevailed—but only, in the long term, if they allowed communities to prosper, or at least survive, in the most basic material and biological terms. The social and ecological processes leading to the European Neolithic had their beginnings here.

Diversification in both ritually and functionally classified artifacts and increasing specialization can be detected as the northwest European Mesolithic develops (Gendel 1987; Verhart 1990; Zvelebil and Rowley-Conwy 1986; Larsson 1995:101; Andersen 1995:41–65). Evidence indicates that animal and plant husbandry and woodland management (e.g., Pedersen 1995:83–84) were practiced (with the use of fire forming an important component in the exploitation of these resources), and marginal areas of northern and western Britain were exploited increasingly (Edwards and Ralston 1984; Zvelebil 1994; Simmons and Innes 1996; Dennell 1983). The use of marine resources throughout the Mesolithic was a fundamental means via which communities supported the overall maintenance of a high population, and there is ample supporting evidence from southern Scandinavia (Zvelebil 1986), Cumbria (Bonsall 1981), western Scotland (Pollard and Morrison 1996), and elsewhere in Britain (Thomas 1988:60; Clutton-Brock and Noe-Nygaard 1990).

The transition from hunting-fishing-gathering to agriculture from the Late Mesolithic is seen by population geneticists (Ammerman and Cavalli-Sforza 1984; Cavalli-Sforza, Menozzi, and Piazza 1994) as having had a major impact on gene distributions in Europe, still detectable today. Most recently, Cavalli-Sforza, Menozzi, and Piazza (1994:292–295) have constructed *principal component synthetic maps* that demonstrate the geographical spread of the major factors accounting for genetic variation in Europe. The first principal component (accounting for 28.1 percent of total variation) travels in a southeast-to-northwest direction (Map 9.3). Furthermore, there are more genetic variants that correlate with the southeast-to-northwest gradient than with the northwest-to-southeast one (Cavalli-Sforza, Menozzi, and Piazza 1994:291), suggesting that the southeastern population maintained higher genetic diversity and hence was of a larger size. The number of different genes and genetic variants involved suggests that natural selection—due to diseases, for example—may not account for the gradient. Neither can the overall pattern of variation be accounted for by simple biogeographical factors such as latitude or climate. The explanation favored by Cavalli-Sforza and others (e.g., Renfrew 1987) is that the gradient

Map 9.3
First Principal Component Synthetic Map of Total Genetic Variation in Europe

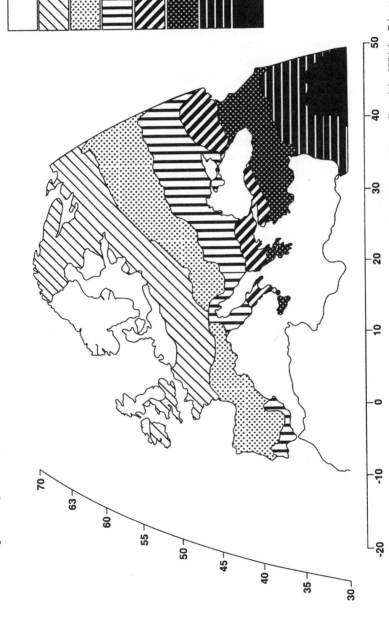

Source: L. L. Cavalli-Sforza, P. Menozzi, and A. Piazza, *The History and Geography of Human Genes.* Copyright 1994 by Princeton University Press. Reprinted by permission of Princeton University Press.

is associated with "demic diffusion"—or population movement—accompanying the transition to agriculture, as this is the only point at which the indigenous population was sufficiently low in numbers and the (presumed) contributing population—originating in the Near East—sufficiently large and distinctive to bring about the pattern (Ammerman and Cavalli-Sforza 1984; Cavalli-Sforza, Menozzi, and Piazza 1994:255–301). In other words, Cavalli-Sforza and his colleagues are proposing the cotransmission of Near Eastern genes and agricultural "culture." Renfrew (1987) adds Indo-European languages to the package.

How well is this cotransmission hypothesis supported by genetic, linguistic, and archaeological data in northwestern Europe? Most archaeologists support the notion of a high Late Mesolithic population in northwestern Europe and cite American northwest coast societies (e.g., Zvelebil 1989:380–381) as being more comparable models than the aboriginal groups chosen by Ammerman and Cavalli-Sforza (1984). A small Mesolithic population could be expected to have led to isolated communities, founder effect, and genetic drift. A distinctive genetic substructure can be detected in and around the Basque region of southwestern France and northern Spain, but only at the level of the fifth principal component of Cavalli-Sforza, Menozzi, and Piazza (1994:295), accounting for only 5.3 percent of total variance (Map 9.4). Topographic and cultural barriers are proposed by Cavalli-Sforza, Menozzi, and Piazza (1994:285–287) to have diminished the effects of gene flow into this part of Europe, thought to have supported a substantial population since the Palaeolithic. When the inundation of the North Sea was complete (around 8,000 B.P.), the extent and frequency of contact, settlement mobility, and any intermarrying between Britain, Scandinavia, and continental Europe must have diminished substantially. Founder effects or genetic drift originating from any isolation of human groups occurring during the Early Mesolithic would have increased from this point on. This would be especially so for Britain and, perhaps, southern Scandinavia, where substantial topographic boundaries would have limited subsequent gene flow. Here a situation comparable to the Basque region might be expected, but clearly this is not apparent (Cavalli-Sforza, Menozzi, and Piazza 1994:268–272). The genetic evidence may not be indicative of a low and dispersed Mesolithic population, and recent studies of maternally inherited mitochondrial DNA (Sykes 1999) suggest that the southeast-to-northwest cline may be older and smaller than Ammerman and Cavalli-Sforza (1984) believed. Pleistocene genetic drift followed by Holocene genetic admixture may explain the southeast-to-northwest gradient.

A specific alternative to a cotransmission or "demic-diffusion" model has been proposed by archaeologists. In southern Scandinavia, archaeological evidence for a thriving Late Mesolithic community is good, and there are indications of continuity in land use and material culture from the Mesolithic to the Neolithic. The arrival of farming in these regions is much slower than the demic-diffusion model might predict (Zvelebil 1986). Zvelebil and Rowley-Conwy (1986) offer an alternative to the demic-diffusion model based on "availability, substitution and consolidation" of agriculture, with fluctuating aquatic resources playing a

Map 9.4
Fifth Principal Component Synthetic Map of Total Genetic Variation in Europe

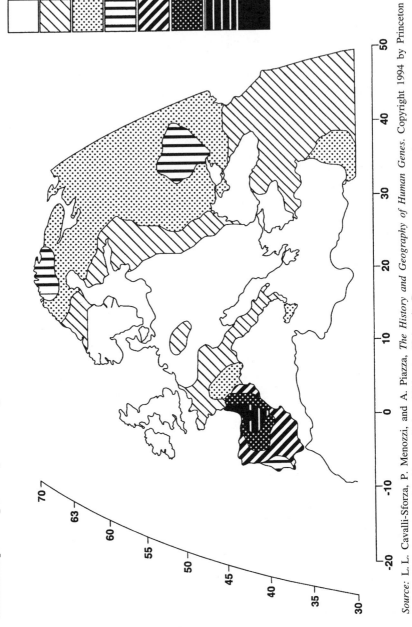

Source: L. L. Cavalli-Sforza, P. Menozzi, and A. Piazza, *The History and Geography of Human Genes.* Copyright 1994 by Princeton University Press. Reprinted by permission of Princeton University Press.

crucial role (cf. Thomas 1988). Evidence for continuity is less convincing in Britain, although Tilley (1994:147) insists on continuity in settlement and patterns of exploitation and dismisses any hiatus as an artifact of categorization and dating (cf. Chamberlain 1996). Thomas (1991) suggests that even during the Neolithic, major buildings, sedentary settlement, and population growth were not prerequisite, and that wild food resources could still have contributed to a substantial part of the diet. The adoption of farming as a single cultural "package" is not well supported by the archaeological evidence. One does not find crop-processing artifacts, agricultural-settlement structures, and archaeozoological and archaeobotanical evidence of farming appearing at the same time and with a uniform geographical distribution (Zvelebil 1986; Thomas 1988, 1991; Tilley 1994). Occasional and limited horticultural or pastoral farming activity is more likely, with much variation according to time and place. It may have been that Mesolithic communities in Britain and elsewhere took up aspects of what was to become farming society gradually, while continuing to forage, and occasionally returned to previous ways of life. Tilley (1994) and Thomas (1991, 1988) portray the eventual shift from hunting-fishing-gathering to farming as an internal social and ideological restructuring of Mesolithic communities. This is the antithesis of the demic-diffusion model, but its proponents have ignored the genetic (and linguistic) evidence. They have resorted to an assumption of "indigenism," which is also ahistorical.

Although archaeologists may see no cause to invoke migration and settlement in Britain as a corollary of the development of agricultural communities, the first principal component map of Cavalli-Sforza, Menozzi, and Piazza (1994: 292) does indicate a genetic contribution from the south and southeast in Britain, southern Scandinavia, the low countries, and the Baltic periphery. While archaeologists such as Thomas (1991) and Tilley (1994) reject the wholesale adoption of farming, even diffusion of the components of farming into Britain poses a logistical dilemma, that of transporting the material and practical necessities across the English Channel. Founding livestock herds and plant-seed crops, and the methods of husbandry, are likely to have derived from the continent. Some settlement of the island seems to be demanded—rather than partial and piecemeal adoption of agriculture by a solely indigenous community—especially in the early stages. Terrestrial or marine voyages of settlement are community activities. Here particular economic, social, and environmental circumstances may have arisen where genetic and cultural traits were transmitted together.

Zvelebil and Rowley-Conwy (1986) accept a demic-diffusion explanation for central Europe, southern Europe, and southern Italy. On the basis of their model for Scandinavia—of a large Late Mesolithic/Early Neolithic population presumably descended from the Palaeolithic inhabitants—one would predict only limited admixture from the continent and a modern genetic structure quite distinct from elsewhere in Europe; one might again expect to see a feature similar to that associated with the Basque region, for example, a structure that does not occur. Can a historical model explain the apparent contradiction between the genetic and archaeological evidence—one that is not driven by presumptions of cotransmission or indigenism?

Modern ethnographic evidence indicates that fluctuating and locally variable contact zones that involve cultural, marital, and linguistic exchange can exist between adjacent hunter-gatherer and farming communities. For the Mesolithic-Neolithic transition in southern Scandinavia (Zvelebil 1986:183) and, despite the presence of the English Channel, Britain (Thomas 1988), a long-lasting process of forager-farmer contact and interaction is probable, and a coastal/maritime social history may have promoted these links. Distinctive labels like "Mesolithic" or "farming" undoubtedly hide complex social and technological changes and fluctuations in space or time, with plant-crop use, animal husbandry and hunting, fishing, and gathering being practiced to various extents by both groups. Adopting aspects of farming may have been a free choice of relatively minor consequence for many Mesolithic communities, but a necessity for others.

Although marriages may have taken place in either direction across the "frontier," farming populations tend to grow relatively quickly. Modern and historical evidence indicates that farming populations would also have developed immunity to diseases associated with animals or increased population density. These would have caused more significant attrition among adjacent Mesolithic communities (Roberts and Manchester 1995:10–12, 136–137), not least as a consequence of their relative genetic homogeneity, a corollary of lower population numbers. These differences may have led to exaggerated genetic consequences for infrequent social events—most marriages could still have been contracted within the communities involved. Adjacent farmers may have begun using the territory of Mesolithic communities, perhaps following marriage or exchange. This may have been the result of social relationships developed over a long period of time and a consequence of a deliberate strategy of one or the other group, or both. This immediate presence of farming may have provided the impetus for people—who may now have been kin—to make a more committed shift. There appears to have been consistent growth in population during the course of the Neolithic in virtually all farming societies (cf. Thomas 1991), although the rate may often have been low and subject to fluctuations resulting from socially or ecologically mediated events (Champion et al. 1984:139–140). Although the majority of the people taking up farming may have been indigenous, there would have been significant demographic input from the farmer community, which itself may have undergone a similar transformation only a generation or two earlier. The rate of intermarriage may have been low; intermarriage may have widely been perceived as only a minor social phenomenon, although one clearly of major significance to those involved.

The substantial variability in material culture and landscape use leading to a distinctive farming economy—comprising the suite of social practices, technology, settlement structure, and architecture associated with animal and plant husbandry—contrasts with the relative homogeneity of material culture apparent during the Upper Palaeolithic and Early Mesolithic periods. While much of the complexity seen in material culture can perhaps be related to diversification in subsistence activities, it is also possible that material-culture traits were at the same time being selected to reflect the development of ethnic identities as social and subsistence structures were continually renegotiated (Table 9.1). Fischer (1995:382, 433–434) discusses how "ownership" and distribution rights may have been maintained within and between fishing communities during the Mesolithic or earlier and notes that settlement sites and graves are often located near permanent fishing structures. Intentionally or unintentionally, such strategies would have promoted the management of socially competitive situations resulting from ecological and climatic changes occurring during the Mesolithic, and socioeconomic changes eventually leading to the adoption of farming. If so, language may have played a similar role, although historical linguistic evidence only begins to emerge with the beginnings of the Neolithic, and then controversially. This period may have been crucial in the development of the Indo-European languages of Europe. The construction of ethnic boundaries for the management of social relations in the relatively competitive environment of the Late Mesolithic may have led, by the Neolithic, to a situation where an Indo-European lingua franca (Zvelebil and Zvelebil 1988) would have been readily adopted by emerging farming communities (a parallel situation may have resulted in the much later adoption of English in Britain; see the following section). Neither indigenist explanations of the Late Mesolithic, which dismiss the importance of significant and perceptible demographic changes, nor cotransmission models, which assume the movement of people, language, and culture in discrete packages, seem to be supported by the archaeological, genetic, and linguistic data, but there may be potential for the development of historically oriented models explaining these diverse sources of evidence.

Early Medieval Period (c. 500–1,100 A.D.)

In Britain, the Early Medieval "migration period" is traditionally explained as a history of invasion and settlement by culturally, linguistically, and racially distinct groups from continental Europe, the "Anglo-Saxons" and the "Vikings." Unlike Mesolithic prehistory, these accounts of invasion are supported by early written texts. Nevertheless, revisionist histories now favor internal social changes as the major explanatory factors in these events. Again, I would like to consider how these competing models are supported by archaeological, genetic, and linguistic evidence and would like to seek historical alternatives.

The historical accounts of Gildas describe substantial migration of groups of "Anglo-Saxon" invaders into Britain following the withdrawal of the Roman Empire and the almost genocidal conflicts that resulted (Higham 1994). These events could be predicted to have clear demographic consequences, but there is little evidence in the distribution of classical genetic markers to support these historical accounts (Evison 2000). Bodmer (1993) notes that certain genes are more frequent in the western part of Britain—in the regions in which British

linguistic and political influence survived the longest. These genes show dwin-
dling frequency gradients across Europe, however, and it would be difficult to
attribute them to the "Celts" (Evison 2000). There are patterns of gene distributions in Britain that are interpreted as reflecting the movements of people
from Scandinavia during the Viking Era, however, movements also well supported by historic, cultural, and linguistic evidence. This probably reflects demographic and sociopolitical differences between the two events, which are
worthy of more detailed consideration.

The historical accounts of Asser (e.g., Keynes and Lapidge 1983) and the
semimythical accounts of the sagas provide a strong indication of extensive
settlement from Scandinavia during the period roughly between 800 and 1066
A.D. Further evidence is provided in the form of both personal and place names
of Scandinavian origin occurring throughout northern England, and there is also
evidence of material culture resembling Scandinavian artifacts in style and construction (Higham 1986). Despite this substantial evidence, language and material culture can be transmitted without large-scale movements of people, and
historical accounts may be unreliable, being written with the social and political
sensitivities of their readership in mind. Studies of gene distributions in northern
England do offer some support to theories of settlement from Scandinavia, however. In Cumbria and north Derbyshire in England, and the northern isles of
Scotland (Roberts 1986, 1990), there are distinctive differences in gene frequency distributions when compared with the surrounding regions. In Cumbria,
the trends in these frequencies tend to resemble gene frequency distributions
detectable in modern Norway (Roberts, Jorde, and Mitchell 1981), and in northeast Derbyshire (Mastana and Sokol 1998) they show affinities with Norway
and Denmark. Although the Danelaw extended over most of northern and central
England, with its southern border roughly in a line from the Mersey to the
Thames (Map 9.5), why is it that it is only in these regions of England that
gene frequency evidence can be explained by Viking settlement?

Central Cumbria and northwest Derbyshire (Map 9.5, inset) are agriculturally
marginal upland areas. Following Roman withdrawal from Britain, there is palaeoenvironmental evidence of woodland regeneration in northwest Derbyshire.
There are surviving British place names in both areas, and historical accounts
indicate that both remained under British political control for some time during
the "Anglo-Saxon" expansion. In northwest Derbyshire, place-name evidence
may indicate that the topographical barriers of the river valleys of the Derwent
and the Wye served as transient borders identifying areas of British and "Anglo-
Saxon" political control. *The Anglo-Saxon Chronicle* refers to the presence of
the Pecsetan (Peak settlers) in north Derbyshire by the late seventh century
(Morris 1973), and substantial Anglian burial mounds have been excavated on
the edge of the region (Hart 1981). The ornamental helmet recovered from the
Benty Grange burial mound is particularly unusual. In structure it resembles a
typical Anglian warrior's helmet. A boar crest, however, seems to have affinities
with Germanic and insular Celtic art styles, and a crucifix is embossed onto the

Map 9.5
Britain, with Insert Showing North Derbyshire

Peak District
Anglian/Anglo-Danish Burials
Scandinavian Place Names

Cumbria

North Derbyshire

Approximate southern
boundary of the Danelaw

front of the helmet. The burial relates to the early period of Christian conversion of the pagan Anglians.

Both Cumbria and Derbyshire were incorporated into Anglian kingdoms prior to the arrival of the Scandinavians. These events occurred late, however, and there is evidence that people of British identity and language remained in these regions after the Anglian "takeover." The term Pecsetan implies the settlement of territory that is somehow "foreign," and references to British settlements are evident in English place names in the region. Were they still in place when the Scandinavian settlers arrived?

The Scandinavian settlers of northwest England tended to originate from Norway and from Norwegian settlements in Gaelic-speaking areas of the Hebrides and the west coast of Scotland; those of northeast England tended to originate from Denmark. It may be no coincidence that the topographies of these regions of England show some resemblance to their Scandinavian counterparts. Studies of Scandinavian place names in England benefit from the recording of place names in the Domesday Book of 1086, within about 200 years of their formation (Fellows-Jensen 1984:148). In both Cumbria and north Derbyshire, place-name evidence indicates Scandinavian influence and is clearly regional, even within the small areas being considered. It is in Cumbria that the largest number of Scandinavian loan words survive in local dialects (Gillian Fellows-Jensen, personal communication). Names of Scandinavian origin recorded in the Domesday Book for north Derbyshire occur exclusively in the eastern part of the region (Morris 1978), adjacent to the Danelaw proper.

Thus both the linguistic and genetic evidence support the idea of Scandinavian settlement in Cumbria and northeast Derbyshire. There is much linguistic, historical, and archaeological evidence to indicate further substantial Scandinavian settlement in northern England, but the genetic evidence elsewhere is less clear (in Yorkshire and Northumberland) or nonexistent (in Lincolnshire and East Anglia). There is evidence from the historical literature of intermarriage between the Norse and the emerging English. Some similarity in vocabulary between Old English and Old Norse would have facilitated communication and eased the transfer of loan words (Fellows-Jensen, personal communication). Despite evident intermittent conflict, there is no evidence to suggest that ethnic boundaries were being constructed using either material or linguistic cultural traits. It could be predicted that any distinction in gene distributions between Norse settlers and the indigenous population would have been quickly eroded by intermarriage, interethnic shift, relocation, and a degree of reverse migration. Why should genetic evidence remain detectable in Cumbria and north Derbyshire?

It is likely that the marginal areas of central Cumbria and north Derbyshire supported relatively low populations, certainly in comparison to adjacent lowland regions. Subsistence in these landscapes is a specialist activity, one in which settlers from Norway would have been well versed and able to transpose or adapt to the local topography (Mahler 1995:501). Norse farming practices, such as the use of heather (*Calluna* sp.) dominated heathland for winter fodder would have been easily adopted here. There is no reason to suppose that the native population would have been any less adept, however (see Mahler 1995:488). Thus Norwegian settlement of Cumbria, the continued presence of British communities in both Cumbria and the High Peak of northwest Derbyshire, and the settlement of Danish communities in lowland northeast Derbyshire are tenable assumptions.

It may have been that preexisting linguistic and cultural differences perpetuated boundaries of ethnic identity in these regions. Old Norse and Brythonic would not have been mutually intelligible, and, as a rule, there may have been little for these communities (especially the Norse) to gain from learning the adjacent language. It is not necessary to propose that boundary construction was being negotiated; rather, existing boundaries, created by happenstance, were not eroding quickly. In contrast, in the Hebrides, there seems to have been a good deal of intermarriage between Vikings and Gaelic-speaking people. Differences in topography between northwest and northeast Derbyshire may have meant that the High Peak area in the west was of little interest to settlers of Danish and Anglo-Danish origin farming in the lower, flatter areas of the northeast, who had tended to choose environments similar to those left behind in Denmark (Fellows-Jensen 1984:149). Place-name evidence and gene frequencies are consistent with this notion, and the survival of British communities in the High Peak may have accentuated any sense of separate community. Scandinavian kinship traditions in areas relatively isolated from the social mainstream may also have influenced the initial genealogical structures in these regions immediately following Scandinavian settlement.

Settlement is a community activity and it is difficult to imagine that groups of settlers numbered less than several hundred; they may well have been substantially larger. Even a few groups of this size arriving in restricted marginal areas of Cumbria and sparsely populated north Derbyshire would have constituted a profound demographic event locally. There is no need to assume that Norse (or Gaelic-Norse) identities or language persisted for more than a few generations, and even then, identity is likely to have been flexible. Intermarriage and cultural and linguistic exchange with the "indigenous" community need not be excluded. Even a few generations of relatively endogamous population growth—which may not have been a conscious political choice—may have been enough to establish a genetic background still detectable today.

Consideration of the historic, archaeological, linguistic, and genetic evidence relating to the negotiation of ethnic structures in Early Medieval northern England reveals a regionally and temporally complex and highly interactive process (Table 9.1). There is little evidence of a biological contribution from northern Europe that can be associated with Anglo-Saxon invasions. Here the selection of Germanic names and linguistic and cultural traits was generally a sociopolitical choice for people who had no connection with the continent by birth or ancestry and may have once identified themselves as "British." Historical evidence for intermarriage between "Anglo-Saxons" and "Britons," and choices of personal names, which would have been seen as identifying with respective communities, indicate that this was an interactive process. The shift in day-to-day language was marked, but the selection of more symbolically important word choices such as personal names indicates that a complex construction of identities was negotiated, and translation between languages is also evident. Although archaeologists continue to describe British communities as "dying out," this is perhaps best seen as a metaphor, not a literal description of events. The British did not die out or give up political influence, but retained it by becoming English. English, Norse, or British were states of mind and not necessarily of language or of birth.

The arrival of Scandinavian settlers leads to a similar, but more complicated, process. Here linguistic similarity would have permitted great flexibility (and ambiguity) in linguistic parameters of identity. Intermarriage is again evident in the historical texts, and place- and particularly personal-name selection, it can be argued, was as much a reflection of the negotiation of social relations as it was a simple indicator of migration. Furthermore, place-name evidence indicates linguistic borrowing from Gaelic by "Norse" settlers, probably made in the Hebrides and Scotland (Fellows-Jensen 1995:403), which reminds us that the Viking period must be seen within the cultural milieu of the Atlantic Fringe typified by diverse communities of origin, migration and return, intermarriage, negotiation of ethnic identities, and linguistic interaction. Fellows-Jensen (1984) suggests that -bý place naming (e.g., Stainsby and Blingsby in northeast Derbyshire) indicates the transfer of units already exploited into small-scale private ownership for the first time in reorganizations following Scandinavian influence or settlement. The complexity and rapidity of local events should not be forgotten. Scandinavian settlements did not long maintain Scandinavian language in Ireland, England, or Normandy (Fellows-Jensen 1984). Although the extent of historical and linguistic evidence for the Early Medieval period is extensive, it remains ambiguous; the genetic evidence is limited and may be contradicted by future research. In Cumbria and north Derbyshire, however, we may perhaps be able to catch a fleeting glimpse of the dynamic processes of interaction and renegotiation of ethnic identities.

DISCUSSION

Eriksen (1993:9) indicates that "to speak of an ethnic group in total isolation is as absurd as to speak of one hand clapping." Ethnicity is an aspect of the relationship between groups of people. Fundamentally, ethnic identity is a structure created, re-created, and manipulated by people for use as a symbolic tool in political negotiations (Cohen 1985). A consideration of British prehistory provides evidence that could be inferred to relate to the maintenance and transcendence of ethnic boundaries, even as far back as the Late Upper Palaeolithic.

The most fundamental aspect of ethnic identity—in contrast to other identities—seems to be a belief in a shared collection of cultural traits (language, religion, kinship system, "way of life"). A belief in shared ancestry is also very common (Eriksen 1993:70–71) and may be accompanied by an ideology of endogamy. Despite this, the evidence from British prehistory indicates that this aspect of ethnic identity has not had any appreciable effect that can be detected in modern gene frequency distributions. While gene frequency distributions, interpreted with other evidence, may provide indicators of demographic events, they indicate extensive interethnic marriage and ethnic shift and the transient nature of any association between people, language, and material culture. Although conflict is evident, British prehistory could be typified by the willingness of ethnic groups to accept outsiders as new members, by a continual process of ethnic interaction and shift, and by the existence of many "anomalous individuals" (Eriksen 1993:159). Within coidentifying groups, various degrees of incorporation and levels of membership could also be inferred (Cohen 1985).

Ethnohistories are written in the present and express present concerns (Eriksen 1993:92). The use and reuse of landscape and of structures in the archaeological record may reflect the construction of histories in the past. Traditions require "real" evidence for their validation. The histories of Gildas, Bede, and Asser would appear to show extensive interethnic conflict, occasionally of genocidal proportions. This is not reflected by the archaeological or the genetic evidence. The contrast between "belief" and historical "reality" presents an ethical dilemma for anthropologists in the present and a problem to be encountered in the interpretation of the past. Eriksen (1993:68) points out that "conspicuous forms of boundary maintenance become important when the boundaries are under pressure." The location of many archaeological monuments is assumed to delineate territorial boundaries. The burial mounds at Benty Grange and nearby may delineate a border between "English" and "British" communities. In contrast, the design of the warrior's helmet from Benty Grange seems to say, "Whoever you are, you can identify with me." Again, ethnic boundaries are amenable to transcendence as well as maintenance. Ethnic identification inevitably involves a degree of stereotyping of members and nonmembers of the group, but it is negotiated and manipulated and is therefore part of a dynamic, ambiguous, and context-dependent process (Eriksen 1993:18–35). It is important to consider the role of men and women and the young and the old in this process. Because children have a clear propensity for language learning and for learning the system of "symbolic metaphors" of material culture, they would have played an important part in "ethnic maintenance" and "ethnic shift." Equally, the older generations are likely to have played a part in passing on histories that enforce ethnic identity and in their renegotiation for the future advantage of the community. Gender roles are likely to have surfaced in patterns of interethnic marriage and in the use of marriage for the symbolic renegotiation of interethnic identity. Matrilocal or patrilocal marriage patterns would have influenced the perceptions of ethnic identity of men and women differently.

Cultural and linguistic evidence for settlement is ultimately ambiguous, but there is genetic evidence for the occurrence of migration and settlement in British prehistory. It is equally clear that any settlement was part of a highly variable and interactive process. Despite the numerous attempts to construct teleologies "proving" or "disproving" settlement or indigenism, it simply is not possible to distinguish between cultural and demic diffusion in British prehistory from the archaeological record alone. The conclusions must be seen as reflections of externally imposed sociopolitical fashions. Although archaeologists rightly criticize the equation of geographically spreading cultural horizons with spreading peoples, they commonly make the same oversight in associating the transmission of material culture traits through time with continuity of residence of indigenous peoples.

The distinction between biology and culture is ultimately misleading. In the same way that one can criticize cladistic models for their theorization of the fissioning and spreading of entirely cohesive and exclusive groups of people displacing or, at best, absorbing indigenous populations, so one can criticize the indigenist stance for failing to incorporate the mobility and plasticity evident in human social relationships and for failing to portray the consistent ability of communities to restructure both their identity and their constitution. Ethnogenetic models (e.g., Moore 1994) can be used to infer negotiation of social relations and ethnicity and of choice in the selection of cultural and linguistic traits and may even allow some perception of self-identity in ancient societies. Such models offer an opportunity for genetic, linguistic, and archaeological evidence to be incorporated into socially driven descriptions of the past. Analogous models for "contextual and contingent" construction of communal or individual identities are available in sociology (Giddens 1984), social theory (Shilling 1993), and psychology (Kelly 1955).

CONCLUSION

I have given a selective and generalized account of issues of ethnicity in contrasting periods of British prehistory. Inevitably, the archaeological, palaeoenvironmental, linguistic, and genetic evidence and any anthropological inferences I have made are all subject to criticism. Nevertheless, I hope that this account has served as an experiment in how questions of identity can be addressed from a multidisciplinary perspective and to illustrate how limiting models that simply equate gene distributions, language, and cultural horizons are. Cladistic models may provide useful information about relationships between sets of traits, but they serve only as (potentially misleading) guidelines for explanations of their origin. In the same way that cladistic models engender interpretations of migration, invasion, displacement, and absorption, indigenist models fail to incorporate the mobility, flexibility, and plasticity evident in human groups and the concomitant ability of individuals and communities to continually restructure their identity, membership, and social relationships. In theory, historical models allow a route out of this impasse and could be tentatively seen as consistent with models of the individual emerging in social theory, sociology, and psychology.

NOTE

This research has been supported by the Natural Environment Research Council; Trent Centre, National Blood Service, United Kingdom; and the University of Sheffield.

REFERENCES

Ammerman, A. J., and L. L. Cavalli-Sforza
1984 *The Neolithic Transition and the Genetics of Populations in Europe.* Princeton: Princeton University Press.

Andersen, S. H.
1995 Coastal Adaptation and Marine Exploitation in Late Mesolithic Denmark, with Special Emphasis on the Limfjord Region. In *Man and Sea in the Mesolithic.* A. Fischer, ed. Pp. 41–66. Oxbow Monograph 53. Oxford: Oxbow.

Barbujani, G., and R. R. Sokal
1990 Zones of Sharp Genetic Change in Europe Are Also Linguistic Boundaries. *Proceedings of the National Academy of Sciences* 87(5):1816–1819.

Barker, G.
1985 *Prehistoric Farming in Europe.* Cambridge: Cambridge University Press.

Beddoe, J.
1885 *The Races of Britain.* Bristol: J. W. Arrowsmith.

Bjerck, H. B.
1995 The North Sea Continent and Pioneer Settlement in Norway. In *Man and Sea in the Mesolithic.* A. Fischer, ed. Pp. 131–144. Oxbow Monograph 53. Oxford: Oxbow.

Boas, F.
1940 *Race, Language, and Culture.* New York: Macmillan.

Bodmer, W. F.
1993 The Genetics of Celtic Populations. *Proceedings of the British Academy* 82:37–57.

Bonsall, C.
1981 The Coastal Factor in the Mesolithic Settlement of North-west England. *Veröffentlichungen des Museums für Ur- und Frühgeschichte Potsdam* 14/15:451–472.

Cavalli-Sforza, L. L., and F. Cavalli-Sforza
1995 *The Great Human Diasporas.* New York: Addison-Wesley.

Cavalli-Sforza, L. L., P. Menozzi, and A. Piazza
1994 *The History and Geography of Human Genes.* Princeton: Princeton University Press.

Chamberlain, A. T.
1996 More Dating Evidence for Human Remains in British Caves. *Antiquity* 70:950–953.

Champion, T., C. Gamble, S. Shennan, and A. Whittle
1984 *Prehistoric Europe.* London: Academic Press.

Clutton-Brock, J., and N. Noe-Nygaard
1990 New Osteological and C-Isotope Evidence on Mesolithic Dogs: Companions to Hunters and Fishers at Star Carr, Seamer Carr, and Kongemose. *Journal of Archaeological Science* 17:643–653.

Cohen, A. P.
1985 *The Symbolic Construction of Community.* Chichester: Ellis Horwood.

Coon, C. S.

1939 *The Races of Europe*. New York: Macmillan.

Dennell, R. W.

1983 *European Economic Prehistory*. London: Academic Press.

Edwards, K. J., and I. Ralston

1984 Postglacial Hunter-Gatherers and Vegetational History in Scotland. *Proceedings of the Society of Antiquaries of Scotland* 114:15–34.

Eriksen, T. H.

1993 *Ethnicity and Nationalism: Anthropological Perspectives*. London: Pluto Press.

Evison, M. P.

2000 All in the Genes? Evaluating the Biological Evidence of Contact and Migration. In *Cultures in Contact: Scandinavian Settlement in England in the Ninth and Tenth Centuries*. D. M. Hadley and J. D. Richards, eds. Pp. 277–294. London: Brepols.

Fellows-Jensen, G.

1984 Viking Settlement in the Northern and Western Isles: The Place-Name Evidence as Seen from Denmark and the Danelaw. In *The Northern and Western Isles in the Viking World: Survival, Continuity and Change*. A. Fenton and H. Pálsson, eds. Pp. 148–168. Edinburgh: John Donald.

1995 Some Orkney Personal Names. In *The Viking Age in Caithness, Orkney, and the North Atlantic*. C. E. Batey, J. Jesch, and C. D. Morris, eds. Pp. 397–407. Edinburgh: Edinburgh University Press.

Fischer, A., ed.

1995 Man and Sea in the Mesolithic. Oxbow Monograph 53. Oxford: Oxbow.

Gendel, P. A.

1987 Socio-stylistic Analysis of Lithic Artefacts from the Mesolithic of North-western Europe. In *Mesolithic Northwest Europe: Recent Trends*. P. Rowley-Conwy, M. Zvelebil, and H. P. Blankholm, eds. Pp. 65–73. Sheffield: University of Sheffield, Department of Archaeology and Prehistory.

Giddens, A.

1984 *The Constitution of Society: Outline of the Theory of Structuration*. Cambridge: Polity Press.

Hart, C. R.

1981 *The North Derbyshire Archaeological Survey to A.D. 1500*. Chesterfield: North Derbyshire Archaeological Trust.

Higham, N. J.

1986 *The Northern Counties to AD 1000*. London: Longman.

1994 *The English Conquest: Gildas and Britain in the Fifth Century*. Manchester: Manchester University Press.

Hodder, I.

1986 *Reading the Past*. Cambridge: Cambridge University Press.

Jones, R. L., and D. H. Keen

1993 *Pleistocene Environments in the British Isles*. London: Chapman and Hall.

Kelly, G. A.

1955 *The Psychology of Personal Constructs*. 2 vols. New York: Norton.

Keynes, S., and M. Lapidge

1983 *Alfred the Great: Asser's Life of King Alfred and Other Contemporary Sources*. London: Penguin Classics.

Larsson, L.
1995 Man and Sea in Southern Scandinavia during the Late Mesolithic: The Role of Cemeteries in the View of Society. In *Man and Sea in the Mesolithic*. A. Fischer, ed. Pp. 95–104. Oxbow Monograph 53. Oxford: Oxbow.

Mahler, D.L.D.
1995 Sheilings and Their Role in the Viking-Age Economy: New Evidence from the Faroe Islands. In *The Viking Age in Caithness, Orkney, and the North Atlantic*. C. E. Batey, J. Jesch, and C. D. Morris, eds. Pp. 487–505. Edinburgh: Edinburgh University Press.

Mastana, S. S. and R. J. Sokol
1998 Genetic Variation in the East Midlands. *Annals of Human Biology* 25(1):43–68.

Megaw, J.V.S., and D.D.A. Simpson
1979 *Introduction to British Prehistory*. Leicester: Leicester University Press.

Moore, J. H.
1994 Putting Anthropology Back Together Again: The Ethnographic Critique of Cladistic Theory. *American Anthropologist* 96(4):925–948.

Morris, J.
1973 *The Age of Arthur: A History of the British Isles from 350 to 650*. London: Weidenfeld and Nicolson.
1978 *Domesday Book: Derbyshire*. Chichester: Phillimore.

Pedersen, L.
1995 7000 Years of Fishing: Stationary Fishing Structures in the Mesolithic and Afterwards. In *Man and Sea in the Mesolithic*. A. Fischer, ed. Pp. 75–86. Oxbow Monograph 53. Oxford: Oxbow.

Pollard, T., and A. Morrison, eds.
1996 *The Early Prehistory of Scotland*. Edinburgh: Edinburgh University Press.

Renfrew, C.
1987 *Archaeology and Language: The Puzzle of Indo-European Origins*. London: Jonathan Cape.
1991 Before Babel: Speculations on the Origins of Linguistic Diversity. *Cambridge Archaeological Journal* 1(1):3–23.

Richards, M. B., H. Côrte-Real, P. Forster, V. Macaulay, H. Wilkinson-Herbots, A. Demaine, S. Papiha, R. Hedges, H.-J. Bandelt, and B. Sykes
1996 Paleolithic and Neolithic Lineages in the European Mitochondrial Gene Pool. *American Journal of Human Genetics* 59:185–203.

Roberts, C., and K. Manchester
1995 *The Archaeology of Disease*. 2nd ed. Stroud: Alan Sutton.

Roberts, D. F.
1986 Who Are the Orcadians? *Anthropologischer Anzeiger* 44(2):93–104.
1990 Genetic Affinities of the Shetland Islanders. *Annals of Human Biology* 17(2):121–132.

Roberts, D. F., L. B. Jorde, and R. J. Mitchell
1981 Genetic Structure in Cumbria. *Journal of the Biosocial Science* 13:317–336.

Roberts, D. F., R. J. Mitchell, and L. B. Jorde
1990 Migration and Genetic Structure in Northumberland. *Human Biology* 62:467–478.

Schmitt, L.
1995 The West Swedish Hensbacka: A Maritime Adaptation and a Seasonal Expression of the North-Central European Ahrensburgian? In *Man and Sea in the Mesolithic*. A. Fischer, ed. Pp. 161–170. Oxbow Monograph 53. Oxford: Oxbow.

Shilling, C.
1993 *The Body and Social Theory.* London: Sage.
Simmons, I. G., and J. B. Innes
1996 Prehistoric Charcoal in Peat Profiles at North Gill, North Yorkshire Moors, England. *Journal of Archaeological Science* 23:193–197.
Simmons, I. G., G. W. Dimbleby, and C. Grigson
1981 The Mesolithic. In *The Environment in British Prehistory.* I. G. Simmons, and M. J. Tooley, eds. Pp. 82–124. London: Duckworth.
Sykes, B.
1999 The Molecular Genetics of European Ancestry. *Philosophical Transactions of the Royal Society of London Series B* 354:131–139.
Terrell, J. E.
1986 *Prehistory in the Pacific Islands.* Cambridge: Cambridge University Press.
Terrell, J. E., and P. J. Stewart
1996 The Paradox of Population Genetics at the End of the 20th Century. *Reviews in Anthropology* 25:13–33.
Thomas, J.
1988 Neolithic Explanations Revisited: The Mesolithic-Neolithic Transition in Britain and South Scandinavia. *Proceedings of the Prehistoric Society* 54:59–66.
1991 *Rethinking the Neolithic.* Cambridge: Cambridge University Press.
Tilley, C.
1994 *A Phenomenology of Landscape: Places, Paths, and Monuments.* Oxford: Berg.
Trigger, B. G.
1989 *A History of Archaeological Thought.* Cambridge: Cambridge University Press.
Verhart, L.B.M.
1990 *Stone Age Bone and Antler Points as Indicators for "Social Territories."* In *Contributions to the Mesolithic in Europe.* P. M. Vermeersch and P. Van Peer, eds. Pp. 139–152. Leuven: Leuven University Press.
Wymer, J. J.
1981 The Palaeolithic. In *The Environment in British Prehistory.* I. G. Simmons, and M. J. Tooley, eds. Pp. 49–81. London: Duckworth.
Zvelebil, M., ed.
1986 *Hunters in Transition: Mesolithic Societies of Temperate Eurasia and Their Transition to Farming.* Cambridge: Cambridge University Press.
Zvelebil, M.
1989 On the Transition to Farming in Europe; or, What Was Spreading with the Neolithic: A Reply to Ammerman (1989). *Antiquity* 63:379–383.
1994 Plant Use in the Mesolithic and Its Role in the Transition to Farming. *Proceedings of the Prehistoric Society* 60:35–74.
Zvelebil, M., and P. A. Rowley-Conwy
1986 Foragers and Farmers in Atlantic Europe. In *Hunters in Transition: Mesolithic Societies of Temperate Eurasia and Their Transition to Farming.* M. Zvelebil, ed. Pp. 67–93. Cambridge: Cambridge University Press.
Zvelebil, M., and K. Zvelebil
1988 Agricultural Transition and Indo-European Dispersals. *Antiquity* 62:574–583.

10

Ethnolinguistic Groups, Language Boundaries, and Culture History: A Sociolinguistic Model

John Edward Terrell

> The Sepik coast of northern New Guinea is an anthropological conundrum. In their ways of living, village communities there are bound to one another by culturally structured and possibly quite ancient relationships of friendship, marriage, commerce, and shared social responsibility. Yet in their ways of speaking, they are divided into scores of separate speech traditions. How can this be? Finding the answer to this question may be key to deciding if the history of language on this coast has much to say about the history of the people living there.—Editor

Is language a reliable guide to history, ethnicity, and human biology? Can linguistics be used to chart historical relationships between societies and their cultures the way that kinship is commonly used to chart human relationships within societies? Consider the Pacific Islands. Here are three anomalies that scholars working there have been unable to resolve with any confidence.

1. New Guinea and its environs comprise what is perhaps the world's most complex language region. Approximately 1,900–2,100 languages, about one-third of all the languages of the modern world, are spoken in the Pacific region (Foley 1986; Pawley and Ross 1993). Roughly 200 of these are (or were) spoken in Australia; 1,000–1,250 languages classified as Austronesian (AN) are spoken in parts of Southeast Asia, much of the Pacific, and as far away from Asia as Madagascar; some 750 "Papuan" or non-Austronesian (NAN) languages are unique to New Guinea and several of the neighboring islands. Both AN and NAN languages are spoken on New Guinea, roughly 900–1,000 languages on an island about 312,000 square miles (808,000 square kilometers) in area (and much of this terrain is nearly uninhabited). While there have been attempts to

do so (e.g., Foley 1986:8–9, 26–29; Laycock 1982; Lynch 1981; Pawley 1981), nobody has explained why this part of the earth has so many languages.

2. New Guinea is also a region of remarkable language differences. While efforts are under way to simplify the picture (e.g., Ross 1995), conservative estimates have suggested that the many hundreds of NAN languages comprise possibly 60 different language families, each on the order of internal relatedness of Romance or Germanic, plus a number of singular language isolates, perhaps a couple of dozen, that cannot be demonstrably related to any other language or language family in the world (Foley 1986:3, 213). While the AN languages are thought to be no older than 5,000–6,000 years, they also exhibit striking diversity in numbers and the degree to which any given AN language resembles the others (Bellwood, Fox, and Tryon 1995; Dutton and Tryon 1994; Pawley 1981). *Homo sapiens sapiens* got to Australia, New Guinea, and the rest of the southwest Pacific (including island Southeast Asia) around 30,000 to 40,000 years ago (35,000 to 40,000 years is the currently favored date; see O'Connell and Allen 1998). There has clearly been enough time for a great many languages to evolve in New Guinea. While 1,000 languages may sound like an astonishing number, this figure is actually many orders of magnitude smaller than we would expect to find based on the conservative estimate that it takes about 1,000 years for a language to develop into two mutually incomprehensible "daughter" languages. Given 40,000 years, say, there actually should be something like 10^{12} languages (Foley 1986:9). The linguistic conundrum, therefore, is not just why there are so many languages in the southwest Pacific but why there are so few.

3. As if to make matters more surprising, the number of languages found on any given island in the southwest Pacific is correlated with the size of the island (Terrell 1986:54–55). Evidently, language numbers in this part of the world have reached an equilibrium where language divergence is balanced by language convergence. What generates and maintains this equilibrium?

POSSIBLE EXPLANATIONS

Five reasons, singly or in combination with one another, have been offered over the years to account for observations such as these.

1. *Isolation.* In the biological sciences, the formula *divergence = mutation + isolation + time* is perhaps the most basic way of thinking about the evolution of taxonomic diversity. Essentially the same formula is at the heart of the comparative method of historical linguistics, except that the word "change" or "innovation" is substituted for "mutation." In talking about people in the Pacific, the word "isolation" has usually been glossed in several alternative ways as (*a*) "genuine barriers to human social interactions" (Foley 1986:9) such as mountains, swamps, and swirling rivers; (*b*) relative barriers to interaction such as empty stretches of open sea that may or may not be passable depending on one's voyaging skills, navigational prowess, and the seaworthiness of one's canoe; and (*c*) social barriers such as warfare, sorcery, and political institutions

that keep people at odds and out of touch with one another. However interpreted, "it must be isolation" is often the first explanation favored to account for the great number of languages in the region and their diversity. "But this is too simple an explanation for Melanesia [and elsewhere in the Pacific; see Terrell, Hunt, and Gosden 1997], where we find, typically, the largest languages (that is, the least diversity) in the most isolated areas (such as the Highlands of Papua New Guinea) and the greatest divergence in areas of easy terrain and extensive trading contacts (as in the north coast of Papua New Guinea, and island Melanesia)" (Laycock 1982:33).

2. *Time*. The equation *divergence = change + isolation + time* is the main reason that reportedly most historical linguists working in the Pacific and not a few archaeologists, as well, think that the ancestral language of all the Austronesian languages (i.e., "proto-Austronesian") was spoken on the island of Taiwan, where three out of the four recognized subgroups of Austronesian are found (Bellwood, Fox, and Tryon 1995; Tryon 1995:20). Exactly how life on this one island has fathered such diversity in a language family that is otherwise so remarkably dispersed is a largely unexplored sociolinguistic issue. Whatever the explanation, one would think that the peculiar diversity of Austronesian on Taiwan would be more than enough evidence to question the historical linguist's rule of thumb (which zoologists and botanists who study species diversity also use) that the homeland of a language family (or biological taxon) should normally be located in the area of its greatest observed diversity (Dyen 1971, 1990). Just as it was recognized years ago that isolation is not sufficient as a general explanation for language divergence, so, too, diversity is not a simple or direct function of time (Swadesh 1971).

3. *Contact*. There are cases in the Pacific (e.g., Dutton 1995; Dutton and Tryon 1994; Lynch 1981; Ross 1988:9) where it is clear that contact between speakers of different languages (usually between AN and NAN) has evidently contributed to language diversity. While linguists using the comparative method may be reluctant to accept that language contact and the development of pidgins and creole languages are historically significant (for discussion, see Nichols 1995:208; Renfrew 1992:448; Ross 1997), nowadays language contact and borrowing are being given closer attention (Bradshaw 1995; Dutton and Tryon 1994; Ross 1996; Thurston 1987). As Edward Sapir (1921:205) observed, "It would be difficult to point to a completely isolated language or dialect, least of all among the primitive peoples. The tribe is often so small that intermarriages with alien tribes that speak other dialects or even totally unrelated languages are not uncommon. It may even be doubted whether intermarriage, intertribal trade, and general cultural interchanges are not of greater relative significance on primitive levels than on our own" (see also Filer 1990; Foley 1986:24; Pawley and Ross 1993:425). Unfortunately, it is too soon to say how influential these processes have been in shaping Pacific language diversity. The fact that there are fewer languages in the region than there perhaps should be after 35,000 to 40,000 years of settlement hints that areal effects have been real enough to make

a difference; yet saying so does not mean that processes favoring language contact and convergence invariably swamp those favoring language divergence. Divergence and convergence are two sides of the same coin. Models and methods must accommodate both kinds of processes (Ross 1997:213).

4. *Intentions*. If one asks people in the Pacific, one will often hear that they see how they speak as a sign of who they are, where they come from, and how they differ from others. Some scholars (e.g., Foley 1986:9, 27–29; Laycock 1982; Ross 1997:232) say that as a result, for example, people in New Guinea are careful to keep their linguistic distinctiveness alive and may be reluctant to abandon altogether their ways of speaking in favor of another dialect or language. "It has more than once been said to me around the Sepik that 'it wouldn't be any good if we all talked the same; we like to know where people come from" (Laycock 1982:34). Others, however, contest the generality of such a claim. Paul Sillitoe (1978:11) notes, for instance, that "where the speakers of different languages meet, they do distinguish between one another, but this does not indicate that they classify themselves as members of discrete cultural groups or that their differences represent barriers to social interaction." As Colin Filer (1990:125) adds, people in New Guinea "may adopt new languages and language-groups may adopt new people; languages may be 'exchanged' without their speakers, and speakers may cross language boundaries without their languages." There is reason to think, therefore, that even if it is important to people in the Pacific to feel that they are special in some way, and however much they may decide to use language diacritics to mark their uniqueness (Barth 1969; Fishman 1972), the desire to be linguistically distinctive may be only part (possibly a small part) of the story of language diversity in the Pacific.

5. *History*. The NAN languages are not all "genetically" related (i.e., unlike the AN languages, linguists cannot show that all these languages may be traced back to a single common ancestral language or protolanguage). When a language is labeled NAN (or "Papuan"), this means nothing more than that the language is not Austronesian (Foley 1986:3). The diversity of the NAN languages is usually taken both as a sign of their great antiquity and as an indication that they have developed in situ. In contrast, the Austronesian languages are said to have attained their extraordinary distribution in the Pacific (and as far away as Madagascar) recently enough that it is possible to reconstruct proto-Austronesian and argue that this way of speaking evolved somewhere to the west of New Guinea (Bellwood, Fox, and Tryon 1995). Therefore, some of the linguistic diversity now found in the Pacific was "preexisting." Such an explanation helps us understand why AN and NAN languages may differ, but it does not explain the origins of the diversity within each of these two linguistic divisions; nor does the hypothesis of separate origins for AN and NAN explain observed convergences between languages on the two sides of this original divide.

While each of these five ways of accounting for the language diversity of the Pacific makes sense, none of them seems sufficient in itself, particularly since each explanation calls for specific circumstances that need not always hold—

isolation is rarely absolute, human intentions are unpredictable, and the like. Furthermore, these different explanations are not mutually exclusive. A suitable formula might even be *diversity = change + isolation + time + contact + intentions + history*. But devising a way to incorporate all these variables into a comprehensive explanation for language diversity would be difficult. It is important, therefore, to decide whether we must pay equal attention to all of them. This is not an easy judgment to make for all 1,900–2,100 languages in the Pacific area. It may be easier if we narrow our focus and consider only a sampling of this diversity. For a number of reasons, the Sepik coast of Papua New Guinea is a good place to weigh possible explanations against actual data.

SEPIK COAST OF NEW GUINEA

Linguists say that over 60 languages belonging to perhaps 24 different language families are spoken along the 700 kilometers of coastline between Jayapura in modern Irian Jaya and Madang in Papua New Guinea (Table 10.1). These many languages have been assigned to five unrelated language phyla: Austronesian and at least three non-Austronesian phyla (Foley 1986; Laycock 1973; Ross 1988, 1991; Wurm 1982; Wurm and Hattori 1981; Z'graggen 1975).

Malcolm Ross (1988) considers all of the Austronesian languages in this region of New Guinea to be members of a single North New Guinea cluster of Oceanic AN languages. He uses the term "cluster" informally to refer to large groupings of languages that are more closely related to one another than to other languages within the 210 or so Austronesian ("Oceanic") languages spoken in Papua New Guinea and the western Solomons. He argues that the languages he includes in the North New Guinea cluster "all originated from the same ancestral linkage [Proto-Oceanic, or POC], which was apparently located in or near the centre of dispersal around the Vitiaz Strait" (Ross 1989:146–147)—the strait running between New Guinea and New Britain. This connection between the north coast and the Vitiaz Strait refutes "the piece of unwritten lore according to which the present-day Austronesian languages of the north coast of New Guinea reflect the west-to-east settlement of Austronesians into Melanesia. Instead, it is claimed [i.e., he proposes] that they reflect settlement in the opposite direction, from the Vitiaz Strait westward" (1989:148).

In Ross's view, the North New Guinea cluster "is probably not descended from a single proto language in the conventional sense of that term, but from a network of dialects which became more or less separated from other communalects" of the ancestral Oceanic linkage (Ross 1988:120; see also 1988:160). The main reason for saying so is that there is no set of linguistic innovations that the languages within the cluster all share to the exclusion of other Oceanic AN languages. Precisely when Oceanic AN languages were first spoken on this coast is unknown. It is commonly said that POC started to break up in the middle of the second millennium B.C. (Pawley and Ross 1993:445–448). How soon afterwards Oceanic speakers settled in northern New Guinea is anyone's

Table 10.1
Languages of Northern Papua New Guinea

AUSTRONESIAN

Schouten chain

Manam chain
Medebur
Sepa
Manam
Bam
Wogeo
Kis

Kairiru chain
Kaiep and Terebu (dialects)
Kairiru

Siau family
Ulau-Suain
Ali, Tumleo (closely related languages)
Sissano, Serra (closely related languages)

Ngero/Vitiaz family

West Bel
Ham
Bilibil
Gedaged
Takia
Megiar
Matukar

NON-AUSTRONESIAN

Sko phylum-level stock
Vanimo family
Sko
Wutung
Vanimo

Krisa family
Krisa
Rawo
Puari
Warapu

Kwomtari phylum-level stock

Kwomtari family
Fas

Torricelli phylum

Wapei family
Valman
Olo

Arapesh family
Mountain Arapesh

Marienberg stock-level family
Mandi
Bungain
Kamasau

Buna
Elepi

Kombio family
Aruek

Monumbo stock-level family
Monumbo
Lilau

Sepik-Ramu phylum
Ndu family
coastal Boiken
island Boiken
Nagum

Ottilien family
Watam
Gamei
Kaian
Awar

Misegian family
Mikarew

Nor family
Murik
Kopar

Trans-New Guinea Phylum
Kaukombaran family
Pila
Pay
Saki
Tani

Kumilan family
Ulingan

Mabuan family
Bunabun
Malas

Kowan family
Waskia
Korak

Hanseman family
Yoidik
Rempi

Nuru family
Erima

Mindjim family
Bom

Dimir family-level isolate
Dimir

Mugil stock-level isolate
Mugil

Source: After Wurm and Hattori (1981) and Ross (1988).

guess (Pawley and Ross 1995:60; Spriggs 1995:122). Based on her archaeological investigations on Muschu Island and in the Wewak area, Pamela Swadling (1990:78) has argued that the string of Austronesian-speaking settlements on the coast may be quite recent, perhaps less than 1,000 years ago. However, there is some evidence in the local NAN languages (Ross 1988:21) to infer that some non-Austronesian people on the coast were once in contact with speakers of a pre-Oceanic AN language (or languages). In other words, contact between AN and NAN may be older than the development of Oceanic somewhere in the Vitiaz Strait/New Britain area (Ross 1988).

The NAN languages listed in Table 10.1 are classified according to the higher-order groupings devised by Wurm and Hattori for their *Language Atlas of the Pacific Area* (1981). After concluding more recently that wider relations among the NAN languages have not yet been conclusively demonstrated, Foley adopted a more conservative approach for his own survey *The Papuan Languages of New Guinea* (1986). As mentioned earlier, he has recognized at least 60 different language families, as well as a couple of dozen language isolates, under the general (and vague) heading "non-Austronesian" or "Papuan." By either interpretation, nevertheless, the points to be remembered are that communities of AN and NAN speakers live right next door to one another on the Sepik coast, and there is marked differentiation within and between the local NAN languages.

New Guinea is famous in the anthropological literature for the intimacy and scale of the integration of local communities into great regional networks of exchange. Trade is not limited to the exchange of food, raw materials, and manufactured commodities. Societies in the Sepik region "engage in an import and export of ritual and artistic culture that reaches intensities almost unparalleled in the nonindustrial world" (Roscoe 1989:219). Since 1987, the New Guinea Research Program at the Field Museum in Chicago has been running a program of ethnographic and archaeological research on the Sepik coast in West Sepik (Sandaun) Province. My colleague Robert L. Welsch and I have been using the ethnological collections at the museum, which were chiefly assembled by Curator Albert B. Lewis during the 1909–1913 Joseph N. Field South Pacific Expedition (Welsch 1998, 1999), as an empirical benchmark for exploring the character of trade and cultural change among Sepik societies.

While he was living on this coast in 1909–1910, Albert Lewis was impressed by the variety, volume, and geographic range of trade in foodstuffs (notably sago and fish), raw materials, and handicrafts taking place among coastal, island, and interior communities (Welsch 1998). Our research is showing us that this is an area of New Guinea where communities have a basically similar material-culture tool kit, other shared cultural practices, unifying economic and socio-political arrangements, and local specializations in the production of certain handicrafts and other economically important items. In sum, these communities are focal points within a shared interaction sphere in which people have a more or less homogeneous material-culture complex but not a common language (Terrell and Welsch 1997; Welsch and Terrell 1991, 1998). Lack of a unifying language or lingua franca has not kept these villagers from sharing in a common pool of resources, material products, and cultural practices.

During fieldwork in 1993–1994, we found out why language and culture do not coincide in this part of New Guinea. People on the coast participate in a vast network of social relationships based on inherited friendship (Welsch 1996a; Welsch and Terrell 1994, 1998) that join people, families, and communities into enduring social fields that ignore not only linguistic differences but even the current international border between Indonesia and Papua New Guinea. On Tarawai Island near Wewak, for instance, one of our informants has had traditional friends (locally called *chem*) in 33 different communities over a distance of 270 kilometers where people, in total, speak 18 languages other than his own Boiken (Welsch and Terrell 1994).

Thus the Sepik coast of New Guinea is an enigma. In their ways of living together, people are tied to one another by social and economic relationships into a vast community of culture, shared interests, and common goals. Yet in their ways of speaking, they are divided into scores of different speech traditions. To use both old and new parlance, they are a "tribe" but not an "ethnolinguistic group." How can this be?

POSSIBLE EXPLANATIONS

Information on the languages spoken along the Sepik coast of New Guinea is limited. Nevertheless, lack of good detailed information has not hindered scholarly reflection on what the complex array of AN and NAN languages may be able to tell us once more complete data are in hand. For example, the German ethnologist Frank Tiesler (1969, 1970), drawing on information available to him about economic relations between these villagers suggested a number of years ago that trade and diffusion across cultural boundaries have blended the disparate ethnic practices of the resident Austronesian and non-Austronesian communities into a fairly uniform way of life that today no longer reflects their formerly divergent history. He accepted the conventional view that New Guinea has seen "specific waves of settlement," the earliest peopled by NAN speakers, the most recent (before modern times) by AN speakers. He surmised that the original non-Austronesian settlers must have all had basically the same culture at the start of their history in the region, but their uniformity must have given way to diversity since they only had (he judged) simple dugout canoes and the density of their settlement along the coast must have been low. Hence their isolation from one another in due time would have led to the creation of different local "cultural types." Each of these local cultures, he concluded, would have grown to became "a separate stone" in the evolving cultural "mosaic of the Sepik region" (Tiesler 1969:121).

In sum, Tiesler assumed that culture (and its reflection in material culture) had once been as diverse on the Sepik coast as language still is today. While he did not attempt to explain why language has stayed so diverse, he did offer a direct way to explain why culture has not. A second wave of settlement, this time by AN speakers, had evidently broken upon the coast. These invaders came in outrigger voyaging canoes that made long-distance trade and communication thereafter much easier and safer. With time, the cultural diversity of the region that had evolved during NAN times gave way once more to a basically uniform way of life, a "mixed culture," within a single and fairly cohesive "northern coastal cultural region." "Wir können mit Recht sagen, dass die Kultur jeder einzelnen Gruppe dieses Beziehungsgebietes zugleich Ausdruck der Leistung aller darin wohnenden Gruppen ist" (Tiesler 1969:114, freely translated, We can legitimately say that the culture of each group in this interconnected network of relationships reflects the achievements of all the groups living within the region).

While Tiesler's reading of human history on the Sepik coast has other elements (notably economic determinism), it can be seen that his formula for explaining diversity relies heavily on the variables *isolation* and *history*. Our studies of over 6,000 ethnographic objects in our museum collections from the coast have confirmed that cultural practices throughout this area of New Guinea are strikingly similar in spite of the coast's linguistic fragmentation (Terrell and Welsch 1990; Welsch 1996b; Welsch, Terrell, and Nadolski 1992), and the little diversity encountered is most directly associated with distance (i.e., geographic propinquity).

Our findings—and, by extension, Tiesler's observations—have been challenged by A. Kimball Romney and his associates (Moore and Romney 1994, 1995, 1996; Roberts, Moore, and Romney 1995). Using our published museum data and several statistical approaches, they find a correlation between cultural diversity on the coast (as exhibited by the ethnographic objects at Field Museum) and a variable they call "language," which is basically a numerical transformation of the fact that linguists divide all of the languages represented in our museum database into seven unrelated major language groupings. However, each of these language groupings, with the exception of AN, has a restricted geographic range on the coast. Collectively, their distribution resembles a few small beads set here and there on a long string of coastline (Welsch 1996b:231). Consequently, in Romney's analyses, the more widely dispersed Austronesian communities must carry the burden of testing his claim that language history makes a significant difference in the distribution of cultural diversity on the coast. If language and modern cultural diversity are associated in historically interesting ways—contrary to what Tiesler, Welsch, and I have argued—then it should make little difference how widely dispersed the Austronesian communities are (Moore and Romney 1996:253; Welsch and Terrell 1994:393). Regardless of where they are located on the coast, these Austronesian communities should all be both distinctly similar to each other and observably different from their non-Austronesian neighbors.

However, our analyses and even those by Romney (Moore and Romney 1996: figures 3, 7–9; Welsch 1996b; Welsch, Terrell, and Nadolski 1992) show that the Austronesian communities on the coast are both similar to their non-

Austronesian neighbors in many respects (as one would expect, for they are the principal voyagers, and they move large quantities of goods and products throughout the area) and are also culturally the most variable group of villages. Furthermore, there is no material-culture trait in our museum database shared by all the AN speakers' communities to the exclusion of their NAN-speaking neighbors (Welsch 1995, 1996b). Other than language, in short, there is nothing that is diagnostically "Austronesian" in a cultural sense.

I have been talking about the coastal Austronesian communities as if they were linguistically undifferentiated, which we know is not true. The Austronesian communities in our database belong to what Malcolm Ross (1991) has called the Schouten chain of AN languages (Map 10.1), a closely related group distributed between Manam Island and Medebur village on the coast southeast of the Sepik-Ramu delta and Serra village west of Aitape. Ross argues that all of these languages are descended from a single earlier language, Proto-Schouten, which he classifies as a member of the North New Guinea cluster of Proto-Oceanic.

Ross shows that the 12 languages he includes in the Schouten chain differ among themselves in a number of respects, both phonological and morphosyntactic (1991: Tables 1–2). The AN language spoken on Manam Island in the east is the most "conservative," that is, Manam is most like Proto-Oceanic/Proto-Schouten. The farther one travels westward away from Manam, the more innovations each language displays (Ross 1991:438). He argues that this clinal patterning of innovations shows that Proto-Schouten must have spread westward from the homeland of Proto-Oceanic in the Vitiaz Strait region as a chain of dialects that eventually differentiated into the array of separate languages recognizable today.

Ross finds it perplexing that this array still has an east-to-west clinal pattern and offers a theory that explains, he says, not only the association between distance and language in the Schouten languages but similar clinal patterns of language variation elsewhere in the Pacific—including, in fact, the entire Austronesian family (the reconstructed family tree for Austronesian shows a geographic progression of increasingly innovative languages as one leaves Taiwan and travels eastward to Fiji and Polynesia). His theory is basically that people who stay at home may be more conservative linguistically than people who leave. Therefore, if people who leave home travel in a fairly orderly direction and set up new communities in a fairly orderly progression, one after another, then they should leave in their wake a linguistic imprint of their migration, and that imprint ought to look like a progressive (that is, clinal) series of increasingly divergent language communities.

Although Ross (1991:448) describes this theory as useful for interpreting linguistic prehistory in Melanesia, there are reasons to be concerned not only about its generality (Blust 1991) but also about its success in accounting for the phonological and morphosyntactic innovations observed in the Schouten languages of northern New Guinea. It is also worth noting that Ross's thesis that new

Map 10.1
Location of the North New Guinea Cluster and Its Subgroups

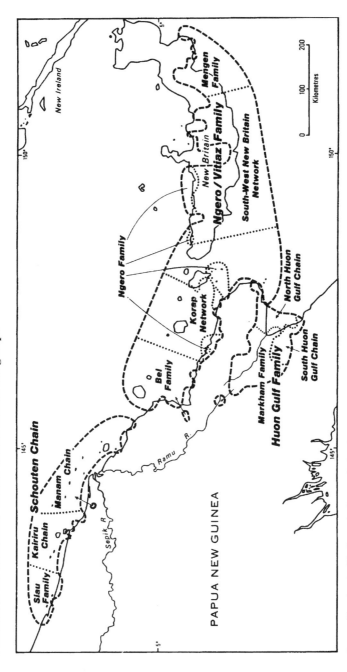

Source: Reprinted with the author's permission from Ross (1988: map 3, page 121).

communities tend to be more innovative than older settlements is not a generally accepted interpretation. Historical linguists have commonly endorsed quite a different view, namely, that languages tend to change more readily in the center of their distribution than at their margins, where older ways of speaking tend to be preserved (Breton 1991:60; Hock 1986:440–442; see also Bradshaw, this volume). Additionally:

1. There is possible circularity in his model, as Ross realizes (1991:435), particularly when he argues that the Manam AN language is "the most conservative" of the Schouten languages. This means that Manam most closely resembles the modern AN languages used in the recognition of the Schouten chain as a minimal group of languages sharing innovations in common relative to Proto–North New Guinea (and that are, of course, also the AN languages instrumental in defining the North New Guinea cluster). Therefore, characterizing Manam as the most conservative of the Schouten languages may just be a bias against geography as an explanation (specifically, against the conventional observation that isolation by distance may lead to clinal patterns of variation). However normal this bias may be in historical linguistics, work in ethnography (Tiesler 1969, 1970; Welsch 1998; Welsch and Terrell 1998) and archaeology (Terrell and Welsch 1997) shows that travel between communities in northern New Guinea, the Vitiaz Strait, the Admiralty Islands, and New Britain has been going on for centuries, probably millennia, as Ross (1988:121) acknowledges. There would seem to be no necessary reason to rule out geography as a plausible explanation for the clinal patterning of innovations seen in the Schouten languages.

2. Ross (1991:441–442) notes that historical linguistics has well-established ways of explaining why innovations in a group of languages may form geographic patterns. Perhaps the best known is the principle underlying the "wave model" of historical linguistics: "namely that if speakers of related communalects are in contact with each other, it is to be expected that an innovation occurring in one communalect will diffuse to its neighbors" (Ross 1991:442). Since there is good reason to say that contact has been a constant of life on the coast for centuries, perhaps millennia, there is also reason to think that the languages in the Schouten chain ought to fit a wave model and other similar ways in historical linguistics of modeling language contact (Bailey 1973; Bloomfield 1933; Hock 1986:444–456; Holmes 1992:218–224; Romaine 1982: 252–273).

3. Ross rejects the applicability of the wave model to the Schouten languages on the basis of an elementary computer simulation showing (in an idealized case) how innovations along a chain of 12 language communities ("communalects") ought to lead to a pattern of variation unlike the clinal pattern observed for the 12 Schouten languages (and elsewhere in the Pacific, including the Austronesian family taken as a whole). Specifically, his simulation indicates that "the communalects at the two ends of the chain are least likely to undergo innovations (because each has only one neighbour from which it can receive a

diffused innovation) and that the communalects in the middle of the chain have the greatest probability of undergoing innovations" (1991:443). In other words, communities at both ends of the chain ought to be—other things being equal— the most conservative (unlike the Schouten chain), and those in the middle ought to be the most innovative. These predictions, however, are correct only if it is assumed that the 12 language communities being modeled comprise a closed system and that distance has no effect on how far an innovation occurring at random in any one of these simulated communities will spread to the others. Since there are ethnographic and archaeological reasons to think that people on the coast have been in contact with their neighbors and with people east of them in the Bismarck Archipelago and the Vitiaz Strait, there is little reason to model the Schouten language communities as a closed system or to think that distance has had no impact on language contact and borrowing.

4. Ross assumes that family trees (1991:Figures 1 and 2) charting the patterns of shared linguistic innovations within the Schouten chain can be read directly as human history (rather than just as a convenient way of summarizing data). He argues specifically that the clinal patterning of innovations in the Schouten languages not only shows that AN speakers moved east to west along the coast from the direction of the Vitiaz Strait (which seems likely), but also that each Austronesian community was established one after another, step-by-step along the coast (1991:446), in such a fashion that where certain villages are located today (e.g., Ulau-Suain on the coast just east of Aitape) may be considered the immediate "homeland" of the remaining language communities yet farther west (1991:445). Yet as Tiesler's earlier work implied, and as our own field studies since 1990 have confirmed, however distinguishable these Austronesian communities may be linguistically, they are each other's neighbors and friends. There would appear to be little reason to think that a language family tree displaying innovations in the Schouten chain maps the settlement history of AN on the Sepik coast, or that where people are living today is where they have always been living (see Bradshaw, this volume).

5. It should also be noted that Ross identifies 12 AN languages on the coast on the evidence of a small number of observed linguistic innovations. His classification, therefore, gives us no clue how mutually unintelligible these speech traditions may be. While AN speakers on Ali Island, as a case in point, report having some difficulty understanding AN speakers at Sissano lagoon (Welsch, personal communication), I suspect that sociolinguistic research on the Sepik coast will show that Ross's classification exaggerates the level of language competence needed for people to move along the coast between the currently recognized AN speech communities.

While I disagree with Malcolm Ross in these several ways, I agree with him that prevailing models in historical linguistics inadequately explain the observed correlation between "the cline of innovativeness" and geography (Ross 1991: 447) on the coast. I see the Schouten languages—ironically, as Ross does, but for a different reason—as a small-scale example illustrating the conundrum of language diversity in the Pacific. What is it about how language is learned and lived in northern New Guinea that gives these communities the linguistic appearance of being isolated from their neighbors in spite of the fact that the people using these speech traditions are tied to one another by culturally structured and possibly quite ancient relationships of friendship, marriage, commerce, and shared social responsibility?

A SOCIOLINGUISTIC MODEL

We have made progress in deciding how much attention to give each of the six elements (*change, isolation, time, contact, intentions,* and *history*) in our formula for diversity. For many purposes, it seems that we may exclude the variable *isolation* if we divide *contact* by a new variable *distance*:

$$diversity = change + time + (\frac{contact}{distance}) + intentions + history$$

What about the other variables? While we might refine what we want *change* and *time* to mean, both seem to be essential elements. Assigning a value to *intentions*, on the other hand, may be so difficult, if not impossible, that including this variable in our formula might make this element little more than a (possibly convenient) "fudge factor" (but see Hill's chapter in this volume). Perhaps instead we need to build *intentions* somehow into a way of estimating the standard error for our calculations, not use it as a separate component in our basic formula.

What about *history*? While both Tiesler and Romney see history as a weighty variable, note that each differs in what he takes the word "history" to mean. Tiesler emphasizes that a historical event—the arrival of Austronesian speakers in their outrigger voyaging canoes from somewhere else in the Pacific—was a crucial turning point in Sepik prehistory. Their expertise in canoe building reversed the drift of culture change toward increasing diversity by making long-distance trade and travel more practicable. Evidently for Romney, on the other hand, history is not about events and change, but about ethnic origins. In short, Tiesler wants us to understand why people in northern New Guinea are so similar in spite of their heritage; Romney wants us to measure how they are different because of it.

It seems unwise, however, to accept that "history" only means "turning points" or "heritage." While our museum data would appear to support Tiesler's interpretation of cultural diversity on the Sepik coast better than Romney's, perhaps our formula can be made more efficient and less cumbersome if *history* is removed as a separate term and reinserted instead as an exponent of *contact* to indicate that the impact or effect of contact, or interaction, on human diversity varies according to the specific events and circumstances involved:

$$diversity = change + time + (\frac{contact^{history}}{distance})$$

Let me hasten to admit that changing our formula in these ways may not make it easier to make useful calculations, and if we really want to be mathematical, we will probably need to make still other alterations in how these variables are related to one another. For example, we might want to make *change* more a function of *time* (say, *change* × *time*), and so on. Nevertheless, our minimally improved formula for diversity has one advantage: it shows us what a reasonable solution to the conundrum of language diversity on the Sepik coast (and elsewhere) might look like. Evidently we need a model incorporating time, change, and the variable ways that human beings are in touch with one another.

It is conventional in linguistics to stress that the coherence or integrity of language is systematic, not situational. Languages in contact, for example, do not blend together like different-colored paints poured into the same pot (Hock 1986:426–455). Even in the face of extensive contact, a language is said to maintain its intrasystemic character, so much so that it is frequently maintained that "mixed languages" do not (and cannot) exist. Such pronouncements, however, presume that languages are bounded objects or entities of some kind (see chapter 1 in this volume) and that we can really tell where one language ends and another begins.

But languages do not come individually boxed. As the linguists Andrew Pawley and Malcolm Ross have observed, "In AN, as in Indo-European, intensive borrowing between dialects and neighboring languages has sometimes created a tangle that is almost impossible to unravel" (Pawley and Ross 1993:431). Even more unsettling, linguists have no sure way to distinguish what is "just a dialect" from what is "a language." As the linguist Mark Sebba says, "From a linguist's point of view, there is no systematic way to decide what is a 'language' and what is a 'dialect': both refer to exactly the same type of communicative system. . . . We have to conclude that the *real* difference between 'languages' and 'dialects' is social" (Sebba 1997:3).

I suspect that most of us would agree that an important difference between what we call a dialect and what we call a language is how easy or difficult it is to understand what someone is saying. Unhappily, while this distinction between "language" and "dialect" may make common sense, language comprehension rarely occurs in an all-or-nothing way. How competently we can "understand" or "translate" what we hear others saying varies with context, content, circumstances, and even how tired or alert we happen to be.

From this perspective, we know as yet far too little about the "communicative competence" (Fishman 1972; Gumperz 1981[1997]; Hymes 1974[1997]) of people on the Sepik coast of New Guinea in languages other than that (or those) they first learned as children. We do know that there is variation in how easily people who know one of the AN languages spoken on the coast are able to communicate with their neighbors who speak other AN languages in the Schouten chain. It is conceivable, therefore, that Malcolm Ross and other linguists have exaggerated the level of linguistic diversity on the Sepik coast when they say that there are 12 AN languages. But what about the communicative competence of people when they visit inherited friends who speak a language in one of the NAN language groupings found on the coast? How do they make themselves understood? How do they use language in these truly "foreign" situations?

Janet Holmes (1992:16) has summarized what scholars working in the relatively new field of sociolinguistics try to accomplish: "The sociolinguist's aim is to move towards a theory which provides a motivated account of the way language is used in a community, and of the choices people make when they use language." To rephrase our questions from this perspective, how do people on the coast use language outside their community? What choices do they have?

Holmes suggests (1992:12) that to develop effective sociolinguistic answers "for why we don't all speak the same way, and why we don't all speak in the same way all of the time," we should pay attention to four basic components of how people make linguistic choices in any situation:

1. The *participants*: *who* is speaking and *whom* is he or she speaking *to*?

2. The *setting* or social context of interaction: *where* are the participants speaking?

3. The *topic*: *what* is being talked about?

4. The *function: why* are they speaking?

Additionally, the concept of "domains of language use" popularized by Joshua Fishman (1972:43–54) may be helpful. Briefly described, "a domain involves typical interactions between typical participants in typical settings" (Holmes 1992:24).

Seen this way, the variable in our model for diversity that we have been calling *contact* is chiefly about the ways (e.g., the "topics" and "functions") that language is used each year in the voyaging season (April–May through September–October) during traditional visiting (the "setting") between inherited friends ("participants") on the coast—a form of contact between people marked by conventionalized social, political, and economic interactions (Welsch and Terrell 1998) that frame a distinctive and locally well-identified "domain of language use." Today in this domain, English and New Guinea Tok Pisin (Sebba 1997) both serve as popular linguae francae. One of the mysteries of language use in this linguistic domain in earlier times, however, is that we have no historical evidence indicating that friends formerly used some other, older lingua franca (say, one of the local AN languages in the widely dispersed Schouten chain). That there appears to have been no prehistoric lingua franca spoken on the coast is a mystery because the option of being otherwise fully competent in the traditional domain of language use that we are talking about—let us call it "when hereditary friends are visiting friends"—does not look like a conceivable option. Every adult on the coast was linked by inherited friendships to at least 5 or 6 and sometimes as many as 25 other communities where people were speaking perhaps a corresponding number of distinguishable languages (Welsch and Terrell 1998:57). Unless people were truly polyglots in former times, the conclusion seems unavoidable that the level of communicative competence needed in this traditional domain must have been fairly elementary. Perhaps also friends may have been genuinely forgiving when visitors were at a loss for words.

Additionally, we should not ignore the possibility that there may have been advantages to having friends who were not genuinely competent in your language (Welsch and Terrell 1994:396). On the coast, we have often been told, at any rate, how difficult it is to entertain friends who understand what you are saying. When visitors are able to speak your language, it may be necessary to be deliberately misleading—saying something to visitors that really means something different to those in the know (i.e., choosing to use what is called *tok bokis* or *tok arere* in Tok Pisin, both meaning "concealed language") so your guests will not understand what is being said.

One other hypothesis should be mentioned as a possibility, although it may now be too late to discover how likely this hypothesis may be, given that Tok Pisin and English are now so widely spoken on the coast. It is conceivable that friends only needed to be sufficiently competent in any one of the many AN languages spoken on the coast to use "basic Austronesian" as a lingua franca.

These observations can be incorporated into our formula if we accept that *contact* on the Sepik coast largely refers to the entangled web (Terrell 1988) of inherited friendships by which and through which people have kept in touch with other people near and far. If so, then to explain why there are so many languages (and dialects?) on the coast, we should accept that the "exponent" of *contact* called *history* in our formula encompasses at least these three sociolinguistic features:

1. *Early childhood language acquisition* (Bavin 1995; Schieffelin and Ochs 1986): On the Sepik coast, a person's "language community" used to be more or less coterminous with his or her residential community, and, therefore, children usually acquired their mother tongue (or tongues) locally.

2. *Language use later in life* (Watson-Gegeo 1986): While the institution of inherited friendships facilitated travel far from home, entrance into this mobile world only began in adolescence; furthermore, these friendships may have favored travel by men more than by women (both men and women "visit" others today, but we are uncertain about the strength of gender differences in mobility in the past).

3. *Communicative competence*: Evidently the conventions of traditional visiting between inherited friends did not require (and may have even discouraged) a high degree of communicative competence in languages other than those learned in childhood.

CONCLUSION

To solve the enigma of language diversity on the Sepik coast, neither Tiesler's view of history, which regards the arrival of Austronesian speakers as a crucial turning point in the past, nor Romney's view, which deems history to be more about the ancient pedigrees of human populations than about what happened in the past, would appear to be sufficient. We have seen how local customs and circumstances structure, or pattern, life history. In this light, the unusual number of languages spoken on the Sepik coast may simply be one unanticipated outcome of *change, time*, and these locally significant conditions and social conventions.

Extrapolating from this suggestion, whether we see language as a guide to human history may depend on what we want history to be and on what it is about people and their lives that we judge worthy of study. Should we see people on the Sepik coast as a "tribe" of diverse village societies that are tied to one another by social and economic relationships into a vast community of culture, shared interests, and common goals? Or should we see them as a string of small "ethnolinguistic groups" living by the sea that are separated by their ways of speaking into scores of different ethnic and historical traditions? One thing at least is sure. In either case, knowing more than we now do about why these societies have the linguistic appearance of being isolated from one another and yet are tied together by inherited relationships of friendship, marriage, commerce, and shared social responsibility would seem key to deciding whether the history of language relationships on this coast has much to say about the history of the people who are living there.

NOTE

I thank Joel Bradshaw, Deborah Bakken, John Hines, Scott MacEachern, Malcolm Ross, William Thurston, Rob Welsch, and Ed Yastrow for their comments on the manuscript of this chapter in one or another of its manifestations.

REFERENCES

Bailey, Charles-James N.
1973 *Variation and Linguistic Theory*. Arlington, VA: Center for Applied Linguistics.
Barth, Fredrik
1969 Introduction. In *Ethnic Groups and Boundaries: The Social Organization of Culture Difference*. Fredrik Barth, ed. Pp. 9–38. Boston: Little, Brown.
Bavin, E. L.
1995 Language Acquisition in Crosslinguistic Perspective. *Annual Review of Anthropology* 24:373–396.
Bellwood, Peter, James J. Fox, and Darrell Tryon, eds.
1995 *The Austronesians: Historical and Comparative Perspectives*. Canberra: Department of Anthropology, Australian National University.

Bloomfield, Leonard

1933 *Language*. New York: H. Holt & Co.

Blust, Robert

1991 Sound Change and Migration Distance. In *Currents in Pacific Linguistics: Papers on Austronesian Languages and Ethnolinguistics in Honour of George W. Grace*. Robert Blust, ed. Pp. 27–42. Canberra: Department of Linguistics, Research School of Pacific Studies, Australian National University.

Bradshaw, Joel

1995 How and Why Do People Change Their Languages? *Oceanic Linguistics* 34:191–201.

Breton, Roland J.-L.

1991 *Geolinguistics: Language Dynamics and Ethnolinguistic Geography*. Translated and expanded by Harold F. Schiffman. Ottawa: University of Ottawa Press.

Dutton, Tom

1995 Language Contact and Change in Melanesia. In *The Austronesians: Historical and Comparative Perspectives*. Peter Bellwood, James J. Fox, and Darrell Tryon, eds. Pp. 192–213. Canberra: Department of Anthropology, Australian National University.

Dutton, Tom, and Darrell Tryon, eds.

1994 *Language Contact and Change in the Austronesian World*. Berlin: Mouton de Gruyter.

Dyen, Isidore

1971 The Austronesian Languages and Proto-Austronesian. In *Current Trends in Linguistics*, no. 8, *Linguistics in Oceania*. T. A. Sebeok, ed. Pp. 5–54. The Hague: Mouton.

1990 Homomeric Lexical Classification. In *Linguistic Change and Reconstruction Methodology*. Philip Baldi, ed. Pp. 211–229. Berlin: Mouton de Gruyter.

Filer, Colin

1990 Diversity of Cultures or Culture of Diversity? In *Sepik Heritage: Tradition and Change in Papua New Guinea*. Nancy Lutkehaus, Christian Kaufmann, William E. Mitchell, Douglas Newton, Lita Osmundsen, and Meinhard Schuster, eds. Pp. 116–128. Durham: Carolina Academic Press.

Fishman, Joshua A.

1972 *The Sociology of Language: An Interdisciplinary Social Science Approach to Language in Society*. Rowley, MA: Newbury House Publishers.

Foley, William A.

1986 *The Papuan Languages of New Guinea*. Cambridge: Cambridge University Press.

Gumperz, John J.

1981[1997] Communicative Competence. In *Sociolinguistics: A Reader*. Nikolas Coupland and Adam Jaworski, eds. Pp. 39–48. New York: St. Martin's Press.

Hock, Hans Henrich

1986 *Principles of Historical Linguistics*. Berlin: Mouton de Gruyter.

Holmes, Janet

1992 *An Introduction to Sociolinguistics*. London: Longman.

Hymes, Dell

1974 [1997] The Scope of Sociolinguistics. In *Sociolinguistics: A Reader*. Nikolas Coupland and Adam Jaworski, eds. Pp. 12–22. New York: St. Martin's Press.

Laycock, Donald C.

1973 *Sepik Languages Checklist and Preliminary Classification*. Pacific Linguistics, series B, no. 25. Canberra: Research School of Pacific Studies, Australian National University.

1982 Melanesian Linguistic Diversity: A Melanesian Choice? In *Melanesia: Beyond Diversity*. R. J. May and Hank Nelson, eds. Vol. 1, pp. 33–38. Canberra: Research School of Pacific Studies, Australian National University.

Lynch, John

1981 Melanesian Diversity and Polynesian Homogeneity: The Other Side of the Coin. *Oceanic Linguistics* 20:95–129.

Moore, Carmella C., and A. Kimball Romney

1994 Material Culture, Geographic Propinquity, and Linguistic Affiliation on the North Coast of New Guinea: A Reanalysis of Welsch, Terrell, and Nadolski (1992). *American Anthropologist* 96:370–392.

1995 Commentary on Welsch and Terrell's (1994) Reply to Moore and Romney (1994). *Journal of Quantitative Anthropology* 5:75–84.

1996 Will the "Real" Data Please Stand Up? Reply to Welsch (1996). *Journal of Quantitative Anthropology* 6:235–261.

Nichols, Johanna

1995 The Spread of Language around the Pacific Rim. *Evolutionary Anthropology* 3: 206–215.

O'Connell, James F., and Jim Allen

1998 When Did Humans First Arrive in Australia and Why Is It Important to Know? *Evolutionary Anthropology* 6:132–146.

Pawley, Andrew

1981 Melanesian Diversity and Polynesian Homogeneity: A Unified Explanation for Language. In *Studies in Pacific Languages and Cultures in Honour of Bruce Biggs*. Jim Hollyman and Andrew Pawley, eds. Pp. 269–309. Auckland: Linguistic Society of New Zealand.

Pawley, Andrew, and Malcolm Ross

1993 Austronesian Historical Linguistics and Culture History. *Annual Review of Anthropology* 22:425–459.

1995 The Prehistory of Oceanic Languages: A Current View. In *The Austronesians: Historical and Comparative Perspectives*. Peter Bellwood, James J. Fox, and Darrell Tryon, eds. Pp. 39–74. Canberra: Department of Anthropology, Australian National University.

Renfrew, Colin

1992 Archaeology, Genetics, and Linguistic Diversity. *Man*, n.s., 27:445–478.

Roberts, John M., Jr., Carmella C. Moore, and A. Kimball Romney

1995 Predicting Similarity in Material Culture among New Guinea Villages from Propinquity and Language. *Current Anthropology* 36:769–788.

Romaine, Suzanne

1982 *Socio-historical Linguistics: Its Status and Methodology*. Cambridge: Cambridge University Press.

Roscoe, Paul B.

1989 The Pig and the Long Yam: The Expansion of a Sepik Cultural Complex. *Ethnology* 28:219–231.

Ross, Malcolm D.

1988 *Proto Oceanic and the Austronesian Languages of Western Melanesia*. Pacific Linguistics, series C, no. 98. Canberra: Department of Linguistics, Research School of Pacific Studies, Australian National University.

1989 Early Oceanic Linguistic Prehistory. *Journal of Pacific History* 24:135–149.

1991 How Conservative Are Sedentary Languages? Evidence from Western Melanesia. In *Currents in Pacific Linguistics: Papers on Austronesian Languages and Ethnolinguistics in Honour of George W. Grace*. Robert Blust, ed. Pp. 433–451. Canberra: Department of Linguistics, Research School of Pacific Studies, Australian National University.

1995 The Great Papuan Pronoun Hunt: Recalibrating Our Sights. In *C. L. Voorhoeve and the Trans New Guinea Phylum Hypothesis*. Connie Baak, Mary Bakker, and Dick van der Meji, eds. Pp. 139–168. Leiden: Department of Languages and Cultures of South-East Asia and Oceania, Leiden University.

1996 Contact-induced Change and the Comparative Method: Cases from Papua New Guinea. In *The Comparative Method Reviewed: Irregularity and Regularity in Language Change*. Mark Durie and Malcolm Ross, eds. Pp. 180–217. New York: Oxford University Press.

1997 Social Networks and Kinds of Speech-Community Event [sic]. In *Archaeology and Language*, vol. 1, *Theoretical and Methodological Orientations*. Roger Blench and Matthew Spriggs, eds. Pp. 209–261. London: Routledge.

Sapir, Edward

1921 *Language: An Introduction to the Study of Speech*. New York: Harcourt, Brace.

Schieffelin, Bambi B., and Elinor Ochs

1986 Language Socialization. *Annual Review of Anthropology* 15:163–191.

Sebba, Mark

1997 *Contact Languages: Pidgins and Creoles*. New York: St. Martin's Press.

Sillitoe, Paul

1978 Exchange in Melanesian Society. *Ethnos* 43:7–29.

Spriggs, Matthew

1995 The Lapita Culture and Austronesian Prehistory in Oceania. In *The Austronesians: Historical and Comparative Perspectives*. Peter Bellwood, James J. Fox, and Darrell Tryon, eds. Pp. 112–133. Canberra: Department of Anthropology, Australian National University.

Swadesh, Morris

1971 *The Origin and Diversification of Language*. Chicago: Aldine Atherton.

Swadling, Pamela

1990 Sepik Prehistory. In *Sepik Heritage: Tradition and Change in Papua New Guinea*. Nancy Lutkehaus, Christian Kaufmann, William E. Mitchell, Douglas Newton, Lita Osmundsen, and Meinhard Schuster, eds. Pp. 71–86. Durham: Carolina Academic Press.

Terrell, John Edward

1986 *Prehistory in the Pacific Islands*. Cambridge: Cambridge University Press.

1988 History as a Family Tree, History as an Entangled Bank: Constructing Images and Interpretations of Prehistory in the South Pacific. *Antiquity* 62:642–657.

Terrell, John Edward, Terry L. Hunt, and Chris Gosden

1997 The Dimensions of Social Life in the Pacific: Human Diversity and the Myth of the Primitive Isolate. *Current Anthropology* 38:155–195.

Terrell, John Edward, and Robert L. Welsch
1990 Trade Networks, Areal Integration, and Diversity along the North Coast of New Guinea. *Asian Perspectives* 29:155–165.
1997 Lapita and the Temporal Geography of Prehistory. *Antiquity* 71:548–572.
Thurston, William R.
1987 *Processes of Change in the Languages of North-western New Britain*. Pacific Linguistics B-99. Canberra: Australian National University.
Tiesler, Frank
1969 Die intertribalen Beziehungen an der Nordkuste Neuguineas im Gebiet der Kleinen Schouten-Inseln (I). *Abhandlungen und Berichte des Staatlichen Museums für Volkerkunde Dresden* 30:1–122.
1970 Die intertribalen Beziehungen an der Nordkuste Neuguineas im Gebiet der Kleinen Schouten-Inseln (II). *Abhandlungen und Berichte des Staatlichen Museums für Volkerkunde Dresden* 31:111–195.
Tryon, Darrell
1995 Proto-Austronesian and the Major Austronesian Subgroups. In *The Austronesians: Historical and Comparative Perspectives*. Peter Bellwood, James J. Fox, and Darrell Tryon, eds. Pp. 17–38. Canberra: Department of Anthropology, Australian National University.
Watson-Gegeo, Karen A.
1986 The Study of Language Use in Oceania. *Annual Review of Anthropology* 15:149–162.
Welsch, Robert L.
1995 Comment on John M. Roberts, Jr., et al. 1995. *Current Anthropology* 36:780–782.
1996a Collaborative Regional Anthropology in New Guinea: From the New Guinea Micro-Evolution Project to the A. B. Lewis Project and Beyond. *Pacific Studies* 19(3):143–186.
1996b Language, Culture, and Data on the North Coast of New Guinea. *Journal of Quantitative Anthropology* 6:209–234.
1998 *An American Anthropologist in Melanesia: A. B. Lewis and the Joseph N. Field South Pacific Expedition, 1909–1913*. 2 vols. Honolulu: University of Hawai'i Press.
1999 Historical Ethnology: The Context and Meaning of the A. B. Lewis Collection. *Anthropos* 94:447–465.
Welsch, Robert L., and John Edward Terrell
1991 Continuity and Change in Economic Relations along the Aitape Coast of Papua New Guinea. *Pacific Studies* 14(4):113–128.
1994 Reply to Moore and Romney. *American Anthropologist* 96:392–396.
1998 Material Culture, Social Fields, and Social Boundaries on the Sepik Coast of New Guinea. In *The Archaeology of Social Boundaries*. Miriam T. Stark, ed. Pp. 50–77. Washington, DC: Smithsonian Institution Press.
Welsch, Robert L., John Edward Terrell, and John A. Nadolski
1992 Language and Culture on the North Coast of New Guinea. *American Anthropologist* 94:568–600.
Wurm, Stephen A.
1982 *Papuan Languages of Oceania*. Ars Linguistica 7. Tübingen: Narr.

Wurm, Stephen A., and S. Hattori, eds.
1981 *Language Atlas of the Pacific Area.* 2 vols. Canberra: Australian National University.
Z'graggen, John A.
1975 *The Languages of the Madang District, Papua New Guinea.* Pacific Linguistics, series B, no. 41. Canberra: Department of Linguistics, Research School of Pacific Studies, Australian National University.

11

Identity and Contact in Three Jewish Languages

Mark R. V. Southern

The degree to which genetics, culture, and language are likely to tell a common story about human history would seem to depend on how restrictively individuals are bound together into enduring and identifiable "races," "ethnic groups," or "human populations." Three distinct Jewish speech communities show how variation in language acquisition by children and how variation in everyday language use by adults can determine how language may become a marker of cultural identity and a sign of a person's affiliation with a conspicuous community of seemingly like-minded and identifiable individuals.—Editor

This inquiry attempts to extend the range and precision of recently developed instruments linking sociolinguistics, creolization, and language change. The broader questions addressed are shared with the other investigations in this volume. How does variation in language acquisition by children (abductive change) and by adults (sociolinguistically marked variation in everyday language use) influence cultural history, definition, and identity? When does language mark ethnic groups? When are language boundaries also cultural and genetic boundaries?

The linguistic profiles of three "convergence" or "cultural-mixture" languages spoken by three distinct Jewish speech communities, exhibiting varying levels of cultural and linguistic assimilation over time, are analyzed for transfer features that are empirically observable properties of language contact in general. What we know about the characteristics of contact-driven feature transfer is far from complete; this analysis tests what we know, thereby building on it.

The extent of creolization in language—the distance between the new post-mixture language (basilect) and its primary structural and genetic linguistic prestige-parent (acrolect)—reflects the conflicting forces of cultural fusion versus maintained separateness of individual cultural components. Partial creolization allows refinement of our linguistic and sociocultural conception of (1) this dialectical tussle between fusion and individuality at community-internal linguistic borders and (2) the interrelationship between fused-cum-disparate language and corresponding cultural community. Dynamics of language change are illuminated by general traits of transfer languages.

The Jewish languages concerned are Yiddish, Judeo-Tat, and Judezmo (Judeo-Spanish). The investigation focuses on contact between languages as an innovation source at the level of language acquisition (by both adults and children).[1] Particular reference is made to linguistic-cultural borderlands and the degree to which such boundaries and overlaps are coextensive.

Ethnocultural Identity and Language Choice

Some underlying notions of ethnic and cultural identity need clarifying. Fishman (1977:44) sees ethnicity as an automatic behavioral feature common to all social groupings, independent of such contact-tinged considerations as intergroup relations, calling it "an aspect of all traditioned, large-scale, self-identifying behavior." Others define any social grouping's construction of ethnic identity as a function of a particular generation's contacts with other ethnic or cultural groups: "ethnicity is essentially a form of interaction between culture groups operating within common social contexts" (Cohen 1974:xi), and it is "constructed" only under certain social conditions (Mercer et al. 1979:16).

Language reflects both these conceptions of ethnic identity while at the same time functioning as its primary identity-diagnostic tool. First, language by definition is the invisible bond welding social units together as a speech community, however imperfectly this maps onto a larger sociocultural grouping; second, language without interactive faultlines (intergroup or intragroup) is clearly impossible. These self-evident properties have served linguists well since Labov, casting new light on the underlying contours of linguistic interaction, variation, and change. We expect every language in a speech community to display low-level variation.[2] Language contact is simply the outward-facing dimension of this interactive force field; the shifting borders of cultural identity and awareness are its equally inevitable corollary.

Boundaries, however mobile, are a structurally predictable attribute of definitions of sociocultural identity, both endocentrically within a community and exocentrically. Language choice is a particularly visible, potent, and highly charged medium for the embodiment and expression of such inherently oppositional definitions. For Fishman, ethnicity is "an aspect of a collectivity's self-recognition as well as an aspect of its recognition in the eyes of outsiders" (1977: 16); "ethnic identity logically requires not only boundaries (contrast) but [consciously recognized] opposition across boundaries for such identity to be most fully articulated" (26). What he calls "the considerable similarity between the nature and functions of ethnicity boundaries and the nature and functions of language boundaries" he attributes to language boundaries' "easy involvement in the implementation and symbolization" of ethnicity boundaries and "the inherent arbitrariness and manipulability" of both boundary types (28).

Coupled with these notions of language boundaries' paramount role in encapsulating and reinforcing the borders set by ethnocultural identity, and equally defining for the cohesion of a community's ideas of ethnicity, are the core sociolinguistic attributes of prestige and value, sometimes explicitly in the form of pride, on the part of a language's speakers. Ethnolinguistic prestige can be maintained either implicitly through simple daily use (as in the history of Yiddish, Judezmo, and Judeo-Tat); or more overtly via a hierarchical ordering of available languages, based on such extralinguistic factors as economic power (conveyed by a nation-state's national language—not the case with the pre-Israel Jewish languages considered here) or religious tradition (as with the functions of the Hebrew/Aramaic hagiolect in Jewish languages).

Giles et al.'s (1977:308ff.) taxonomy of groups' ethnolinguistic vitality depends on three variables: status (economic, sociohistorical, internal/external linguistic prestige), demography (territory, concentration, exogamy), and institutional support (government, media, education, religion).[3] Central to the first, status, is "a language's history, prestige value, and . . . the pride or shame . . . of a linguistic community" (312). Mercer et al. (1979) identify conscious ethnolinguistic choices between the attitudinal poles of assimilation and pluralistic cultural maintenance: language selection centrally focuses perceptions of ethnic self-identity.

Language choice can have a similarly defining function within social groupings that are not specifically demarcated along ethnocultural lines. Milroy's work with urban-industrial speech choices in Belfast English showed that change in network structure contributes to linguistic change (1982). The dynamics of close-knit localized social groupings eloquently support a view of language choice as a token of perceived sociocultural self-definition linked to sociolinguistic prestige or pride. A consequence of loosened close networks may be the blurring of codes' and variables' "symbolic function . . . as markers of various social identities" (Romaine 1982a:10), paving the way for language change. Local network structure can be correlated with adherence to a vernacular norm, explaining why speakers continue to choose ostensibly "low-status" vernaculars despite pressure from more socially prestigious standard or coterritorial languages.

Comparison with the three Jewish speech-community languages is instructive. Forces of religious cohesion have worked hand in hand with a mix-absorbing convergence language (maintaining a particular kind of de facto prestige within each speech community, and thus functional use, as a vernacular in sometimes-diglossic relationship with more economically prestigious outside languages) to ensure linguistic and hence cultural continuity, even in the face of extreme sociopolitical adversity. Language choice here is overwhelmingly self-identifying and is embraced within the speech community. Language continuity is buttressed by the living solidity of the hagiolectal language of religious tradition and socially defining adherence, threaded through the strata of daily life—above all including the traditional requirements of literacy. Ethnic identity is vigorously maintained. It is a remarkable fact that despite, for example, the defiantly Yiddish-rejecting, germanophone post-*Haskalah* Jewish population of German-speaking central Europe in the nineteenth and twentieth centuries, Yiddish, Judezmo, and Judeo-Tat speech communities have historically been relatively immune to the depredatory effects of linguistic and (to some extent) cultural assimilation, even at times of evidently extensive assimilationist tides. The linguistic task is to assess these Jewish languages' convergence-driven development, backed by the Hebrew/Aramaic hagiolect as religious unifier and by the ostensibly low-prestige but nonetheless culturally preferred convergence vernacular as linguistic unifier, in the light of this ethnic, religious, and cultural record of survival against the odds.

Language Contact

Until recent advances in language-contact studies (Holm 1988–1989; Romaine 1982b; Sankoff 1980; Hancock 1979; Todd 1974), processes in contact-driven language change in general lacked a rigorous framework. Thomason and Kaufman (1988:37–45, 110–46) and van Coetsem (1988:7–23), following Uriel Weinreich (1953), identified two categorically distinct transfer types between languages. These determine how linguistic material is transferred between two speech communities (SCs) in contact or within a single mixed or heterogeneously layered one.[4]

These constraints urge empirical testing. Blending historical linguistics and sociolinguistics, the three exemplars of Jewish contact languages are investigated to identify the interplay between their historical components.[5] Divergent sociolinguistically motivated traits help separate the two transfer types: simple borrowing (Type 2), as against interference through shift, or creolizing feature innovation (Type 1). With Type 2, direct loans, the recipient language enacts change, and the process is strongly speaker-motive dependent, hence sociolinguistically molded. With Type 1, interference-prompted innovation, the source language enacts change, and the process is more unaware and hence less speaker-motive dependent (Table 11.1; see note 4 for definitions).

In transfer Type 2 (borrowings), factors such as (*a*) prestige-driven replacement and (*b*) the need to fill a semantic-functional gap in the speaker's language are crucial. Pervasively expressive, affective connotations point to sociolinguistic speaker-motives behind the transfer of linguistic forms or features: hence Type 2, borrowing. Separating out Type-2 effects (loans and other sociolingu-

Table 11.1
Language-Contact Transfer Types

TYPE 1:	source-language enacts change	interference-bred innovation	structural innovations	more unwitting: less speaker-motive dependent
TYPE 2:	recipient-language enacts change	loans	prestige-driven replacement, including affect-words; semantic gaps filled ("culture"-words, calques)	strongly speaker-motive dependent: sociolinguistically molded

istically constrained transfers) from Type-**1** interference-driven innovations among language acquirers is especially revealing for mixed Jewish-SC languages such as Yiddish, Judezmo, or Judeo-Tat, alternatingly hospitable to SC-external linguistic influences (Type-**2** transfers) and resistant to them, as in each case heterolectal Jewish-language SCs encountered one another and a mixed convergence-creole language emerged (Type-**1** transfers).

Historical evidence concerning contact-induced change must be assessed against cross-linguistic creole features. This provides insights into the dynamics of language change, the Grail of both diachronic and sociolinguistic researchers.

Sociolinguistic Variation, Interference, and Bilingual Communities

Variation is the norm in language. Weinreich, Labov, and Herzog (1968) pointed out that the key to a rational conception of language itself lies in the possibility of describing orderly differentiation in a language by breaking down the identification of structuredness with homogeneity. "Nativelike command of heterogeneous structures is not a matter of multidialectalism of 'mere' performance, but is part of unilingual competence. . . . in a language serving a complex (i.e. real) community, it is the absence of structured homogeneity that would be dysfunctional" (1968:101). This predicts low-level variation operating in even the most introverted speech community, linguistically and a fortiori culturally. "A linguistic community is *never* homogeneous and hardly ever self-contained" (Martinet 1963:vii).

This predictable intra-SC heterogeneity also applies closely to Jewish languages' SCs within the broader commonality supplied by religious tradition, sociocultural cohesion, and hagiolect-driven literacy.[6] As Fishman points out (1981:11f.), "Jewish society is never homogeneous, and . . . some networks within it stand far closer to the gentile world and interact far more with it than others. These networks are change-agents within the Jewish fold if the rewards that their services and skills bring them in the gentile world are also translated into increased status in the Jewish world per se. These change agents . . . acquire the gentile language first and best. . . . they are also the ones that utilize it, first and most, for *intra*-group purposes with one another and with other Jews [my italics]. . . . *It is only in the intra-group context . . . that the requirements of the Jewish tradition then impose themselves* [my italics]. . . . One of these internal influences is recurringly the LK [Hebrew, *loshn-koydesh*] literacy tradition."

The ubiquity of sociolinguistic variability in fact presents an opportunity, particularly in assessing the results of language contact and their implications for cultural-internal heterogeneity. Given the inevitability of linguistic cross-currents between SCs in prolonged contact with each other, as Gumperz argues (1968), the SC can be seen (both inter- and intralinguistically) as "a dynamic field of action where phonetic change, borrowing, language mixture, and language shift all occur because of social forces, and where genetic origin is secondary to these forces" (383). Romaine (1982b) argues that if linguistics is to be conceived of as sociolinguistic in nature, then sociolinguistics must be "tested" on new kinds of evidence, including diachronic, and "move beyond the description of synchronic phonetic and phonological data to a more general body of linguistic data" (1f.).

Yiddish

Components, Interference, Loans

Germanic-based Yiddish is an interference-born "compromise" mesolect (U. Weinreich 1953:37, 44). It has at least four historical components (M. Weinreich 1980): Germanic, Slavic, Semitic, and a tiny lexical constituent from Romance.[7] Recent Yiddish linguists (Harshav 1990:28; Prince 1996) see Yiddish as an incomplete fusion, emphasizing Yiddish's absorptive openness and the discourse-conditioned and speaker-determined multilingual ease with which it has always borrowed usages from its component languages, overstepping strict linguistic boundaries. Yiddish speakers have apparently always been livingly, synchronically aware of the constituent languages of their own speech, recognizing their imprint and incorporating it freely; hence the code-switching and shifts back and forth within a single discourse characteristic of Yiddish speech patterns.

In the history of Yiddish, the facts do not support simple Type-**2** adstratal convergence in the form of straight loans. Structural innovations here are creolization features, entailing clear Type-**1** phonological and morphosyntactic reworkings. They result from linguistic convergence in the early Middle Ages (ninth and tenth centuries) between two speaker groups, Judeo-German and Judeo-Slavic. With the arrival of the superimposed Judeo-German Ashkenaz overlayer, these two groups, speaking different languages, came into coterritorial, culturally blending contact in the preexisting Judeo-Slavic SC in east-central Europe. This cultural and linguistic mixture probably developed in the southeast German speech area, centered around Regensburg on the Danube and moving east, judging from the powerful evidence of Yiddish's dialectal closeness to Bavarian, along with some East Middle German features (King 1992:426–428,

King 1993). Some local dialect of Judeo-Slavic functioned as the "substratum" or source language.[8] What this structurally innovative transfer type (Type **1**) involves is either feature imposition on a target or recipient language, or else innovation of new, creolized, typically contrast-simplifying features. The domains affected are the linguistically stabler ones, such as phonology and morphology.

Yiddish's evolution has now been shown to exhibit both types of contact-driven feature transfer, Types **1** and **2** (Louden 1993). Its linguistic structures reveal convergence-creolized features of phonology and morphosyntax via Type **1**, interference-bred innovation. The Judeo-Slavic source-language (SL) speakers enact change through acquiring a new language, Judeo-German.[9] A comparable second-language-acquisition structure is a learner's evolving system of "interlanguage." Additionally, Yiddish displays direct borrowing, Type **2**, with the Judeo-German recipient-language (RL) speakers enacting change.[10] For Yiddish, this is a secondary, later process, fed by speakers of the new "SL + RL blend" interacting with Slavic, non-Jewish neighbors.

Yiddish fuses the Middle High German forebears of two varieties of German, Bavarian and East Middle German, as foundational Germanic components, together with external Hebrew (*loshn koydesh*: "holy language") and later-Slavic components (King 1992:427). With Germanisms proliferating in the form of *daytshmerish*,[11] the creolization layerings deepened. The genesis of Yiddish can also be traced via its stratified "non-native" components (Wexler 1987), principally the secondary Slavic overlayer.

Linguistic convergence's nondeliberate causality contradicts the conscious language-based demarcation of a speech community's self-defined ethnicity. As in many so-called convergence creoles (Gilbert 1993) and as with Judezmo and Judeo-Tat, Yiddish's multicomponent layering reflects interaction between cultural identity (fusion versus separation) and linguistic absorptiveness (fusion versus transparently separable strata).[12] The borderlands straddled by the absorptive but separate sociocultural development of Yiddish involve (*a*) Ashkenaz/Jewish customs and cultural patterns and (*b*) Jewish/host cultural blending, as well as (*c*) the mixture of the Judeo-German base with the Judeo-Slavic base. Yiddish, the comfortable, familiar folk language or *mame-loshn* ("mama-tongue"), is a contact lect: a "mid-course formation" (M. Weinreich 1967), culturally and linguistically a cohesive SC by being all-inclusive.[13]

Latter-day contact effects, both interference (structural innovations, Type **1**) and borrowing (prestige-driven substitution or addition, Type **2**), show up in the interaction between Yiddish and its chief partner languages: German, East and West Slavic, Lithuanian, Hungarian, Rumanian, and, recently, English. The two feature-transfer types produce different outcomes. Code-switching by the convergence-creole speaker is diagnostic of sociolinguistically conscious, prestige-focused feature transfer, Type-**2** direct borrowing (usually lexicosemantic). Register-dependent variation and normativism—likewise prestige effects—also suggest straight borrowing, not interference-prompted structural innovations. Expressive or subjective connotations (mostly morphological) comprise a third Type-**2** characteristic, indicative that sociolinguistic speaker-motives underlie the transfer of linguistic features. The structural innovations marking Type **1**, on the other hand, are typically phonological and morphosyntactic. Yiddish and Judezmo, and to a lesser extent Judeo-Tat, present features that match phonological and morphosyntactic patterning in more fully creolized languages. This type of analysis uses these transfer types as testable mechanisms for contact-induced change in general, allowing reconfigured perceptions of cultural identity, mixture,[14] and assimilation.

Cultural Nationalism and Identity

Historically, Yiddish's sociolinguistic status has been low-prestige. It is the folk tongue, developing since the 1200s as the Ashkenazi Jewish speech community's secondary literary language (like Aramaic in the pre-Islamic Middle East before it) and the comfortable diglossic complement to the holy language: low-genre *mame-loshn* Yiddish to high-genre *loshn-koydesh* Hebrew. For Max Weinreich, Yiddish-Hebrew symbiosis evolved through rabbinic religious learning in cheders and yeshivas, where oral learning was conducted in Yiddish, rote learning in Hebrew. Yiddish was tainted with inferiority Jewish-internally as a half-breed *zshargon*, but its stigmas have also been external. Speakers of successive host languages—German, Polish, Lithuanian, Rumanian, Hungarian, Ukrainian, Russian, English—have associated it with lack of social and political power.

The Yiddish Golden Age at the turn of the twentieth century saw fierce polarity of Yiddish versus Hebrew. This was essentially the battle for the cultural identity of the Eastern European Ashkenazi Jewish community. Identity-maintaining struggles (assimilation versus separateness) stretch back over the entire history of Yiddish, harking back to successively bilingual Jewish eras: (1) the original postexilic and first-millennium Hebrew/Aramaic epoch, followed by (2) the Hebrew/Aramaic flowering in Islamic Spain, alongside the Spanish Diaspora host, and the Judeo-Spanish (Judezmo) that developed from this linguistically composite SC. Other Jewish languages (Judeo-Persian, Judeo-Greek/ "Yavanic," and Judeo-Arabic) arose from similar partially interwoven blends (linguistic and cultural) of Hebrew/Aramaic continuations with local languages across the Diaspora.[15] Given Yiddish's linguistic status as a substandard, hybrid language (*zshargon* and *Yidish-Teitch* imply "off" German), sociolinguistically far inferior to Hebrew, with Yiddish maintaining a complementarily symbiotic relationship, this self-definition fight also reflects Yiddish's origins as a convergence language between Judeo-German and Judeo-Slavic, with Hebrew always as a diglossic, reciprocal partner hagiolect.

Yiddish's evolving postmedieval position within the Jewish community emerges from contemporary comments and speakers' behavior. In 1534, Reb Anshel of Cracow commented that Old Yiddish glossaries on difficult words in the Tanach were written as a composite, in "the Holy Tongue and Ashkenasi"—

exemplifying the historically close relationship between Hebrew and *Yidish-Teitch* (Judeo-German). Aggadic tales and biblical legends were certainly bilingual in Hebrew and Yiddish (such as the 1602 *Ma'aseh Buch*), as were Musar ethical writings.[16]

Yiddish *zshargon* was not consciously considered a Jewish language (as opposed to either a folk vernacular or a Jewishized German) until very late. Even late-eighteenth-century Chasids deal with it as a folk language, and only incidentally as Jewish. It was only referred to as "Yiddish" toward the end of the 1800s, as part of a self-conscious cultural renaissance. Yiddish was no more viewed as primarily Jewish than was Aramaic. Written sources often referred to Aramaic as "Targum" ("translation") or "Ashurith" ("Assyrian"). Reb Nachman of Bratzlav urged followers to converse with God "in the mundane spoken tongue."

The only groups viewing Yiddish as explicitly Jewish, not simply a vernacular, were socially progressive *Maskilim* (Jewish propagators of the European Enlightenment/*Haskalah*) like Moses Mendelssohn, who loathed it as debased German and encouraged Jews to speak German instead. Ironically, in the western-European *Haskalah*, favoring a cultured Hebraist atmosphere, the modes of expression quickly became fully Germanized, and most Hebrew publications died away; but by the mid-nineteenth century, the Jewish *Haskalah* in Russia and Lithuania pioneered a modernization movement and Hebrew revival, with modern Hebrew weeklies appearing under Tsar Aleksandr II's liberal patronage.

In the late nineteenth and early twentieth centuries, Yiddish removed the religious-educational class barrier, furthering progressive Jewish nationalism and egalitarianism; Hebrew kept the class barrier in place. Yiddish was the national folk language, the vital cultural instrument for all, gradually effacing the distinction between intelligentsia and masses. Writing in Yiddish kept late-nineteenth-century European intellectuals from assimilating: the absence of a Hebrew readership no longer forced them to seek their intellectual fortunes in the local non-Jewish prestige language (mostly German, Russian, or Polish). The bilingual poet Bialik, seeing Hebrew-Yiddish bilingualism as an enforced burden of nationless Jews, pointed out that Yiddish (by translating Hebrew, educationally and in rabbinic scholarship) had kept Hebrew living, constantly infusing it with the vernacular lifeblood of daily life.

The 1908 Czernowitz Yiddish Conference (the Yiddish Golden Age's high-water mark) proposed Yiddish's recognition as a national language. Yiddish/Hebrew linguistic parity was debated hotly at the time. Culturally inclusive Yiddishists insisted on the coexistence of Yiddish-speaking Jewish secularism with extensive knowledge of Hebrew, guaranteeing living connection with the gamut of Jewish tradition. Baal Machshoves proposed state recognition of Yiddish throughout Jewish social institutions (schools, courts) and acknowledgment by the state, religious leaders, and educators that Hebrew is the national classic language uniting Jews to their past and nationhood. The historian Simon Dubnov, an impassioned advocate (in Russian) of Jewish cultural autonomy as the preferred mode of unified Diaspora existence, insisted on European-Jewish tri-lingualism, in other words, multilingualism within a single culture: Yiddish, Hebrew, and the local non-Jewish linguistic-cultural medium.[17] He foregrounded Yiddish, the folk tongue, as the vital heart of Ashkenazi national unity and as the Ashkenazi SC's most powerful weapon against cultural and linguistic assimilation both in the United States and Europe.

At this point, Yiddish's self-defined intra-SC cultural profile is clearly far more complex and politically conditioned (with respect to Hebrew, the European and U.S. nation-states and languages, and Jewish cultural nationalism) than even half a century earlier, let alone the previous six centuries. Previously, Yiddish's evolution had been a successive process of loose hybridization (Judeo-German and Judeo-Slavic), bilingualism (external languages), and diglossia (Yiddish and Hebrew): fluid internal-external linguistic absorbency mapped onto the Ashkenazi interweave of internal cross-Jewish cultural autonomy and cultural interdependence within the external, non-Jewish European setting. Harshav (1990) identifies the two-decade-long pogrom wave following Tsar Aleksandr II's assassination in 1881 as the seminal event shaping the shift in Jewish intellectual and cultural sensibilities. It should be added that this post-*Haskalah* shift occurred in the wake of the rising international and Enlightenment-inspired tide of secularization, alongside the societywide effects of urban industrialization, political self-enfranchisement, and vocal nationalism.

Judeo-Tat

Components

Judeo-Tat is another strongly self-defining Jewish speech-community language. Like Yiddish, Judeo-Tat, which developed from South-West Iranian, represents an absorptive, incomplete fusion or "convergence creole." Judeo-Tat is also known natively as Juhuric or Tat, although non-Jewish Tat speakers speak a separate Iranian dialect of their own. The Tat ethnonym is probably abbreviated from *Tatar'* ("Tartar"), a locally exotic-familiar but unrelated group of "Other." Judeo-Tat is spoken by the culturally self-contained "Mountain Jews" in the foothills of the southeastern Caucasus, far removed from centers of political or economic power, on the borders between Azerbaijan and Dagestan. They are geographically and linguistically isolated, wedged between Turkic and other non-Iranian languages. There were 6,800 speakers at the official 1979 census (Haarmann 1985:163), down from 11,500 in 1959, but the number of speakers has been estimated at roughly double the official figure (Grjunberg 1963). There are enough speakers in Moscow to constitute a separate Judeo-Tat congregation.

The language was formed from a South-West Iranian linguistic base approximately 1,600 years ago (when the remote mountainous area was settled by garrisoned Sassanid troops), with convergent overlayers of local North-West

Iranian dialects and later blending with neighboring Turkic (Turkish and Azeri). Judeo-Tat is written in Farsi script, with Hebrew words often kept in the original alphabet.

Hebrew/Aramaic Reflexes

The non-Iranian, non-Turkish derivates in Judeo-Tat fall into two unequal groups. First, there are a handful of indirect lexical borrowings via Aramaic: for example, *evir* "air" <Aramaic *avir* <Greek ἀήρ [aḗr]; *leket* "kick" <Aramaic *lakat* <Greek λακτίζω[laktízō]. A second, much larger corpus of Hebrew/Aramaic words or phrases has directly maintained in Judeo-Tat. Forty of the commoner instances are given here.

ʿ*ani* "poor" < Hebrew/Aramaic ʿ*ani*

ʿ*arävo* "evening" (before the seventh day of a festival) < ʿ*arvāh*

ʿ*a'il* "child" < ʿ*avil,* ʿ*aileti* "childhood"

ʿ*ölom* < ʿ*olām* "world/age"

Ašgenazi "European Jew" < *'Aškenazī*

bedeq (*der-bedeqa sokhde*) "smash to pieces" < *bedeq*

borukho "blessing" < *brākhāh* (with anaptyctic vowel)

däʿam "taste" < *taʿam*

dofus "seal, stamp" < *dəfus* "shape"

gelgel "whirling" < *galgal*

hezi "this" < *hazeh* (< ʿ*olām hazeh* [Judeo-Tat *ölom hezi*] "this world," ritualized phrase from prayers)

homunu "Purim" (festival involving the folk story of the foiling of Hāmān, whose historical counterpart occurred in Southern Iran in the fifth century B.C.E.) < *Hāmān*

hüšiʿano "festival's seventh day" < Aramaic *hošiʿāhnā', hošaʿnā'*

ketobo "marriage-contract" < *kətubāh*

khaliso "ritual putting on and taking off of shoes" (marking a divorce) < *khəlitsāh*

khalo "bread" < *khalāh*

khašodi "envious slander" < *khašād* (+ Middle Iranian *ezāfe* attributive marker -*i*)

khəllo'i "sly cunning" < *khilul* "profanation"

mähanäf "flatterer" < *məkhanēf* "hypocrite"

meläkh "angel" < *mal'akh* (*meläkh hemovit* "angel of death" < *mal'akh hamāvet, meläkh hedümi* "angel of death" < *mal'akh hadōmāh*)

memizir "bastard" < *mamzēr* (with anaptyctic vowel)

mihəlo (*bire*) "forgive" < *məkhilāh* (*mihəlo* "Quiet!" < *məkhilāh*)

mile "circumcision" < *milāh*

mito "corpse" < *met* (*móto* "death to X!" < *mōtō*)

mozuzä < *məzūzāh*

nešumo "soul" < *nəšāmāh*

nisonu "Pesakh" < *Nīsān*

ovili "mourning" (*e ovili bire* "wear mourning") < *'āvēl*

pä'a "sidelock" < *pēāh*

qadiš "kaddish" < *qadīš*

qofo "donation-cup" < *qufāh*

qudere "vessel" < *qədērāh*

rabi "teacher" < *rabī*

sokuni, sokune'i "fear" < *səkānāh*

šobot "sabbath" < *šabāt*

šolum "greeting" < *šālōm*

tonoi "engagement" < *tənā'īm*

tühüm (raba), tühün "abyss", *töhmek* "pit" < *təhum (rabāh)*

zere "offspring" ("son" in kin compounds: niece, nephew) < *zera'*

züno "whore" < *zōnāh*[18]

Judeo-Tat's Hebrew/Aramaic component is clearly more than simply a ha-giolect. As with Yiddish and Judezmo, everyday words and cultural expressions are represented as well. The evidence indicates straightforward continuity: He-brew > Aramaic > Judeo-Tat. This recalls Katz's terms for the continuity of the Hebrew/Semitic component in Yiddish: Hebrew > Aramaic > Yiddish, "the Jewish chain" (1985:100): "an unbroken chain of language . . . links ancient He-brew to Aramaic to Yiddish."

In both Judezmo and Judeo-Tat, as in Yiddish, this unbroken continuation of Hebrew/Aramaic functions as a "metahagiolect": hagiolect plus culture-word repository.[19]

Linguistic Transfer, Sociolinguistic Profile

Judeo-Tat displays Type-**2** sociolinguistically conditioned lexicosemantic loans, including calques and idioms, direct from the Iranian and Turkic source languages (Haarmann 1980, 1985; Kreindler 1985; Vinogradov 1966). Here Turkish and North-West Iranian are functionally parallel to Slavic in Yiddish's emergence from the converging of Judeo-German with Judeo-Slavic. Type-**1** morphological and phonological innovations are also attested in Judeo-Tat, pre-cisely the a priori more stable and conservative domains of a grammar.

In Judeo-Tat, unlike modern Yiddish, there is no concern with linguistic "pu-rity" or normativizing. The same is true for Judezmo, aside from the authorita-tive influence of the canonical Ladino used in the 1553 Ferrara translation of the Tanach (Hebrew Bible). These two Jewish languages' sociolinguistic con-figurations, especially this absence of purist impulses, mirror Yiddish's independent-interdependent cultural image and absorptive-fluid linguistic character within its own SC prior to the advent of the political and nationalistic currents, Jewish-internal and European-external, that swept across it in the modern era.

Judezmo

Components

Judezmo (Judeo-Spanish) offers a third point of comparison for contact features. Historically the language of Sefarad, or Jewish Spain prior to the 1492 expulsion,[20] Judezmo's structural ingredients are (1) Ladino/Old Spanish, (2) a large admixture of Turkish, as well as a handful of North African Arabic words via Old Spanish and/or Levantine Arabic words via Turkish later on, (3) a substantial Hebrew(/Aramaic) contribution, mostly lexical, (4) a moderate Greek component, and (5) a few lexical items from Italian, Bulgarian, Rumanian, and other southeastern European languages. The relative dialectal mixture of (2), (4), and (5) varies depending on each Judezmo dialect's host-country language.[21] Judezmo SCs (Malinowski 1983, 1985; Harris 1983, 1994) offer illuminating parallels with Yiddish and Judeo-Tat, namely, (a) speakers' attitudes and adherence to Judezmo within a weightedly bilingual SC and (b) the degree of creolization traceable in the Spanish-Turkish-Hebrew-Arabic layers of Judezmo's composition.

Unlike Judeo-Tat, which has kept its linguistic and cultural autonomy mostly intact, largely by virtue of the Judeo-Tat communities' ideally isolated mountainous locale on either side of the Russian-Azeri border, Judezmo has recently been subjected to relentless external pressure from English and now Israeli Hebrew. This sociolinguistic imbalance has presented uneven bilingual situations in which Judezmo could not maintain itself. Prior to the twentieth century, with its overwhelming assimilatory pressures following the European Holocaust and the twin dominance of Hebrew in Israel and English in émigré Sephardi communities in anglophone countries, Judezmo had been more or less holding its own, chiefly in the Ottoman world. Judezmo's Jewish-internal prestige profile has historically been higher than Yiddish's. But its mix of a Spanish structural base with Hebrew hagiolectal and cultural material and subsequent substantial Turkish, Arabic, and Balkan contact admixtures in the respective Turkish-controlled host communities matches the sociolinguistic profile of Yiddish (German structural base, Hebrew hagiolectal-cultural material, subsequent substantial Slavic contact admixtures in Slavic-controlled host communities). Both languages are signally absorptive.

Cultural Boundaries and Hybridization

Defining the nature of cultural borders, Streeck (1997) argues that culture is an underlyingly intercultural mass noun: not a collection of separate entities nor a monolith, but a shifting structure of forces. Within this intercultural structure, linguistic separateness is only the most obviously difference-maintaining feature, since communication depends on shared linguistic material. Gestural divides and other physical, nonlinguistic assumptions (communicative or otherwise) are less sharply coextensive with the boundaries of political units than are politically conditioned linguistic borders. Abruptly bordered linguistic (and cultural) difference seems to be always politically conditioned.

Exceptionless political and cultural underpinning of linguistic self-definition is intuitively predictable and certainly fits the Yiddish facts. It applies equally well to Judezmo, but the differences in Judezmo's sociocultural and especially sociolinguistic configuration are as instructive as the similarities. The central differences hinge on sociolinguistic value and the consequent extent of acculturation (promoting absorptive, adaptive language contact) versus cultural isolation (promoting crystallization of newly formed linguistic systems, such as independent creoles). A continuum links these two poles. Seeing culture as a structural force field in flux, rather than as a homogeneous bloc or as a set of discrete cultures, also helps supply a cross-applicable framework for the dialectic between cultural autonomy and interdependence that characterizes Judezmo, Judeo-Tat, and Yiddish. Absence of nationally defined identity and political borders enables fluid contact-driven transfer of linguistic material.

With its various SCs' historically diverse cultural-exposure configurations, Judezmo shows variable linguistic syncretism along lines comparable to the West African/European syncretism observable in creolized languages of the Caribbean, especially in morphosyntax. The wide variation in Atlantic creoles can be attributed to a continuum of "differential acculturation among Africans placed in contact with European culture" (Alleyne 1971:170). Analyzing the emergence of the Atlantic creoles as originating in interference (Type 1), with Africans interpreting European languages' grammatical patterns in terms of their own linguistic structures, Alleyne argues that "socio-cultural factors everywhere determined the degree of [Type-1] interference. . . . this resulted in *linguistic variation and instability which is characteristic of any dynamic acculturative process* [my italics]. At the beginning of the process [of crystallization of a linguistic medium (creole) within a group effectively in contact only with themselves], this creole was in fact only a major segment of a continuum of variation and marked the first stage in the process of adaptation to a cultural model" (182). Linguistic acculturation is clearly quite distinct from situations where simple sociolinguistically driven bilingualism develops, for example, with the introduction of an elite or prestige language.

Judezmo's linguistic and acculturative matrix shows a wider spectrum of variation than does Yiddish's, although historically the two languages enjoy similar degrees of componential richness. The explanation is again to be found in sociolinguistic prestige and the accompanying cultural and political self-definition over time, though this diachronic self-definition does not necessarily equate with a given synchronic situation.

First, unlike Yiddish, Judezmo's livingly felt cultural association with the

Sephardi Golden Age in Spain harks back to a time when its Sephardi speakers, as a community, had abundant access to economic, political, and cultural power and prestige. In addition, the political circumstances of the subsequent postexpulsion refugee settlements in the Ottoman Empire were more favorable than the living conditions of ghettoized Yiddish speakers of central and eastern Europe, who from century to century were under perpetual threat (however dormant) of a renewed outbreak of violent attacks. Second, although its names are not noticeably revealing of any very different factors than Yiddish's (*Judezmo, Judyó,* and *Jidyó* all refer to the Jews or the Jewish religion, as does the late-attested cultural-nationalist name *Yidish,* and *Ladino* refers to Spanish origins, as *Teitch* does to German origins), Judezmo's postexpulsion cultural profile is characterized by a sociolinguistically far less overtly "low-end" self-image than Yiddish's even with regard to Hebrew, although in terms of registers, genres, and usage within their respective Jewish SCs, Judezmo and Yiddish were historically fairly comparable. Both are hybrids, in SC perception and in reality; both are quintessentially folk tongues; both are products of successively bilingual societies; and both show extraordinary capacity for absorption of linguistic input. Yiddish also clearly displays considerable dialectal diversity. But internally and externally, Judezmo's sociolinguistic character was less confining, in addition to being less socioculturally ghettoized and isolated. Culturally, this evidently translated into a broader continuum spread of the degrees to which acculturation could take place. One byproduct, assisted by a greater number of source languages for Judezmo's syncretic mixture, was linguistic variety.

Linguistic Diversity and Contact Features

Judezmo's linguistic ingredients are chronologically layered. To illustrate their compositional complexity, reflexes of the major components are presented here.[22]

A. Structural core: Old Spanish (the contact "recipient language")

por módre "because" < OSpan. *por modo + modro* "order"

ánde "where" < OSpan. [*a +*] *onde*

favlár "speak" < OSpan. *fablar* (~ *avladéro* "talking-place"), *fásta* "until" < Arabic *khàttà,* with the *f ~ h* alternation including hypercorrect forms (cf. Span. *hasta*); *fíja/o* in fixed collocations "daughter/son," *fijóla* "baby girl naming-feast," beside *íja/o*

golór, golyendo "smell" < OSpan. *holór, holiendo*

yazér "lie down, sleep" < OSpan. *yacer* (< Lat. *iacēre*)

Code-switching (Spanish + Turkish/Hebrew)

Phrasal blends:

kump[l]ír minyán "reach age of 13" (a Bar Mitzvah boy counts for a minyan) < Span. *cumplir* + Heb.

kon tenay ke "on condition that" < Span. + Heb. *tenā'i* = "condition"

bevér tutún "drink tobacco," hence "smoke" < Span. + Turk. *tütün* "tobacco"

rizúm "grape" < Span. *racimo* "cluster" + Turk. *üzüm* "raisin"

Word-internal compound blends:

holiénte "sick" < Heb. *kholeh* + Span. *-iente*

mazalózu, desmazaládo "(un)lucky" < Heb. *mazāl* + Span. *-oso, des- -ado.*

Relexification:

arrib'abásho "more or less" < Span. *de arriba abajo* "top to bottom," based (internal calquing) on Jdzm. *malámata* < Heb. *ma'alā-matāh*

hahán = *sávyo* "rabbi" ("wise one") < Heb. *khākhām*, Span. *sabio*

B. Hebrew

hilúl Ashém "profanation of the Name of God" < *khilul HaŠēm*

masá "unleavened bread" < *matzāh* (cf. Turkish-derived *hamursúz* = *matzot*)

peá, plural *peót* "sidelock" (cf. Turkish-derived *ulúfya* "sidelocks" < *zülüf* with met-analysis: *la zulúf* > *las/z uluf* + Span.-derived *-ya*)

olám abá "the world to come" < *'olām haba'āh*

hanéf "hypocrite" / *hanífero* "flatterer" (with Span. *-ero*) < *khānēf*

mamásh "real" < *mamāš* (cf. Yidd. *máməsh* "that of all things")

amáres "idiot, ignoramus" < *'am ha'arets* lit. "countryfolk" > "bumpkin"

Yintó, Intó (personal name) < *yom tov* "holiday (good day)": unstressed *ə* > *i*

rishhódish "first of the month" < *rō'š khōdeš* "head of the month"

lashón acódis "Hebrew" < *ləšōn haqōdeš* "holy language"[23]

Reborrowing back into Judezmo of a Hebrew term, with new features from the borrowing (non-Judezmo) language

haburá "chaos" < Bulgarian *xavra* "synagogue, noise" < Heb.-in-Jdzm. *khavurāh/khevrāh* "society"

Cf. Yidd. *shakhermakher* "a slick operator/shady deal[ings]" (Wexler 1996:215) < Heb. verb *sakhar* "trade" + Ger. *Macher* "wheeler-dealer," with Yiddishized *sh-* < Heb. *s-* influenced by the conditioned *s-* > *sch-* of German (not Yiddish) phonology, since Yiddish initial *s-* would pose no phonotactic problems. Hence the Yiddish *shakher-* form reflects transfer and then retransfer, Hebrew-in-Yiddish > German > Yiddish.[24]

C. Turkish

kojá (nominal prefix *kojá-*) "big"

kim bilír "who knows" (Maimon 1980:145)

janúm "my darling, my life" < *jan-um* (grammaticalized: Turk. *-um* "my")

bash ustuné "with pleasure" < *baš üstüne*

garéz "grudge, shackle"

jennét, je'eném "paradise," "hell"

yok "none"

Taboo replacement

el taván "roof" (< Turk.) for *el Dió* "God" < Span. *Díos*. Jdzm. *Dió* replaces archaizing Span. *Díos* (< Lat. *Deus*), since *-s* as the distinctive plural marker would be unsuitable or taboo (carrying pluralitarian connotations of the Trinity): hence (1) Judezmo's disambiguating addition of the deictic *el* and (2) the removal of *-s*.[25]

Playful labial-initial disparagement-pairs (Turkic derived), as a productive *X-* ~ *m-* phrasal configuration

Jdzm. *konde . . . monde* "count and whatever," extended to *X-* ~ *sX-*, especially with labials: so Jdzm. *shpudre, shmudre* "father, mother" for *padre, madre*. Turkish (like other Turkic languages like Baškir)[26] has a fully productive *X-* ~ *m-* pair matrix: *šapka mapka* "hat or whatever," *kim mim* lit. "who or what's-his-name," *sonu monu* "end or whatever," *dergi mergi* "journals and stuff," *reform meform* "reform and things." These are comparable to Yiddish derogatory twin formulas (see the Borrowing section later in this chapter),[27] typologically and etymologically, since the Yiddish feature probably derives from Turkic via Slavic.

Apotropaic substitution

blánko "coal" < Span. "white" by apotropaic taboo replacement. Compare Yidd. *der guter yor* for *shvarts-yor* "black year" (M. Weinreich 1980:133).

D. Arabic

aljáma "community" < Arab. (via OSpan.), along with other "congregational" socio-cultural words

hazíno "sick" < OSpan. *hacino* "sad, troubled" < Arab. *khazīn* "sad," with the perceived formal closeness here to Judezmo derivates of Hebrew triliteral root-structure templates (*CVCVC-* + *-o* etc.) perhaps helping to ensure—by morpheme-structure association— that this word found a safe niche in Judezmo users' lexicons

alhá[d] "Sunday" < Arab. *al-khad* "(the) [Day] One." Compare Heb. *yom 'alef*, biblical Heb. *yom 'ekhad/yom ri'šon* "day one/day first." This is conscious, culturally determined, Christendom-avoiding lexical replacement for Span. *domingo* with its taboo connotations of the Christian "Lord's day." Yiddish parallels: *benshn* "bless" replaced Middle High German *segnen* "bless" < *segen* "sign of the cross"; diminutive *kinderlekh* (plural) "children" (with the derivational morpheme placed after the inflectional morpheme), but no **kindl (singular), to avoid Christian connotations of German *[Christ]kindl* (Santorini and Prince 1996); Yidd. **Maria is avoided as a proper name, *Miriam* poses no problem (Prince 1996).

Interference and Borrowing: Evidence

As discussed in the "Language Contact" section, sociolinguistically conditioned language traits separate transfer Type **2**, borrowing, from transfer Type **1**, feature imposition[28] or creolizing feature innovation.[29] Type-**2** transfers are *loans*, mostly lexicosemantic, affecting the less conservative linguistic domains. They can be strongly speaker-motive dependent, hence *language-external* and sociolinguistically molded. Type-**1** transfers are interference-prompted *structural innovations*: they are *system-internal*, affecting more change-resistant linguistic domains such as phonology and morphosyntax. They are more unwitting and less speaker-motive dependent. Foreign accents are a comparable Type-**1** contact feature—a phonological trace imposed on the RL by a speaker of an SL in acquiring the RL.

Two "loan channels" are central to Type **2** (chiefly lexical borrowings), involving *substitution* (**2A**) and *addition* (**2B**): **2A**, prestige-driven *replacement*, the borrowing of forms that are marked for prestige, positively or negatively, including emotionally or expressively charged "affect words"; **2B**, the need to fill a semantic-functional *gap* in the speaker's language, such as "culture" words; this category also includes calques (RL forms, SL meanings) and idioms. Affective connotations, a predominantly morphological extension of loan channel **2A**, point to sociolinguistic speaker-motives behind feature transfer and are diagnostic of borrowing (Type **2**). As mentioned earlier, in the section on Yiddish, code-switching is a discourse pointer to this Type-**2** transfer; register-conditioned variation and normative effects also reflect it.

Judezmo and Judeo-Tat historically share with Yiddish particular SC features, such as the Hebrew/Aramaic hagiolect and culture-word source. Do they also show evidence of both types of contact-driven change, as Yiddish does?

Type 1: Interference

Type-**1** linguistic evidence for creolized features[30] appears when an RL has been adopted by SL speakers in an adapted mixed version of RL; the SL speakers' language shift generates the linguistic interference effects.[31] The restructured features, usually phonological and morphosyntactic, are imposed from the SL by transfer or else innovatively developed.[32] The following sections consider creolelike linguistic features of phonology and morphosyntax that enrich our perspective on Yiddish, Judezmo, and Judeo-Tat as convergence creoles, developing out of particular kinds of cultural blending.

Phonology

Cross-linguistically plausible changes become likelier when universal tendency and substratal influence converge (Holm 1988:107). Both Judezmo and Judeo-Tat, as well as Yiddish (Louden 1993), display features that match familiar phonological patterns in creolized languages.

Initial alternation: hypercorrection

Jamaican [haɪlan] "island" ~ [aɪlan] "highland[s]", nonnative Eng. *Heinar Augen* (a "linguistonym"), *w* ~ *v* in Ger. nonnative Eng. *telewision*: a post–"critical-age" type of change phenomenon. This type of hypercorrection may underlie Judezmo *f-* ~ *h-* alternation (OSpan. *f-* > *h-*) and conceivably extraneous nasals in Jdzm. *ansína* "like this" < Span. *así*, *múncho* < *múcho* (cf. Byzantine Greek *sambaton* < *sabb-*, Jdzm. *zinganó* < Byz. Gk. *tsiganos* ~ Modern Gk. *tsingáno*). E Yidd. *a ferd hest ey*, cf. German *ein Pferd iβt Heu*, W Yidd. *a ferd est hey* "a horse eats hay" (M. Weinreich 1980:557).

Near-regular metathesis (resonants/sibilants)

/rd/: *bódre* "border, around" < *bord-*, *modrér-* "bite" < *mord-*, *acodrár* < *-cord-* "remember," *gódro* "fat" < *gordo*; /rk/: *Trukesko* "Turkish" < *Turk-*; /rp/: *trepentína* < *terp-*; /br/: *próve* "poor" < *pobre*; /rS/: *trezéru* "third" < *tercero*; /dl/ imperatives: Jdzm. *tómalda* "take it" < *tómad-la*, *búshkadla* "look for it," *mételda* "put it," *dáldo* "give it"

< *dád-lo, tráeldo* "bring it." Cf. Virgin Is. *pistarckle* "publicly obnoxious person" < Negerhollands *pistắkəl* < Dutch *spektakel* (Stolz 1986:98); Príncipe *kiryá* "raise a child" < Port. *criár*; older Haitian *drōni*, Papiamentu *drumi* < *dormir* (Holm 1988:111).

Front-round vowels lost

Jdzm. *shukiúr* "thanks" < premodern Turk. *šükür*, *borékas* "cheese pastry" < Turk. *börek*, Yidd. *sheyn, grin* (MHG /ö/, /ü/), etc. This is not true in Judeo-Tat: /ü/, /ö/ are alive and well, in fact spreading: *ʿölom* < Heb. *ʿolām*, *tühüm* "abyss", *töhm-ek* "pit" < *təhum*.

Unstressed shwa > Judezmo [ɛ] / [ɪ] / [a]; [Λ] > [o] / [ɔ]

Jdzm. *tefilá* < Heb. -*ə*, *lashón acódis* < *ləšōn haqōdeš*, *Yintó* < *yəntóv* < Heb. *yom tov*, *fistók/fustúk* "peanuts" < Turk. *fistik* (Spanish-based vowel system); Yidd. *guter* < German -*ə*; *mekhutónim* "in-laws" < Heb. *məkhutoním*, *pénim-er* "face" < Heb. plural-marked *paním* [Λ]; Atlantic creoles (based on the seven-vowel shwa-less system of many West African languages): Jamaican *bɪta* < Eng. *bitter* [bitə], Saramaccan *kóti* < *cut*, Krio *fɔs* < *first*. This is not always true in Judeo-Tat, although there is vowel resolution via accommodation to the Iranian-base vowel system, with partial Turkish-influenced vowel harmony: e.g., *mozuzä* < Heb. *məzūzāh*, *nešumo* < *nəšāmāh*, *tühüm*, *töhm-ek* < *təhum, zere* < *zeraʿ, memizir* < *mamzēr*. Turkish vowel harmony is notorious for its contagious contact effects on neighboring and convergent languages.

Distinctive vowel length lost, a creole near-universal (Holm 1988:118–119)

Judeo-Tat *nisonu* < Heb. *Nīsān, sokuni* < *səkānāh, šolum* < *šālōm*; Yidd. *geshribn, gegebn*, where *e* = [ɛ]. This reflects the more general phonology/phonetics porosity (i.e., between the levels of structural sound-system features versus raw sounds) characteristic of creoles. Kay and Sankoff (1974:62ff.) call this transparency—marked by a relative lack of allophony—"shallowness" in creoles' or contact languages' phonology.

Morphology/syntax

Morphosyntactic features shared by Yiddish or Judezmo with creole or semi-creole grammars are detailed here.[33] Nearly all creoles rely on free morphemes more than inflected morphemes to carry grammatical information—a tendency familiar from second-language acquisition to isolate this information through lexicalization (Holm 1988:144).

Gender breakdown

Judezmo proverb *cása mío, nído mío* "my home, my nest" (cf. Palenquero *un kasa má bonito*); SE Yidd. *bukh* "book" is masculine, not neuter as in MHG and modern German (a common switch; Louden 1993:24).

Inflectional isomorphism

Yidd. *shrayber-s* "writers" (≠ German *Schreiber* [plural], with -*s* plural marker confined to loans, slang, neologisms); {+ pl.} is frequently marked in creoles by a generalized affix based on a third-person-plural morpheme: Krio/Jamaican/Miskito *dem* < pron., Palenquero *ma* < Bantu inanimate plural prefix *ba-*, nonstandard Afrikaans *hulle* {+ definite pl.} < Afrikaans *hulle* "[and her/his] people" (Holm 1988:193).

Morpheme-boundary shift (metanalysis)

Jdzm. *ulúfya* "sidelocks" < Turk. *zülüf: la zulúf* > *laz uluf; lonso* "bear" < OSpan. *el-onso*; cf. Haitian *zié* "eyes" < French *les yeux, nonm* "adult male" < *un homme, lèzòm* "mankind" < *les hommes*; OSpan. *algebra* < Arab. *al jabr* "the reduction."

TMA (tense-manner-aspect) particles[34]

Yidd. *fleg-* {+ preterite iterative} without nonfinite forms: cf. Eng. *used to* ~ **to use to*; {+ completive} Jamaican (and other Atlantic creoles) *don*; {+ progressive} Haitian *ap*, Cajun *[a]pé* < French *après*, cf. Hiberno-English progressive-intentional "you'll be after sleeping"; {+ irrealis} Papiamentu *lo* < Port. *logo* "right away," Guyanese {+ irrealis} *go*, {anterior + irrealis} *bin go* > "would have": *awi bin go kom out seef* "we'd have come out all right" (Holm 1988:164); Negerhollands *[h]a* < *hab* {+ anterior} < dialectal Dutch *habben, lo* < *loop* < Dutch *lopen* {+ progressive}.

Invariant question marker

Yidd. utterance-initial Slavic-derived *tsi*; asymmetrical word order lost—sentential iso-morphism again: Yidd. ***tsi** darf der mentsh nokh mer?*; cf. Haitian *apa*, Namibian Eng. sentence-final *intit?*, Jamaican *duonit?* (< tag questions, irrespective of main-clause ver-bal syntax).

Type 2: Borrowing

Loan-influencing of the RL by a coterritorial SL instigates change (adstratal convergence).

Lexicon

Lexically borrowed function words, verbs, nouns, and adjectives are abun-dantly attested in Yiddish (< Slavic, Hebrew), Judezmo (< Turkish, Arabic, Hebrew), and Judeo-Tat (< Turkish, North-West Iranian, Hebrew) as gap fillers (loan channel **2B**).

Affect words (intimacies, nicknames, value words [positive/negative], slang), including positively or negatively marked prestige forms, indicate loan channel **2A**.

Calques (RL forms, SL meanings) include idioms, compounds, and aspectual markers, thus partly overlapping with the internally code-switching morpholog-ical material in the following section (SL forms, SL meanings). Judezmo calques readily: Jdzm. *arrib'abásho* "more or less" < Span. *de arriba abajo* "top to bottom," internally calqued on Jdzm. *malámata* < Heb. *ma'alā-matāh; sávyo* "rabbi" < Span. *sabio* < Heb. *khākhām*. Judeo-Tat calques mostly on Turkish idioms and agglutinative grammatical affixes. Yiddish verbs are frequently calqued on Slavic originals: *unterhern* "overhear" to Pol. *podsłuchiwac* (≠ Ger. *unterhören*); *iberarbitn* "act up" ≠ Ger. *überarbeiten* "revise, overwork."

Some semantic areas are immune to loans (e.g., preexisting cultural or reli-gious terms: no gap needs filling).

Morphology and Iconicity

Typically these are expressive affect forms, betokening subjective involve-ment and sociolinguistic evaluation. They are strongly marked for *prestige* (en-dearment or contempt).

Judezmo is laced with figurative or mildly expressively loaded code-switching phrases or compounds: *bevér tutún* "drink tobacco," *cumpír minyán* "reach puberty," *kon tenáy ke* "on condition that."

Yiddish boasts a rich roster of morphological Slavicisms, including bound morphemes from different sources:

- Derivational {+scornful/affectionate} affixes attached to roots (Germanic, Semitic, Romance): e.g., {+scornful} *-nik*, on nouns or verbs (or *got+enyu* "dear Lord"); *-inke* marking {+ endearment} < Slav. *-inka*: *esinken* nursery-talk "eat", *nayinke* "brand new"
- {+ Intimate} suffixal *-e* on names
- Derogatory Yiddish ∅- ~ *shm-* twin formulas (cf. the Judezmo playful disparagement pairs mentioned earlier)
- Expressive palatalization: consonantal /-y-/ added to certain syllable-onset consonants, marking {+ scornful/affectionate}, sometimes partially grammaticalized.[35]

Productive, derogatory Judezmo affect suffixes are plentiful: *avladéro* "chatterbox" < *[f]avlár; fedorénto* "stuck-up" < *fedór* < *odór* (> Span. *olór*), *afedénto* "pain in the butt [task]", *ahariénta* "rotten food/taste", *gaaviénto* "braggart, boastful" < *gaavá* "vanity" < Heb. *ga'aváh* "arrogance."

Jdzm. *amáres* < Heb. *'am ha'arets* "bumpkin" occupies a similar affective lexicosemantic and cultural niche to that of Yidd. *nebekh* (< Slavic: Czech *nebohý*; comparable to Russian *bédnyj*, Polish *bedny* "poor"): ~ "poor slob." *Amáres*, like *nebekh* (Yiddishized Eng. *nebbish*), is everywhere in proverbs: e.g., *Guáy! cuándo el amáres fávla lashón acódis* "Watch out when slobs start talking Hebrew!"

CONCLUSIONS

Linguistic Absorbency and Prestige in Jewish Languages

All three languages display both types of convergence-driven feature transfer. Judeo-Tat is less creolized overall than Yiddish, despite some restructuring (such as partial vowel harmony). Judezmo indicates blending of transfer types 1 and 2 along lines similar to Yiddish (imposition through shift, plus loans), but with a more multiplicitous and sequential profile, reflecting the larger number and wider scatter of important source languages in the Judezmo diachronic mix.

The ratios of this linguistic picture roughly coincide with the three SCs' cultural configuration. Cultural self-identification is a tricky commodity to quantify, but proportionally, the degree of both Yiddish and Judezmo speakers' cultural self-identity is characterized by a more or less conscious blend of separateness and mixture (*mestizaje*) down the centuries, rather than by assimilation. Judeo-Tat is historically the most isolated of the three speech communities, and its sociocultural profile shows less evidence of cultural hybridization and blending than do Yiddish and Judezmo. Religious cohesion and autonomy, together with such notable attendant cultural effects as the tradition and explicit prominence of literacy, have clearly played a significant part in determining all three Jewish SCs' linguistic as well as sociocultural continuity (Katz's "unbroken Jewish chain of language") and in shaping the contours of language change in each case through degrees of linguistic convergence with coterritorial host or neighbor languages.

Absence of national or nationalist power centers, and absorbent linguistic and cultural compositional diversity, heighten the importance of the analytic testimony of these languages. Their contribution to our notions of culture and linguistic-cultural mapping is enhanced in the light of such steady factors as Jewish-SC layered bilingualism and internal diglossia (with culturally and educationally prestigious Hebrew) and such recent, secondary anomalies as the prewar rise of Yiddish-speaking European Jewish cultural nationalism.

Political conditioning always underlies sharply boundaried linguistic (and cultural) difference and self-definition. Obviously, linguistic reality is inevitably and intuitively implicated in political and cultural identity. This applies just as well to Judezmo as it does to Yiddish. But switching the question around to investigate the nature of linguistic identity, the focal differences between languages or dialects, and the divide between nonnormative dialectal continuums and SCs dominated by a standard language, turn on sociolinguistic prestige. Yiddish and Judezmo both maintained their identity without an attendant political power base by constituting the vibrant vernacular heart of their communities. The relative extent of their speech communities' consequent adaptive acculturation over time (as opposed to assimilation, acculturation's extreme form) is determined by their differential sociocultural and especially sociolinguistic configurations. Here the differences between languages' separateness-versus-mixture blends are as culturally telling as the componential similarities.

Linguistic Plurality, Cultural Identity

Grace (1997:178f.) points out that the isolation of ethnic traditions is an artificial working assumption of many cultural anthropologists: "We linguists have treated *languages* as isolates. . . . communities (and the linguistic usages of speakers) are often not at all uniform. . . . [In a given speech community] not all people are monolingual. . . . A language is likely to show the effects of frequent use by its speakers of their languages or different dialects, but these effects are deliberately overlooked in genetic classification. We have hardly begun to learn how to look for them." With Jewish languages, urging awareness of natural-language heterogeneity has particular resonance.

The studies in the present volume attempt sharper definition of the overlap between linguistic and ethnocultural identity—age-old questions that in Western traditions have fueled heated debate at least since the Enlightenment. Central to these is interlanguage contact, which molds culturally determined patterns of expression far more vitally and pluralistically than familial classification implies. Neither language relationships nor language/culture relationships are homogeneous within a speech community. Degrees of assimilation and identity can be as hard to freeze-frame as linguistic change itself. The "cultural matrix" (Alleyne 1971) is a structurally essential component of an SC's language, which becomes more slippery to measure the more it is matched to phenomena as layered as language contact.

It is this methodological paradox that lies at the heart of the question. The present chapter has explored the linguistic phenomena arising from contact (or cultural mixture) as indicators of cultural identity. Jewish SCs offer a number of advantages for analysis. Cultural continuity is bound up with linguistic continuity both at the level of religious language (hagiolect), with its accompanying traditions of literacy,[36] and in the absence of the sociolinguistic and political framework of a nation-state. The language—convergence vernacular as well as Hebrew/Aramaic—*is* the culture to an even greater degree than with many language communities exposed over centuries to the possibility of cultural assimilation. As with creolization, contact mechanisms of language change do not lend themselves neatly to conventionally assigned categories. Genetic adherence to a language family is far less structurally relevant here than the nature of the mix itself.

For each of the three Jewish SCs considered here, the range of cultural contact has been historically somewhat circumscribed, largely as a result of their religious coherence as a larger social unit (made more urgent for Yiddish and Judezmo by recurrent ethnic persecution and expulsions). Trade has been the chief vehicle of language contact, carrying little threat for ethnic or group self-identity; intermarriage and other more radically culture-mixing trends seem to have been periodically either avoided, discouraged, or otherwise offset by each culture's norms. These SCs have each consciously fought against assimilatory currents, successfully maintaining their integrity along self-aware lines of ethnocultural and religious unity. At the same time, the language itself in each case shows clear evidence of convergence effects.

The nature of the boundaries themselves needs to be reformulated. In these instances, cultural delimitation is not the same commodity or necessarily susceptible to the same types of convergence-driven inroads as linguistic definition. Linguistic identity can be simultaneously absorptive (all three of these languages rely on non-Semitic primary language bases to supply morphosyntactic structure and show substantial convergence effects with secondary non-Semitic languages), functionally prestigious for users, and an autonomous, continuity-preserving standard-bearer and vital indicator of strongly defined cultural identity.

Nationless Jewish Diaspora languages have emerged, converged, survived, and flourished in apparently unfavorable settings. It is hard to draw a convincing language boundary of any kind in the context of Yiddish or Judezmo; their respective linguistic and cultural-genetic boundaries roughly coincide because of their speakers' religious and national-without-a-nation internalized self-identification. Historically, all three of these languages have fortified themselves through external and internal cross-fertilization within a culturally and ethnically autonomous setting. For Yiddish and Judezmo, convergence languages of the overlapping linguistic-cultural borderlands, linguistic autonomy has been maintained through their flexibly absorbent fluidity, anchored to a remarkably independent and culturally unified community existence robustly centered around religious belief, national self-awareness, traditions of literacy and respect for the word, and, preeminently, love of the Holy Tongue of the Torah. In this sense, the Yiddish *mame-loshn* and the Judezmo and Judeo-Tat colloquial languages are absolute embodiments of sociocultural markers. Each convergence language demarcates its own ethnic, social, and sociolinguistic formations under the notionally unified cultural umbrella of Jewish group identity, sufficient unto itself.

NOTES

I wish to express my heartfelt thanks to my colleagues Ian Hancock, Mark Louden, and Robert King for their generous assistance and guidance with earlier versions of this chapter, including the form in which it was presented at the Second Germanic Linguistics Annual Conference (GLAC 2) in Madison, Wisconsin, in April 1996. All misconceptions and misstatements are of course my own.

1. For further discussion of creolization specifically in Jewish languages, see Fishman 1987.

2. See the section "Sociolinguistic Variation, Interference, and Bilingual Communities." See Cedergren 1973 (*s*-aspiration and *s*-deletion in Panamanian Spanish), however, for an analysis of instances of language variation in a speech community without language change occurring as a necessary consequence. For an early call for assessment of contrastive, variational sociolinguistic patterns across social dialects as indicators of the mechanisms of linguistic change, compare Bright and Ramanujan's investigation (1964) of caste dialects in a South Asian context, namely, Tamil ("no language is as monolithic as our descriptive grammars sometimes suggest" [1107]).

3. Compare Le Page and Tabouret-Keller 1985:234–249, who point out cases illustrating the complex relationship between language and ethnic identity: the first is frequently but not inevitably an arm of the second. They can certainly be related through what Eastman and Reese (1981) called "associated language": "language is an aspect of our self-ascription" (110). But "the language we can somehow associate with" (109) is plainly "not a *necessary* part of ethnic . . . identity" (Le Page and Tabouret-Keller 1985: 238). After all, supported by the institutional maintenance of political or cultural traditions, including religion, "feelings of ethnic identity . . . can survive total language loss" (239f.). Nor, clearly, is self-definition as belonging to a particular group always the same as ethnicity.

4. The following standard terms and abbreviations are used in the present analysis:

1. *SC*s refer to speech communities.

2. *Sociolinguistic* factors are socially determined, extralinguistic forces that affect the nature of an SC's linguistic profile.

3. A *creole* is a new grammatical system emerging from the mixture—not necessarily equal—of two autonomous languages. It becomes a creole, rather than simply a *pidgin* or trade language, as soon as a generation of children starts to acquire it as a mother tongue; thus pidgins' typical complexity-reducing character is replaced by new, coherent, and autonomously complex grammatical formations (morphosyntactic, phonological).

4. *Creolization* refers to the process of this productively hybrid emergence; it is a linguistic development, but it has clear cultural implications. Creolization is therefore not necessarily always fully complete.

5. *Partial creolization*, or *linguistic convergence*, takes place in situations of language contact and cultural mixture. The languages concerned are referred to as *convergence creoles*. Culturally, as linguistically, the degree of creolization is contingent on dialectical forces of cultural (or linguistic) fusion versus individual cultural constituents' continuing separateness.

6. In language-contact situations, speakers of a *source language* (SL) acquire a new language, and in so doing, they unconsciously bring features from their own language to their version of the new language they are acquiring; this form of innovation is known as linguistic *interference*. This is referred to in the present discussion as *Type 1* contact-driven transfer of linguistic features. Speakers of a *recipient language* (RL) directly borrow features from a neighboring language; this *direct borrowing* is *Type 2* contact-driven transfer, and it is often far more dependent on speakers' sociolinguistic motivations.

7. A *lect* is a speech form or grammatical system, whether idiolect (an individual's speech systems), sociolect (a speech community's), dialect, or language. A *standard language* is therefore simply a prestige lect or dialect supported in some way by social or political power. *Normativism* is a language's tendency, either intentional or unplanned on the part of an SC, to adhere to a prestige norm or standard at the expense of naturally emerging dialectal divergences.

8. In creolization terms, a *basilect* refers to the new postmixture language; an *acrolect* denotes the new language's primary genetic and structural prestige-parent. The distance between these two is a spectrum or continuum; each intervening stage is a *mesolect*.

9. A *hagiolect* is a language, or linguistic component, used by a culture or SC for religious or sacred purposes.

10. {+ X} denotes a given linguistic feature—morphological, phonological, syntactic, or lexico-semantic: e.g., a form marked {+ affectionate} shows that it carries the semantic feature "affectionate" in its feature matrix.

5. The present analysis takes its cue explicitly from Louden's penetrating discussion (1993) of Yiddish's possible classification as a creole language. I wish to thank Professor Louden for his kindness in discussing with me many of the central issues, as well as making his conclusions and his Yiddish materials available to me.

6. See M. Weinreich 1968 (specifically for Yiddish) on religion and language.

7. The percentage figures are approximately as follows: German, 75 percent; Slavic, 10–15 percent (or more, depending on the dialect), with Hebrew/Aramaic as a cultural hagiolect, and Romance, 1 percent.

8. Note that the linguistic evidence in Yiddish, with its overwhelmingly Germanic structure and specifically Bavarian phonology, together with the population evidence, shows that the original contact mixture cannot have been southwest German blending with Judeo-French and Judeo-Italian in the Rheinland (Loter), *pace* M. Weinreich 1980. There is simply not enough significant linguistic material from Romance; in addition, the Jewish populations involved would have been straightforwardly insufficient for this kind of contact change to be plausible, as King has convincingly demonstrated (1992, 1993).

9. Good evidence of a Type-**1** phonological effect seems to be the so-called *sábes-diker losn* dialectal phenomenon in Litvak Yiddish, as explained by U. Weinreich (1952: 360ff., esp. 373f.). *Sábesdiker losn* entails absence of the s $\neq$ š [and c $\neq$ č] hissing-hushing phonemic distinction that is intact elsewhere in Yiddish: literally, *sábesdiker losn* means "language that says *sábes* instead of *shábes*" [Heb. *shabát*]. This is a giveaway speech shibboleth much derided by speakers of other dialects. Following Weinreich's account, by far the most plausible so far presented, this can now be seen as a Judeo-Slavic "foreign-accent" kind of trace in Yiddish, and the facts can be incorporated into the Judeo-Slavic/Judeo-German model for Yiddish's convergence origins. In the original areas of Poland where *sábesdiker losn* started, speakers of the Judeo-Slavic source language (before Yiddish itself developed) were in linguistic contact with the local coterritorial Polish dialect in which hushing and nonpalatal hissing phonemes merged, a dialectal Polish feature known as *mazurzenie*; through its influence, their speech had lost the hissing-hushing phonemic distinction. As these *mazurzenie*-influenced Judeo-Slavic speakers acquired Judeo-German, blending with early waves of Judeo-German immigrants, this phonological-loss feature was simply transferred into the new Yiddish convergence language in these SCs. Subsequent migration brought speakers of this dialect of Yiddish further to the northeast, to Lithuania and Belorussia. Weinreich (369ff.) also offers an alternate, secondary Slavic-based solution to the question of the emergence of *sábesdiker losn*, centering on similar facts in Belorussian, though their causality is much less secure, as he shows.

10. See note 4.

11. The term *daytshmerish* was popularized by the editor and critic Shmuel Niger (1912a, 1912b), who saw it as the sociolinguistic result of "a parochial contempt for Yiddish" (Hutton 1993:16). As a post-*Haskalah* trend, this excessive "Germanizing" was bemoaned and excoriated, along with allegedly excessive American-Yiddish usages, by Noyekh Prilutski (1938) and Max Weinreich (1938), head of the newly founded Vilna YIVO (Yidisher Visnshaftlekher Institut [Institute for Jewish Research], founded in 1925), in their purist criticisms of earlier editions of the American lexicographer Alexander Harkavy's 1928 trilingual Yiddish-English-Hebrew dictionary. Later, Harkavy's revised, expanded edition was in turn attacked for containing too many Slavicisms. Purity-pleading critiques of dialectal diversity are perhaps the surest sign of a mature language's robust linguistic health.

12. On bilingualism in the light of intralinguistic relationships within Jewish speech communities, see Gold 1981.

13. Another convergence-creole property of Yiddish is the traceable process of Yiddish/German lexical cross-fertilization, such as via *Gaunersprache* (medieval "thieves' slang") or modern German urban vernaculars (e.g., Berlin; Nachama 1995). These typologically similar "rolling-loan" processes point to a successive two-way sociolinguistic osmosis, with Judeo-German reciprocally influencing German in its turn.

14. When describing the mixing of identity and originally autonomous folkways at cultural border zones—the enriched strata that make up the intercultural "frontier"—sociocultural analysts now increasingly use a term borrowed from its Latin American context, *mestizaje*.

15. See Fishman 1981.

16. See M. Weinreich 1972.

17. Dubnov's 1897–1907 *Pis'ma o starom i novom evrejstve* (Letters on the Old and New Judaism) were published individually, then in a single-volume collection in 1907,

in the heady internationalist years following the 1905 Russian near-revolution, and a year before the Czernowitz Yiddish Conference. Dubnov's role as eloquent upholder of a reconciliation position between rival linguistic partisans of Yiddish and Hebrew (partly mirroring political Bundists-versus-Zionists antagonisms) is reflected still 20 years later in his 1929 *Fun "zshargon" tsu yidish* and consistently throughout his career as social philosopher and historian of Judaism, till his death at age 81 at the hands of a Latvian soldier in 1941 during the liquidation of the Riga ghetto.

18. See Miller 1892; Bakšiev 1932.

19. It makes little sense to speak either of loans and adstratal coterritorial contact influence (Type-**2** transfer) or of recipient language.

20. Cf. Gold 1991.

21. Ladino is the sacred-text written language used for translation from Hebrew into the Judeo-Spanish vernacular that emerged in the "Golden Age" centuries of pre-1492 Jewish Spain. Judezmo, also known natively as Judyó, Jidyó, and Khakitía in the North African Maghreb, is Ladino's spoken version, developing when Arabic-speaking Jews judaized Castilian Spanish in the eleventh to the fourteenth centuries C.E. (Wexler 1988: 17). It is the approximate Sephardi vernacular counterpart of Yiddish. The Judezmo name for the language, *judésmo/judézmo*, means "Judaism."

22. See Wagner 1930; Sala 1976.

23. Comparable to this last formulaic phrase for "Hebrew" are similarly derived West Germanic underworld words for "street slang," arriving via Yiddish: Dutch *lachoudisch*, Schwäbisch *loschnekaudisch*, Alsatian *loschnekaudisch kaudesch* "slang, deliberately incomprehensible thieves' cant," and probably the first element of German ***Kauder**welsch*. So Rotwelsch *kochumloschen* "robber's night-signal" < Heb. *khākhām* + *ləšōn* "smart language." Palpable Hebraisms, via Yiddish, underlie (1) Dutch *gabbertaal* "slang" < Hebrew *khāvēr* "friend, accomplice" + Dutch *taal* "language" ("buddy-talk"); (2) Rotwelsch *laker-schmus* "slang" < dialectal German *lattech* "poor" + Yiddish *shmusen* (Yidd.-Eng. *shmooze*) < Heb. *šmū'ōt* "rumors" ("poor-tales"); (3) Rotwelsch *laufdibbern* "slang" < Hebrew *lo'* "no" + *dibbēr* "said" + German infixed prefix *-auf-* + inf. *-n* ("saying 'no' aloud").

24. As a reborrowing parallel in African-European-blended Atlantic creoles, compare Eng. *boss* < Dutch *baas* (which underwent a connotational shift in seventeenth-century Dutch to pejorative "slave overseer": Afrikaans *baas*): so Sranan *basja*, Ndjuká *basía* "overseer" (both English-based creoles in contact with Dutch), Jamaican *buša* (beside *laša* < *las yiia* "last year," *diša* < *dis yiia*: Holm 1988:134). All these Caribbean English-creole forms are derivable from (*r*-less) English *overseer*, with aphesis, leftward stress shift, and *v* > *b*. English *boss* results from convergence of anglophone Caribbean Creole /basja/ with Dutch *baasje*, interpreted as *baas* + *-je*, thus: *r*-less Eng. *overseer* > (1) Atlantic-creole phonemic /vasía/ (accentually this stage is preserved in the Ndjuká form *basía*) > (2) /vásia/ > (3) /básia/, with the /i/ realized as a glide /y/ in the Sranan, Jamaican, and Dutch/Afrikaans forms: respectively, *basja*, *buša* < /bosyia/ (with /a/ > /o/ > /u(o)/), and *baasje* (with unstressed final /a/ realized as the central shwa default vowel). For a typologically similar, contemporaneous creole-based example of a widespread form in a standard European language whose usage has been determined by creole linguistic features, cf. Span. *palo* "stick" > (sixteenth-century+) "wood," based on creoles influenced by Yoruba and its neighboring West African languages (Holm 1988:82–83).

25. There are two incidental consequences. First, Jdzm. *diós* is always plural, and the referent is "gods," not the Jewish God. Second, the authoritative Ladino version of the Tanach (Ferrara 1553) translates Heb. (originally plural) *'Elōhim* "God" as Jdzm. *Dioses*—doubly characterized as a plural, but for deliberate linguistic-cultural-religious reasons. For a parallel phenomenon elsewhere in monotheistic, singulative Semitic, compare Arabic *Allāh* < *al-'elāh* "the one God," a direct cognate of the Heb. grammatical plural *[ha-]'elōh-im* (< PSem. *hal-'elāh* "the God").

26. See Dmitriev on Baškir (1962:133–152).

27. Cf. Stankiewicz 1985 on Slavic-derived expressives in Yiddish.

28. Thomason and Kaufman's term for this is "interference through shift."

29. For any kind of creolization to develop, clearly RL and SL speakers must lack a shared intracommunity language.

30. Holm labels these contact features "semi-creolized" (1988:9–10). Thomason and Kaufman call this type of change "language-shift with normal transmission": that is, it attests to both *disrupted* (hence creolizing) and *continuous* (unbroken) genetic transmission of RL input.

31. Another term for this kind of mixture is a compromise mesolect, formed when a native acrolect and a nonnative basilect merge. For its application to Yiddish, see the "Yiddish" section.

32. Strata-based models ("substrate"/"superstrate" and acrolect /basilect [literally, "top talk"/"bottom talk"]) distortively reflect only the sociohistory of two languages' interactions. Viewing contact in terms of transfer types clarifies the *relative* dynamics of interacting linguistic structures (interference and imposition-via-shift, versus borrowing) without resorting to an artificially homogeneous, static, or hierarchy-centered picture.

33. Once again, I am indebted to Louden's 1993 pathbreaking analysis for much of the Yiddish morphosyntactic data in this section.

34. Cf. Kay and Sankoff 1974:64ff., who broaden the "TMA" category to embrace propositional qualifiers in general (also including indicators of negatives, yes-no questions, and locatives): they argue that in "contact vernaculars," these are predictably likely to "appear in surface structure exterior to the propositions they qualify, or not at all." Compare the question-marker example in the following category.

35. Again, see Stankiewicz 1985.

36. Cf. Fishman 1987:7 ff., who explicitly differentiates "post-exilic Jewish languages"—convergence creoles each with a componentially diverse genesis—from the development of creoles per se on the basis of their continuously formative interaction with the Hebrew/Targumic hagiolect, through literacy: "PEJLs have a *historically recurring and predictable relationship with a sanctified classical language* [my italics] and, therefore, manifest the recurring development of calque varieties with traditional read/written and spoken functions . . . which ultimately influence the linguistic nature of all PEJLs even in other, modern secular functions" (18).

REFERENCES

Alleyne, Mervyn C.
1971 Acculturation and the Cultural Matrix of Creolization. In *Pidginization and Creolization of Languages*. Dell Hymes, ed. Pp. 169–186. Cambridge: Cambridge University Press.

Bakšiev, Z.
1932 *Antologija tatskikh poetov*. Moscow: Akademija Nauk SSSR.
Bright, William, and A. K. Ramanujan
1964 Sociolinguistic Variation and Language Change. In *Proceedings of the Ninth International Congress of Linguists*. Horace Lunt, ed. Pp. 1107–1113. The Hague: Mouton.
Bunis, David M.
1981 A Comparative Linguistic Analysis of Judezmo and Yiddish. *International Journal of the Sociology of Language* 30:49–70 (*The Sociology of Jewish Languages*). The Hague: Mouton.
Cedergren, Henrietta J.
1973 The Interplay of Social and Linguistic Factors in Panama. Ph.D. dissertation, Cornell University.
Coetsem, Frans C. van
1988 *Loan Phonology and the Two Transfer Types in Language Contact*. Dordrecht: Foris.
Cohen, Abner, ed.
1974 *Urban Ethnicity*. London: Tavistock.
Dmitriev, Nikolai K.
1962 O parnykh slovosočetanijakh v baškirskom jazyke. In *Stroj tjurkskikh jazykov*. Pp. 133–152. Moscow: Akademija Nauk SSSR.
Dubnov, Simon M.
1907 *Pis'ma o starom i novom evrejstve* (Letters on the Old and New Judaism). St. Petersburg: Landau. Published individually 1897–1907 in Voskhod, St. Petersburg, and elsewhere. (Translated into French and edited by Renée Poznanski as *Lettres sur le judaïsme ancien et nouveau*. Paris: Cerf, 1989.)
1929 *Fun "zshargon" tsu yidish, un andere artiklen: Literarishe zikhroynes*. Vilna: Kletskin.
Eastman, Carol M., and Thomas C. Reese
1981 Associated Language: How Language and Ethnic Identity Are Related. *General Linguistics* 21(2):109–16.
Fishman, Joshua
1972 Historical Dimensions in the Sociology of Language. In *Sociolinguistics: Current Trends and Prospects*. Roger W. Shuy, ed. Pp. 145–155. Washington, DC: Georgetown University Press.
1977 Language and Ethnicity. In *Language, Ethnicity and Intergroup Relations*. Howard Giles, ed. Pp. 15–57. London: Academic Press.
1981 The Sociology of Jewish Languages from the Perspective of the General Sociology of Language: A Preliminary Formulation. *International Journal of the Sociology of Language* 30:5–16 (*The Sociology of Jewish Languages*). The Hague: Mouton; = 1985 *Readings in the Sociology of Jewish Languages*. J. Fishman, ed. Pp. 3–21. Leiden: Brill.
1987 Post-exilic Jewish Languages and Pidgins/Creoles: Two Mutually Clarifying Perspectives. *Multilingua* 6(1):7–24.
Gilbert, Glenn G.
1993 Popular Brazilian Portuguese: A Convergence Creole, Derived from a Dual Source. Unpublished manuscript, Society for Pidgin and Creole Languages/University of Texas at Austin.

Giles, Howard, R. Y. Bourhis, and D. M. Taylor
1977 Towards a Theory of Language in Ethnic Group Relations. In *Language, Ethnicity and Intergroup Relations*. Howard Giles, ed. Pp. 307–348. London: Academic Press.
Gold, David L.
1981 Jewish Intralinguistics as a Field of Study. *International Journal of the Sociology of Language* 30:31–46 (*The Sociology of Jewish Languages*). The Hague: Mouton.
1991 Judezmo: Once the Chief Language of Sephardic Jewry. *Language International* 3(5):32–34.
Grace, George
1997 Comments on "Dimensions of Social Life in the Pacific" (Terrell, Hunt, & Gosden). *Current Anthropology* 38(2):178–179.
Grjunberg, Aleksandr L.
1963 *Jazyk severoazerbajdžanskikh tatov*. Leningrad: Akademija Nauk SSSR.
Gumperz, John J.
1968 The Speech Community. In *International Encyclopedia of the Social Sciences*. David L. Sills, ed. 9:381–386. New York and London: Macmillan.
Haarmann, Harald
1980 *Studien zum Multilingualismus aschkenasischer und orientalischer Juden im asiatischen Teil der Sowjetunion*. Hamburg: Buske.
1985 Yiddish and Other Jewish Languages in the Soviet Union. In *Readings in the Sociology of Jewish Languages*. Joshua Fishman, ed. Pp. 151–176. Leiden: Brill.
Hancock, Ian F., ed.
1979 *Readings in Creole Studies*. Gent: Story-Scientia.
Harkavy, Alexander
1928 *Yidish-English-Heibreisher verterbukh*. New York: Hebrew Publishing Co.
Harris, Tracy K.
1983 Foreign Interference and Code-Switching in the Contemporary Judeo-Spanish of New York. *Spanish in the U.S. Setting: Beyond the Southwest*. L. Elías-Olivares, ed. Pp. 53–68. Rosslyn, VA: National Clearinghouse for Bilingual Education.
1994 *Death of a Language: The History of Judeo-Spanish*. Newark: University of Delaware Press.
Harshav, Benjamin
1990 *The Meaning of Yiddish*. Berkeley and Los Angeles: University of California Press.
Holm, John
1988–1989 *Pidgins and Creoles, 1–2*. (1:1988; 2:1989). Cambridge: Cambridge University Press.
Hutton, Christopher
1993 Normativism and the Notion of Authenticity in Yiddish Linguistics. In *The Field of Yiddish: Studies in Language, Folklore, and Literature: Fifth Collection*. David Goldberg, ed. Pp. 11–57. Evanston: Northwestern University Press; New York: YIVO.
Katz, Dovid
1985 Hebrew, Aramaic and the Rise of Yiddish. In *Readings in the Sociology of Jewish Languages*. Joshua Fishman, ed. Pp. 85–103. Leiden: Brill.
Kay, Paul, and Gillian Sankoff
1974 A Language-universals Approach to Pidgins and Creoles. In *Pidgins and Creoles:*

Current Trends and Prospects. David DeCamp and Ian Hancock, eds. Pp. 61–73. Washington, DC: Georgetown University Press.

King, Robert D.

1992 Migration and Linguistics as Illustrated by Yiddish. In *Reconstructing Languages and Cultures*. Edgar Polomé and Werner Winter, eds. Pp. 419–439. Berlin and New York: Mouton de Gruyter.

1993 Early Yiddish Vowel Systems: A Contribution by William G. Moulton to the Debate on the Origins of Yiddish. *The Field of Yiddish: Studies in Language, Folklore, and Literature: Fifth Collection*. David Goldberg, ed. Pp. 87–98. Evanston: Northwestern University Press; New York: YIVO.

Kreindler, Isabelle T., ed.

1985 *Sociolinguistic Perspectives on Soviet National Languages: Their Past, Present, and Future*. New York: Mouton.

Le Page, Robert B., and Andrée Tabouret-Keller

1985 *Acts of Identity: Creole-based Approaches to Language and Ethnicity*. Cambridge: Cambridge University Press.

Louden, Mark L.

1993 Is Yiddish a Creole Language? Unpublished manuscript, Society for Pidgin and Creole Languages/University of Texas at Austin.

Maimon, Sam

1980 Ladino-English Dictionary. In *Studies in Sephardic Culture*. Marc D. Angel, ed. Pp. 107–178. New York: Sepher-Hermon.

Malinowski, Arlene

1983 Judeo-Spanish Language Maintenance Efforts in the United States. *International Journal of the Sociology of Language* 44:137–151.

1985 Judezmo in the USA Today: Attitudes and Institutions. In *Readings in the Sociology of Jewish Languages*. Joshua Fishman, ed. Pp. 212–224. Leiden: Brill.

Martinet, André

1963 Preface to U. Weinreich, *Languages in Contact: Findings and Problems*. The Hague: Mouton.

Mercer, Neil, Elizabeth Mercer, and Robert Mears

1979 Linguistic and Cultural Affiliation amongst Young Asian People in Leicester. In *Language and Ethnic Relations*. Howard Giles and Bernard Saint-Jacques, eds. Pp. 15–26. Oxford: Pergamon.

Miller, Vsevolod F.

1892 *Materialy dlja izučenija evrejskogo-tatskogo jazyka*. St Petersburg: Imperatorskaja Akademija Nauk.

Milroy, Lesley

1982 Social Network and Linguistic Focusing. In *Sociolinguistic Variation in Speech Communities*. Suzanne Romaine, ed. Pp. 141–152. London: Arnold.

Nachama, Andreas

1995 *Jiddisch im Berliner Jargon*. Berlin: Stapp.

Niger, Shmuel

1912a *Daytshmerish. Lebn un visnshaft* 11–12:49–55.

1912b *Vegn yudishe shrayber: kritishe artiklen*. Warsaw: Shreberk.

Prilutski, Noyekh

1938 Methodological Remarks on the Problem of Daytshmerish. *Yidish far ale* 8:201–209.

Prince, Ellen
1996 Personal communication.
Romaine, Suzanne
1982a Introduction. In *Sociolinguistic Variation in Speech Communities*. S. Romaine, ed.
     Pp. 1–11. London: Arnold.
1982b *Socio-historical Linguistics*. Cambridge: Cambridge University Press.
Sala, Marius
1976 *Le judéo-espagnol. Trends in Linguistics 7*. The Hague and Paris: Mouton.
Sankoff, Gillian
1980 *The Social Life of Language*. Philadelphia: University of Pennsylvania Press.
Santorini, Beatrice, and Ellen Prince
1996 Personal communication.
Stankiewicz, Edward
1985 The Slavic Expressive Component of Yiddish. *Slavica Hierosolymitana* 7:177–187.
Stolz, Thomas
1986 *Gibt es das kreolische Sprachwandelmodell? Vergleichende Grammatik des Neg-*
     erholländischen. Frankfurt: Lang.
Streeck, Jürgen
1997 Remodeling Cars and Intercultural Communication. Unpublished manuscript, De-
     partment of Speech Communication, University of Texas at Austin.
Thomason, Sarah Grey, and Terrence Kaufman
1988 *Language Contact, Creolization, and Genetic Linguistics*. Berkeley and Los An-
     geles: University of California Press.
Todd, Loreto
1994 (rev. ed. 1990) *Pidgins and Creoles*. London: Routledge.
Vinogradov, Viktor V., ed.
1966 *Jazyki narodov SSSR*, vol. 1, *Indoevropejskie jazyki*. Moscow: Akademija Nauk
     SSSR.
Wagner, Max Leopold
1930 *Caracteres generales del Judeo-Español de Oriente*. Madrid: Hernando.
Weinreich, Max
1938 Daytshmerisms Are Not Acceptable. *Yidish far ale* 1:97–106; = 1975 *Yidishe*
     shprakh 34(1–3):23–33.
1967 The Reality of Jewishness versus the Ghetto Myth: The Sociolinguistic Roots of
     Yiddish. In *To Honor Roman Jakobson* 3. Pp. 2199–2211. The Hague: Mouton.
1968 Yidishkayt and Yiddish: On the Impact of Religion on Language in Ashkenazic
     Jewry. In *Readings in the Sociology of Language*. Joshua Fishman, ed. Pp. 382–
     413. The Hague: Mouton. (Originally in *Mordecai M. Kaplan Jubilee Volume*.
     Pp. 481–514. New York: Jewish Theological Seminary of America, 1953.)
1972 Internal Bilingualism in Ashkenaz. Lucy S. Dawidowicz, trans. In *Voices from the*
     Yiddish. Irving Howe and Eliezer Greenberg, eds. Pp. 279–289. Ann Arbor: Uni-
     versity of Michigan Press.
1980 *History of the Yiddish Language*. Shlomo Noble and Joshua Fishman, trans. Chi-
     cago: University of Chicago Press; = *Geshikhte fun der yidisher shprakh*, Vols.
     1–2 of 4. New York: Yidisher Visnshaftlekher Institut (YIVO Institute for Jewish
     Research), 1973.
Weinreich, Uriel
1952 *Sábesdiker losn* in Yiddish: A Problem of Linguistic Affinity. *Word* 8:360–377.

1953 *Languages in Contact: Findings and Problems.* New York: Publications of the Linguistic Circle of New York (repr. The Hague: Mouton, 1963).

Weinreich, Uriel, William Labov, and Marvin I. Herzog

1968 Empirical Foundations for a Theory of Language Change. In *Directions for Historical Linguistics: A Symposium.* Winfred P. Lehmann and Yakov Malkiel, eds. Pp. 97–195. Austin: University of Texas Press.

Wexler, Paul

1987 Reconceptualizing the Genesis of Yiddish in the Light of Its Non-native Components. In *Origins of the Yiddish Language.* Dovid Katz, ed. Pp. 135–142. Oxford: Pergamon.

1988 *Three Heirs to a Judeo-Latin Legacy: Judeo-Ibero-Romance, Yiddish, and Rotwelsch.* Wiesbaden: Harrassowitz.

1996 *The Non-Jewish Origins of the Sephardic Jews.* Albany: State University of New York Press.

12

Languages on the Land: Toward an Anthropological Dialectology

Jane H. Hill

How widespread or localized a language appears to be may depend on what people are using language for. Those who have secure claims over vital resources in their cultural environment can afford to set themselves apart from others, and they may use language to help them do so. People who need to rely on people elsewhere because their circumstances are less reliable and secure may instead be more open to adopting new ideas and sharing the linguistic innovations of others far and wide.—Editor

The historical, evolutionary, and ecological grounds for the distribution of human languages over the globe and their varieties pose a classic problem that has recently been reopened by linguists Robert Dixon (1997) and Johanna Nichols (1992), who emphasize the possibilities for what John Terrell (chapter 1 of this volume) calls "trellis" formations in history, and archaeologists Peter Bellwood (1997) and Colin Renfrew (1988), who emphasize the importance of family-tree branching. I last examined these questions in an article written more than 20 years ago (Hill 1979). There I attacked the then-dominant notion of the "dialect tribe" (Birdsell 1957) as the organizing unit for linguistic diversity in ancient human populations, arguing that large-scale, multilingual, multiethnic areal systems were at least as important in ancient human adaptations. However, when we examine linguistic maps of the world, we are struck by a pattern of alternation that appears at all levels between clusters of local diversity contrasting with zones of widespread homogeneity. This phenomenon occurs at every level of the historical-linguistic hierarchy. At the level of linguistic stocks[1] themselves, we can contrast the very local distribution of the Mixe-Zoquean languages in Mesoamerica with the relatively far-flung distribution of the Otomanguean, Mayan, and Uto-Aztecan families, shown on Map 12.1. Within families, we can see contrasts like the cluster of small and relatively differentiated Numic languages around the southern and eastern flanks of the Sierra Nevada, compared to the large geographical scale of the Numic languages in the Great Basin, shown on Map 12.2. At the level of dialect differentiation in individual languages, an excellent example is the local differentiation of English among populations of urban working-class whites in the United States, compared to the nationwide relative homogeneity of African-American Vernacular English.

To characterize these contrasting patterns, I borrow from Nichols's (1992) discussion of the global patterning of language differentiation the terms "residual zones" and "spread zones." Residual zones, which Nichols exemplifies by the Caucasus Mountains, exhibit great linguistic diversity, great antiquity of this diversity, and stability of location of linguistic communities and lack widespread linguae francae. In contrast, spread zones, such as Nichols's case of the Eurasian steppe, exhibit low linguistic diversity, with relatively recent origin of this diversity, geographical mobility of linguistic communities, and linguae francae used over large areas.

These patterns tempt the prehistorian to think about "spreads" and "migrations" of human communities. Migration theorists like Bellwood (1997) and Renfrew (1988) would argue that in the case of Map 12.1, speakers of Mixe-Zoquean stayed put, while speakers of Otomanguean, Mayan, and Uto-Aztecan moved. Map 12.2 suggests that speakers of Mono, Panamint, and Kawaiisu stayed put, while speakers of Northern Paiute, Shoshone, and Southern Paiute moved. Speakers of Philadelphia Italian-American Vernacular English stayed put, while speakers of African-American Vernacular English moved.

A problem with migration theory is that it requires that people have, first, reasons to move ("push factors," "pull factors") and, second, the ability to expand at the expense of their neighbors, usually made possible by some important technological innovation. One difficulty with these ideas is that every migration then requires a singular set of explanations.[2] Another is that for many proposed migrations, the archaeological record does not yield unequivocal evidence in support of these explanations. We need good alternative models, and a genuinely anthropological dialectology can help. I propose here what one approach developed from the perspective of anthropological dialectology might look like.

Human beings do, of course, migrate sometimes; history provides many examples. Indeed, I now believe that historical-linguistic evidence supports the proposal by Bellwood (1997) for a migration out of Mesoamerica by the Uto-Aztecan peoples (Hill 1999). But, as Nichols has pointed out, this cannot be the reason for all of the linguistic spread zones in the world, since this would require that we postulate repeated cycles of singular historical events that we know did not occur—or, at least, they did not always occur at the right times and places.

Map 12.1
Distribution of Major Language Stocks in Mesoamerica

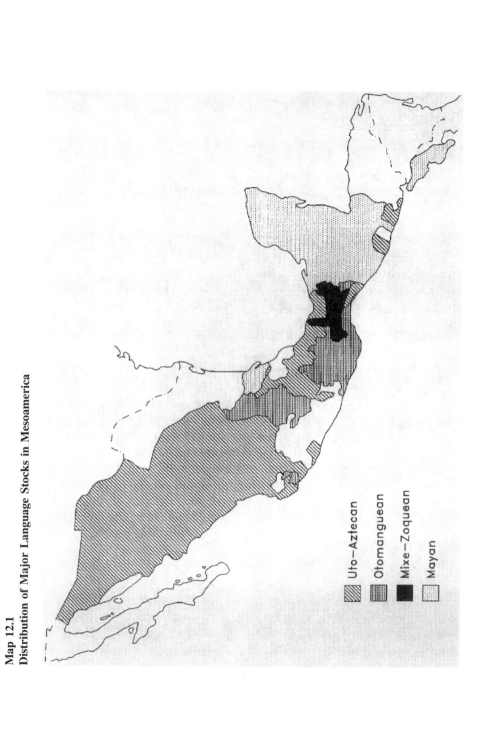

Uto-Aztecan

Otomanguean

Mixe-Zoquean

Mayan

Map 12.2
Distribution of the Numic Languages

Source: Madsen and Rhode 1994:i. Reprinted by permission of University of Utah Press.

Dialectology, the discipline that attends most closely to the geographical distribution of language variation, hardly invokes migrations at all. Instead, dialectologists tend to see human communities as stable ground across which advancing and retreating waves of linguistic innovation are in motion. I discuss here a small-scale example of this type, using data from two dialect communities of the Tohono O'odham language. I generalize from this case to argue that the movement—or lack thereof—of linguistic innovation across the relatively stable ground of human populations is due to the relative dominance among speakers of two major strategies or stances toward the variation available in their sociolinguistic universe. In a "localist" strategy, the speaker decides, "I will select a particular kind of person as my model, and I will try to sound as much like that kind of person as I can." In a "distributed" strategy, the speaker decides, "I am not sure what kind of person I want to sound like. I will try to sound like a variety of different kinds of people." The speech of any single person and the patterns of variation in any community will always be the product of a combination of these two strategies, but I focus on cases where one or the other is clearly dominant, with a conspicuous effect on the local distribution of variation.

What is "anthropological" about this proposal is that I associate localist and distributed strategies each with a different set of ecological, sociocultural, and biological constraints. Ecological constraints come from environment and technology. By "environment," I mean the cultural construction of a system of resources, accessible through local technologies, on which the well-being of a community depends. There are, of course, certain minimal constraints on how resources may be construed, and indeed, my central case involves ultimate necessities in a particularly straightforward way: the possibility of death by thirst was by no means remote for the Southwestern Tohono O'odham. Yet "environment" is a cultural, not a natural, phenomenon. In the localist case, speakers behave as if they hold an opinion that we might express as "I have a rightful and primary claim on valuable and dependable local resources that are necessary to my well-being." In the distributed case, speakers seem to have a different thought: "I have no rightful and primary claim on valuable and dependable local resources adequate to sustain my well-being. However, I might be able to add to my limited primary claims secondary claims on a sufficient range of a distributed inventory of resources to sustain my well-being."

The ways in which language variation is distributed across human populations must be linked to these construals of environmental rights and opportunities by a local culture of language, including those interested stances toward language structure and use usually called language ideology (Woolard and Schieffelin 1994; Woolard 1998). A culture of language can define the various options in systems of language variation as relevant or irrelevant to critical distinctions, including that of "insider" versus "outsider" to a community with a primary claim on resources. It can even define language variation in general as quite irrelevant to such claims. However, this is unlikely: since the way people talk is such an essential and transparent dimension of identity, most "cultures of language" permit speakers to imagine, "One way I can license my claim on resources is through speaking in a certain way."

Localist strategies especially are constrained by the biological nature of language acquisition, which operates within a critical period of human development. Infants begin to respond to the distinctive phonological features of their native language as early as two to three months of age (Kuhl et al. 1992). Quantitative analysis of variation can distinguish speakers who joined a community after about the age of eight from those who joined it before that age, and in one notable case, the complex lexical patterning of the raising of English short *a* (the vowel in *glad* and *plan*) in King of Prussia, Pennsylvania, speakers whose parents came from the community were different from speakers who were raised in the community but by nonnative parents (Payne 1980). Speakers who acquire languages after early adolescence usually have foreign accents that are detectable even to the nonlinguist. So a successful localist strategy must usually be established early in life and must orient toward usages among the speaker's primary relatives and childhood playmates. Distributed strategies permit greater flexibility both across the life course and across diverse reference groups, but their expression is likely to be both less systematically dense and less perfectly conforming than localist usages.

If we think of localist and distributed strategies as stances toward innovation, we can see that they are likely to be associated with particular types of social networks. The work of James and Leslie Milroy (1985) has shown that in relatively dense and closed social networks, within which members are bound to one another by multiplex or "strong" ties (that is, where each member sustains multiple relationships with most others, such as sibling, workmate, sports teammate, co-member of religious sodality, and so on), speakers exhibit "sociolinguistically focused" variation: members of the network are relatively homogeneous in their speech and are unlikely either to innovate or to accept innovation. In contrast, innovations spread rapidly among speakers where relatively open network structures favor the presence of many "weak" ties (for instance, a slight acquaintance with the checkout clerk in a local supermarket) among members of different networks. The Milroys argue that the relative dynamism of urban in contrast to rural speech in western languages develops because the urban context favors the development of weak ties along which innovations can spread into new networks.

TWO TOHONO O'ODHAM DIALECTS

Two dialect communities within the Tohono O'odham language that contrast sharply in dominant sociolinguistic strategy can provide a case that illustrates the general outline just presented. Tohono O'odham, formerly known as "Papago," is a member of the Upper Piman dialect system within the Tepiman family of the Uto-Aztecan stock. Upper Piman dialects[3] were spoken aboriginally roughly from the Altar River valley in the present-day Mexican state of Sonora to the Gila River in Arizona, and from the San Pedro River in southeastern Arizona probably as far west as the Colorado, as shown in Map 12.3. Among the surviving dialects, the distinction often made between "Pima" (*Akimel O'odham* "River People") and "Papago" (*Tohono O'odham* "Desert People")[4] is a political, not a historical-dialectological, division.

Between 1986 and 1989, Ofelia Zepeda and I, assisted by Molly DuFort and Bernice Belin, conducted a survey of 91 speakers of Tohono O'odham, representing almost all major villages on the main reservation. All but 4 speakers were over 55 years of age. Based on the survey, on the largest scale we distinguish "peripheral" from "central" regional dialect systems of Tohono O'odham. The peripheral system subdivides into at least four major varieties; the center

Map 12.3
Area Inhabited Historically by Speakers of Upper Piman

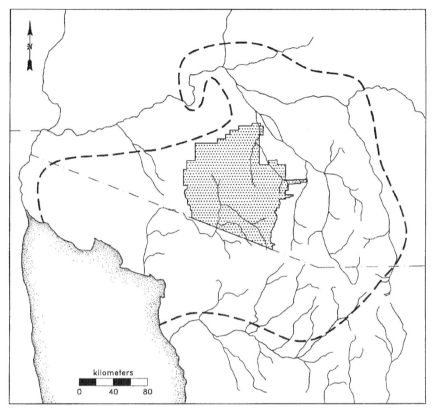

Note: The shaded area is the contemporary Tohono O'odham Reservation.

exhibits a variety of less differentiated subdialects. Several of the major iso-glosses that define this system are shown in Map 12.4.[5]

Joseph, Spicer, and Chesky (1949), who recognized six distinctive dialects,[6] thought that each came historically from the dispersal of patrilines associated with a single "defense village" or closely associated cluster of defense villages established during the Apache wars. Examination of local topography and drain-age systems suggests how the dispersal of these patrilines may have been shaped. These dialect areas and their major subdivisions are strongly associated with drainage systems that provide simultaneous access to two types of water resources: permanent tanks or springs that provided water during the relatively dry season from October to June, usually located in mountains, and seasonally flowing washes that provided lowland sites for cultivation in moist silts during the summer rainy season from July to September. The major drainage systems

Map 12.4
Some Major Isoglosses Dividing Dialects of Tohono O'odham

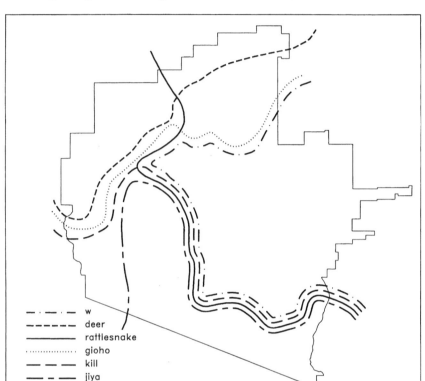

on the reservation are shown on Map 12.5, which should be compared with the distribution of major dialect boundaries shown on Map 12.4.

Widespread development of permanent stock tanks and deep wells did not occur until the 1930s. Until that decade, most O'odham (including many of the people in our survey) were entirely dependent on surface water. This dependency required that communities move at least twice yearly, from "winter villages" located in the hills near springs and rock tanks that would usually last through the dry season, to "summer villages" located along seasonally flowing washes where crops of the fast-growing local cultigens of corn and beans could be planted in damp silts left by retreating floods caused by intense summer thunderstorms (Hackenberg 1983). Thus access to surface water was emphatically the major resource constraint affecting Tohono O'odham survival until quite recent times.

The ethnographic literature on the Tohono O'odham (Underhill 1939; Joseph, Spicer, and Chesky 1949), as well as our interviews with speakers, confirms the presence of a "culture of language" within which regional variation was highly

Map 12.5
Major Drainage Systems on the Tohono O'odham Reservation

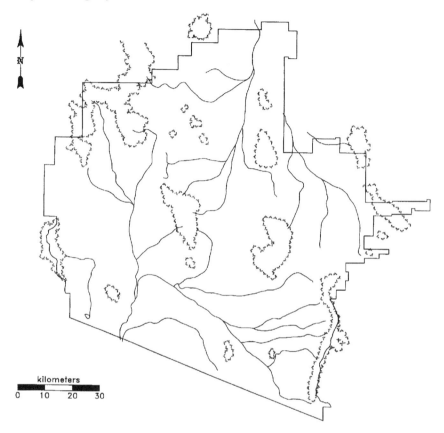

salient. There are at least six names for dialects, which are different from the names for regions, districts, and villages. Speakers are highly aware of lexical and phonological shibboleths. Speakers report being teased about their speech when they went visiting, went away to school, or married across dialect boundaries (which does not seem to have been very common). Speakers who left their natal dialect areas often report trying to sound like their new neighbors in order to avoid being teased. Regional dialect variation is a problem for bilingual education, since parents, teachers, and children often concur that speakers of other dialects, or curricular materials prepared in other dialects, are simply "wrong," not just different. Given the excellent match between dialect systems and drainage systems, it seems highly likely that this intense awareness of dialect differences constituted one component of a complex set of filters that matched people to critical resources, especially access to surface water.[7] In extremis, the Tohono O'odham did have an escape valve: they could become marginal dependents of communities of the "river people," both Pimans and speakers of Maricopa, a Yuman language, who lived along permanent streams such as the Santa Cruz or the Gila. Today, many O'odham leave their natal communities for seasonal farm labor, which sometimes turns into long periods of off-reservation residence.

As might be guessed from the culture of language described here, speakers of Tohono O'odham generally lean toward the localist end of the continuum of sociolinguistic stances—although Hackenberg (1983) characterizes overall O'odham subsistence strategies as diffuse and opportunistic, in most cases their patterns of language variation are relatively localist. However, the extreme Southeast is especially striking in its devotion to localism. Eleven speakers in the dialect survey sample come from (that is, claim to be *si ki:kam*, "real home people"; cf. Hill and Zepeda 1991) five villages in the extreme southeastern corner of the Tohono O'odham Reservation: Ce'ul Ṣa'i (Fresnal Canyon), Cu:lig, South Komalig, Cold Fields, and San Miguel. They are speakers of the larger Kokolo:di dialect, but exhibit some locally distinctive traits. In contrast, speakers of the Southwestern dialect, called Huhuwosh by Joseph, Spicer, and Chesky (1949) and Saxton, Saxton, and Enos (1983), manifest such an extreme distributed strategy that the dialect is best characterized not by identifying the local innovations, but by enumerating combinations of features that probably originated elsewhere, but that do not cluster together in other dialects. The Southwest does not retain an unusually large number of archaisms, as we might expect on a linguistic periphery. On the contrary, it is a sort of catch basin for relatively recent innovations. From this much less densely populated area the dialect survey data include only six speakers, who claim origin in two villages, Pi Oikk and Ali Jek (Menager's Dam).

These two groups of speakers, which are both part of the "peripheral" dialect system, contrast sharply along several major sociolinguistic dimensions. On each of these, the Southeastern Kokolo:di speakers are more "localist," while Southwestern speakers are more "distributed." These dimensions include willingness to accept innovation, degree of sociolinguistic focus or diffusion, consistency of usage by individual speakers, and willingness to accommodate to other dialects. I now take these dimensions up in turn, providing examples for each one.

Southeastern speakers resist innovation. Southeastern speakers have innovated independently on only two major variables that I am sure about and are much less likely to accept innovations originating in other dialect areas than are Southwestern speakers. Southeastern speech preserves high frequencies of realization of a number of archaisms at loci where every other area has innovated. By contrast, Southwestern speakers have adopted almost 20 major innovations that must have come from outside in fairly recent times.

One example of the tendency of Southwestern speakers to be more likely to innovate appears in a series of lexical items where one vowel in a word assimilates to the other.

1a. *nonha* "eggs" > *nonho*

SE: No innovation.   SW: S50, S75 show innovation.

1b. *weho* "it's true" > *woho* (a stereotype)

SE: Only S48 shows innovation.   SW: S50, S74, S75 show innovation.

In a series of variable pronunciations of Spanish loan words, innovation moves away from the Spanish pronunciation in the direction of assimilation of adjacent consonants.

2a. *wa:ldi* "bucket" > *wa:ndi, wa:nni, wa:lli*

SE: No innovation.   SW: S50, S67, S55 have *wa:lli*.
                                                    S74 has *wa:ndi*.
                                                    S28 has *wa:nni*
                                                    S66 preserves *wa:ldi*.

2b. *wandi:ho/a* "bread tray" > *wanni:ho/ a, waññi:ho/a*

SE: Only S48 shows innovation.   SW: All speakers except S74 show inno-
                                                    vation. Furthermore, two speakers palatal-
                                                    ize /n/ to /ñ/.

In the pronunciation of Spanish loan words, an innovation moves stress to the initial syllable, canonical for Tohono O'odham, while conservative forms retain Spanish stress. This is a stereotyped variable.

3. *milgá:n* "white person" > *mílgan*

SE: No innovation.   SW: S66 shows *mílgan*.

Several cases involve lexical variables. A good example is a shift of meaning of the word *ga:t* "bow" to mean "rifle," replacing conservative *gawos* (Saxton, Saxton, and Enos 1983 suggest that this is a loan word from Spanish *arquebús*).

4. *gawos* > *ga:t*

SE: No innovation.   SW: S50, S74, S67 show ga:t.

An important innovation involves a shift in the permissible membership of vowel clusters. The innovation prohibits both members of a vowel cluster from exhibiting tongue-root retraction. Thus clusters /eo/, /ea/, and /oa/ become /io/, /ia/, and /ua/, respectively. This innovation has gone to completion in the central dialect, with nearly all speakers exhibiting percentages in the 90s or at 100 percent, and the isophone of the 90 percent level is one of the best markers of the boundary of the Central dialect. Given this complete domination by the innovation among speakers of the Central dialect, we can assume that the innovation originated there and is now diffusing into the periphery. In dialects where the innovation is not yet well advanced, it exhibits so-called lexical diffusion: some lexical items are more likely to be affected by it than others. Thus we must look at speaker behavior in quantitative terms. Here are the percentages for tongue-root advancement of *e, and *o to i and u, respectively, for the two areas:

5.		%i	%u
SE:	S90	0	0
	S81	10	12
	S58	18	0
	S69	19	53
	S48	65	92
	S83	20	95
	S15	5	17
	S59	20	0
	S43	6	30
	S23	39	20
	S61	5	28
SW:	S50	13	21
	S74	44	60
	S28	11	16
	S66	75	63
	S67	59	53
	S75	11	7

Here we see that in the group of speakers from the Southeast, only S48 is well along toward categorical /i/. Two speakers, S48 and S83, exhibit near-categorical /u/. Several speakers exhibit values of 0 or percentages under 10 percent for these innovations. In contrast, in the Southwest, no speakers exhibit zero values, and three of the six speakers are well advanced.

A second example of a phonological innovation involves one dimension of a larger process, the elision of unstressed vowels (see Hill and Zepeda 1992 for details). In the Southeast and in the Kokolo:di dialect more generally, this process has been inhibited where /i/ follows /l/; /i/ is variably retained, and this is a conspicuous feature of this dialect (the Spanish, and hence English, name for the O'odham sacred mountain, Baboquivari, reflects this feature: Southeastern speakers say /wáwə gíwulikị/, while speakers of other dialects say /wáwə gí-wulk/). Elsewhere (except in the Southwest), unstressed /i/ is categorically lost after all coronal consonants including /l/. The percentages of retention of /i/ after /l/ for the two areas are as follows:

6.		%li
SE:	S90	27
	S81	59
	S58	75
	S69	25
	S48	13
	S83	56
	S15	43
	S59	62
	S43	80
	S23	69
	S61	56
SW:	S50	2
	S74	2
	S28	11
	S66	2
	S67	14
	S75	39

Here S48 again is the outlier in the Southeastern group. However, three of the Southwestern speakers exhibit this archaism, although they use it at a relatively low frequency compared to most of the Southeasterners. Three others exhibit the otherwise-universal innovative pronunciation (retention values at 2 percent are found even in the Central and Northern varieties, although 0 percent retention is more common).

Southeastern speakers are more "focused." They constitute a strikingly homogeneous group. For 77 sociolinguistic variables that appear to display patterning in space (as opposed to being associated with gender, for instance), Southeastern speakers exhibit greater variability than speakers in the Southwest on only 10. In contrast, Southwestern speakers are heterogeneous, exhibiting greater internal variability on 37 variables. (Among the remaining 30 variables, either they are not relevant in the south, or I have insufficient data, or I judge the two groups to be similarly heterogeneous or homogeneous.) Furthermore, Southeastern speakers attend more carefully to boundaries, frequently mentioning ways in which their speech differs from that of the Central-dialect speakers who are their neighbors (for the Southeast is a dialectally "mixed" area). Speakers in the Southwest are certainly aware of dialect, but with one exception (S67, who has the most education of any Southwestern speaker and more than that of most Tohono O'odham), they do not talk much about it.

The greater sociolinguistic focus of Southeasterners can be illustrated by cases where particular pronunciations of individual lexical items are closely associated with particular dialect areas. Such lexical variables are highly salient for Tohono O'odham speakers, and the Southeast invariably exhibits a very high level of focus. For instance, there are three major pronunciations of the word for "creosote/greasewood bush" (*Larrea tridentata*):

7. *ṣegai* (Central and North) / *ṣegoi* (General South) / *ṣegio* (Pisinmo'o)

SE: *ṣegai* for 10 speakers (S83 has *ṣegio*, the Pisinmo'o variant)

SW: *ṣegoi* for 5 speakers (S66 has *ṣegai*)

The word meaning "one person arrives" has three pronunciations:

8. *jiya* (Southern) / *jiwa* (Central) / *jiwia*
(North and Northwest)

SE: *jiya* everywhere (except S82, who has *jiwaye* ʤíwayɛ], a unique pronunciation)

SW: S50 *jiwa*
    S74 *jiwia*
    S28 *jiwia/jiya*
    S66 *jiwa*
    S67 *jiwia*
    S75 —

Among Southwestern speakers, every possible pronunciation can be observed. Southeastern speakers are focused on a single form; the deviant pronunciation by S82 may have been intended to illustrate a nonlocal usage.

A third example of this type is the pronunciation of the word meaning "rattle." Here three pronunciations are known, and they have strong regional associations. We would expect the Southwest to exhibit the first pronunciation. Instead, all possible pronunciations of this word were produced by Southwesterners.

9. *ṣawǐkuḍ* "rattle" (Southern) / *ṣawkuḍ*
(Central and North) / *ṣaikuḍ* (Northwest)

SE: *ṣawǐkuḍ* only

SW: S50, S74, S28 *ṣawkuḍ*
    S66 *ṣawǐkuḍ*
    S67 *ṣaikuḍ*
    S75—

Southeastern speakers are more consistent in their use of focused speech. As can be seen from examining the preceding data, most cases of deviation from their central tendencies were produced by a single individual, S48, a man who has lived outside the dialect area for 50 years. For the Southwest, every one of the six speakers was an outlier on one or more variables.

Southeastern speakers are less likely to change their speech when they move.

Table 12.1
Number of Variables on Which Women Changed or Did Not Change in the
Direction of the Dialect Area of Residence

AREA OF ORIGIN	CHANGED	UNCHANGED
SOUTHEAST		
S23	7	29
S69	8	16
S43	2	38
CENTRAL		
S42	24	19
S82	20	9
S85	16	13
S73	32	7
S70	17	13
SOUTHWEST		
S74	16	6

Here our best evidence is from a study of three Southeastern women (S23, S69, S43) who are married to, and living with, men from villages in other areas (Hill and Zepeda 1991). They contrast both with the one woman (S74) who had married out of the Southwestern area and with five women of Central-dialect origin who live in peripheral areas. Southeastern women did not seem to accommodate their speech to that of their husband's communities in spite of very long residence there. Indeed, in one notable case, the husband seemed to be accommodating to his wife's speech in spite of the fact that they had lived for 30 years in his family's summer village in a Central-dialect area. In contrast, Central-dialect women did accommodate. In several cases, women chose to mention that they either had or had not chosen to accommodate, so this issue is salient for them. There is not time to repeat this study in detail here, so I summarize the difference in a chart of the grossest measure, the number of variables that are definitional for the natal dialect area on which women either changed or did not change in the direction of the dialect area of residence (as retrievable from interview data) (Table 12.1).

In addition to this gross pattern of modifying fewer variables, Southeastern women exhibited the least accommodation, in quantitative terms, on the variables on which they did change their speech. Interestingly, the two women who moved into Southeastern communities, S82 and S85, exhibit extreme hyperaccommodation, shifting their usage, in quantitative terms, even past the outer limits on native Southeast usage.

I proposed earlier that localist versus distributed sociolinguistic stances would associate with speakers' construals about rights and access to resources. Probably the most obvious difference between these two dialect communities is differential access to surface water. The villages in the Southeast are strung along the western flanks of the Baboquivari Range, which includes Baboquivari Peak (7,730 feet), the highest mountain on the Tohono O'odham Reservation. There is a general east-to-west gradient of average annual rainfall in the Sonoran Desert regions of Arizona. The Baboquivari Range marks the western edge of a region that averages 15 inches of annual rainfall. In contrast, the Southwestern villages lie between the Mesquite Mountains on the east, with the highest elevations barely above 3,000 feet, and the Ajo Mountains on the west, with the highest peak just over 4,000 feet. This region falls in a zone marked on climate maps for 0–5 inches of annual rainfall. However, the difference is even greater than the rainfall maps of the Sonoran Desert suggest: Baboquivari is a rain catcher in both winter and summer, with annual rainfall over the range itself probably averaging closer to 20 than to 15 inches and in some years reaching as much as 30 inches. Even in years of extreme drought, the area is unlikely to receive less than about 10 inches of rain. In contrast, years with no rainfall at all are fairly common in the Southwest. The biogeographic contrast between the two regions is stark. In the context of the Sonoran Desert, the foothills of Baboquivari are a virtual earthly paradise, with oak woodlands dipping low in the canyons, many permanent springs, and lush grassland on the alluvial outflow plains that provide superb forage for cattle, the principal measure of wealth for the contemporary Tohono O'odham. The broad washes west of the range run with great reliability; the main channel of the Vamori Wash (which I know because a main road goes along it and crosses it several times) is marked by dense thickets of mesquite and reeds, and the beds of sand and silt along its course spread over a wide area and are damp during a large part of the year. People from the Southeast are widely regarded as wealthier than other O'odham.

The Southwest has quite a different aspect. The best water sources in the low hills are not springs, but semipermanent rock tanks where rainwater lasts through the dry season only in good years. The flanks of these mountains provide no forage except in unusually wet years, and the sandy beds of the washes cross creosote desert with only scattered mesquite and palo verde. During the 1930s, the confluence of the Sweetwater, Ali Jek, and Pi Oikk washes was dammed to form a stock pond, grandly dubbed "Menager's Lake," which is usually little more than a mudpuddle (it is shown in the southwest corner of Map 12.5). Deep wells in the area were provided between 1934 (at Sweetwater) and 1938 (at Ali

Jek [Menager's Dam]). The people of this area are not thought of as wealthy; indeed, they are often teased about being "Sand Papago"—foragers—a point discussed in more detail later.

Both the Southeastern and Southwestern communities of speakers are thought to be relatively recent migrants from Mexico into their respective regions. If this is true, the contrast between the two groups is all the more remarkable. The southeastern regions of today's Baboquivari and Chukut Kuk districts (the districts, founded as grazing districts, are the units of tribal government) are mixed areas in which both Central-dialect Totoguañ speakers and Kokolo:di speakers live. The Kokolo:di speakers, the population under consideration here, are said to have entered the area from Mexico after the pacification of the Apaches in the 1870s, displacing the Central-dialect Totoguañ from the most desirable sites; one Kokolo:di man opined, in a way that is rather unusual for the egalitarian O'odham, that Kokolo:di people are simply technically more advanced than the Totoguañ. I am agnostic about this theory, since, as I pointed out earlier, the Spanish orthography of the word "Baboquivari," which appears on late-seventeenth-century maps, reflects Kokolo:di, not Totoguañ, phonetics.

People currently living in the Southwest are believed by other O'odham, and by ethnohistorians, to be recent immigrants from Mexico. They are often referred to as "Sand Papago," a mildly insulting epithet implying that they originated among the foragers of the extreme western deserts, who are said to have subsisted primarily on *hia tatk* "sand root" (*Ammobroma sonorae*), an edible plant that grows only on dunes. While a few families in the area may be descendants of genuine "Sand Papago," this designation seems to be most frequently used by the O'odham simply to mean something like "rustics who come from west of my own area of origin." Autobiographical data from these speakers (and information collected from their parents in the early 1960s; King and Jones 1974) suggest that most of these families have probably been at least occasional seasonal cultivators for over 100 years and probably took refuge at the spring-fed oases at Wa:kk (Quitovac, Sonora) and A'al Waippia (Quitobaquito Springs, now in Organ Pipe Cactus National Monument) for drinking water in the worst dry seasons. However, permanent populations at the oases were necessarily small, and the community at the A'al Waippia oasis was removed in 1957 (cf. Nabhan 1982).[8]

Brief life-history information that we collected from speakers in the two areas reveals that families in the Southwest moved with much greater frequency and among a wider range of sites than those in the Southeast. Only one of the six Southwestern speakers, S74 (born in 1926 at Ajo), reports a regular two-village migration pattern during her childhood. The rest report living at as many as half a dozen different village sites, some of them in Kokolo:di territory east of the Mesquite Mountains, moving when water ran out and occasionally seeking refuge with relatives at the Quitovac oasis in Mexico or in employment in the cotton fields near Casa Grande. Four of these six speakers report that at least one parent came from the Mexican side of the border. These biographies contrast with those offered by speakers from the Southeast, where 4 of the 11 speakers report living as children in regular two-village migration patterns between a single winter village in the Baboquivari Range and a single summer village on the Vamori Wash system. The other 7 report stable residence in a single location as children. Two of these speakers also have Mexican relatives, at the important village of Ce:dagĭ Wahia (Pozo Verde) just south of the border.

While I cannot reconstruct the social networks of these people's natal families, the residential patterns they report imply that there must have been important differences between the two areas. Speakers whose families were involved in stable two-village migrations, or even permanent residence in one of the summer villages with reliable surface water along the big washes, would have probably had many stable strong ties to coresidents. Speakers in the Southwest, lacking residential stability, would have found it difficult to maintain strong ties outside the nuclear family and would have required weak ties in a variety of potential residence sites in order to obtain permission to settle, albeit briefly.

It is interesting to speculate about the social environment of the primary socialization of these consultants. Wick Miller (1970) once pointed out that children among the Western Shoshone probably lacked stable peer groups of age mates, since local groups were so small. It seems very likely that this was also the case among the Southwestern Tohono O'odham. Group size would have been sharply constrained by available water, and repeated moves would have frequently reshuffled any small groups of age mates that might have formed. Thus the sort of sociolinguistic focusing that seems to occur mainly in such peer groups may not have been a major factor in their language socialization. In contrast, the relatively large villages and greater stability of residence in the Southeast would permit peer groups to play an important role in language socialization.

SOME EXTENSIONS OF THE MODEL

Let me now return to my original point: what does an anthropological dialectology have to contribute to our understanding of the alternations of residual zones and spread zones on our maps of language variation? The case shown here is especially interesting if it is indeed true, as is claimed by the people themselves and by ethnohistorians, that the two groups are rather recent arrivals in their areas. But regardless of the specific history of these groups, most features of the Tohono O'odham dialect system are unlikely to date from before 1870, because of the extreme disturbances of residence that this group experienced during the 200 years that they were under siege by the Apaches. Thus these striking contrasts are the result of a rather brief history, suggesting that these sociolinguistic stances can develop very quickly in speech communities. Note that in neither case have the contrasts developed because actual human beings are "migrating." While Southwesterners frequently lived outside of their home area, all of them claim to be "from" there and have chosen to live there when they can. Southeasterners also have been a relatively stable population since at least 1870. Furthermore, the two groups used identical technologies of subsistence, although Southwesterners report many years when they were unable to plant crops. The question is not, have these groups moved? It is, have linguistic innovations moved into these groups? In the case of the Southwest, the answer is, largely, "Yes." In the case of the Southeast, it is, largely, "No." That is, behavior of people in the Southeast models, on a very small scale, the formation of a residual zone, while the behavior of people in the Southwest models, again on a small scale, the formation of a spread zone.

Let us now return to Map 12.2, the map of the Numic languages. The traditional explanation for this pattern is that of "expansion" or "spread" of Numic-speaking peoples (e.g., Steward 1940; Lamb 1958; Bettinger and Baumhoff 1982), who are said to have replaced a sparse population of pre-Numic peoples in the Great Basin about a thousand years ago. The complex of small languages in the west is said to be the point of origin of this spread, showing the most diversity simply because it is where Numic speakers have lived for the longest time. This model requires that prehistorians postulate some specific reason for Numic speakers to migrate, and some reason why they were able to replace their predecessors in the Basin. Sutton and Rhode (1994) mention a variety of proposals. All of them require some specific innovation that advantaged the Numic migrants, and none are clearly confirmed by the archaeological data. A more general explanation that can account universally for the residual-zone/spread-zone contrast would be preferable.

The distinction between localist and distributed sociolinguistic stances proposed here can provide such an explanation, permitting a model of "differentiation in situ," perhaps including the "Numicization" of pre-Numic populations in the Basin, but definitely involving the distribution of language variation among Numic speakers themselves, who probably began to penetrate the basin by about 3000 B.P.[9] The ecological facts fit: It is easy to imagine that people living in the Great Basin felt "poor" compared to people living in the well-watered eastern foothills of the Sierra Nevada. We know that people in the Great Basin moved frequently, and that they lived in relatively small groups. We know that a principal resource, pinyon nuts, was relatively unreliable; a grove might yield well in one year and hardly at all in the next. Access to drinkable water is also a problem throughout the Great Basin. Thus we do not require any special innovations: we need only postulate that the Great Basin is a "spread zone" because human adaptation there lent itself to a distributed stance. The "culture of language" fits: Miller (1970) reports that the Shoshone attended little to dialect differentiation, claimed not to be able to tell where people came from based on their speech, and had a highly flexible attitude toward innovation. Within such a culture, innovations could spread with great rapidity, overriding the centrifugal forces that create linguistic divergences when people are separated at great distances. Note that we need not postulate (as I have in the past, Hill 1979, and as has been suggested by Shaul 1986) any particular patterns of marriage, visiting, or whatever. The only thing that is needed is a distributed stance toward sociolinguistic variation. We also do not need to postulate any particular cultural innovations or environmental catastrophes, although it seems likely that the zones where distributed stances were in dominance must have enlarged as the Basin became increasingly dry. In contrast, the Sierra foothills remained a part of the larger California "residual zone," an area where people perceived themselves to have primary rights to desirable resources and developed localist sociolinguistic stances accordingly.

Now let us look again at Map 12.1, of Mixe-Zoquean languages versus Otomanguean and Mayan languages. Some of the linguists most expert in matters Mesoamerican think it likely that the very earliest complex societies based on maize agriculture developed among Mixe-Zoquean–speaking peoples. Campbell and Kaufman (1976) propose that many words in the agricultural complex in other Mesoamerican languages are Mixe-Zoquean loanwords.[10] Mixe-Zoquean writing is some of the most ancient in Mesoamerica (Justeson and Kaufman 1993). Mixe-Zoquean languages are very limited in their geographical spread compared to the other major language families in the region. Why did not Mixe-Zoqueans expand at the expense of foraging neighbors, according to the models of Bellwood (1997) and Renfrew (1988)? One possibility, of course, is that Campbell and Kaufman and others are wrong about the priority of Mixe-Zoqueans as agriculturalists, and that the first cultivators were ancestral to the speakers of the large language families of the region, Otomanguean, Mayan, and Uto-Aztecan. However, the model I propose here would permit Mixe-Zoquean priority. A very early adoption of agriculture with a consequent sense of entitlement would have permitted Mixe-Zoqueans to develop localist sociolinguistic strategies and continue to use them. The much larger geographical spread of the Otomanguean, Uto-Aztecan, and Mayan languages suggests that these language groups might have formed in spread zones where distributed strategies associated with a sense of relative resource impoverishment were in dominance. As the new technologies of cultivation permitted a sense of trust in the reliability of local resources, new "residual zones" could form, yielding the contemporary linguistic complexity of highland Mesoamerica.[11]

Thus far, I have discussed only indigenous North American cases. However, the model can be applied in other contexts as well. Many distributions of variation in social space in contemporary societies lend themselves to accounts in its terms. I have already mentioned the case of African-American vernaculars contrasted to white-ethnic dialects of American English. Here the obvious relative economic insecurity of African Americans would favor a distributed strategy. A second interesting example involves gender: Working-class and lower-middle-class female speakers of European languages are notoriously receptive to innovation, in contrast to men. Among the many proposed explanations of this phenomenon, Eckert (1993) argues that it occurs because these women control little material capital, so they seek to control cultural capital. Within my model, the claim would be a little different: These women do not feel that they have primary rights to reliable resources, so they practice the distributed strategy, in contrast to more localist men, who feel more secure in their primary rights. My model predicts that working-class women will be just as receptive to stigmatized as to prestigious variants; Eckert predicts that they will favor prestige variants. There almost certainly exist enough data to test these predictions.[12]

A second phenomenon that might be modeled in my terms is language shift. The model can describe language shift as a change from dominant localism vis-à-vis a language to a distributed stance that accepts a new language. It suggests that this shift in sociolinguistic stance will be driven by new cultural construals of environmental rights and values far more than by relative population size, relative intimacy of contact, or the panoptical power of speakers of the new language (as in boarding schools for Native Americans in the United States, which did not in fact stamp out languages in spite of trying explicitly to do so). One of the phenomena that this understanding accounts for is the extreme power of television to provoke language shift; linguist Michael Krauss of the Alaskan Native Language Center at the University of Alaska has often remarked that television works like "cultural nerve gas." Television advertising is precisely designed to accomplish the necessary shift in evaluation of resources that will take a community from a localist to a distributed strategy: It makes you think that what you have is not good enough, and it provides images of people who have what you want who are so much more perfect than you will ever be that your claims to what they have can never be primary.

CONCLUSION: ANTHROPOLOGICAL DIALECTOLOGY AND TRADITIONAL DIALECTOLOGY

This very general anthropological model of the distribution of language variation in space is distinct from "traditional" dialectological models, a term I use in an extended sense to include studies of language variation that employ quantitative methods, as developed by scholars like Trudgill (1983) and Labov (1966, 1972). First, it is intended to generalize across all the different kinds of human societies that we can observe throughout history. This contrasts, for instance, with models proposed by Trudgill (1983) that depend on differential population density, in which innovation will diffuse from areas of high density to areas of low density. This generalizes the phenomenon of the diffusion of urban forms into rural areas. In the Neolithic, of course, there were no cities, and it is unclear that Trudgill's demographic generalization will hold up in every case of residual-zone/spread-zone differentiation. It should usually be the case that spread zones will have lower population density than residual zones, but the theory does not require this (for instance, distributed-stance African-American vernacular speakers live at population densities at least as high as those found among localist white ethnics). Second, Trudgill proposes that distance is crucial: innovation spreads faster over short distances than over long ones. This variable breaks down when we notice the difference between residual zones, where innovations spread slowly if at all, and spread zones, where they spread rapidly over long distances. The model of localist versus distributed strategies does not require either a demographic or a distance component. A third dimension that has been important for contemporary students of language variation is Labov's distinction of "change from below," innovations that emerge in lower-status social zones, and "change from above," innovations that begin in high-status sectors. The present model has nothing to say about differential prestige or rank. It requires only that a variant be associated with a primary or secondary claim on resources. It may be that variants of the "change-from-below" type, which are highly regular and seem to manifest the basic "drift" of a language, will develop and spread even without this licensing function, however, which would be of great interest.

My notion of "localist" versus "distributed" stances toward variation owes much to the idea of "focused" versus "diffuse" linguistic communities proposed by Le Page and Tabouret-Keller (1985). However, the model is distinct from theirs in that "localist" and "distributed" stances are taken up by individuals (although they may be quite general in communities) and can be taken up differentially toward different variables. Furthermore, they are associated with specific ecological and cultural contexts. My incorporation of the biology of language also distinguishes my position from Le Page and Tabouret-Keller's argument that every choice among sociolinguistic variables is an "act of identity." I agree with their basic point, but I argue that because of biological constraints on the language-acquisition process, such "acts of identity" directed outside the primary community are likely to be less easily accomplished than are those that perpetuate the usage of the primary family and peer group. They will thus be vulnerable to the perfectionist ideologies of localists and will usually constitute merely partial and secondary claims on resources. Finally, my position differs from the "accommodation theory" of Giles (1973) in generalizing beyond microinteraction to broad stances toward variation that are constrained by the total contexts in which speakers live. In summary, the dialectological model proposed here differs from previous proposals in that it is genuinely anthropological: it requires attention to the two basic stances, to human ecology, to human biology, to the culture of language, and to social organization. By encompassing all of these dimensions of human adaptation, we may be able to generalize dialectology and add it to the inventory of models that anthropologists use to account for the nature of human diversity.

NOTES

This research was supported by the National Science Foundation (NSF BNS 8608009) and by the Social and Behavioral Sciences Research Institute of the University of Arizona. This chapter is a slightly revised version of my David Skomp Distinguished Lecture, presented to the Department of Anthropology at Indiana University on March 21,

1996. The chapter is dedicated to the memory of Robert M. Netting, who believed in the power of a unified vision of anthropology.

1. I use "stock" here in the sense of Nichols (1992), as the largest linguistic group of languages known to share a common ancestry, and "family" for the highest-level subordinate units of stocks.

2. Renfrew (1988) and Bellwood (1997) have of course argued that many of the large-scale language spreads visible on today's maps reflect a single series of events in human history: the domestication of plants and animals and the origins of agriculture, which permitted agriculturalists to expand at the expense of foragers.

3. I use the term "dialect" here in its technical sense: "a regional (or social) variety of a language." Upper Piman probably constitutes a single language; today's speakers can understand one another across the entire area.

4. The official spelling is *Tohono O'odham*. However, the word meaning "desert" should be transcribed for linguistic purposes as *tohonno*, with a geminate /n/.

5. The isoglosses are as follows: (1) *w*: east of the boundary (inside it), the phoneme /w/ is pronounced [w]; outside it (north, west, and south), it is often pronounced [β]; (2) *deer*: northwest of the line, the pronunciation of "mule deer" is *huai* [hwái]; south and east of the line, *huawī* [húaβī]; (3) *rattlesnake*: east and north of the line, the pronunciation is *ko'owi* [kó'oβī]; west and south of the line, *ko'oi* [kó'oi]; (4) *gioho*: west and north of the line, words containing the sequence V_1hV_2 (where V is a vowel) correspond to $V_1V_2hV_2$; e.g., *giho* "basket" corresponds to *gioho*; (5) *kill*: north of the line, the pronunciation is *mua* [múa]; south of the line, the pronunciation is *mea* [mía]; (6) *jiya* "one person arrives": north of the line, the pronunciation is *jiwia* [dʒíβia] or *jiwa* [dʒíβa]; south of the line, *jiya* [dʒíja].

6. The main distinction that Joseph, Spicer, and Chesky (1949) and Saxton, Saxton, and Enos (1983) make that we do not is the recognition of a "Hu:hu'ula" dialect in the Northwest. We have only two speakers from this area in our sample. However, based on their speech, we would have to rank Hu:hu'ula as a subdialect; it is no more different from the speech of the neighboring Gigimai and Kohadk dialects than is, for instance, the speech of people in Pisinmo'o different from the rest of the Southern or Kokolo:di dialect, or the speech of the people of Iron Stand and Big Fields different from the speech of other speakers of the Central or Totoguañ dialect. However, what is most distinctive about our proposal is our recognition of a relatively conservative "Periphery" that includes Pima, distinguished from the innovating "Central" or Totoguañ speakers.

7. Workman and Niswander (1970) found considerable population-genetic differentiation among the administrative districts of the Tohono O'odham Reservation, which largely overlap dialect areas. They found this to be consistent with a high level of endogamy within each district.

8. Most ethnographers and ethnohistorians believe that the genuine "Sand Papago," dwellers in the Pinacate Desert, never numbered more than 150 and died out over a century ago. However, Mexican Papago from Quitovac and neighboring villages were also known as "Areneños." Whatever the source of the current population of the Southwestern region, they seem to have gone through some sort of genetic bottleneck. Workman and Niswander (1970) found that subjects from District 4 (Ge Wo'o, which includes also speakers of the Gigimai or Western dialect who are not part of the Southwestern dialect group) showed a striking departure from populations in other districts in frequency of the Diego blood antigen, at 11.5 percent. No other group had a frequency of Diego above 3.2 percent.

9. This estimate is based on new radiocarbon dates on early maize in the Southwest; the earliest date for maize on the fringes of the Great Basin is 3445 B.P. (uncalibrated), at Lukuchukai in northeastern Arizona (*Archaeology Southwest* 13:8–9). Numic is a closely related group of Uto-Aztecan languages. Maize cultivation was probably brought into the U.S. Southwest by Uto-Aztecan migrants from Mesoamerica (Bellwood 1997; Hill 1999).

10. Dakin and Wichmann (1995) have challenged some of Campbell and Kaufman's etymologies, suggesting a Uto-Aztecan origin for some elements of Campbell and Kaufman's (1976) "Olmec" vocabulary.

11. While Mesoamerica is linguistically very diverse (there are four languages generally considered isolates, and five major language stocks are represented, with Otomanguean having many subfamilies), Nichols (1992) considers it a spread zone; linguistic innovations definitely cross languages and even families in this region, constituting it as a "linguistic area" (Campbell, Kaufman, and Smith-Stark 1986).

12. Working-class men have been said to exhibit devotion to variants that exhibit "covert prestige," that is, they are valued in working-class communities, even though people do not articulate this value and may even deny it in favor of an advocacy of overtly-prestigious "standard" forms. My model does not require prestige, either covert or overt; it simply requires that use of a particular set of ways of speaking license access to resources.

REFERENCES

Bellwood, Peter
1997 Prehistoric Cultural Explanations for Widespread Linguistic Families. In *Archaeology and Linguistics: Aboriginal Australia in Global Perspective*. Patrick McConvell and Nicholas Evans, eds. Pp. 123–134. Melbourne: Oxford University Press.
Bettinger, Robert L., and Martin A. Baumhoff
1982 The Numic Spread: Great Basin Cultures in Competition. *American Antiquity* 47: 485–503.
Birdsell, Joseph
1957 Some Population Problems Involving Pleistocene Man. *Cold Spring Harbor Symposia on Quantitative Biology* 22:47–69.
Campbell, Lyle, and Terrence Kaufman
1976 A Linguistic Look at the Olmecs. *American Antiquity* 41:80–89.
Campbell, Lyle, Terrence Kaufman, and Thomas C. Smith-Stark
1986 Mesoamerica as a Linguistic Area. *Language* 62:530–570.
Dakin, Karen, and Soren Wichmann
1995 Cacao, chocolate, y los nahuas y mixezoques en el sur de Mesoamerica. *Revista Latina de Pensamiento y Lenguaje, 1995–1996. Monográfico: Estudios de filología y lingüística náhuatl* 2(28):455–475.
Dixon, Robert M. W.
1997 *The Rise and Fall of Languages*. Cambridge: Cambridge University Press.
Eckert, Penelope
1993 Cooperative Competition in Adolescent "Girl Talk." In *Gender and Conversational Interaction*. Deborah Tannen, ed. Pp. 32–61. New York: Oxford University Press.

Giles, Howard

1973 Accent Mobility: A Model and Some Data. *Anthropological Linguistics* 15:87–105.

Hackenberg, Robert A.

1983 Pima and Papago Ecological Adaptations. In *Handbook of North American Indians.* Vol. 10, *Southwest.* Alfonso Ortiz, ed. Pp. 161–177. Washington, DC: Smithsonian Institution Press.

Hill, Jane H.

1979 Language Contact Systems and Human Adaptations. *Journal of Anthropological Research* 34:1–26.

1999 Why Is Uto-Aztecan So Big? Paper presented to the Department of Anthropology Colloquium Series, University of California at Davis, 24 May 1999.

Hill, Jane H., and Ofelia Zepeda

1991 "Some People Say I Sound Just Like I'm from around Here": The Speech of Tohono O'odham Dialect Outsiders. Paper presented to the Annual Meeting of the Southwestern Anthropological Association, Tucson, AZ, April 1991.

1992 Derived Words in Tohono O'odham. *International Journal of American Linguistics* 59:355–404.

Joseph, Alice, Rosamond B. Spicer, and Jane Chesky

1949 *The Desert People.* Chicago: University of Chicago Press.

Justeson, John S., and Terrence Kaufman

1993 A Decipherment of Epi-Olmec Hieroglyphic Writing. *Science* 259:1703–1711.

King, William S., and Delmos J. Jones

1974 *Papago Indians II: Papago Population Studies.* New York: Garland Publishing.

Kuhl, P. Katherine, K. A. Williams, F. Lacerda, K. N. Stevens, and B. Lindblom

1992 Linguistic Experience Alters Phonetic Perception in Infants by 6 Months of Age. *Science* 255:606–608.

Labov, William

1966 *The Social Stratification of English in New York City.* Washington, DC: Center for Applied Linguistics.

1972 *Sociolinguistic Patterns.* Philadelphia: University of Pennsylvania Press.

Lamb, Sydney

1958 Linguistic Prehistory in the Great Basin. *International Journal of American Linguistics* 24:95–100.

Le Page, R. B. and Andrée Tabouret-Keller

1985 *Acts of Identity.* Cambridge: Cambridge University Press.

Madsen, David B., and David Rhode, eds.

1994 *Across the West: Human Population Movement and the Expansion of the Numa.* Salt Lake City: University of Utah Press.

Miller, Wick

1970 Western Shoshoni Dialects. In *Languages and Cultures of Western North America.* E. Swanson, ed. Pp. 17–36. Pocatello: Idaho State University Press.

Milroy, James, and Leslie Milroy

1985 Linguistic Change, Social Network, and Speaker Innovation. *Journal of Linguistics* 21:339–384.

Nabhan, Gary

1982 *The Desert Smells like Rain.* San Francisco: North Point Press.

Nichols, Johanna

1992 *Linguistic Diversity in Space and Time.* Chicago: University of Chicago Press.

Payne, Arvilla
1980 Factors Controlling the Acquisition of the Philadelphia Dialect by Out-of-State
       Children. In *Locating Language in Time and Space*. William Labov, ed. Pp. 143–
       178. New York: Academic Press.
Renfrew, Colin
1988 *Archaeology and Language*. Cambridge: Cambridge University Press.
Saxton, Dean, Lucille Saxton, and Susie Enos
1983 *Dictionary Papago/Pima–English, O'othham–Mil-gahn; English–Papago/Pima,
       Mil-gahn–O'othham*. Tucson: University of Arizona Press.
Shaul, David
1986 Linguistic Adaptation and the Great Basin. *American Antiquity* 51:415–416.
Steward, Julian
1940 Native Cultures of the Intermontane (Great Basin) Area. In *Essays in Historical
       Anthropology of North America, Published in Honor of John R. Swanton*.
       Pp. 445–502. Smithsonian Miscellaneous Collections No. 100. Washington, D.C.
Sutton, Mark, and David Rhode
1994 Background to the Numic Problem. In Madsen and Rhode 1994:6–15.
Trudgill, Peter
1983 *On Dialect*. New York: New York University Press.
Underhill, Ruth
1939 *Social Organization of the Papago Indians*. Columbia University Contributions to
       Anthropology, vol. 30. New York: Columbia University Press.
Woolard, Kathryn
1998 Introduction: Language Ideology as a Field of Inquiry. In *Language Ideologies*.
       Bambi Schieffelin, Kathryn Woolard, and Paul Kroskrity, eds. Pp. 3–47. New
       York: Oxford University Press.
Woolard, Kathryn A., and Bambi B. Schieffelin
1994 Language Ideology. *Annual Review of Anthropology* 23:55–82.
Workman, P. L., and J. D. Niswander
1970 Population Studies on Southwestern Indian Tribes. II. Local Genetic Differentiation
       in the Papago. *American Journal of Human Genetics* 22:24–49.

13

Language, Culture, and Community Boundaries around the Huon Gulf of New Guinea

Joel Bradshaw

Villages around the Huon Gulf of New Guinea have exceedingly permeable linguistic and social boundaries. Multilingualism is widespread; neighboring languages are easily translatable. Traditionally, patterns of language, culture, and community rarely coincided, and it is difficult to identify any former groupings of people to which the adjectives "ethnic" or "tribal" might apply. Today, however, social and linguistic boundaries may be starting to synchronize as people speaking mutually intelligible varieties of speech increasingly act together and identify themselves as language-defined village alliances, even though, as individuals, they continue to be bilingual and often multilingual.—Editor

Melanesia in general and New Guinea in particular have long been recognized as convergence areas, where many residential communities show decidedly ambiguous linguistic and cultural affiliations. This case study of language relationships, social networks, and population movements around the coast of New Guinea's Huon Gulf finds little evidence of enduring ethnicity. Instead, it paints a kaleidoscopic picture of ever-changing patterns of fission and fusion among small, fragile communities where language, culture, and community have rarely coincided.[1]

DIFFERENT PATTERNS OF CONVERGENCE

In their oft-cited work on linguistic convergence in Kupwar village, Gumperz and Wilson (1971) described a situation in which the local varieties of (Indo-

European) Marathi and Urdu and (Dravidian) Kannada have converged to the point that all three share *"a single syntactic surface structure"* (original emphasis) and "are also identical in phonetics although they have different morphophonemic rules" (1971:256). "Marathi is the principal literary language" and "the main local medium of intergroup communication" (1971:253). Although multilingualism and code switching are the norm in public discourse, each language also plays an important role as a home language and marker of caste identity (1971:252–254). "While language distinctions are maintained, actual messages show word-for-word or morph-for-morph translatability, and speakers can therefore switch from one code to another with a minimum of additional learning" (1971:270). Although historical linguists are accustomed to think of "grammar as most persistent, lexicon as most changeable," Gumperz and Wilson note that "in Kupwar, it is grammar that has been most adaptable, lexical shape most persistent" (1971:271). The convergent syntax and phonology of the three main local languages in Kupwar apparently results from persistent code switching over a very long time. "There is every indication that the Kannada-speaking Jain cultivators and the Marathi-speaking service castes have both been in the region for more than six centuries" (1971:253), while the Urdu-speaking Muslims date from the Mughal era three to four centuries ago.

Although the patterns of linguistic convergence in many multilingual areas of New Guinea resemble those in Kupwar village, the ethnolinguistic context shows some striking differences. In the first place, the three major linguistic groups in Kupwar village have apparently been in constant, face-to-face contact for about 300 to 600 years. During that time, the syntax, semantics, and phonology of their local speech varieties appear to have converged very thoroughly, leaving only the sounds of the individual words in each language as the most salient marker of group identity. Second, the linguistic boundaries in Kupwar village are strongly reinforced by inherited differences of religion, caste, and socioeconomic status, allowing very little possibility of intermarriage or socioeconomic movement across linguistically marked community boundaries. Geographical mobility is also rather limited. In short, it would be hard to imagine linguistic boundaries less socially permeable than those in Kupwar village. The social context strongly encourages language maintenance and discourages language shift, even in the face of widespread multilingualism.

Villages around the Huon Gulf of New Guinea, by contrast, have extremely permeable linguistic and social boundaries. The typical village of 200 or so people is too small to be endogamous, husbands and wives often come from different language communities, and children often grow up speaking more than one language even at home. Social status is typically achieved rather than inherited, and multilingual skills are often an important tool for those who seek to mobilize allies from other villages in cooperative endeavors. Thus, as in Kupwar village, multilingualism is widespread, and neighboring languages are often easily intertranslatable on a morpheme-by-morpheme basis. The frequent need to translate from one language to another over many centuries will easily explain why the languages in both regions display such a high degree of syntactic and semantic convergence.

However, the linguistic results are rather different when it comes to phonology. The three languages in Kupwar village have achieved a very high degree of phonological convergence in the 300 to 600 years they have been spoken there, while the languages around the coast of the Huon Gulf display far more fractured patterns of phonological convergence after a period of perhaps five or ten times as long—assuming that the first Austronesian (AN) languages had arrived in the gulf by at least 3,000 years ago.[2] How can we explain this very spotty and localistic pattern of phonological convergence in the face of very widespread convergence in syntax and semantics? If we assume that phonological convergence requires direct, face-to-face contact while syntactic and semantic convergence can result from mediated, secondhand translationese, then the answer may lie in the extraordinary geographical mobility as well as social fluidity of village communities in New Guinea. As Ross (1988:135) notes, "It is likely that a number of Huon Gulf languages have been in close contact with different languages, both AN and non-AN, at different times." This case study assembles evidence of such ethnolinguistic "turbulence" (Watson 1990:39) and considers some of its effects on identifiable linguistic, cultural, and community boundaries in the region. It concludes with some thoughts on the origins of language-defined communities in the modern era.

LANGUAGE-BASED GROUPINGS IN THE HUON GULF

Ross (1988) was the first to amass qualitative evidence for a Huon Gulf family of languages that consists of four subgroups: (1) a Markham family that stretches up the tributaries of the Markham River, which empties into the western head of the gulf; (2) a North Huon Gulf (NHG) chain that stretches all along the north and south coasts of the gulf; (3) a South Huon Gulf (SHG) chain primarily in the mountains above the south coast of the gulf; and (4) an isolate that is the last Austronesian language along the southeast coast of the gulf (see Map 13.1). In Ross's usage, a "family" is a group that evolves by separation, while a "chain" is a grouping that evolves by dialect differentiation along a linear trajectory (1988:7–11). The languages of all four of Ross's groups are often intertranslatable on a morpheme-for-morpheme basis, as the following examples from four coastal languages illustrate. Our sample consists of Jabêm (Ja.), Labu (La.), Iwal (Iw.), and Numbami (Nu.).[3] Optional elements are parenthesized.

Resultatives

Ja.	(êsêàc)	sêjac	bôc	`ĕndu
La.	(êsôha)	sêya	mba	hônô
Iw.	(eisir)	es	bwelk	vunu
Nu.	(ai)	tilapa	bola	uni
	(them)	they-hit	pig	dead
	"They killed the pig."			

Map 13.1
Huon Gulf Language Groups

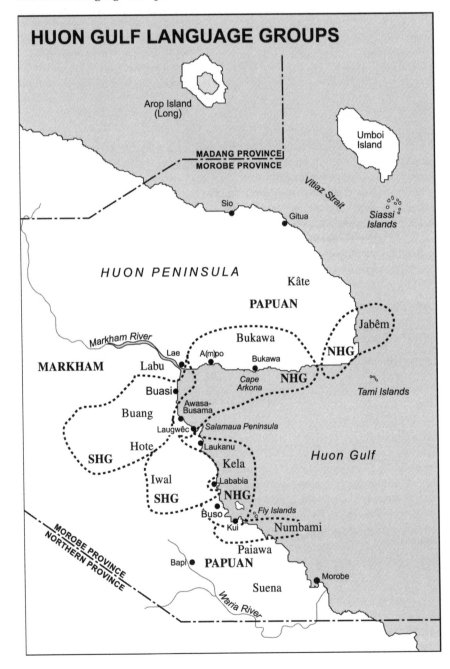

HUON GULF LANGUAGE GROUPS

Arop Island
(Long)

Umboi
Island

MADANG PROVINCE
MOROBE PROVINCE

Vitiaz Strait

Siassi
Islands

Sio

Gitua

HUON PENINSULA

Kâte

PAPUAN

Jabêm

Markham River

Bukawa

NHG

MARKHAM

Lae

A(m)po

Bukawa

Labu

Cape
Arkona

NHG

Buasi

Tami Islands

Buang

Awasa-
Busama

Laugwêc

Salamaua Peninsula

Hote

Laukanu

Huon Gulf

SHG

Kela

Iwal

Lababia

SHG

NHG

Buso

Fly Islands

Kui

Numbami

MOROBE PROVINCE
NORTHERN PROVINCE

Paiawa

Bapi

PAPUAN

Morobe

Suena

Waria River

Dative Noun Phrases

Ja.	eng	kêkêng	i	gêdêng	aê
La.	ini	yô	ê	ta	ai
Iw.	ei	geb	ih	gitangi	ayeu
Nu.	e	iki	iya	de(nga)	woya
	him	he-put	fish	(it)reach/ to	me

"He gave/sent fish to me."

Benefactive/Purposive Noun Phrases

Ja.	aêàc	akwê	àndu	kêtu	lau	nga
La.	êmaha	môsôhô	hanô	kô	du	
Iw.	amei	atav	nam	ve	apmol-mol	ane
Nu.	i	matawi	kapala	iu	lawa	ndi
	us	we-build	house	it-become/ for	people	Genitive

"We (exclusive) built a house for the people."

Abilitatives

Ja.	aê	katôm	gebe	jasôm	bing
La.	ai	natô	mba	ndôkô	yà
Iw.	ayeu	gatangi	ve	nanei	yaun
Nu.	woya	inden-gama	inggo	nanggo	binga
	me	(I)suffice/ able	say/for	I'll-say	talk

"I can talk."

Desideratives

Ja.	aê	gabe	jana	Lae	atom
La.	ai	mba	ndakô	Walêmu	ki
Iw.	ayeu	ve	navang	Lae	ite
Nu.	woya	wanggo	nawasa	Lae	kote
	me	I-say	I'll-go	Lae	not

"I don't want to go to Lae."

Hooley (1971) had earlier assigned all four of these languages to a single "Gulf subfamily" within a more widespread "Siasi family" that stretched along the coast and islands around the Huon Peninsula to the north of the gulf. Using only lexicostatistics compiled from 100-word lists, Hooley calculated that the coastal languages shared their highest cognate percentages (roughly 25–40 percent) with each other (see Bradshaw 1978b for further discussion). On the basis of shared phonological and morphological innovations, however, Ross (1988) assigns each of these languages to a different subgroup. Jabêm is the most conservative member of the NHG chain, Labu is an aberrant member of the Markham family, Iwal is the most conservative member of the SHG chain, and Numbami is a phonologically well-preserved but morphologically eroded isolate.

The NHG chain consists of only three languages, Jabêm, Bukawa, and Kela, but most of the villagers along the coast speak one or the other of them as home languages (Ross 1988:148–152). They are most likely to have provided the targets for the convergent syntax of the other coastal languages. (This tendency would have accelerated during the first half of the twentieth century, when Jabêm was propagated as the Lutheran mission's lingua franca among the Austronesian languages of Morobe Province.) The most striking phonological feature of this group presumably arose to compensate for the severe erosion of final segments. Jabêm and Bukawa show tonal contrasts on vowels (Dempwolff 1939; Capell 1949; Bradshaw 1979; Ross 1993), while Kela shows distinctive nasalization, but may lack tone (Collier and Collier 1975). Either Kela had tone and lost it, or else Jabêm and Bukawa developed tone after all the Kela speakers had moved to the south coast, where they now reside.

The only other tonal language on the coast is Labu, the sole coastal member of the Markham (Mk) family (Ross 1988:152–154). While Labu displays innovations diagnostic of Lower Mk languages, such as the merger of Proto-Oceanic (POC) *t, *r, and *R as PMk *r, and the presence of a numeral classifier *sV- (Ross 1988:152–154), it also shows the effects of strong influence from neighboring Bukawa. For instance, while PMk had a five-vowel system without phonemic tone, had a base-two counting system, and had lost nearly all of its inherited maritime vocabulary, Labu has reacquired maritime vocabulary, recreated a base-five counting system, and now has a seven-vowel system with phonemic tone. The particular influence of Bukawa phonology and morphology is clear in each case (Holzknecht 1994).

Iwal (known to Jabêm speakers as Kaiwa) is likewise a rather divergent member of the SHG chain, which otherwise consists of Hote and the more tightly knit Buang group, with quite distinctive phonological and morphological innovations (Ross 1988:154–160). Iwal follows the SHG pattern of showing a voiced, usually liquid, reflex of POC *s (Iw. *aru* "smoke" < POC *qasu; ruru-* "breast" < POC *susu; ur* "rain" < POC *qusan), but is unique among SHG languages in having merged POC *r and *R, as non-SHG neighbors have done.

It is also unique among the SHG group in retaining POC *t as t (not l or y) and POC *mw as mw (not my or ny) and in retaining the distinction between the first-person-plural inclusive and exclusive subject prefixes (*Iw.ta-* "we including you," *a-* "we excluding you"). It also preserves more of its inherited morphology than the rest of its congeners.

Finally, the isolate Numbami (also known as Siboma) appears to be the most phonologically conservative member of the Huon Gulf family (Ross 1988:135). It should be noted, however, that while Numbami appears to have preserved the shapes of inherited words better than most of its congeners, it has abandoned almost all of its morphology, apart from subject prefixes. The POC possessive suffixes on inalienable nouns, for instance, are well preserved in Iwal and are still visible but underdifferentiated in Jabêm, but are preserved in only a handful of kin-term compounds in Numbami. The preservation of POC final consonants has also been aided by the addition of a final supporting vowel /a/ to inherited words that ended in consonants, as in *awila* "fishhook" < POC *kawil, ilama* "adze" < POC *kiRam, dimila* "caulking substance" < POC *jimiR, niwila* "coconut" < POC *niuR, samana* "outrigger float" < POC *saman, walasa* "rope, vine" < POC *waRoc, wata* "four" < POC *pat, usana* "rain" < POC *qusan*. This is one of several indications that earlier generations of Numbami speakers may have begun to eliminate final vowels on many words, but that later generations may have restored more conservative-looking, vowel-final syllable shapes by adding a new supporting vowel (either /a/ or an echo vowel) after each final consonant—perhaps as speakers of neighboring Papuan (non-Austronesian) languages shifted to Numbami. If Suena is typical (see Wilson 1976), the neighboring non-Austronesian languages of the Binandere family have even simpler syllable structures than Numbami's Austronesian neighbors. A community of Papuan speakers shifting to Numbami may also have been responsible for eliminating virtually all of Numbami's inherited morphology and for regularizing what little remains. In short, Numbami may not be as phonologically conservative as it first appears.

CONSERVATIVE = SEDENTARY?

One feature of interest is the apparent phonological conservatism of Jabêm, Iwal, and Numbami within their respective subgroups. The readiest explanation may be that all three languages lie on the peripheries of their subgroups and are thus farthest from the centers of innovation. Jabêm and Numbami lie at the far eastern edges of the Huon Gulf and the HG family of languages. Iwal is spoken in nine villages, four on the coast and the rest in the mountains, but far below the high valleys where most of the SHG languages are concentrated. However, Ross (1991) has proposed another explanation that equates conservatism and sedentariness. He argues that the SHG languages spread westward and inland from initial settlements on the southeastern coast, near where Numbami is today

(1991:448). He thus assumes that Numbami and Iwal are the conservative "stay-at-home" languages on the south coast whose communities have remained sedentary for a very long time while more linguistically innovative speakers migrated inland. Neither of these two explanations is without difficulties.

While generally corroborating the existence of a correlation between amount of sound change and lineal distance from probable earlier homelands among Austronesian languages, Blust (1991) rejects Ross's explanation for why such a correlation exists. Ross suggests that migrating populations are likely to be younger than their stay-at-home compatriots and thus not only more innovative in their speech patterns, but also less restrained by the more conservative "gerontocrats" of the village after their departure (Ross 1991:447–448). However, if an innovation were already under way at the time of departure, "we would expect change in a language to follow immediately upon [or soon after] the physical relocation of its speakers," and not "*many generations after* the major moves," as Blust demonstrates must have happened in many cases (Blust 1991: 40; original emphasis).

A further problem for both the "conservative = sedentary" and the "center versus periphery" explanations is that both assume that the current locations of language communities reflect essentially one major wave of migration, with each group remaining fairly stable after branching off and settling in a new location. In fact, to help make his point, Ross indulges in a questionable—and since-retracted (personal communication)—reconfiguration of his South Huon Gulf "chain" (1988) into a "family" (1991) with the (1988) isolate Numbami attached to the top node of a neat, right-branching tree. He even goes so far as to appeal to Grace's (1986) "principle of shortest moves," which states that "in the absence of evidence to the contrary, it is to be assumed that each new Oceanic settlement was made from the geographically closest Oceanic-speaking place then in existence" (1986:5). I believe that this principle was formulated to reduce the number of possible hypotheses about the point of origin of each new migration beyond the old periphery of Oceanic habitation. However, I have doubts about its utility even within remote Oceania and remain firmly convinced that it has no place at all in constraining hypotheses about movements within long-settled areas of western Oceania. The following reconstruction of patterns of contact and movement around the Huon Gulf in the recent past casts considerable doubt on the assumption that any of the language communities around the gulf have remained sedentary since they first arrived.

SOCIAL NETWORKS AND MOVEMENTS AROUND THE HUON GULF

Recent Interaction Spheres

Harding (1967) has given the most complete account of trade relationships around the Huon Peninsula. He describes three major overlapping networks, each served by one principal long-distance carrier and each tying together groups with complementary resources and specializations. The Bilibili Islanders were the voyagers and potmakers of a network centered on Astrolabe Bay in present-day Madang Province. The Siassi Islanders were the voyagers and coconut growers of a network centered on the Vitiaz Strait between the southwestern tip of New Britain and the northeastern tip of New Guinea. The Tami Islanders were the voyagers and bowl carvers of a network that stretched from the south-eastern tip of the Huon Peninsula all around the gulf as far as Morobe Harbor at the mouth of the Waria River.

According to Harding (1967:241), the most distinctive feature of these New Guinea–area trading systems is their degree of economic integration in the absence of any overarching political institutions. He cites three factors that may have encouraged the Austronesian latecomers to the region to develop and rely on such trade networks: (1) they encountered a very diverse but very compact geographic environment; (2) they possessed the sailing technology required for overseas trading; and (3) most of the larger land areas they encountered were already occupied, so they were often restricted to environments too marginal for independent subsistence (1967:239–246). With rare exceptions, such as Busama and Sio, the typical population of one of these coastal villages was around 200 (see Harding 1967:14n; Hogbin 1951:15, 30), so that most villages were not even self-sufficient in suitable marriage partners. Indeed, gift giving among kin-folk residing in different villages was the principal means by which goods circulated around the coast; only strangers relied on direct barter exchanges (Harding 1967:165–184; Hogbin 1951:83–86).

The other foundation of the trade network was local specialization. According to Hogbin (1951:81–95), Salamaua Peninsula was the only good source of work-able stone, which the nearby Kela- and Bukawa-speaking villagers made into extra adze blades for their kin in other villages. One of the Fly Islands farther down the south coast was the only good source of clay, which the nearby Kela-, Numbami-, and (Papuan) Paiawa-speaking villagers made into extra pots for trade. The marsh-dwelling Labu speakers specialized in weaving baskets, hand-bags, and purses from the abundant lakeside grasses available to them. The Bukawa speakers on the north coast specialized in mats and stringbags, while the resource-starved Tami Islanders relied on their bowl-carving, canoe-building, and navigational skills to obtain enough food and other necessities. The villagers near Salamaua produced surplus taro and sago to reciprocate for the baskets, bowls, mats, and pots their less well-fed kinsmen gave them. My Numbami hosts told me that Lababia used to be the site of a periodic pig market for the villages on their stretch of the south coast. One quantitative measure of this exchange system is the fact that about 270 of the more than 500 material objects that the Field Museum's A. B. Lewis collected from Huon Gulf villages in 1910 "were traded into the villages where he acquired them, rather than having been made there" (Welsch 1998:192).

Besides material goods and marriage partners, a common set of myths and local lore also circulated around the gulf. The Bukawa speakers north of Sala-maua trace the origin of their ritual bullroarers to a village near the mouth of the Waria River far to the south (Hogbin 1951:214). Many people know the story (recorded in Sack 1976:110–111) of the hill Luamung in the center of Lae, which is said to have once been located in the Fly Islands. Luamung's cousin and neighboring hill Bombieng was so greedy that he ate all the food the villagers supplied to them, leaving only scraps for Luamung. The latter therefore uprooted himself one night and moved far enough away that Bombieng could no longer see him, leaving behind only a pit where Numbami, Paiawa, and Kela villagers get clay for making their pots.[4]

Another widely shared story (also recorded in Sack 1976:111–113) involves a woman who cuts herself on sugarcane and fills two holes in the ground with her own blood. The blood turns into two boys who, after learning from the woman how to build canoes and fish and take care of themselves, go on to slay monsters who had long threatened the local population. In the Lae account recorded by Sack, the boys are called "strongboy" and "weakboy," the story is set near Luamung, and the monsters are wild boars. In the Numbami version I heard, the boys were called "righthand man" (Nu. Anokole) and "lefthand man" (Nu. Kazekole), the story was set in their own locale, and the monsters were two giants in a cave, followed by a moray eel, an octopus, and a sea eagle. The cave monsters reflect inland versions of the same story cycle, while the latter menagerie betrays a strong orientation toward the sea. I believe that this sort of dual heritage is fairly typical of many coastal villages in New Guinea (see Dutton 1994, 1995; and especially Pomponio, Counts, and Harding 1994).

Recent Migration Patterns

Since most of the trade goods were presented as gifts to relatives and most people found spouses from villages not too far away, most of the people and goods moved only fairly short distances along the arc of the coastline at any one time (Hogbin 1951:87–88). The Tami Islanders were the only ones in the gulf who regularly undertook long-distance voyages. When famine, warfare, or other disasters struck, villagers would migrate or disperse to their kinfolk along the most familiar trade routes. The following reconstruction of the most recent such population movements by speakers of various languages around the Huon Gulf starts from Hogbin (1951), who did most of his fieldwork among speakers of Bukawa (Ja. Kawac, Bu. Gawac) near Salamaua.

Before the advent of the Lutheran missionaries, who propagated Jabêm as a lingua franca, Bukawa was the most widely spoken language around the Huon Gulf. Bukawa-speaking villages stretched all along the north and west coast of the gulf and as far as Salamaua on the south coast, with a total population of about 7,000 in 1950. By contrast, Labu, Kela, and Iwal only had about 1,500 speakers each in the 1970s, and Numbami only had about 250. The earliest known Bukawa-speaking settlement was near the mouth of the river in the center of the north coast (at Cape Arkona) from which the current name of the language derives (*bu* "freshwater, river" + Kawac). From there, they spread west to the mouth of the Markham River (Ja. Busi), where Labu speakers now reside, and east as far as the Jabêm-speaking territory at the southern tip of the Huon Peninsula. Sack (1976) chronicles some of these movements, especially in the vicinity of present-day Lae. After a drought sometime during the 1700s, a group of Bukawa speakers crossed the gulf to Lutu, at the tip of Salamaua Point, near the only good stone quarry in the region. (Hogbin's precontact dates derive primarily from genealogies and must be treated cautiously, as he himself admits [1951:102 n.], but the settlement sequences are likely to be more reliable.) In 1950, Busama villagers still maintained close trade ties with the village of Bukawa, which was traditionally hostile to visitors from Kêla, Busama's Kela-speaking neighbor.

The villagers of Kêla, for their part, maintained close trade ties with Apo (or Ampo), between Cape Arkona and Lae on the north coast. It is tempting to infer from this that Apo, or a portion of it, may have been Kela-speaking at one time. When the first Bukawa villagers arrived at Salamaua, there were already Kela-speaking villages along the coast to the south. Kêla is the Jabêm name for the closest one, which was no doubt the first one encountered by the German missionaries when they established their first station on the south coast at Malaclo in 1907.[5] The Jabêm name for the other Kela-speaking village just south of Salamaua is Laugwêc, "sea people." Stretching along behind the coast at that time were several groups of inlanders (Ja. Kai). The first such group the new Bukawa immigrants encountered when they established gardens and later settlements on the neighboring mainland were speakers of what is now called Hote. The language of another group of Kai villages is now known as Kaiwa (Ja. Kaiwac, probably < Kai Iwac; cf. Iw. Iwal, Nu. Yuwala), ranged behind the Kela villages along the coast to the south and well into the interior. Kai who lived behind the first range of mountains (therefore known in Jabêm as Kaidê-môê "backside Kai") spoke one or more of the Buang languages. One isolated community of Buang speakers, the Vehes, have apparently occupied an inland village on the lower reaches of the Buasi (north of Salamaua) since before European contact.

The Jabêm label Kai has cognates in the other coastal languages (Bu. Gai, Nu. Kaila). It applies to all inlanders, wherever they might be encountered. (Its adjectival cognate *kaikaila* in Numbami denotes not just "characteristic of inlanders," but also "shoddy, of poor quality.") This is but one indication that before the coming of the Europeans, the most salient cultural divide recognized by the coastal peoples around the Huon Gulf was that between inlanders and themselves. Watson (1990:32–34) describes a similar distinction between "forest" and "grassland" peoples at higher elevations (around Kainantu in neighboring Eastern Highlands Province), where the lowland grasslanders are characterized as politically and culturally dominant and more sophisticated, while the highlanders are characterized as more knowledgeable about their natural surroundings. (See Pomponio 1990 for an analysis of the effects of the Siassi maritime identity on Mandok attitudes toward development opportunities.)

In Morobe Province, speakers of Austronesian languages fall on both sides of the coastal–inland divide. The Markham and South Huon Gulf groups are now thoroughly oriented toward the land, while the North Huon Gulf groups and Numbami remain firmly tied to the sea. Hogbin (1951:28–29) cites the case of the Kai (probably Hote-speaking) village of Wamasu, which in 1910 was induced by the missionaries to move down from the foothills to within 50 meters of the coast. By 1950, they had still not learned to swim, fish, or handle canoes. In contrast, when the coastal Busama were forced to move about 500 meters inland during the war, they petitioned almost monthly to return to within sight and sound of the sea, and many individuals would temporarily move back down to the shore whenever they felt ill (Hogbin 1951:112–113).

The spread of the Bukawa speakers after their initial settlement at Lutu may be typical of similar migrations in the past. For a generation or two, they planted and harvested food on the adjacent mainland, but retreated to their easily defended village on the promontory each night. As their own population increased or they acquired more allies, they built villages on the mainland, first at Asini, then at Busama. The population of the latter village was augmented first by the incorporation of a dozen or so families of inlanders from Kaiwakuc (Ja. "new Kai"), then by a whole village called Awasa whose inhabitants had been driven off their lands near present-day Lae. Hogbin (1951:28) thinks that the Awasa were originally a Bukawa group, but Sack (1976:116n) thinks that they were a Markham group. In 1950, the Busama villagers of Lutu origin outnumbered those of Awasa origin by about two to one, and each villager (even those known to descend from Kaiwakuc) identified with one or the other of these two primary divisions. Thus the largest Bukawa-speaking village on the south coast has incorporated peoples representing as many as three of the four major linguistic subgroups in the Gulf: Bukawa of the NHG chain, Kaiwakuc of the SHG chain, and Awasa (possibly) of the Markham family.

At least during the most recent round of migrations, Kela speakers clearly arrived on the south coast before Bukawa speakers, but I suspect not much more than a century or two before. Perhaps they fled south when the cataclysmic eruption of Arop (Long) Island in the mid-1600s (Blong 1982:177–194) set off a wave of migrations around the Huon Peninsula (see Pomponio 1994). According to my most reliable Numbami sources (two leaders whose court testimony had helped establish their land claims), there had been only two Kela villages below Salamaua until fairly recently, one on a promontory at Laukanu (Ke. Apoze, Nu. Bazela) and another on the small offshore island of Lababia. After an epidemic struck the island, the Lababia people (Nu. Ya) dispersed to the coastal villages of Lababia, Buso (Nu. Ya Tinaso), and Kuwi (Nu. Ya Keula). The Kuwi group settled on Numbami land provided by some of their kinfolk. After pacification, several Iwal-speaking villages moved down to the coast, generally shadowing their Kela-speaking rivals. Iwal Nuknuk borders

Kela Laugwêc, Iwal Buansing borders Kela Laukanu, Iwal Duali faces Lababia Island, and Salus lies on its left flank. Rival land claims mar the relations between the traditionally inland Iwal-speaking and the coastal Kela-speaking villages. (Numbami speakers may have had a similar relationship with Iwal speakers earlier; cf. *Yuwala* "Iwal people," *yuwayuwala* "enemy.)" Numerous precolonial conflicts are recounted in Lechner and Male's (1955) Jabêm school reader.

The first Numbami speakers probably arrived on the south coast before the first Kela speakers, since their language is not a member of the NHG chain. (Or they may have come directly from one of the islands in the Vitiaz Strait, bypassing the north coast.) By their own account, they first settled on the lee side of Awayagi Island just west of Cape Kubumi and at Ulingi Point across the bay. Both sites would have been easily defensible from inlanders, but they began to suffer repeated raids from the coastal Lababia people to the north and from the Papuan (Binandere family) speakers of Suena (Nu. Zena) from the mouth of the Waria River, near Morobe Harbor. There are tantalizing bits of lexical evidence that coastal Suena speakers may have had some friendlier contact with local Austronesian speakers as well, perhaps absorbing a coastal settlement or two.[6] The successful Numbami land claim to their piece of the coast in the face of rival claims by their Papuan Paiawa-speaking neighbors hinged on Suena testimony that the Numbami (known to them as Siboma) were the first people they used to encounter when they traveled north. The Paiawa (Nu. Kembula) apparently came down to the coast later.

The Numbami story then takes several sharp turns. To escape the coastal raiders, they moved to Karsimbo, at the head of the deeper and more defensible neighboring bay, perhaps around 1850. There they were surrounded and attacked in a dawn raid by a combined party from Lababia, Buso, and Kuwi, suffering many losses (see Lechner and Male 1955:99–100 [in Jabêm] for one account of this event). They later retaliated in a similar attack on Buso and were about to slaughter everyone when they found some of their own kin among their prospective victims, so they killed one Buso villager for each of the Numbami killed in the earlier attack. Perhaps to escape the inevitable counterattack, they moved farther up into the hills above Karsimbo and joined up with a Papuan-speaking Bapi (Nu. Wapi) village farther inland.[7] In 1976, the former Numbami village head, a man everyone called Abu Bamo "Big Grandfather," told me that he was really a Bapi man. (By contrast, his successor—and my host—had close ties to Kela-speaking Laukanu.) This joint Numbami-Bapi village at a site called Yawale broke up after some European prospectors came through and massacred some of the Bapi for refusing to carry for them, perhaps between 1890 and 1910 (see Idriess 1933:8–12). The remaining Bapi then fled farther up toward their present location on the upper reaches of the Waria River, while the Numbami moved back down to the coast, where they were living when the Lutheran missionaries contacted them and named their bay Braunschweig Harbor.[8] Perhaps a generation or so later, they moved back to the bay between their ancestral settlements at Ulingi Point and Awayagi Island. The new village also had the advantage of being closer to the South Pacific Timber Company compound at Natter Bay (Nu. Nadubai), between the Numbami and Paiawa villages. (The timber royalties were split three ways among the Numbami, Paiawa, and Bapi villages.) By 1976, the former village site at Karsimbo was still marked by tall old coconut trees, while Ulingi Point no longer had any signs of former habitation.

Similarities Elsewhere in New Guinea

The narrative of recent migrations presented here, although clearly quite sketchy and tentative, strikes me as altogether typical of many areas of the relatively unpopulated coastal lowlands of Papua New Guinea. Similar tales of "substantial population movements" in the Lae area during the early period of European contact have been compiled by Sack (1976). In his field diary during a 1910 visit to the Sattelberg region above Finschhafen, the anthropologist A. B. Lewis noted that "the villages are moved, divided or united every few years, and each time have a new name" (Welsch 1998:210). In reconstructing the history of the Markham languages, Holzknecht (1989) also found a tangled series of relocations that seemed to follow Watson's (1970:114) principle of "relocation at a distance" (or what we might call the "leapfrog" principle). It is not hard to imagine how the particular local conditions that induce a group to seek refuge elsewhere in the first place—whether drought, warfare, volcanic eruptions, or disagreements with kinfolk—might also induce them to seek refuge at a safer distance, rather than as close as possible to the origin of their troubles.

Harding (1967, 1985) has also described complex relationships of trade and migration among the peoples of the Vitiaz Strait, focusing especially on the coastal Sio. "The theme of Sio history is unity out of diversity. Culturally and linguistically differentiated groups and settlements joined forces on an offshore island to form a large compact village that became a monolingual and culturally homogeneous society" (Harding and Clark 1994:36). Harding also found the "leapfrog" principle to apply: "The Sios found their enemies closer to home. . . . People from afar were friends" (1967:116). No doubt this is why Ross (1988: 160) found such "a bewildering variety of [crosscutting] isoglosses" despite the "reasonable similarity" in the typology of the Vitiaz languages.

Chowning, after exploring the linguistic effects of such population mixing in the same region, concluded, "All of the historic evidence suggests that a considerable stretch of the north coast of New Guinea, including the offshore islands, has been subject to constant movements of people" (1986:429). "I do not think that most of New Britain was settled in one wave of AN speakers, as Grace (1986) suggests" (1986:425). In fact, Chowning has established an honorable tradition of injecting an antidote of what one might call "social anthropologist realism" every time linguists threaten to fall too blindly in love with a new Melanesian subgroup whose beguiling image is depicted in the clean lines of an abstract tree structure. At the first Austronesian linguistics conference in Honolulu (Chowning 1973), she administered a dose to those enamored of Milke's (1965) "New Guinea cluster." At the fourth Austronesian conference in Suva (Chowning 1986), she countered several new subgrouping proposals involving the languages around the Vitiaz and Dampier straits. At the fifth Austronesian conference in Auckland (Chowning 1989), she attempted to cure Ross's (1988) increasing attachment to his Papuan Tip Cluster (PTC) in the region known to anthropologists as the Massim. "Given that Ross has expressed many doubts about how well his Kilivila chain fits into PTC, I suggest that it is time he and others re-considered the possibility that the Massim was not settled by a single migration of speakers of one Oceanic proto-language. If it were, it would be an extraordinary event in the apparently complicated prehistory of western Melanesia" (Chowning 1989:137). In this particular instance, Chowning suggested that the Kilivila may represent a later intrusion from either New Britain or the Solomons long after the initial Austronesian colonization of the Papuan Tip. This illustrates the difficulty of always finding a clear distinction between settlement and relocation, that is, between colonizing migrations from afar and later population movements within an established local network.

Others have issued similar caveats of a more general nature. In his now-classic work on direct and indirect inheritance in Rotuman, Biggs (1965) warned about the linguistic effects of much movement and long-continued contact in Melanesia, and in 1972 he warned that contact and resettlement make the derivation of human population movements from linguistic subgrouping relationships far from straightforward. Unfortunately, the increasing attention by Austronesian linguists to issues of contact—so evident in Dutton and Tryon's (1994) major compilation of case studies spurred by the appearance of Thomason and Kaufman (1988)—does not seem to have been matched by equally close attention to patterns of movement and migration within Melanesia. Perhaps this has something to do with the comparatively unspectacular achievements of Melanesian navigators relative to their Polynesian and Micronesian counterparts, at least in more recent times. Perhaps it also reflects a long-term reaction against earlier attempts by Ray (1926) and Capell (1943) to account for Melanesian diversity almost exclusively in terms of multiple migrations and substrate effects.

This peripatetic lifestyle is not peculiar to the Austronesian-speaking peoples of Oceania. Foley's (1986) survey of Papuan languages briefly explores some of the broader linguistic implications of population movements, multilingualism, and prehistoric changes in geomorphology in New Guinea. Watson (1970, 1990) outlines a model of community fission, migration, and fusion among Papuan highlanders that applies very well to the coastal Austronesians described earlier, even down to the typical size of the village communities:

The aboriginal peoples of Papua New Guinea's Eastern Highlands are organized in autonomous polities, some with as few as one or two hundred members. Many if not most of these local peoples experience episodes of radical revision in their membership. Most groups are formed in a highly fluid sociopolitical field, intermittently marked by relocations, realignments, and the patriation of alien immigrants who have been expelled by hostile neighbors from their own lands elsewhere. Restless or disgruntled insiders split off to form new groups; refugee outsiders are recruited from time to time to reinforce the ranks of those remaining. To the literal-minded genealogist, the long-term kinship and continuity of each such group seem confused, even compromised.

A truncated local sense of history nevertheless contains the frequent events of fission and fusion. In spite of ongoing exchanges of personnel, a common and ostensibly continuous local identity immerses not only long-established elements of the community but, in time, the descendants of recent immigrants. (1990:17)

In his earlier work, Watson considers in some detail the wider implications of "the recurrent fission of kinsmen and the recruitment of outsiders" (1970: 107), including spatial mobility unwarranted by rules of descent and residence, short (or "shallow") genealogies, fragmentation and changing realignments of local and descent groups, and lack of formal offices, positions of seniority, and hierarchy of any sort. In his later work, he also considers some of the linguistic implications:

Over half a dozen languages are spoken in the immediate vicinity of Kainantu, and all the communities I resided in have close social ties to at least one community of alien speech. Often two or three other languages are represented in these linkages. Many communities of the vicinity have incorporated refugees who arrived speaking a language other than that of their hosts. With time, if the refugees remain, their original language may be lost, but probably not without a distinct residue of the sounds, words, attitudes, and cultural practices they brought with them. In some communities in the 1960s there were refugees or their descendants still speaking their original language, . . . resulting in their designation by the community (from Pidgin) as "hapkas" [half-caste].[9] (1990:26)

Thurston (1987, 1989, 1994) has perhaps been the most persistent in investigating the effects of such ethnolinguistic turbulence, especially in the area of New Britain where he did fieldwork. However, Thurston's valuable findings are somewhat marred by his commitment to a model that reduces virtually all language change to cycles of simplification (or "exoterogeny," akin to pidginization) and complication (or "esoterogeny," akin to creolization).[10] Ross (1987, 1994, 1996) has also been actively investigating issues and cases of language contact within a more conservative theoretical framework.

EPILOGUE: ON THE ORIGINS OF MODERN LANGUAGE COMMUNITIES IN NEW GUINEA

In his broad-ranging attempt to explain differing degrees of complexity and power among human societies, Diamond (1997) is careful to distinguish between his usage of "tribe" for a level of small-scale political organization and the more common earlier usage of "tribe" for a group sharing a distinct language and culture, in other words, what is now usually called an "ethnic" group. Diamond's example is drawn from his experience working among the Foré-speaking high-landers of New Guinea in 1964.

By linguistic and cultural standards, there were then 12,000 Foré, speaking two mutually intelligible dialects and living in 65 villages of several hundred people each. But there was no political unity whatsoever among villages of the Foré language group. Each hamlet was involved in a kaleidoscopically changing pattern of war and shifting alliances with all neighboring hamlets, regardless of whether the neighbors were Foré or speakers of a different language. (Diamond 1997:270–271)

This description actually implies that the non-Foré-speaking neighbors who form periodic alliances with groups of Foré speakers also share many common elements of culture with the latter. What does it mean, then, to speak of "the Foré"? In the context of traditional New Guinea, political boundaries usually divide groups sharing a common language, while shared cultural complexes often unite groups speaking different languages. Moreover, all such boundaries shift constantly as people physically relocate their residences or simply realign their allegiances. In the modern context, however, language boundaries have become increasingly salient primarily because people speaking mutually intel-ligible varieties of speech constitute a single market for vernacular literacy and Bible-translation efforts, not unlike Europe on the eve of its modern era. These efforts can turn language-defined markets into language-defined communities by creating a powerful new symbol of common identity: a vernacular language objectified and made tangible by reduction to writing, and standardized and legitimized by virtue of its educational and religious uses.

Iwal provides a case in point. There is no indication that the members of the four coastal and five inland villages of Iwal speakers that existed in 1990 had ever previously formed a unified multivillage alliance apart from speakers of all other neighboring languages. In other words, one could not speak of "the Iwal" as anything other than a linguistic grouping. However, Cobb and Wroge (1990) describe recent multivillage efforts to start a vernacular literacy program. Most Iwal speakers are already literate to some degree in one or more of either Jabêm, the church language; Tok Pisin, the national lingua franca; or English, the of-ficial language of government and education. Older people know Jabêm, and everyone speaks Tok Pisin, but Iwal is still the dominant language in village conversation. In 1985, an Iwal New Testament was dedicated after being trans-lated by a native speaker of Iwal working with the Bible Translation Association (BTA) of Papua New Guinea. In 1986, three Iwal speakers attended that year's National Literacy Course. In 1990, they and the three other members of a re-cently constituted Iwal Language Committee helped two members of the Sum-mer Institute of Linguistics conduct a workshop for vernacular writers and teachers, to which six of the nine Iwal villages sent participants. (It would be interesting to know why the other three villages failed to send participants after being invited to do so.) The six villages supplied food for the duration of the course, and several sent men and materials to build facilities for the course and for a future classroom and office. Moreover, the Language Committee assessed each adult K1.20 per annum to help fund its work. (Again, it would be interesting to track payments and delinquencies among the various villages.) These efforts are clearly creating a broader multivillage community united and defined by a distinct common language, even though each of its speakers is at least bilingual and often multilingual.

It is instructive to compare the Iwal case with the earlier creation and dissolution over the past century of two large language communities in response to the propagation by German Lutheran missionaries of Jabêm and Kâte as local linguae francae for religious and educational purposes among speakers of Austronesian and Papuan languages, respectively (see Hogbin 1947; Streicher 1982: iv–ix; Zahn 1996). As noted, the most salient cultural divide around the Huon Gulf before European contact was between coastal people and inlanders, regardless of whether each particular community spoke an Austronesian or a Papuan language. However, in choosing whether to assign a particular community to the Jabêm or the Kâte circuit, the missionaries considered first its language-family affiliation.[11] Besides providing for the first time a reified institutional symbol of the Austronesian-Papuan language-family boundary, the Lutheran mission's evangelical efforts around the gulf managed to standardize and richly describe two local languages; to produce a significant body of religious and secular literature, including many original contributions by New Guineans as well as translations and textbooks by Europeans; and to build a larger and stronger multivillage community—unified by both language and religion—than had ever existed there before.

At the mission's height, before and after World War II, about 30,000 pupils attended Jabêm elementary schools, and at least twice that number achieved minimal literacy in the language (Streicher 1982:v). Hogbin (1947:21) noted that in the Bukawa-speaking village of Busama immediately after the war, every child of 14 was fluent in three languages—his own, Jabêm, and Tok Pisin. During my fieldwork in 1976, one Numbami man told me that of all the older people in the village at that time, only his mother had failed to attend Jabêm school. By then, however, the government and mission schools had long since changed their medium of instruction to Tok Pisin and English, and the former had supplanted Jabêm as the lingua franca, except in church contexts, where the Jabêm-educated elders would regularly switch into their old lingua franca.[12] By now, many of those elders have passed from the scene, and the formerly Jabêm-speaking religious community is no longer demarcated by a language boundary, apart from hymns and liturgy. Instead, the lingua franca of the state, Tok Pisin, now unites the various religious communities of Papua New Guinea, at least until Bible-translation and vernacular schooling efforts manage to unify as well as set off villages speaking mutually intelligible varieties of speech.

The demarcative function of language use in New Guinea has long been recognized, but the failure of language to act as a unifier seems not to have been widely acknowledged. This case study of language, culture, and community boundaries around the Huon Gulf shows that in the traditional context, these boundaries have rarely coincided, making it difficult to find any cohesive collectivities to which the adjective "ethnic" or "tribal" might be applied. Efforts to build vernacular-language literacy in village schools may yet create multivillage communities united and set off from their neighbors by a common language, but such communities will be a product of the modern era.

NOTES

1. Another version of this chapter with a rather different focus appeared in the *Journal of the Polynesian Society* (Bradshaw 1997). Other earlier versions were presented to the Austronesian Circle at the University of Hawai'i on 19 September 1996 and to the Third International Conference on Oceanic Linguistics at the University of Waikato on 18 January 1997. Comments from Bob Blust, George Grace, Terry Hunt, Ken Rehg, Jeff Siegel, and anonymous referees helped much to improve various drafts, as did responses from members of both audiences at the formal presentations. All remaining flaws are my responsibility.

2. These dates must be regarded as very rough estimates. There is not yet any firm archaeological evidence of Austronesian settlements on the New Guinea mainland as early as 3000 B.P. (Andy Pawley, personal communication), and Jeff Siegel (personal communication) has suggested that the phonologies of regional varieties of Marathi, Urdu, and Kannada may have already begun converging before local varieties of all three began to be spoken in Kupwar village.

3. Jabêm examples are based on data from Dempwolff (1939) and Zahn (1940); Labu on data from Siegel (1984); Iwal on data from Davidson and Davidson (1976); and Numbami on data from Bradshaw (1982, 1993, and field notes). Fieldwork on Numbami was supported by National Science Foundation grant no. BNS 75–1945–1 to the University of Hawai'i Oceanic Comparative Linguistics Project under the direction of George W. Grace and Andrew K. Pawley.

4. This island is called Ulangawa "clay pit" in Numbami and Abudubu "clay pit" in Papuan Paiawa. The Numbami name for its larger neighboring island is Biananggutu "trochus-shell island," which may be partially cognate with Bombieng, whose initial *bo-* may be related to Nu. *bou*, Ja. *bau* "hill, land (versus sea)."

5. Iwal speakers call the Kêla village locale Busin, while Numbami speakers call it Buzina and call Salamaua Peninsula Buzina Bubusu "Buzina Point," perhaps named after some previous community residing there.

6. Compare Suena (Su.) *gutu*, Nu. *gutu* "island"; Su. *bamu*, Nu./Iw. *bamo* "big"; Su. *ma*, Ja. *mo*, POC **mwapo* "taro"; Su. *wa*, Ja./Bu./Ke. *wang* "canoe"; Su. *mama*, Nu. *mama* "father" (Suena data from Wilson 1976). Note also the offshore islands named Babagutu, Matebinagutu, Mindrugutu, and Morobegutu.

7. Perhaps it is only a curious coincidence that the complex of villages in the Lae area at the time of European intrusion also had a dual heritage that included an inland-oriented "Wapi" component among its Kamkumun group in addition to its more sea-oriented (and Bukawa-speaking) Butibam group (Sack 1976:110).

8. The inland origins of (at least part of) the Numbami community and its battles

with Kela-speaking neighbors are corroborated by two traditional stories that appear in *Buku Sêsamnga II*, the Jabêm school reader (Lechner and Male 1955:98–100).

9. Watson notes an interesting case in which one community regarded its neighbors as alien, even though both spoke the same language, because the latter community was "closely allied to a third group—likewise enemies of the first—that did in fact speak a foreign language" (1990:39).

10. Thurston's model may apply somewhat more appropriately to the lifecycle of linguistic theories, which seem to be abandoned after a period of esoterogeny that progressively reduces the ability of outsiders to learn them, after which groups of former adherents begin shifting toward radically simplified models that are initially much easier to learn but that remain far from adequate to meet the full needs of the linguistic community until they have undergone another period of increasingly intolerable esoterogeny.

11. Whether from lack of knowledge or from overriding logistical considerations, some communities were assigned to the wrong circuit. For instance, Papuan-speaking Paiawa children attended Jabêm school in neighboring Austronesian-speaking villages, while Austronesian-speaking Gitua villagers on the northeast coast of the Huon Peninsula were evangelized in Kâte.

12. Sankoff (1968) also observed this contextual shift in choice of language.

REFERENCES

Biggs, Bruce G.
1965 Direct and Indirect Inheritance in Rotuman. *Lingua* 14:383–415.
1972 Implications of Linguistic Subgrouping with Special Reference to Polynesia. In *Studies in Oceanic Culture History*, vol. 3. R. C. Green and M. Kelly, eds. Pp. 143–152. Pacific Anthropological Records, no. 13. Honolulu: Bernice P. Bishop Museum.

Blong, R. J.
1982 *The Time of Darkness*. Seattle: University of Washington Press.

Blust, Robert
1991 Sound Change and Migration Distance. In *Currents in Pacific Linguistics: Papers on Austronesian Languages and Ethnolinguistics in Honour of George W. Grace*. Robert Blust, ed. Pp. 27–42. Pacific Linguistics C-117. Canberra: Australian National University.

Bradshaw, Joel
1978a Multilingualism and Language Mixture among the Numbami. *Kivung (Journal of the Linguistic Society of Papua New Guinea)* 11:26–49.
1978b Notes on Subgrouping in the Huon Gulf Area. *Working Papers in Linguistics* (University of Hawai'i) 10:49–83.
1979 Obstruent Harmony and Tonogenesis in Jabêm. *Lingua* 49:189–205.
1982 Word Order Change in Papua New Guinea Austronesian Languages. Ph.D. dissertation, University of Hawai'i.
1993 Subject Relationships within Serial Verb Constructions in Numbami and Jabêm. *Oceanic Linguistics* 32:133–161.
1997 The Population Kaleidoscope: Another Factor in the Melanesian Diversity v. Polynesian Homogeneity Debate. *Journal of the Polynesian Society* 106:222–249.

Capell, Arthur
1943 *The Linguistic Position of South-Eastern Papua.* Sydney: Australasian Medical Publishing Co.
1949 Two Tonal Languages of New Guinea. *Bulletin of the School of Oriental and African Studies* 13:184–199.
Chowning, Ann
1973 Milke's "New Guinea Cluster": The Evidence from Northwest New Britain. *Oceanic Linguistics* 12:189–243.
1986 Refugees, Traders, and Other Wanderers: The Linguistic Effects of Population Mixing in Melanesia. In *FOCAL II: Papers from the Fourth International Conference on Austronesian Linguistics.* Paul Geraghty, Lois Carrington, and S. A. Wurm, eds. Pp. 407–434. Pacific Linguistics C-94. Canberra: Australian National University.
1989 The "Papuan Tip" Languages Reconsidered. In *VICAL 1, Oceanic Languages: Papers from the Fifth International Conference on Austronesian Linguistics,* part 1. Ray Harlow and Robin Hooper, eds. Pp. 113–140. Auckland: Linguistic Society of New Zealand.
Cobb, Elyce, and Diane Wroge
1990 Iwal Transfer Primer and Teachers' Training Course. Summer Institute of Linguistics. *Read* 25(2):40–44.
Collier, Ken, and Margaret Collier
1975 A Tentative Phonemic Statement of the Apoze Dialect, Kela Language. *Workpapers in Papua New Guinea Languages* 13:129–161.
Davidson, Ian, and Doris Davidson
1976 Essentials for Translation: Iwal Language. Manuscript.
Dempwolff, Otto
1939 *Grammatik der Jabêm-Sprache auf Neuguinea.* Abhandlungen aus dem Gebiet des Auslandskunde, vol. 50. Hamburg: Friederichsen, de Gruyter.
Diamond, Jared
1997 *Guns, Germs, and Steel: The Fates of Human Societies.* New York: W. W. Norton.
Dutton, Tom
1994 Motu-Koiarian Contact in Papua New Guinea. In *Language Contact and Change in the Austronesian World.* Tom Dutton and Darrell T. Tryon, eds. Pp. 181–232. Trends in Linguistics: Studies and Monographs, vol. 77. Berlin: Mouton de Gruyter.
1995 Language Contact and Change in Melanesia. In *The Austronesians: Historical and Comparative Perspectives.* Peter Bellwood, James J. Fox, and Darrell Tryon, eds. Pp. 192–213. Canberra: Australian National University.
Dutton, Tom, and Darrell T. Tryon, eds.
1994 *Language Contact and Change in the Austronesian World.* Trends in Linguistics: Studies and Monographs, vol. 77. Berlin: Mouton de Gruyter.
Foley, William A.
1986 *The Papuan Languages of New Guinea.* Cambridge Language Surveys. Cambridge: Cambridge University Press.
Grace, George W.
1986 Further Thoughts on Oceanic Subgrouping. In *FOCAL II: Papers from the Fourth International Conference on Austronesian Linguistics.* Paul Geraghty, Lois Car-

rington, and S. A. Wurm, eds. Pp. 1–12. Pacific Linguistics C-94. Canberra: Australian National University.

Gumperz, John J.
1971 Communication in Multilingual Societies. In *Language in Social Groups: Essays by John J. Gumperz*. Selected and introduced by Anwar S. Dil. Pp. 230–250. Stanford, CA: Stanford University Press.

Gumperz, John J., and Robert Wilson
1971 Convergence and Creolization: A Case from the Indo-Aryan/Dravidian Border in India. In *Language in Social Groups: Essays by John J. Gumperz*. Selected and introduced by Anwar S. Dil. Pp. 251–273. Stanford, CA: Stanford University Press.

Harding, Thomas G.
1967 *Voyagers of the Vitiaz Strait: A Study of a New Guinea Trade System*. Seattle: University of Washington Press.
1985 *Kunai Men: Horticultural Systems of a Papua New Guinea Society*. Berkeley and Los Angeles: University of California Press.

Harding, Thomas G., and Stephen A. Clark
1994 The Sio Story of Male. *Pacific Studies* 17(4):29–51.

Hogbin, Ian
1947 Native Christianity in a New Guinea Village. *Oceania* 18:1–35.
1951 *Transformation Scene: The Changing Culture of a New Guinea Village*. London: Routledge and Kegan Paul.

Holzknecht, Suzanne C.
1989 *The Markham Languages of Papua New Guinea*. Pacific Linguistics C-115. Canberra: Australian National University.
1994 Mechanisms of Language Change in Labu. In *Language Contact and Change in the Austronesian World*. Tom Dutton and Darrell T. Tryon, eds. Pp. 351–376. Trends in Linguistics: Studies and Monographs, vol. 77. Berlin: Mouton de Gruyter.

Hooley, Bruce A.
1971 Austronesian Languages of the Morobe District, Papua New Guinea. *Oceanic Linguistics* 10:79–151.

Idriess, Ion L.
1933 *Gold-Dust and Ashes: The Romantic Story of the New Guinea Goldfields*. Sydney and London: Angus and Robertson.

Lechner, M., and Nêdeclabu Male, eds.
1955 *Buku Sêsamnga II*. 2nd ed. Madang: Lutheran Mission Press. (First edition comp. and ed. by F. Bayer in 1928.)

Milke, Wilhelm
1965 Comparative Notes on the Austronesian Languages of New Guinea. *Lingua* 14: 330–348.

Pomponio, Alice
1990 Seagulls Don't Fly into the Bush: Cultural Identity and the Negotiation of Development on Mandok Island, Papua New Guinea. In *Cultural Identity and Ethnicity in the Pacific*. Jocelyn Linnekin and Lin Poyer, eds. Pp. 43–69. Honolulu: University of Hawai'i Press.
1994 Namor's Odyssey: Mythical Metaphors and History in Siassi. *Pacific Studies* 17(4): 53–91.

Pomponio, Alice, David R. Counts, and Thomas G. Harding, eds.

1994 *Children of Kilibob: Creation, Cosmos, and Culture in Northeast New Guinea.* Special Issue. *Pacific Studies* 17(4).

Ray, Sidney H.

1926 *A Comparative Study of the Melanesian Island Languages.* Cambridge: Cambridge University Press.

Rehg, Kenneth L.

1995 The Significance of Linguistic Interaction Spheres in Reconstructing Micronesian Prehistory. *Oceanic Linguistics* 34:305–326.

Ross, Malcolm D.

1987 A Contact-Induced Morphosyntactic Change in the Bel Languages of Papua New Guinea. In *A World of Language: Papers Presented to Professor S. A. Wurm on His 65th Birthday.* Donald Laycock and Werner Winter, eds. Pp. 583–601. Pacific Linguistics C-100. Canberra: Australian National University.

1988 *Proto Oceanic and the Austronesian Languages of Western Melanesia.* Pacific Linguistics C-98. Canberra: Australian National University.

1991 How Conservative Are Sedentary Languages? Evidence from Western Melanesia. In *Currents in Pacific Linguistics: Papers on Austronesian Languages and Ethnolinguistics in Honour of George W. Grace.* Robert Blust, ed. Pp. 433–451. Pacific Linguistics C-117. Canberra: Australian National University.

1993 Tonogenesis in the North Huon Gulf Chain. In *Tonality in Austronesian Languages.* Jerold A. Edmondson and Kenneth J. Gregerson, eds. Pp. 133–153. Oceanic Linguistics Special Publication no. 24. Honolulu: University of Hawai'i Press.

1994 Areal Phonological Features in North Central New Ireland. In *Language Contact and Change in the Austronesian World.* Tom Dutton and Darrell T. Tryon, eds. Pp. 551–572. Trends in Linguistics: Studies and Monographs, vol. 77. Berlin: Mouton de Gruyter.

1996 Contact-Induced Change and the Comparative Method. In *The Comparative Method Reviewed: Regularity and Irregularity in Language Change.* Mark Durie and Malcolm Ross, eds. Pp. 180–217. New York: Oxford University Press.

Sack, Peter G.

1976 *The Bloodthirsty Laewomba? Myth and History in Papua New Guinea.* Canberra: Australian National University Press.

Sankoff, Gillian

1968 Social Aspects of Multilingualism in New Guinea. Canadian Theses on Microfilm, no. 3213. Ottawa: National Library of Canada.

Siegel, Jeff

1984 Introduction to the Labu Language. *Pacific Linguistics* A-69:83–159.

Streicher, J. F.

1982 *Jabêm-English Dictionary.* Rev. ed. Pacific Linguistics C-68. Canberra: Australian National University.

Thomason, Sarah Grey, and Terrence Kaufman

1988 *Language Contact, Creolization, and Genetic Linguistics.* Berkeley and Los Angeles: University of California Press.

Thurston, William R.

1987 *Processes of Change in the Languages of North-Western New Britain.* Pacific Linguistics B-99. Canberra: Australian National University.

1989 How Exoteric Languages Build a Lexicon: Esoterogeny in Western New Britain.

In *VICAL 1, Oceanic Languages: Papers from the Fifth International Conference on Austronesian Linguistics*, part 2. Ray Harlow and Robin Hooper, eds. Pp. 555–579. Auckland: Linguistic Society of New Zealand.

1994 Renovation and Innovation in the Languages of North-Western New Britain. In *Language Contact and Change in the Austronesian World*. Tom Dutton and Darrell T. Tryon, eds. Pp. 573–609. Trends in Linguistics: Studies and Monographs, vol. 77. Berlin: Mouton de Gruyter.

Watson, James B.

1970 Society as Organized Flow: The Tairora Case. *Southwestern Journal of Anthropology* 26(2):107–124.

1990 Other People Do Other Things: Lamarckian Identities in Kainantu Subdistrict, Papua New Guinea. In *Cultural Identity and Ethnicity in the Pacific*. Jocelyn Linnekin and Lin Poyer, eds. Pp. 17–41. Honolulu: University of Hawai'i Press.

Welsch, Robert L., ed.

1998 *An American Anthropologist in Melanesia: A. B. Lewis and the Joseph N. Field South Pacific Expedition, 1909–1913*, vol. 1, *Field diaries*. Honolulu: University of Hawai'i Press.

Wilson, Darryl

1976 Paragraph and Discourse Structure in Suena. *Workpapers in Papua New Guinea Languages* 15:5–125.

Zahn, Heinrich

1940 *Lehrbuch der Jabêmsprache*. Zeitschrift für Eingeborenensprachen, Beiheft 21. Berlin: Reimer.

1996 *Mission and Music: Jabêm Traditional Music and the Development of Lutheran Hymnody*. Philip W. Holzknecht, trans. Don Niles, ed. and intro. Boroko: Institute of Papua New Guinea Studies.

Index

About the Contributors

JOEL BRADSHAW currently serves as journals manager at the University of Hawai'i Press and as editorial advisor to *Language and Linguistics in Melanesia*. He is a frequent contributor to the journal *Oceanic Linguistics*. After fieldwork in Morobe Province, Papua New Guinea, in 1976, he completed his Ph.D. dissertation at the University of Hawai'i in 1982 on word-order change in Papua New Guinea Austronesian languages.

MARTIN PAUL EVISON graduated in genetics and completed a six-year career in computing before returning to postgraduate studies in environmental archaeology and ancient DNA. He is Lecturer in Forensic and Biological Anthropology at the University of Sheffield with research interests in computer modeling, forensic archaeology, skeletal DNA analysis, and the interdisciplinary synthesis of genetic and archaeological evidence of the past. He is presently conducting research on gender and kinship in Bronze Age burials in Crete.

JANE H. HILL is Regents' Professor of Anthropology at the University of Arizona. She is a specialist in the languages of the Americas, focusing on languages of the Uto-Aztecan family and especially on sociolinguistic and historical questions. She is author or editor of four books, including *Speaking Mexicano* (with Kenneth C. Hill), and has published many chapters and articles in journals including *American Anthropologist, Language*, and *Language in Society*; she is currently editor-in-chief of the last. In 1998 and 1999, she was president of the American Anthropological Association. Professor Hill is a member of the American Academy of Arts and Sciences.

JOHN HINES worked as a field archaeologist in Britain and Scandinavia before taking a first degree in English language and literature at Oxford. He returned to archaeology for his doctoral research and was appointed to teach English literature and language history at the University of Wales, Cardiff, in 1983. He is currently a professor in the School of History and Archaeology at that university.

RICHARD W. LINDSTROM is a doctoral candidate in the Department of Anthropology, University of Chicago. His research is focused on the Bronze Age of the Eurasian steppe and includes considerations of the relationships between ethnicity, material culture, language, and human biology. He is currently working as a research assistant in Collection Development and Research at the Getty Research Institute in Los Angeles, California.

SCOTT MacEACHERN is Assistant Professor in the Department of Sociology and Anthropology, Bowdoin College. He received his Ph.D. from the University of Calgary in 1991 and has directed the Project Maya-Wandala since 1992. His publications include "Foreign Countries: The Development of Ethnoarchaeology in Sub-Saharan Africa" (*Journal of World Prehistory* 10[3]:243–304, 1996) and "Scale, Style, and Cultural Variation: Technological Traditions in the Northern Mandara Mountains" in *The Archaeology of Social Boundaries* (1998).

JOHN H. MOORE is Research Professor of Anthropology at the University of Florida. He has done extensive fieldwork with the Cheyennes and Mvskoke Creeks and has published widely on evolutionary theory. He received his Ph.D. from New York University in 1974 and taught sixteen years at the University of Oklahoma and seven years at the University of Florida. He is a Fellow of the American Association for the Advancement of Science.

MARK R. V. SOUTHERN received his doctorate from Princeton University in 1997 and teaches historical linguistics in the Department of Germanic Studies, University of Texas at Austin. His dissertation, "The Wandering *S*: The Problem of the *s-mobile* in Germanic and Indo-European," appeared in revised form as *Sub-grammatical Survival* (Journal of Indo-European Studies Monograph 34) (1999). He conducts research in Indo-European and Semitic linguistics, Germanic linguistics, comparative/historical linguistics, sociolinguistics, creoles, Yiddish, Indo-Iranian, Greek, Latin, Celtic, phonology/morphology, discourse analysis, poetics, comparative religions, and anthropological linguistics.

JOHN EDWARD TERRELL received bachelor's, master's, and doctoral degrees from Harvard University and is Curator of Oceanic Archaeology and Ethnology at the Field Museum of Natural History in Chicago, where he directs the New Guinea Research Program and is responsible for Ruatepupuke II, the only New Zealand Maori *whare whakairo* (carved meeting house) in the New World. He is especially interested in biogeography, the evolution of human diversity, and the dynamics of human social life.

LINDSAY J. WHALEY is Associate Professor of Linguistics and Cognitive Science and Classics at Dartmouth College in Hanover, New Hampshire. He earned his Ph.D. in theoretical linguistics at the State University of New York at Buffalo in 1993. His research interests include language typology, language endangerment, Tungusic languages, and Bantu languages. He is currently the codirector of the Tungusic Research Group at Dartmouth.

PAMELA R. WILLOUGHBY is Associate Professor of Anthropology at the University of Alberta, Edmonton, Alberta, Canada. Her research interests are in Paleolithic archaeology, paleoanthropology, and African prehistory. Since 1988, she has directed an archaeological field project in the Western Rift valley of southwestern Tanzania, investigating the beginnings of modern human behavior. Among other duties, she edits *Nyame Akuma*, the research bulletin of the Society of Africanist Archaeologists.